Open Access to Knowledge in Nigeria

This book provides an analysis of the legal and policy dimensions of open access to research, education and public sector information, with a focus on Nigeria. It shows how open access has evolved across the world and how such initiatives could be implemented in Nigeria and other countries in the developing world.

The author argues for a platform where Nigerians would be able to freely connect to the "global library", through the open access dual platforms of self-archiving and open access publishing, thereby providing access to knowledge. The importance of connecting local works to the global library to increase visibility and impact of such works is also underscored. This book furthers our understanding of open educational resources as alternative avenues to accessing education. It seeks to foster citizenry participation, good governance, accountability, democratic values and spurs creativity and innovation through open governance and access to public sector information.

Providing a framework for open access in developing countries is imperative and *Open Access to Knowledge in Nigeria* is an important read for anyone interested in developing such a framework. It is also important for those interested in the development of knowledge economies, the open access and Access to Knowledge movements.

Kunle Ola is a lecturer at the Thomas More Law School, Australian Catholic University.

Routledge Contemporary Africa Series

The Media and Aid in Sub-Saharan Africa
Whose News?
Lena von Naso

Political Culture, Change, and Security Policy in Nigeria
Kalu N. Kalu

African Science Education
Gendering Indigenous Knowledge in Nigeria
Jamaine Abidogun

Power in Contemporary Zimbabwe
Edited by Erasmus Masitera and Fortune Sibanda

Unfolding Narratives of Ubuntu in Southern Africa
Edited by Julian Müller, John Eliastam and Sheila Trahar

Reimagining Science and Statecraft in Postcolonial Kenya
Stories from an African Scientist
Denielle Elliott with Davy Kiprotich Koech

Food Security for Rural Africa
Feeding the Farmers First
Terry Leahy

African Language Digital Media and Communication
Abiodun Salawu

Open Access to Knowledge in Nigeria
A Framework for Developing Countries
Kunle Ola

Open Access to Knowledge in Nigeria

A Framework for Developing Countries

Kunle Ola

Routledge
Taylor & Francis Group
LONDON AND NEW YORK

First published 2019
by Routledge
2 Park Square, Milton Park, Abingdon, Oxon OX14 4RN

and by Routledge
52 Vanderbilt Avenue, New York, NY 10017

First issued in paperback 2020

Routledge is an imprint of the Taylor & Francis Group, an informa business

British Library Cataloguing-in-Publication Data
A catalogue record for this book is available from the British Library

Library of Congress Cataloging-in-Publication Data
A catalog record for this book has been requested

ISBN 13: 978-0-367-66517-3 (pbk)
ISBN 13: 978-1-138-33223-2 (hbk)

Typeset in Times New Roman
by Apex CoVantage, LLC

Contents

1 Introduction*

1 Introduction

Content is King,[1] and Knowledge is Power.[2] This is the knowledge dispensation, the knowledge economy. This generation and probably the next one will be dominated by knowledge. Acquiring knowledge is therefore imperative for development, and the currency for acquiring knowledge is "access". If there is no knowledge, there is no development; if there is no access, there is no knowledge.

The importance of development through access to knowledge is imperative because Africa is the second-largest continent in the world, and Nigeria has the largest population in Africa.[3] It has been estimated that the continent's current 1 billion population will more than quadruple over the next 90 years. This will no doubt make Africa more important than ever.

> And it's not just that there will be four times the workforce, four times the resource burden, four times as many voters. The rapid growth itself will likely transform political and social dynamics within African countries and thus their relationship with the rest of the world.[4]

This work therefore seeks to provide a framework that enables access to knowledge to all Nigerians, and if this is achieved, it will bring about multiple platforms for development in Nigeria. The book holds an important key to Nigeria's development. It is a key that provides opportunity for development to all Nigerians. If Nigeria attains true development via open access to knowledge, the spread of development to all of Africa becomes tangible, and the journey to African development becomes easier.

2 Background

We all live on the same planet, but definitely not in the same world. Global inequality is on the rise, and whereas it has been postulated that all men are equal, it is however apparent that some are more equal than others.[5] A world where billions of people live on less than two dollars per day, while others live in luxury and wastefulness, a world where some have unlimited access to power supply, good water, good roads and quality education, while others live in squalor, without power supply, good roads, pipe-borne water, and access to quality education, information and knowledge.[6] We live in a digitally divided world with those on the advantaged divide being able to maximize the benefits of information communication technology, while those on the other divide struggle to make sense of it and are mostly *cut off* as a result of the inhumanity of men and the many societal inequalities.[7] There are many challenges facing humanity with no current concrete solution.[8] The challenge of access to knowledge, the closure and locking up of knowledge are some of the fundamental challenges facing humanity today, but fortunately these problems can and are being addressed.[9] The open movement (open access, open educational resources [OER], open government, or public sector information and other such initiatives) is taking active steps to open what has been hitherto closed.

Open access to knowledge is the central focus of this work, and as the open movement is dynamic and has a wide spread, this work narrows down its analysis and discussions to three fields, namely, open access to journal articles (Chapter 4), OER (Chapter 5) and public sector information (Chapter 6). These three areas play a vital role in any society, and they are of particular interest to Nigeria as they form the bedrock of scientific and academic research, socio-economic and political development.[10] This work draws attention to the creative and innovative abilities of Nigerians but also notes that Nigerian authors are facing accessibility, visibility and impact challenges with respect to scholarly works. It also showcases the growth in Nigeria's higher education institutions, particularly her universities and discusses OER as a tool for addressing several challenges in Nigeria's educational system. The work discusses the introduction of the Freedom of Information Act in Nigeria as part of Chapter 6 where public sector information is discussed. It highlights their similarities and differences and discusses the importance of public sector information in Nigeria. The work discusses several strategies the open movement has adopted in addressing challenges of accessing knowledge. These strategies include self-archiving, open access journals, open access mandates, aggressive public enlightenment, lobbying and licensing.

3 The position in Nigeria

Lack of access to knowledge and information is a fundamental challenge to the average Nigerian, and it is a key determinant for development.[11] The fact that there is a wealth of information freely available but mostly inaccessible and that at the same time 57 percent of Nigerians are rated as illiterate without any formal education or access to education, 40 million of whom are adults, with approximately 7 million children not in school is worrisome and should be of great concern to the Nigerian government and the international community.[12]

In an article written in furtherance of the 2012 World Literacy Day organized in Nigeria, it was noted that

> The United Nations Education Scientific and Cultural Organisation lists [sic] Nigeria as one of the nine countries with the largest population of illiterate

> people. The nine countries, namely: Bangladesh, Brazil, China, Egypt, India, Indonesia, Mexico, Nigeria and Pakistan, account for 53 per cent of the world's illiterate population. These nations account for the world's largest population of illiterate adults and over half of the world's population of out-of-school children.[13]

If the illiteracy level in Nigeria is to be tackled, there must be access to knowledge, and it is imperative that strategies be put in place to effectively address the barriers to accessing knowledge.[14] High illiteracy levels affect virtually all sectors, in the sense that an illiterate community is often an unhealthy, sick, poor and disadvantaged community, and this is not unconnected to their lack of general and specific knowledge.[15] The former Secretary General of the United Nations Ban Ki-moon captured it succinctly when he noted that "Illiteracy exacerbates cycles of poverty, ill-health and deprivation. It weakens communities and undermines democratic processes through marginalization and exclusion. These and other impacts can combine to destabilize societies."[16]

The illiteracy level is one challenge, but other issues around information management, distribution and sharing also exist in Nigeria. There are problems associated with poor visibility, lack of access, low impact and utility of works authored and published by Nigerian academics, researchers and writers.[17] The private and public sector in Nigeria are also faced with challenges of accessing, using and reusing government-held information. The difficulties associated with cultural beliefs, terrorism (Boko-Haram), high cost of school fees, school/educational textbooks, and other teaching aids and materials, as well as access, use, and reuse of research and educational materials by students and researchers are serious challenges to access to knowledge in Nigeria.

Other issues both in the private and public sectors are beginning to emerge from the steady growth of Nigeria's higher education institutions (HEI),[18] to the growth in the software industry,[19] to the dynamism of Nigeria's entertainment industry and the fast growth of the telecommunication industry.[20] These four industries constantly make use of knowledge products and hence the constant need to access, use and reuse contents. These knowledge products often enjoy proprietary rights, and the proprietary issues around the contents accessed, used and reused need to be addressed within a legal, policy and/or regulatory framework to achieve balance. This balance is meant to provide a system that enables sharing in the interest of users and the general public, and at the same time, it incentivizes right owners to continue creating and innovating.[21] Achieving this balance could be difficult with the constant extension of copyright duration and the increasing limitations on user rights. Fortunately, the Canadian Supreme Court has asserted the rights of users' and has made it clear that use within certain specified ambits are not merely a defence but are actually user rights. The Chief Justice noted this when he said that

> the fair dealing exception is perhaps more properly understood as an integral part of the Copyright Act than simply a defence. Any act falling within the

> fair dealing exception will not be an infringement of copyright. The fair dealing exception, like other exceptions in the Copyright Act, is a user's right. In order to maintain the proper balance between the rights of a copyright owner and users' interests, it must not be interpreted restrictively.[22]

Part of the strategy of the open movement is to ensure that the freedoms guaranteed in the current legal framework under compulsory licensing, limitations and exceptions to copyright are adequately explored and sufficiently protected.[23] These principles, often referred to as *fair use* or *fair dealing*, provide a safe haven where users are free to use knowledge products. The major challenge for Nigeria and indeed the global community when it comes to the interface between access to knowledge and fair use/fair dealing are the limitations placed on exploiting such knowledge products through use and reuse.

One cannot begin to imagine the level of frustration one has to go through in search of available but inaccessible knowledge. We are talking about knowledge that is crucial to the completion of an educational endeavour, knowledge without which one cannot complete an assignment and therefore cannot complete the course, meaning that the chance for a better life is dashed due to inaccessibility of available knowledge. This is knowledge that was produced by authors who are more than happy to share it with curious minds, but which have been locked up behind pay walls, and these lock-up systems enjoy legal protection.[24]

This frustration is aggravated by the knowledge that what is been sought for is actually available, but one's local circumstances, that is, the inability of Nigerian institutions to afford subscription fees, or the inability of one's country to provide the requisite Information and Communication Technology (ICT) infrastructure for speedy Internet connectivity and access amongst other things is what has caused inaccessibility to available information.[25]

In recognition of the importance of accessing knowledge to development, particularly knowledge within peer-reviewed literatures, school textbooks (educational resources), and that within the broader public sector (public sector information) and the challenges faced in accessing requisite information, this prompted the question of how many people in Nigeria and other developing countries could be experiencing this frustration. These thoughts call to memory the words of Ghandi's "be the change you wish to see,"[26] and it prompted several questions such as what can be done, what is the way out from this dark tunnel of knowledge inaccessibility, is there a way that available knowledge can be made accessible without all the restrictions currently on it, and what platforms need to be put in place to enable impact, visibility and utility of Nigerian works? Open Access to knowledge provides some answers.

4 The meaning of open access

Open access refers to free immediate unrestricted online access to peer-reviewed literature. It seeks to allow users access to knowledge by providing a legal platform to open up what the knowledge distribution system has legally closed up[27]

There are many definitions of the term. Suber, one of the pioneers in this field provides this definition; "open access (OA) literature is digital, online, free of charge, and free of most copyright and licensing restrictions."[28] To Harnad, it is "free, immediate, permanent online access to the full text of research articles for anyone webwide".[29] Fitzgerald opines that open access "aims to disseminate knowledge broadly and freely across the internet in a timely fashion".[30] Hubbard says it is "to make the full text of the research article freely available".[31] Willinsky who was one of the first to publish a book (access principle) on the subject sees open access as a tool for extending the frontiers of knowledge through the extension of the circulation of research outputs.[32] A concise definition is found on the Public Library of Science (PLOS) website, which defines open access as "unrestricted access and unrestricted reuse".[33] One central theme running through the definitions of open access is the freedom to access, use and reuse information within legally defined frameworks. The formal foundations of open access can be traced back to several meetings where the initiative was given formal definition and crafted and shaped into what has become a global initiative today. The term open access[34] was first coined at a meeting in Budapest, where the Budapest Open Access Initiative (BOAI) was crafted and signed.[35] The Bethesda Statements on Open Access Publishing, which was released on the 20th of June 2003, are similar in context to that of the Budapest initiative.[36] The Berlin Declaration on Open Access to Knowledge in the Sciences and Humanities is similar to Bethesda's definition. The declaration which was signed on the 22nd of October 2003 also defines the term by providing a definition of an open access contribution and the conditions it must satisfy.[37]

The Bethesda and Berlin Declarations particularly provide that for a work to be open access, prior consent by the copyright owner permitting users is required to "copy, use, distribute, transmit and display the work publicly and to make and distribute derivative works, in any digital medium for any responsible purpose, subject to proper attribution of authorship".[38] These two documents provide for use and reuse rights, thereby providing a wider scope for exploiting the work in comparison with that of the Budapest Declaration, which provides for only use rights. Whereas, permission to "make and distribute derivatives of works" (reuse rights) was specifically included in the Bethesda and Berlin Declarations alongside use rights (reproduction and distribution which cover exploitations such as to read, download, copy, distribute, print, search, or link to the full texts of these articles, crawl them for indexing, pass them as data to software, or use them for any other lawful purpose), the Budapest Declaration on the other hand has no clear provision for reuse rights, but it basically permits users to reproduce and distribute works (use rights) but does not contain permission to make and distribute derivatives of work (reuse rights).

5 BBB definition

The outcome of the Budapest, Bethesda and Berlin meetings, now referred to as the BBB definitions, are generally accepted as the standard definitions for open access.[39] These definitions are all agreed on the need to spread and extend the reach of knowledge, particularly peer-reviewed literature. The need for such knowledge to be freely available, that is, at no cost to users, is a recurring decimal in these definitions. Similarly, it is that the knowledge be available via the platform of the Internet. Some of the definitions use the terms online, public Internet and others webwide to describe the platform on which knowledge should be made available. The central focus with regard to platform is that information which would be considered open access is such that should be in a digital form and available on the Internet.[40]

Not all the definitions use the same term and address the same issues. Whereas Suber's definition has some peculiarity with regard to open access being free from most copyright and licensing restrictions, Harnad's definition is peculiar for his call that open access be immediate. Willinsky on the other hand adopts a liberal perspective towards open access and considers every little opportunity that opens up the access gate to knowledge as part and parcel of open access. He explains this in his "Ten Flavors of Open Access",[41] which basically shows that the more restrictions that are removed from a work, the more open it becomes. The restrictions which the open access movement seek to address were identified in the Budapest declaration as price, technical and legal. These restrictions can be individually or collectively removed.[42] Where all three restrictions are removed, the access gate is apparently opened the widest. Harnad however opines on the need to maximize the opportunities of open access and notes that removal of price restriction (that is, the cost associated with gaining access to peer-reviewed journal articles via subscription and pay-per-view fees) alone is actually sufficient to constitute open access.[43] In the same vein, Suber notes that removing price restriction alone will provide most users and open access proponents with requisite access to basic peer-reviewed literature.[44]

Considering the different flavours to open access which opens the access gate wider and wider depending on the type of rights granted, that is, the quantum of restriction that has been lifted, the need to explain the different levels and clarify grey issues became imperative, and hence both Suber and Harnad came up with the terms *libre* and *gratis*.[45]

Whereas, *gratis open access* refers to access that is delivered free of charge to users (without price restriction);[46] *libre open access* on the other hand is a combination of access that is free from prices and also free from technical and legal restrictions.[47] The latter are the restrictions which Suber referred to in his definition when he said, "and free of most copyright and licensing restrictions".[48]

The BBB definitions appear to have provided the building blocks upon which the discussions on open access definitions have rested. They provide important clarifications as to what exactly is open access, what can be done with content termed open access, the target audience (authors, funders, library, publishers, users, funding agencies, universities, research institutions, and international and non-governmental agencies) the mode of implementation, the interface with the law, the specific barriers it seeks to remove, as well as the funding options. Identifying funding options coupled with the willingness of several stakeholders to sponsor and see to the success of this initiative has contributed immensely to the success of the open access initiative.[49]

Below are some of the fundamentals of open access enunciated from the definitions of open access, but particularly from the BBB definitions.

6 Fundamentals of open access[50]

It was at the Budapest meeting that the term *open access* was first coined and defined.[51] Apart from defining the term, the meeting provided the framework on which open access still operates and identified certain crucial issues that have shaped the developments and discussions around open access.[52] The meeting addressed the need to remove barriers to accessing knowledge and focused on what would enable access to knowledge such as the need to structure effective and proactive management systems for copyright.[53] It advocated for a copyright system that will have a default pre-granting of "permission to use", rather than the current default "prohibition from use".

It further advocated for the removal of fees which constitute price barriers to access and for the discovery of business models that would ensure payment of publication. In addition to this, it recommended two strategies for the actualization of open access, namely self-archiving (green road) and open-access journals (gold road).[54]

Several other statements have endorsed the BOAI such as the Bethesda Statement on Open Access Publishing,[55] the Berlin Declaration on Open Access to Knowledge in the Sciences and Humanities,[56] and the Declaration on Access to Research Data from Public Funding.[57] Fundamental to all of these initiatives and statements are some of the issues mentioned hereunder.

6.1 An old tradition

The academic community is knowledge based. It builds and feeds on knowledge and thrives through the expansion of knowledge. It has a practice of publishing its articles for free and provides editorial and refereeing services to publishers also for free.[58] The structure for promotion, advancement and academic recognition is directly connected to the number and quality of papers published and has promoted a "publish or perish culture".[59] The BOAI took cognizance of this old tradition, that is, the willingness of academics and researchers to publish their works for free and was able to use it as one of the building blocks of the open access movement. The open access movement reasons that if academics and researchers are willing to release their work to the public for free (publishing for free), then the public should be allowed to access these works for free.

6.2 A new technology

The switch from the Advanced Research Project Agency Network (ARPANET) to Transmission Control Protocol/Internet Protocol (TCP/IP) marked the birth of the Internet, and the world has not been the same ever since. The enabling ability of the Internet to grant access to, as well as distribute content is unprecedented. This enabling ability of the Internet constitutes probably the most important building block in the open access structure. The Internet has been described as a

> global system of interconnected computer networks that use the standard Internet protocol suite (often called TCP/IP, although not all applications use TCP) to serve billions of users worldwide. It is a network of networks that consists of millions of private, public, academic, business, and government networks, of local to global scope, that are linked by a broad array of electronic, wireless and optical networking technologies. The Internet carries an extensive range of information resources and services, such as the interlinked hypertext documents of the World Wide Web (WWW) and the infrastructure to support email.[60]

6.3 Public good

The objective of the open access movement is larger than any individual's interest and seeks to serve the common good by providing platforms capable of enabling access to knowledge. The merger of the old tradition with the enabling ability of the Internet would have the potential of granting access to research output as well as instantaneous worldwide electronic distribution of such outputs, and this will no doubt result in the good of all of mankind.[61]

6.4 Quality

The open access movement is concerned about the quality of published information and is thus not advocating for just any kind of literature; it has made it clear that the information it would like to put out for free, without permission and price restrictions are literatures that have been peer-reviewed.[62] The BOAI puts it this way "Open access to peer-reviewed journal literature is the goal."[63]

6.5 Delivery

Peer-reviewed literature in the closed access model is delivered through a subscription-/fee-paying model. On the other hand, it is the objective of the open access movement that peer-reviewed articles and literature would be delivered free and without any access restrictions to the general public.

6.6 Barriers

The three barriers identified in the BOAI are financial, legal and technical.

1 Financial barriers include price barriers in the form of subscription fees.

2 Legal barriers refer to intellectual property rights that grant exclusive rights to owners, restrict access to works, and require intending users to seek and obtain permission to use such works.
3 Technical barriers refer to technologies deployed by right-owners to restrict and control access to copyrighted digital contents. They are referred to as Technological Protection Measures (TPM) and Digital Rights Management (DRM).

6.7 Focus

The Budapest meeting identified five classes of people as beneficiaries of the free and unrestricted access to peer-reviewed literatures. They include scientists, scholars, teachers, students and other curious minds. The inclusion of the category "other curious minds" must have been intended to capture any group not specifically mentioned, as well as the general public.

6.8 Potential benefit

Five potential benefits of a system where peer-reviewed literature is delivered for free and without any form of access barrier include

1 Accelerate research
2 Enrich education
3 Share the learning of the rich with the poor and the poor with the rich
4 Make the literature as useful as it can be
5 Lay the foundation for uniting humanity in a common intellectual conversation and quest for knowledge

6.9 Area of operation

One important point to note is that the terrain for the free and unrestricted access to these peer-reviewed literatures is only online. The BOAI only dealt with online availability and online accessibility on the public Internet.

6.10 Exploitation

The BOAI interestingly mentions in detail what it expects users to be able to do with works that are within the open access regime, and it is clear that the BOAI seeks to open up the access door as wide as possible and at the same time allay any fears regarding infractions of the law by potential users. The types of use noted include the following:

1 Reading
2 Downloading
3 Copying

4 Distributing
5 Printing
6 Searching
7 Linking to the full text
8 Crawling for indexing
9 Passing the information as data to software
10 Use for any other lawful purpose

6.11 Nexus to intellectual property rights

This movement is not anti-copyright or anti-intellectual property.[64] It actually builds on intellectual property (IP) rights to achieve its objectives.[65] For instance, the open access movement, in reliance on the right of an author which is traditionally to prohibit (negative by default) exploitation of a work without permission, turns around its traditional default position and grants permission in advance to prospective users. In doing this, copyright becomes the building block upon which permission is granted, but this time, permission is not prohibitively used; rather, it is used for empowerment by advanced authorization. Hence, the restrictions placed by copyright are no longer present, except for the moral rights of the copyright owner to be appropriately acknowledged as the author and to exercise control over the integrity of his or her work.

6.12 Who pays the bills?

If subscription fees are no longer paid by the users, who then funds production? After all, publishing, including facilitating peer review and editing, costs money, and since it is a business concern, issues as to how to cover the costs must be considered. The BOAI made some suggestions on how these costs could be defrayed and opens the door for more ideas. It stated that

> While the peer-reviewed journal literature should be accessible online without cost to readers, it is not costless to produce. However, experiments show that the overall costs of providing open access to this literature are far lower than the costs of traditional forms of dissemination. With such an opportunity to save money and expand the scope of dissemination at the same time, there is today a strong incentive for *professional associations, universities, libraries, foundations, and others*[66] to embrace open access as a means of advancing their missions. Achieving open access will require new cost recovery models and financing mechanisms, but the significantly lower overall cost of dissemination is a reason to be confident that the goal is attainable and not merely preferable or utopian.[67]

Article processing charges (APC) have been introduced as a means of paying the bills, but just like the BOAI suggested, these fees are often (but not always) covered by funding agencies, universities and professional associations.[68]

7 Barriers to open access

7.1 Legal

The open access movement takes cognizance of the fact that access to the results of either public or private research is often not possible due to protections on such materials as stipulated by intellectual property laws: for example, copyright laws which prohibit unauthorized persons from exploiting the output of research without having first obtained permission.[69] In essence, only persons who have obtained permission from the copyright owner or who are covered by some form of exceptions or limitations to copyright may exploit research outputs.[70]

7.2 Price

Permission is not the only barrier to gaining access to the results of research. The price barrier[71] is another restriction referring to costs such as licensing fees, fees for pay-per-view, as well as subscription fees payable to journal publishers who are responsible for publishing,[72] warehousing, marketing and distributing the results of research. In recent times, it has become impracticable for most institutions to pay the subscription fees for all the journals they would wish to access. This frustrating view was recently expressed by Harvard.[73] The high cost of paying the journal fees is an example of the price restriction; it means that those who are unable to pay are unable to access the needed information.

The involvement of government and funding organizations in research all over the world is such that research outputs can to a large extent be considered the product of taxpayers' money (at least to the extent that it was funded by the government), and it is only reasonable that if taxpayers have funded research,[74] outputs of such research should be freely available to taxpayers without legal or price restrictions.[75]

7.3 Technical

The advent of digital technology and online access to information raised concerns amongst right owners as to ensuring that due protection is given to their copyrightable works.[76] To this end, the World Intellectual Property Organization (WIPO) passed the WIPO Copyright Treaty[77] and the WIPO Performance and Phonogram Treaty,[78] both referred to as the Internet Treaties,[79] which provide a legal regime for technological protection measures and digital rights management on works in which copyright subsists. Both treaties place an obligation on contracting States to provide adequate legal protection and effective legal remedies against circumvention of effective technological measures and against anyone knowingly doing, inducing, enabling, facilitating or concealing the removal or alteration of any electronic rights management in information without due authorization.[80] The open access movement advocates that for free unrestricted online access to be achieved, technological lock ups via the deployment of technological protection measures and digital rights management need to be removed.[81]

8 Major stakeholders

The implementation of open access involves multiple strategies and several players.[82] These players include universities,[83] research institutions,[84] government,[85] funding agencies, libraries, learned societies and professional agencies. Five broad groups could however be considered directly involved in all open access publications namely,[86] *authors* who generate content such as literary works; *funders/employers*, who provide funding for carrying out research, for example National Institute of Health (NIH), Australian Research Council (ARC) and Research Councils UK (RCUK); *publishers* who publish works of authors and markets them; and *libraries* who are the major clients of the publishers and serve the multi-purpose of providing storage of literary works as well as access to literary work (usually to a select audience); and lastly, the *user* public.[87] The strategies will now be discussed.

9 Strategies to achieving open access

Two major strategies were recommended by the BBB statements, namely self-archiving and open access journals. Other strategies such as contracts, licensing and open access mandates are being explored in the implementation of open access, and the movement encourages the discovery of new strategies for the implementation of open access.[88] The two strategies suggested in the BBB definitions are as follows.

9.1 Self-archiving (green road)

This is a system that enables authors to deposit their refereed journal articles in open electronic archives such as personal websites, blogs and repositories.[89] This strategy also referred to as green open access could be implemented by the deposit of an e-print in an institutional repository. Electronic prints (e-prints) are made up of pre- and post-prints. Whereas the former refers to author documents that are yet to be peer reviewed, the latter refer to those that have been peer reviewed and may also be called publishers' version. The University of South Africa (UNISA)[90] and that of the Queensland University of Technology are examples of repositories.[91] The Directory of Open Access Repositories (DOAJ),[92] the Register of Open Access Repositories (ROAR)[93] and the Registry of Open Access Repositories Mandate Archiving Policies (ROARMAP)[94] hold important information about repositories. Whereas the DOAJ and ROAR provide a comprehensive list of most of the repositories, the latter provide information on institutions that have adopted policies mandating deposits in repositories. Both DOAJ and ROAR currently list on their databases over 2,000 registered institutional repositories. The SHERPA/RoMEO website provides a list of publishers that support green open access.[95]

9.1.1 Origin of self-archiving

The origin of self-archiving has been traced to the field of computer sciences where researchers developed the practice of depositing their research output in the ftp archives since the early 1980s.[96] This practice was for purposes of establishing priority, ownership, expansion of knowledge, as well as to receive constructive criticism and suggestions which could be used in revising the work before it was finalized and sent for publication with one of the journals. The practice was that prior to the documents undergoing peer review, the document would be sent out to colleagues in print form. However, with the advent of the digital age and the Internet, sharing moved online. In the field of physics, the practice of sharing research outputs was also prevalent. The era of the Internet saw sharing within this field move online and lead to the establishment in 1991 of an electronic pre-print archive, which was called ArXiv.[97] The archive which is hosted by Cornell University is still fully operational.[98]

9.1.2 Rationale of self-archiving

Prior to the open access movement, some publishers responding to calls from the United Nations and the World Health Organization as well as a number of other international organizations provided platforms through which peer-reviewed literature would be made accessible on a limited basis to certain under developed and developing countries based on the world bank's indicators for poor countries. The projects HINARI,[99] AGORA[100] and INASP[101] were all commendable when initiated, but as implementation progressed, the challenges became apparent. Although the initiatives were noble, they were highly restricted in terms of content, in that only specific literatures within specific fields, particularly the scientific fields were made available. The use of the literatures was geographically confined to the location where the computers were located. It was also limited in terms of the number of people who could use it simultaneously.[102] There was therefore the need to expand the access gate, and self-archiving appeared to provide the needed widening.

Self-archiving of the e-print of a peer-reviewed literature provides the user with access to information which before now was inaccessible.[103] The responsibility of putting this information out no more lies in the hands of a third party, the publisher, but now rests on the author who is anxious to maximize the potentials in his or her work by getting it cited and for it to achieve strong impact factors.[104] Self-archiving does two major things, it removes the major obstacle which users are confronted with and that is the problem of price, and once this is resolved, there is the freedom to access requisite literature, and this resolves the second problem, an access/impact problem. This problem is resolved in favour of the author, because with access comes the opportunity for willing minds to read and cite the work, and impact is therefore made possible.[105] Putting it in a succinct form: no access, no reading, no reading, no impact.

The opportunity afforded users to freely access requisite literature and authors for impact through self-archiving, coupled with the absence of the need to negotiate with publishers for rights form important rationales for self-archiving.[106]

9.1.3 Self-archiving strategies

Self-archiving is currently implemented in either of four ways namely; personal websites, disciplinary archives, institutional-unit archives or institutional repositories.[107]

9.1.3.1 PERSONAL WEBSITE

Individuals are able to set up personal webpages where they provide information about themselves and from where they relate to the world as they wish. Such sites often contain personalized information about the individuals who set them up. One of such pieces of information is usually a list of publications and a link to the full documents of such publication. Several authors now make their works available via the platform of their personal websites. See for example the personal webpage of Peter Yu.[108]

9.1.3.2 SPECIALIZED OR DISCIPLINARY ARCHIVE

Particular disciplines have cultivated the practice of sharing research output with one another even prior to the digital and online age. Experts in the field of Computer Science and Physics are particularly known for such practices. Authors within these disciplines have an archive where they deposit their research outputs. ArXiv was the first electronic archive to be set with a focus on the field of physics.[109] It has extended to most of the physical sciences today and now includes fields like mathematics, astronomy, computer sciences and quantitative biology. Other examples of such archives are the Archaeological Data Services[110] and the Analytical Sciences Digital Library (ASDL).[111]

9.1.3.3 DEPARTMENTAL OR UNIT REPOSITORY

These are departmental, unit or school specific archives dedicated to hosting e-prints of members only. This type of repositories are often not that large as they majorly host the deposits made by members of a specific unit, department or school within an institution. See for example the repository hosted by the Duke Law School[112] and that hosted by the Queensland Department of Agriculture, Fishery and Forestry.[113]

9.1.3.4 INSTITUTIONAL REPOSITORY

This strategy is similar to the departmental or unit repository but is different in the sense that institutional repositories are set up by institutions. These repositories are usually larger in capacity than the ones run by departments, units or schools. They operate as one stop shops for archiving the output of research and other similar information within such institutions. Most universities today have institutional repositories. Queensland University of Technology (QUT)[114] and Covenant University in Nigeria[115] are two examples.

The four strategies to self-archiving highlighted above are all aimed at enabling access to knowledge. There are other initiatives that support access to knowledge from a policy framework perspective (open access mandates), as well as by the creation of platforms for easy detection of resources (open archive initiatives).

9.1.4 Open archive initiative

This is an initiative that ensures easy location of resources. It was set up to ensure that despite the large numbers of repositories, anyone conducting a search for information that should be in a repository would be able to harvest, that is, extract such information from any repository. The OAIster database is an example of a site powered by the open archive initiative providing resources from multiple repositories that can be easily harvested.[116] This is achieved by the development and promotion of standardized formats to enable interoperability and seamless searching, which in turn would enhance dissemination and sharing of information.[117] This initiative achieves centralization as it enables a single search via a database to run through all repositories that are compliant with the open archive initiative, and therefore, high numbers of repositories cannot constitute a challenge to those seeking information thanks to the interoperable nature of repositories enabled by the open archive initiative.[118]

9.1.5 Open access mandate

These are policies adopted by institutions (employers, funding agencies, government etc.) to ensure the output of academic scholarship inclusive of peer-reviewed journal publications, research findings, conference papers, theses, dissertations and institutional information are made open access by self-archiving such documents in a freely accessible central or institutional repository.[119] Prior to the issuance of mandates, it was observed that authors were not depositing their works.[120] This may have been due to a general lackadaisical attitude on the part of authors or the age-long practice of assigning all author rights to publisher.[121]

It has been discovered that open access via self-archiving help authors achieve accessibility, visibility and impact on their work but breaking the age-old practice of turning over the entire copyright to the publisher now stands as the challenge.[122] This is where open access mandates play a key role in that they are able to swing the negotiating pendulum in favour of authors due to institutional influence.

9.1.6 How open access mandate works

These open access mandates make open access a requirement for researchers and people under the charge of a mandating institution, thus placing on authors' an obligation to make the output of their research available via the platform of self-archiving. It also places authors in a position of strength to bargain with publishers for the right to self-archive the output of their research and thus provide open access to such journal articles.[123] In addition, it places a responsibility on authors who would ordinarily not have bothered, to ensure that their works are deposited in an institutional repository.[124] A good example is the National Institutes of Health (NIH) in the United States of America, which has made it mandatory that the output of all funded research be deposited in its institutional repository, PubMed.[125]

Open access self-archiving has been mandated by over 200 universities,[126] including Harvard University,[127] Queensland University of Technology (QUT),[128] Massachusetts Institute of Technology (MIT),[129] University College of London,[130] research organizations in the United States (NIH),[131] United Kingdom (RCUK)[132] and Europe (European Research Council – ERC),[133] the Australian Research Council (ARC),[134] the World Bank,[135] and the major global funding organizations.[136] A comprehensive list of registered repositories can be found on the website of the ROARMAP.[137]

10 The gold road

The other road to achieving open access is the gold road; open access journal publishing. The DOAJ defines open access journals as journals that use a funding model that does not charge readers or their institutions for access.[138] This new model of publishing, provides a free platform to the general public read and reuse peer-reviewed literature.[139] It however charges an APC to cover the publication cost.[140] These are scholarly journals readily available online to the public without "financial, legal or technological barriers other than those inseparable from gaining access to the internet itself".[141] Open access journals are not free to produce but are free to access. Users are therefore not required to make any form of payment to be able to access such materials. In addition, a number of journals allow for reuse rights. The scope of reuse is often made known by means of the application of a licence on the work.[142] Examples of open access journals are *PLoS*,[143] *BioMed Central*,[144] *The New Journal of Physics*[145] and *Murdoch University Law Review*[146].

The paths to open access are not all together straightforward. Several approaches have been adopted to provide free unrestricted access to the output of scholarly research. Some publishers maintain the traditional journal system and at the same time make particular articles available online subject to payment of a fee by the author or the authors sponsor (hybrid open access).[147]An example is the Thomas Walker's *Florida Journal of Entomology*.[148] Another practice is to make a particular article published in the traditional journal available after an embargoed period, which refers to an agreed period of time within which the work shall not be made open access (delayed open access).[149] *Journal of the Physical Society of Japan* is an example of a traditional journal with delayed open access.[150] The SHERPA/RoMEO website provides, among other things, a list of publishers and their embargo period for each of the publishers.[151]

11 Strategies in action

To further underscore the importance of access to knowledge, the positive impacts made by the open movement, particularly the successes made by the policy and licensing strategies, three of the largest not-for-profit funding organizations in the United States, Ford Foundation,[152] Bill & Melinda Gates Foundation,[153] and the William and Flora Hewlett Foundation[154] have all adopted open access policies requiring that the output of funded research be made available under creative commons licences, thereby granting free access for use and reuse to the general public.[155] Similarly, on the 20th of January 2011, the Obama Administration pledged US$2 billion for purposes of making available, accessible and reusable educational resources and required that they be released under a Creative Commons attribution (CC BY) licence.[156] The NIH (the largest source of funding for medical research in the world[157] and home to the largest hospital totally dedicated to medical research)[158] has adopted and mandated open access by making available online all its research findings and requiring that all NIH funded research be made available in line with the Institute's open access policy.[159] In the same vein, similar policies have been adopted by the Research Councils United Kingdom (RCUK),[160] the European Research Councils (ERC),[161] the Australian Research Council (ARC)[162] and the World Bank. The World Bank reiterating the well-known phrase that "knowledge is power" announced its adoption of an open access policy. It requires that all research outputs and knowledge products published by the Bank be licensed under a Creative Commons attribution licence (CC BY) as a default and as a first phase of the policy, the Bank on the 10th of April, 2012 launched the Open Knowledge Repository[163] with more than 2,000 books, articles, reports and research papers under a CC BY licence,[164] thus making those materials freely available and accessible to the general public.[165]

Although access to knowledge is critical to societal development, it is imperative to note that the default setting for the grant of access for the vast stores of knowledge is closed.[166] This closure is architecturally structured within a legal framework known as IP, which requires that permission/consent be sort and obtained before content with IP protection can be exploited, thereby giving the closure mechanism not only legal rights, but also protection against non-compliance.

Notes

* This chapter contains excerpts from one of the authors articles titled 'Fundamentals of Open Access'. The material was first published by Sweet & Maxwell in *European Intellectual Property Review* 36 (2) (2014), 112–123 and is reproduced by agreement with the publishers.

1 Craig Bailey, *Content Is King by Bill Gates*, available at www.craigbailey.net/content-is-king-by-bill-gates/.

2 See generally, J. Henry, *Knowledge Is Power: Francis Bacon and the Method of Science* (Icon, 2002). See also, *The Economist*, 'Knowledge Is Power: Do We Need a New Competition Policy for the New Economy?' available at www.economist.com/node/375597.

3 UNdata, *Nigeria*, available at https://data.un.org/CountryProfile.aspx?crName=NIGERIA. See also, Robert Kunzig, A. 'World with 11 Billion People? New Population Projections Shatter Earlier Estimates: Dueling Projections of Population Growth Present Different Visions of the World's Future', *National Geographic* (2014), available at http://news.nationalgeographic.com/news/2014/09/140918-population-global-united-nations-2100-boom-africa/.

4 Max Fisher, 'The Amazing, Surprising, Africa-Driven Demographic Future of the Earth' (2013) in nine charts, *The Washington Post*.

5 See G. Orwell & M. Bradbury, *Animal Farm* (Penguin Press, 2003), 112. "All animals are equal but some animals are more equal than others." See the, U.S. Congress, *Declaration of Independence* (1776), available at www.archives.gov/exhibits/charters/declaration_transcript.html. "We hold these truths to be self-evident, that all men are created equal." See also, The Constitution of the Federal Republic of Nigeria, available at www.nigeria-law.org/ConstitutionOfTheFederalRepublicOfNigeria.htm: "And to provide for a Constitution for the purpose of promoting the good government and welfare of all persons in our country, on the principles of freedom, equality and justice".

6 World Bank, *Poverty Overview* (2015), available at www.worldbank.org/en/topic/poverty/overview. See also, World Bank, *Poverty & Equity Data* (2015), available at http://povertydata.worldbank.org/poverty/home/. See also, David Pannell, *278-Global Wealth Inequality* (2012), available at www.pannelldiscussions.net/2015/02/278-global-wealth-inequality/.

7 R. Burns & L. Brander, *Poems of Robert Burns* (Oxford University Press, 1950), 91. "Man's inhumanity to man makes countless thousands mourn!"

8 United Nations, *The Millennium Development Goals Report 2014*, 3–4 (2014), available at www.un.org/millenniumgoals/2014%20MDG%20report/MDG%202014%20English%20web.pdf. "But more needs to be done to accelerate progress. We need bolder and focused action where significant gaps and disparities exist. . . . Substantial progress has been made in most areas, but much more effort is needed to reach the set target."

9 Nagla Rizk and Lea Shaver (eds.), *Access to Knowledge in Egypt: New Research on Intellectual Property, Innovation and Development* (Bloomsbury Academic, 2009), 176, where it was noted that "Knowledge and ICT innovation are becoming important values for business, socioeconomic development and wealth creation – with implications at the macro and micro levels."

10 Kunle Ola, 'Fundamentals of Open Access' 36 (2) (2014) *European Intellectual Property Review* 112, 119.

11 See generally, Krikorian Gaëlle & Kapczynski Amy, *Access to Knowledge in the Age of Intellectual Property* (Zone Books, 2010), 20–21, where it was noted that "The rise of new forms of knowledge management and the application of sophisticated information-processing schemes to fields such as health and agriculture means that our relationships to our very bodies – how we eat, whether we live – are more intimately governed by scientific and technical knowledge and information than ever before."

12 United Nations Educational, Scientific and Cultural Organization, Major Push for Adult and Youth Literacy in Nigeria, *UNESCO* (2012), available at www.unesco.org/new/en/dakar/about-this-office/single-view/news/major_push_for_adult_and_youth_literacy_in_nigeria/.

13 John Alechenu, Nigeria, Still in the Throes of Illiteracy, *Punch*, available at www.punchng.com/education/nigeria-still-in-the-throes-of-illiteracy/.

14 Chris Armstrong et al., *Access to Knowledge in Africa: The Role of Copyright in Africa* (UCT Press, 2010), 1. Education is integral to development. It is a catalyst for poverty reduction and economic growth, a pillar of public health and community building. Beyond its social and economic utility, education betters' people's lives by increasing their scope for individual choice and helping to fulfil human potential.

15 *Dying for Change Poor People's Experience of Health and Ill-Health, a Joint Undertaking Between WHO and World Bank*, available at www.who.int/hdp/publications/dying_change.pdf.

16 UN News Centre, *Literacy Vital for Beating Poverty and Disease and Reinforcing Stability – UN*, available at www.un.org/apps/news/story.asp?NewsID=39485&Cr=literacy&Cr1#.USQB_h1BP-Y.107.

17 Kunle Ola, 'Scholarly Publication in Nigeria: Implications of Open Access' 6 (2015) *The WIPO Journal* 117, 127. "The choice of where to publish often determines accessibility, visibility, impact and utility of the work. Most works published in Nigeria suffer low global and local visibility."

18 National Universities Commission, *List of Nigerian Universities and Years Founded*, available at www.nuc.edu.ng/pages/universities.asp?ty=1&order=inst_name.

19 Jide Awe, *Software Nigeria – The Software Industry in Nigeria*, available at www.jidaw.com/nigeria/nigeriasoftware.html. See also, *Microsoft Corporation v Frankie Associates Ltd* LPELR-8987 (CA) (Court of Appeal).

20 See, *Comrade Victor Ashaolu v Prince Muyideen Alade Aromire and Ors.*, Suit No. FHC/L/CS/949/97 (Federal High Court, Lagos), where the plaintiff brought and succeeded in his action for infringement of copyright.

The fact that these works were being marketed outside of Nigeria is testimony of the growth in the Nigerian film industry.

21 Jerome H. Reichman & Ruth L. Okediji, 'When Copyright Law and Science Collide: Empowering Digitally Integrated Research Methods on a Global Scale' 96 (2012) *Minnesota Law Review* 1367, 1370.

22 *CCH Canadian Ltd. v Law Society of Upper Canada* [2004] 1 S.C.R. 339.

23 Kevin Smith, *Are Fair Use and Open Access Incompatible?* (Duke University, 2014), available at https://blogs.library.duke.edu/scholcomm/2014/09/25/fair-use-open-access-incompatible/: "the solution is to help them understand that fair use and open licensing are NOT incompatible."

24 Peter Suber, *Open Access* (MIT Press, 2012), 15, 16, 39, 44. See where he noted that "For 350 years, scholars have willingly, even eagerly, published journal articles without payment, freeing them to consent to OA without losing revenue."

25 G. E. Christian, *Issues and Challenges to the Development of Open Access Institutional Repositories in Academic and Research Institutions in Nigeria*, available at https://idl-bnc.idrc.ca/dspace/bitstream/10625/36986/1/127792.pdf, International Development Research Centre (IDRC) (2008). See also, E. S. Gbaje, *Open Access Journal Publishing in Ahmadu Bello University, Zaria, Nigeria*, 76th IFLA: World Library and Information Congress, available at http://conference.ifla.org/past-wlic/2010/138-gbaje-en.pdf.

26 Carmella B'Hahn, 'Be the Change You Wish to See: An Interview with Arun Gandhi' 10 (2001) *Reclaiming Children and Youth* 6.

27 Ola, 114 (2014).

28 Suber, 4 (2012).

29 Stevan Harnad, *What Is Open Access*, available at www.eprints.org/openaccess/.

30 Brian Fitzgerald et al., OAK LAW PROJECT NO.1: Creating a Legal Framework for Copyright Management of Open Access Within the Australian Academic and Research Sector (Report for the Department of Education and Science and Training (DEST) 79 (2006), where he also noted that "the OA movement has captured worldwide attention and support."

31 Bill Hubbard, *Transcript of a Conversation Between Bill Hubbard and Steve Burholt*, available at https://radar.brookes.ac.uk/radar/file/77294217-6d7d-04a0-db9a-ef4d-ba94c6e3/1/RADAR_BillHubbard.pdf.

32 John Willinsky, *The Access Principle: The Case for Open Access to Research and Scholarship* (MIT Press, 2006), xii. The Access Principle: "A commitment to the value and quality of research carries with it a responsibility to extend the circulation of research output as far as possible and ideally to all who are interested in it and all who might profit by it."

33 See *PLOS*, Open Access (2013), available at www.plos.org/about/open-access/, 18 February.

34 Mellisa Hagemann, *Budapest Open Access Initiative*, available at www.opensocietyfoundations.org/openaccess/read

35 Mellisa Hagemann, *Ten Years on, Researchers Embrace Open Access*, available at www.opensocietyfoundations.org/voices/ten-years-on-researchers-embrace-open-access.

36 *Bethesda Statement on Open Access Publishing*, available at www.earlham.edu/~peters/fos/bethesda.htm. (2003).

37 *Berlin Declaration on Open Access to Knowledge in the Sciences and Humanities*, available at http://oa.mpg.de/files/2010/04/berlin_declaration.pdf. (2003).

38 See Peter Suber, *Open Access Overview: Focusing on Open Access to Peer-Reviewed Research Articles and Their Preprints* (2013), available at www.earlham.edu/~peters/fos/overview.htm (Peter Suber ed.). On 18 February, Bethesda Statement on Open Access Publishing, www.earlham.edu/~peters/fos/bethesda.htm. 2003, on 18 February, Berlin Declaration on Open Access to Knowledge in the Sciences and Humanities, http://oa.mpg.de/files/2010/04/berlin_declaration.pdf. 2003. at 18 February.

39 Suber (2013), See also, Peter Suber, 'Praising Progress, Preserving Precision' *SPARC Open Access Newsletter*, available at www.earlham.edu/~peters/fos/newsletter/09-02-04.htm#progress.

40 Charles W. Bailey, 'What Is Open Access' in N. Jacobs ed., *Open Access: Key Strategic, Technical and Economic Aspects* (2006), available at www.digital-scholarship.org/cwb/WhatIsOA.htm.

41 Willinsky, 211 (2006). See Appendix A Table A.1. See also, Sha. Li Zhang, 'The Flavors of Open Access' 23 (2007) *OCLC Systems & Services* 229.

42 Stevan Harnad et al., *The Green and Gold Roads to Open Access*, Nature Publishig Group, available at www.nature.com/nature/focus/accessdebate/21.html?a_aid=3598aabf.

43 Stevan Harnad, *The Green Road to Open Access: A Leveraged Transition*, available at http://users.ecs.soton.ac.uk/harnad/Temp/greenroad.html.

44 Suber, 58–60 (2012).

45 Peter Suber, *Green/Gold OA and Gratis/Libre OA* (2008), available at http://legacy.earlham.edu/~peters/fos/2008/08/greengold-oa-and-gratislibre-oa.html.

46 Peter Suber, *Gratis and Libre Open Access*, available at http://legacy.earlham.edu/~peters/fos/newsletter/08-02-08.htm#gratis-libre.

47 Suber (2008).

48 Suber, 4 (2012).

49 Several funding agencies have contributed to the success of open access and continue to contribute. The Open Society Foundation sponsored and hosted the meeting where the Budapest Open Access Initiative was adopted and signed. See also, Bill & Melinda Gates Foundation, *Bill & Melinda Gates Foundation Open Access Policy*, available at www.gatesfoundation.org/how-we-work/general-information/open-access-policy. See also, The William and Flora Hewlett Foundation, *Commitment to Open Licensing*, available at www.hewlett.org/about-us/values-policies/commitment-open-licensing. See also, Philanthrophy News Digest, *Ford Foundation Announces Open Licensing Policy for Grantees* (2015), available at http://philanthropynewsdigest.org/news/ford-foundation-announces-open-licensing-policy-for-grantees. See also, Creative Commons, *Hewlett Foundation Extends CC BY Policy to All Grantees* (2014), available at http://creativecommons.org/tag/the-william-and-flora-hewlett-foundation. See also, Creative Commons, *Ford Foundation to require CC BY for All Grant-Funded Projects* (2015), available at https://creativecommons.org/weblog/entry/44865. See also, Tate Williams, Why Big Foundations Ganging Up for Open Access Is Important, *Inside Philanthropy* (2015), available at www.insidephilanthropy.com/home/2015/2/6/why-big-foundations-ganging-up-for-open-access-is-important.html.

50 This excerpt on fundamentals of open access is an earlier work written by the author and was first published by Sweet & Maxwell in *European Intellectual Property Review* 36 (2) (2014), 112–123 and is reproduced by agreement with the publishers.

51 Hagemann, on 20 February 2013.

52 Budapest Open Access Initiative, *Ten Years on from the Budapest Open Access Initiative: Setting the Default to Open*, available at www.opensocietyfoundations.org/openaccess/boai-10-recommendations.

53 See Suber, 9 (2012), where he said "OA is made possible by the Internet and copyright-holder consent."

54 *Budapest Open Access Initiative*, available at www.opensocietyfoundations.org/openaccess/read (2002), www.opensocietyfoundations.org/openaccess/read. See generally, Cutler Kim-Mia, *Elsevier's Research Takedown Notices Fan Out to Startups, Harvard, Individual Academics* (2013), available at http://techcrunch.com/2013/12/19/elsevier/.

55 PetersonAndrea, *How One Publisher Is Stopping Academics from Sharing Their Research* (2013), available at www.washingtonpost.com/blogs/the-switch/wp/2013/12/19/how-one-publisher-is-stopping-academics-from-sharing-their-research/.

56 *Berlin Declaration on Open Access to Knowledge in the Sciences and Humanities*, available at http://oa.mpg.de/files/2010/04/berlin_declaration.pdf. 2003.

57 Organisation for Economic Co-operation and Development, *Declaration on Access to Research Data from Public Funding* (2004), available at www.oecd.org/science/sci-tech/sciencetechnologyandinnovationforthe21stcenturymeetingoftheoecdcommittee forscientificandtechnologicalpolicyatministeriallevel29-30january2004-finalcommu nique.htm, www.oecd.org/science/scienceandtechnologypolicy/38500813.pdf.

58 Suber, 17 (2012)." In general, scholarly journals don't pay editors or referees. . . "

59 Phil Davis, Publish-or-Perish Culture Promotes Scientific Narcissism, *The Scholarly Kitchen*, available at http://scholarlykitchen.sspnet.org/2012/05/07/publish-or-perish-culture-promotes-scientific-narcissism/.

60 See Internet (2014), available at http://en.wikipedia.org/wiki/Internet, 15 January.

61 Peter Suber, Knowledge as a Public Good, *SPARC* (2009), available at www.sparc.arl.org/resources/articles/knowledge#sthash.R1nBSlQF.dpuf.

62 Stevan Harnad, Open Access – Stevan Harnad Im Interview 65 (2012) *Mitteilungen Der* VÖB.

63 Kim-Mia (2013).

64 See Lawrence Lessig, The Vision for the Creative Commons: What Are We and Where Are We Headed? Free Culture, in Brian Fitzgerald ed., *Open Content Licensing: Cultivating the Creative Commons* (Sydney University Press, 2007), 42, where he said "I want to be clear about something, intellectual property is good. I am in favour of it."

65 See Jeremy De Beer et al., *Innovation & Intellectual Property Collaborative Dynamics in Africa* (UCT Press, 2014), 7. Here, it was noted that "It seems clear that IP does, to some extent, have a positive role to play in incentivising innovation and creativity." See also, note 64, where he said, "We want to use IP to enable free culture."

66 Emphasis mine, for the category of those who suggested to be able to cover the cost.

67 See, *Read Budapest Open Access Initiative* (2014), available at www.opensociety foundations.org/openaccess/read, 15 January.

68 David Solomon & Bo-Christer Bjork, 'A Study of Open Access Journals Using Article Processing Charges' 63 (2012) *The Journal of the American Society for Information Science and Technology* 1485.

69 See for example Section 6 of the Nigerian Copyright Act, which provides that works protected under copyright are under the exclusive control of the copyright holder. See also, Caralee Adams, *Open Access in Latin America: Embraced as Key to Visibility of Research* (2013), available at www.sparc.arl.org/news/open-access-latin-america-embraced-key-visibility-research-outputs.

70 Olukunle Ola, *Copyright Collective Administration in Nigeria Lessons for Africa* (Springer, 2013), 4.

71 Stevan Harnad et al., 'The Access/Impact Problem and the Green and Gold Roads to Open Access' 30 (2004) *Serial Review* 310–314.

72 Nigerian Copyright Commission NCC, 'STRAP and CLAMP – Nigeria Copyright Commission in Action' (2008) *WIPO Magazine*, September. At 12. Op Cit.

73 See, Justin Norrie, 'Harvard Decries the High Cost of Journal Subscription', *The Conversation* (2012), available at http://theconversation.edu.au/harvard-journal-subscription-fees-are-prohibitive-6659, 24 April. Where it was reported that "Harvard

library says it can no longer afford the vast cost of academic journal subscriptions. Subscription prices for online content from two publishers have increased by 145% over the past six years, far in excess of not only the consumer price index but also the higher education and the library price indices."

74 See Carolyn Deere, *The TRIPS Agreement and the Global Politics of Intellectual Property Reform in Developing Countries* (Oxford University Press, 2009), 3.

75 See MIT, *Working with the MIT faculty Open Access Policy*, available at https://libraries.mit.edu/scholarly/mit-open-access/open-access-policy/.

76 David Fewer, *The Genie in the Information Bottle* Index On Censorship, available at www.eurozine.com/articles/2005-10-24-fewer-en.html.

77 World Intellectual Property Organisation (WIPO) Copyright Treaty, adopted in Geneva on 20 December (1996), available at www.wipo.int/treaties/en/ip/wct/pdf/trtdocs_wo033.pdf WCT.

78 WIPO Performances Phonograms Treaty, adopted in Geneva on 20 December (1996), available at www.wipo.int/treaties/en/ip/wppt/pdf/trtdocs_wo034.pdf WPPT.

79 Nigerian Copyright Commission (NCC), *Copyright Notification Scheme* (2005), available at www.copyright.gov.ng/index.php/regulatory-schemes/copyright-notification.

80 WCT (1996). See Articles 11 and 12. See also, WPPT (1996) Articles 18 and 19.

81 Lucie Guilbault, 'Owning the Right to Open Up Access to Scientific Publications' in Lucie Guilbault & Christina Angelopoulos eds., *Open Content Licensing from Theory to Practice* (Amsterdam University Press, 2011), 158–159.

82 See Zhang, 231 (2007) where it was mentioned that "there are many players in the open access movement. Some are advocates, some are spectators, and other take quite opposite stands."

83 Most universities have put in place a repository for the deposit of final version of articles. The QUT and UNISA repositories are examples.

84 The NIH in America and Wellcome Trust in the United Kingdom are examples of players in the research industry.

85 Many government bodies are adopting open access and have opened up the results of publicly funded research to the public on several platforms inclusive of the Creative Commons licensing system. See available information at http://wiki.creativecommons.org/Government_use_of_Creative_Commons about the adoption of CC licences by the Australian Bureau of Statistic for its census. Also mentioned are AusGOAL and the adoption by the Netherland government of a CCO as the default policy for the nation's single government website "Rijksoverheid".

86 See Knowledge Unlatched, *A New Model for Academic Publishing*, available at www.knowledgeunlatched.org/. Where four of the five groups was mentioned.

87 See Esther Hoorn & Maurits Graaf, 'Copyright Issues in Open Access Research Journals, The Authors' *Perspective*' 12 (2006) *D-Lib Magazine*, available at www.dlib.org/dlib/february06/vandergraaf/02vandergraaf.html, where the open access movement was said to have stimulated discussions on copyright in the scholarly communication system and noted that stakeholders in that system include publishers, academic institutions, libraries and academics authors.

88 See, *Ten Years on from the Budapest Open Access Initiative: Setting the Default to Open*, available at www.opensocietyfoundations.org/openaccess/boai-10-recommendations.

89 Steven Harnad, *What Is Open Access*, available at www.eprints.org/openaccess/ See also, Steven Harnad, *Open Access Archivangelism*, available at http://openaccess.eprints.org/

90 UNISA, *Unisa Institutional Repository*, available at http://uir.unisa.ac.za/.

91 QUT has both an e-print repository, available at http://eprints.qut.edu.au/ and a digital repository available at www.digitalrepository.qut.edu.au/. The e-print repository warehouses and showcases some of the research output of QUT staff and postgraduate students, and the digital repository makes available the current QUT research repositories and digitized collections.

92 Directory of Open Access Journals (DOAJ), *Open Access Journal*, available at www.doaj.org/doaj?func=loadTemplate&template=faq&uiLanguage=en.
93 ROAR, *Registry of Open Access Repositories*, available at http://roar.eprints.org/cgi/roar_search/advanced?location_country=&software=&type=institutional&order=-recordcount%2F-date.
94 ROARMAP, *Registry of Open Access Repositories Mandatory Archiving Policies*, available at http://roarmap.eprints.org/.
95 SHERPA/RoMEO, *Publisher Copyright Policies & Self-Archiving*, available at www.sherpa.ac.uk/romeo/PDFandIR.html.
96 Stevan Harnad, 'The Open Challenge: A Brief History. Public Service Review: European Science & Technology' 9 (2010) *Public Service Review: European Science & Technology*, 13–15. See also, Alma Swan & Sheridan Brown, *Open Access Self-Archivng: An Author Study* (Key Perspective Limited, 2005), 1. See the introduction where Alma noted that "the practice of self-archiving has its roots in the field of computer sciences."
97 See the report by Leslie Chan et al., *Open Access and Development: Journals and Beyond* (Institute of Development Studies [IDS], 2012), 16. See where it was noted that "The ArXiv electronic archive of self-archived preprints was founded in 1991."
98 Cornell University Library, *arXiv.org*, available at http://arxiv.org/.
99 World Health Organization, *About HINARI* (2014), available at www.who.int/hinari/about/en/.
100 Access to Global Online Research In Agriculture, *About Agora* (2014), available at www.aginternetwork.org/en/.
101 INASP Annual Review (2012–2013).
102 Willinsky (2006).
103 Stevan Harnad, *Gold Open Access Publishing Must Not Be Allowed to Retard the Progress of Green Open Access Self-Archiving*, available at http://eprints.soton.ac.uk/271818/1/logospaper.pdf.
104 Suber (2004).
105 Stevan Harnad et al., 'The Access/Impact Problem and the Green and Gold Roads to Open Access' 30 (2004) *Serial Review,* 310–314
106 See generally, Tim Brody et al., 'Incentivizing the Open Access Research Web. Publication-Archiving, Data Archiving and Scientometrics' 3 (2007) *Ctwatch Quarterly* 42. See also, Swan & Brown (2005).
107 Bailey (2006).
108 See for example the home page of Peter K. Yu, *Peter Yu*, available at www.peteryu.com/publications.htm Where a list of all his publications are listed and made available.
109 Cornell University Library.
110 ADS, *Archaeology Data Service*, available at http://archaeologydataservice.ac.uk/.
111 ASDL, *Analytical Sciences Digital Library (ASDL)*, available at http://home.asdlib.org/.
112 Duke Law, *Duke Law Scholarship Repositories*, available at http://scholarship.law.duke.edu/.
113 E Research Archive eRA, *Queensland Department of Agriculture, Fisheries and Forestry Archive of Scientific and Research Publications*, available at www2.dpi.qld.gov.au/extra/era/index.html.
114 Queensland University of Technology, *QUT ePrints*, available at http://eprints.qut.edu.au/.currently.
115 Covenant University, *Covenant University Repository*, available at http://eprints.covenantuniversity.edu.ng/.
116 See, Online Computer Library Centre (OCLC), *OAIster* (2015), available at www.oclc.org/oaister.en.html?urlm=168646. OAIster is built upon the Archive Initiative Protocol for Metadata Harvesting (OAI-PMH) "Today, OAIster includes more than 30 million records representing digital resources from more than 1,500 contributors."

See also, MOAI Server, *MOAI, an Open Access Server Platform for Institutional Repositories*, available at http://infrae.com/products/moai.

117 Open Archives, *Open Archive Initiative*, available at www.openarchives.org/.

118 See, Open Archives, *Open Archives Initiative Protocol for Metadata Harvesting*, available at www.openarchives.org/pmh/tools/tools.php. This site has a list of sites that are powered by the open archive initiative.

119 See Stevan Harnad et al., 'The Access/Impact Problem and the Green and Gold Roads to Open Access' 30 (4) (2004) *Serial Review* 310–314, available at www.sciencedirect.com/science/article/pii/S0098791304001480, where it was noted that to reach 100 percent open access, self-archiving needs to be mandated by researchers' employers and funders, as the United Kingdom and the United States recently recommended, and universities need to implement that mandate.

120 Tom G. Cochrane & Paula A. Callan, 'Making a Difference: Implementing the Eprints Mandate at QUT' 23 (2007) *International Digital Library Perspectives*.

121 Swan & Brown (2005). See also, Bailey (2006). See also, Harnad (2007).

122 Harnad (2012). See also, Suber (2013).

123 *The Conversation*, Princeton goes open access to stop staff handing all copyright to journals – unless waiver granted, available at http://theconversation.edu.au/princeton-goes-open-access-to-stop-staff-handing-all-copyright-to-journals-unless-waiver-granted-3596.

124 See, Swan Alma, *Open access self-archiving: An Introduction* (2005), available at http://eprints.soton.ac.uk/261006/1/jiscsum.pdf.

125 National Institutes of Health (NIH), *NIH Public Access Policy*, available at http://publicaccess.nih.gov/.

126 See, ROARMAP, *Registry of Open Access Registries Mandatory Archiving Policies*, available at http://roarmap.eprints.org/.

127 See, *OA Self-Archiving Policy: Harvard University: Faculty of Arts and Sciences*, available at www.eprints.org/openaccess/policysignup/fullinfo.php?inst=Harvard%20University%3A%20Faculty%20of%20Arts%20and%20Sciences.

128 See, QUT ePrints.

129 See, Massachusetts Institute of Technology (MIT), available at http://roarmap.eprints.org/122/.

130 See, OA Self-Archiving: University College London (UCL), available at www.eprints.org/openaccess/policysignup/fullinfo.php?inst=University%20College%20London%20%28UCL%29.

131 NIH.

132 RCUK, *RCUK Policy on Open Access*, available at www.rcuk.ac.uk/research/Pages/outputs.aspx.

133 Open-access mandate, available at http://en.wikipedia.org/wiki/Open-access_mandate.

134 ARC, *ARC Open Access Policy*, available at www.arc.gov.au/applicants/open_access.htm.

135 The World Bank, *World Bank Announces Open Access Policy for Research and Knowledge, Launches Open Knowledge Repository* (2012), available at www.worldbank.org/en/news/press-release/2012/04/10/world-bank-announces-open-access-policy-for-research-and-knowledge-launches-open-knowledge-repository.

136 Bill & Melinda Gates Foundation. See also, Digest (2015).

137 See ROARMAP.

138 DOAJ.

139 Quin Sarah, *Open Access by IOP Publishing* (2013), available at http://australe.upmc.fr/access/content/group/fcMED_infoScient/seminaire_2012/UPMC_IOP_2012_11_anglais.pdf.

140 JISC, Report on the JISC Collections Workshop: 'Open Access Fees and the Hybrid Journal' (2011).

141 Suber (2013).

142 (CC) Creative Commons, *About the Licenses*, available at http://creativecommons.org/licenses/.
143 PLoS, 'PLOS ONE is a Peer-Reviewed, Open Access *Journal' PLOS One*.
144 BioMed Central, 'BioMed Central the Open Access Publisher' *Biomed Central*.
145 IOPscience, *New Journal of Physics The Open Access Journal for Physics*, available at http://iopscience.iop.org/1367-2630.
146 Murdoch University, *Murdoch University Law Review*, available at https://mdulr.murdoch.edu.au/index.php/mdulr.
147 These are referred to as Hybrid open access journals.
148 Ben Mudrak, 'New Study Tracks Growth of Open Access Publishing' *Expert Edge* (2012), available at http://expertedge.aje.com/2012/11/10/new-study-tracks-growth-of-open-access-publishing/. See also, David W. Lewis, 'The Inevitability of Open Access' 73 (2012) *College & Research Libraries* 494. See also, Wikipedia, *Hybrid Open Access*, available at http://en.wikipedia.org/wiki/Hybrid_open-access_journal, where it was noted that this was the first journal to have been recorded to have used this model. It was later extended to the other publications of the Entomological society of America and later refined by David Prosser in 2003 in the journal Learned Publishing.
149 These are referred to as delayed open access journals.
150 See, B.-C. Bjork et al., *Analysis of Economic Issues Related to Open Access to Scientific Publications* (Wydawnictwa ICM, 2014), 20 & 36. Mikael Laakso & Bo-Christer Bjork, 'Anatomy of Open Access Publishing: A Study of Longitudinal Development and Internal Structure' 10 (2012) *BMC Medicine* 2. See also Wikipedia, *Delayed Open Access*, available at http://en.wikipedia.org/wiki/Delayed_open-access_journal. Where it was noted that Molecular Biology of the Cell has a 1 month embargo, whereas Journal of the Physical Society of Japan has a 15-year embargo period.
151 See, *Publisher Copyright Policies & Self-Archiving: Embargoes Required*, available at www.sherpa.ac.uk/romeo/PDFandIR.html, where it categorized the embargo periods into 1 month (one publisher), 3 months (one publisher), 6 months (25 publishers), 12 months (22 publishers), 18 months (three publishers), 24 months (10 publishers), 3 years (two publishers), 4 years (two publishers), 5 years (two publishers), and Various embargo lengths (one publisher).
152 Digest (2015).
153 Bill & Melinda Gates Foundation.
154 Foundation.
155 See, Commons (2015).
156 Timothy Vollmer, *New Federal Education Fund Makes Available $2 Billion to Create OER Resources in Community Colleges* (2011), available at http://creativecommons.org/weblog/entry/26100. The announcement was jointly made by the Secretary of Labor Hilda L. Solis and Secretary of Education Arne Duncan.
157 NIH, *About NIH*, available at www.nih.gov/about/.
158 Ibid.
159 NIH.
160 RCUK.
161 ERC, *Open Access Guidelines for Researchers Funded by the ERC* (2012), available at http://erc.europa.eu/sites/default/files/document/file/open_access_policy_researchers_funded_ERC.pdf.
162 ARC, "ARC requires that any publications arising from an ARC supported research project must be deposited into an open access institutional repository within a twelve (12) month period from the date of publication."
163 The World Bank, *Open Knowledge Repository*, available at https://openknowledge.worldbank.org/.
164 Creative Commons.
165 The World Bank (2012).
166 Fitzgerald et al., 113 (2006).

Bibliography

Access to Global Online Research in Agriculture, *About Agora* (2014), available at www.aginternetwork.org/en/.

Adams, Caralee, *Open Access in Latin America: Embraced as Key to Visibility of Research* (2013), available at www.sparc.arl.org/news/open-access-latin-america-embraced-key-visibility-research-outputs.

ADS, *Archaeology Data Service*, available at http://archaeologydataservice.ac.uk/.

Alechenu, John, Nigeria, Still in the Throes of Illiteracy, *Punch*, available at www.punchng.com/education/nigeria-still-in-the-throes-of-illiteracy/.

Andrea, Peterson, *How One Publisher Is Stopping Academics from Sharing Their Research* (2013), available at www.washingtonpost.com/blogs/the-switch/wp/2013/12/19/how-one-publisher-is-stopping-academics-from-sharing-their-research/.

ARC, *ARC Open Access Policy*, available at www.arc.gov.au/applicants/open_access.htm.

Armstrong, Chris, et al., *Access to Knowledge in Africa: The Role of Copyright in Africa* (UCT Press, Cape Town 2010).

ASDL, *Analytical Sciences Digital Library (ASDL)*, available at http://home.asdlib.org/.

Awe, Jide, *Software Nigeria-the Software Industry in Nigeria*, available at www.jidaw.com/nigeria/nigeriasoftware.html.

B'Hahn, Carmella, 'Be the Change You Wish to See: An Interview with Arun Gandhi' 10 (2001) *Reclaiming Children and Youth*.

Bailey, Charles W., 'What Is Open Access' in N. Jacobs ed., *Open Access: Key Strategic, Technical and Economic Aspects* (Chandos publishing, Oxford 2006).

Bailey, Craig, *Content Is King by Bill Gates*, available at www.craigbailey.net/content-is-king-by-bill-gates/.

Berlin Declaration on Open Access to Knowledge in the Sciences and Humanities (2003), available at http://oa.mpg.de/files/2010/04/berlin_declaration.pdf.

Bethesda Statement on Open Access Publishing (2003), available at www.earlham.edu/~peters/fos/bethesda.htm.

BioMed Central, *BioMed Central the Open Access Publisher* (Biomed Central), available at https://www.biomedcentral.com/

Bjork, B-C., et al., *Analysis of Economic Issues Related to Open Access to Scientific Publications* (Wydawnictwa ICM, 2014).

Brody, Tim, et al., 'Incentivizing the Open Access Research Web. Publication-Archiving, Data Archiving and Scientometrics' 3 (2007) *CTWatch Quarterly* 42.

Budapest Open Access Initiative (2002), available at www.opensocietyfoundations.org/openaccess/read.

Budapest Open Access Initiative, Ten Years on from the Budapest Open Access Initiative: Setting the Default to Open, available at www.opensocietyfoundations.org/openaccess/boai-10-recommendations.

Burns, R. & L. Brander, *Poems of Robert Burns* (Oxford University Press, 1950).

(CC) Creative Commons, *About the Licenses*, available at http://creativecommons.org/licenses/.

CCH Canadian Ltd. v Law Society of Upper Canada (2004) 1 S.C.R. 339.

Chan, Leslie, et al., *Open Access and Development: Journals and Beyond* (Institute of Development Studies (IDS), 2012).

Christian, G. E., *Issues and Challenges to the Development of Open Access Institutional Repositories in Academic and Research Institutions in Nigeria*, available at https://idl-bnc.idrc.ca/dspace/bitstream/10625/36986/1/127792.pdf, International Development Research Centre (IDRC) (2008).

Cochrane, Tom G. & Paula A. Callan, 'Making a Difference: Implementing the Eprints Mandate' 23 (2007) *International Digital Library Perspectives*.

Comrade Victor Ashaolu v Prince Muyideen Alade Aromire and Ors., Suit No.FHC/L/CS/949/97 (Federal High Court, Lagos).

The Constitution of the Federal Republic of Nigeria (1999), available at www.nigeria-law.org/ConstitutionOfTheFederalRepublicOfNigeria.htm

Cornell University Library, *arXiv.org*, available at http://arxiv.org/.

Covenant University, *Covenant University Repository*, available at http://eprints.covenantuniversity.edu.ng/.

Creative Commons, *Ford Foundation to Require CC BY for All Grant-Funded Projects* (2015), available at https://creativecommons.org/weblog/entry/44865.

Creative Commons, *Hewlett Foundation Extends CC BY Policy to All Grantees* (2014), available at http://creativecommons.org/tag/the-william-and-flora-hewlett-foundation.

Davis, Phil, Publish-or-Perish Culture Promotes Scientific Narcissism, *The Scholarly Kitchen*, available at http://scholarlykitchen.sspnet.org/2012/05/07/publish-or-perish-culture-promotes-scientific-narcissism/.

De Beer, Jeremy, et al., *Innovation & Intellectual Property Collaborative Dynamics in Africa* (UCT Press, Cape Town 2014).

Deere, Carolyn, *The TRIPS Agreement and the Global Politics of Intellectual Property Reform in Developing Countries* (Oxford University Press, 2009).

'Directory of Open Access Journals (DOAJ)' *Open Access Journal*, available at www.doaj.org/doaj?func=loadTemplate&template=faq&uiLanguage=en.

Duke Law, *Duke Law Scholarship Repositories*, available at http://scholarship.law.duke.edu/.

Dying for Change Poor People's Experience of Health and Ill-Health, a Joint Undertaking Between WHO and World Bank, available at www.who.int/hdp/publications/dying_change.pdf.

The Economist, 'Knowledge Is Power: Do We Need a New Competition Policy for the New Economy?' available at www.economist.com/node/375597.

ERC, *Open Access Guidelines for Researchers Funded by the ERC* (2012), available at http://erc.europa.eu/sites/default/files/document/file/open_access_policy_researchers_funded_ERC.pdf.

E Research Archive eRA, *Queensland Department of Agriculture, Fisheries and Forestry Archive of Scientific and Research Publications*, available at www2.dpi.qld.gov.au/extra/era/index.html.

Fewer, David, *The Genie in the Information Bottle*, Index on Censorship, available at www.eurozine.com/articles/2005-10-24-fewer-en.html.

Fisher, Max, 'The Amazing, Surprising, Africa-Driven Demographic Future of the Earth' (2013) in 9 charts, *The Washington Post*.

Fitzgerald, Brian, et al., OAK LAW PROJECT NO.1: Creating a Legal Framework for Copyright Management of Open Access Within the Australian Academic and Research Sector (Report for the Department of Education and Science and Training (DEST) (2006).

Gaëlle, Krikorian & Kapczynski Amy, *Access to Knowledge in the Age of Intellectual Property* (Zone Books, New York 2010).

Gbaje, E. S., *Open Access Journal Publishing in Ahmadu Bello University, Zaria, Nigeria*, 76th IFLA: World Library and Information Congress, available at http://conference.ifla.org/past-wlic/2010/138-gbaje-en.pdf.

Guilbault, Lucie, 'Owning the Right to Open Up Access to Scientific Publications' in Lucie Guilbault & Christina Angelopoulos eds., *Open Content Licensing from Theory to Practice* (Amsterdam University Press, 2011).

Hagemann, Mellisa, *Ten Years on, Researchers Embrace Open Access*, available at www.opensocietyfoundations.org/voices/ten-years-on-researchers-embrace-open-access.

Harnad, Stevan, *Gold Open Access Publishing Must Not Be Allowed to Retard the Progress of Green Open Access Self-Archiving*, available at http://eprints.soton.ac.uk/271818/1/logospaper.pdf.

Harnad, Stevan, *The Green Road to Open Access: A Leveraged Transition*, available at http://users.ecs.soton.ac.uk/harnad/Temp/greenroad.html.

Harnad, Stevan, 'Open Access – Stevan Harnad Im Interview' 65 (2012) *Mitteilungen der VÖB*.

Harnad, Stevan, 'The Open Challenge: A Brief History. Public Service Review: European Science & Technology' 9 (2010) *Public Service Review: European Science & Technology*, 13–15.

Harnad, Stevan, *What Is Open Access*, available at www.eprints.org/openaccess/.

Harnad, Stevan, et al., 'The Access/Impact Problem and the Green and Gold Roads to Open Access' 30 (2004) *Serial Review*, 310–314

Harnad, Stevan, et al., *The Green and Gold Roads to Open Access*, Nature Publishing Group, available at www.nature.com/nature/focus/accessdebate/21.html?a_aid=3598aabf.

Henry, J., *Knowledge Is Power: Francis Bacon and the Method of Science* (Icon, Cambridge England 2002).

Hoorn, Esther & Maurits Graaf, 'Copyright Issues in Open Access Research Journals: The Authors' Perspective' 12 (2006) *D-Lib Magazine*.

Hubbard, Bill, *Transcript of a Conversation Between Bill Hubbard and Steve Burholt*, available at https://radar.brookes.ac.uk/radar/file/77294217-6d7d-04a0-db9a-ef4d-ba94c6e3/1/RADAR_BillHubbard.pdf.

Hubbard, Bill & Melinda Gates Foundation, *Bill & Melinda Gates Foundation Open Access Policy*, available at www.gatesfoundation.org/how-we-work/general-information/open-access-policy.

INASP Annual Review (2012–13).

IOPscience, *New Journal of Physics the Open Access Journal for Physics*, available at http://iopscience.iop.org/1367-2630.

JISC, Report on the JISC Collections Workshop: 'Open Access Fees and the Hybrid Journal' (2011).

Kim-Mia, Cutler, *Elsevier's Research Takedown Notices Fan Out to Startups, Harvard, Individual Academics* (2013), available at http://techcrunch.com/2013/12/19/elsevier/.

Knowledge Unlatched, *A New Model for Academic Publishing*, available at www.knowledgeunlatched.org/.

Kunzig, Robert, A World With 11 Billion People? New Population Projections Shatter Earlier Estimates: Dueling Projections of Population Growth Present Different Visions of the World's Future, *National Geographic* (2014), available at http://news.nationalgeographic.com/news/2014/09/140918-population-global-united-nations-2100-boom-africa/.

Laakso, Mikael & Bo-Christer Bjork, 'Anatomy of Open Access Publishing: A Study of Longitudinal Development and Internal Structure' 10 (2012) *BMC Medicine*.

Lewis, David W., 'The Inevitability of Open Access' 73 (2012) *College & Research Libraries*.

Li Zhang, Sha, 'The Flavors of Open Access' 23 (2007) *OCLC Systems & Services* 229.

Microsoft Corporation v Frankie Associates Ltd LPELR-8987 (CA) (Court of Appeal).

MIT, *Working with the MIT Faculty Open Access Policy*, available at https://libraries.mit.edu/scholarly/mit-open-access/open-access-policy/

MOAI Server, *MOAI, an Open Access Server Platform for Institutional Repositories*, available at http://infrae.com/products/moai.

Mudrak, Ben, *New Study Tracks Growth of Open Access Publishing* (Expert Edge, 2012), available at http://expertedge.aje.com/2012/11/10/new-study-tracks-growth-of-open-access-publishing/.

Murdoch University, *Murdoch University Law Review*, available at https://mdulr.murdoch.edu.au/index.php/mdulr.

National Universities Commission NCC, *List of Nigerian Universities and Years Founded*, available at www.nuc.edu.ng/pages/universities.asp?ty=1&order=inst_name.

Nigerian Copyright Commission NCC, *Copyright Notification Scheme* (2005), available at www.copyright.gov.ng/index.php/regulatory-schemes/copyright-notification.

Nigerian Copyright Commission NCC, 'STRAP and CLAMP – Nigeria Copyright Commission in Action' (2008) *WIPO Magazine*, September.

NIH, *About NIH*, available at www.nih.gov/about/.

NIH, *NIH Public Access Policy*, available at http://publicaccess.nih.gov/.

Norrie, Justin, Harvard Decries the High Cost of Journal Subscription, *The Conversation* (2012), available at http://theconversation.edu.au/harvard-journal-subscription-fees-are-prohibitive-6659, 24 April.

Organisation for Economic Co-operation and Development, *Declaration on Access to Research Data from Public Funding* (2004), available at www.oecd.org/science/sci-tech/sciencetechnologyandinnovationforthe21stcenturymeetingoftheoecdcommitteefor scientificandtechnologicalpolicyatministeriallevel29-30january2004-finalcommunique.htm, www.oecd.org/science/scienceandtechnologypolicy/38500813.pdf.

Ola, Kunle, 'Fundamentals of Open Access' 36 (2014) *European Intellectual Property Review* 112.

Ola, Kunle, 'Scholarly Publication in Nigeria: Implications of Open Access' 6 (2015) *The WIPO Journal* 117.

Olukunle OLA, *Copyright Collective Administration in Nigeria Lessons for Africa* (Springer, New York 2013).

Online Computer Library Centre (OCLC), *OAIster* (2015), available at www.oclc.org/oaister.en.html?urlm=168646.

Nick Shockey ed., Open Access Empowers 16-Year-Old Jack Andraka to Create Breakthrough Cancer Diagnostic, *SPARC* (2013), available at www.sparc.arl.org/news/enews/june13

Open Archives, *Open Archive Initiative*, available at www.openarchives.org/.

Open Archives, *Open Archives Initiative Protocol for Metadata Harvesting*, available at www.openarchives.org/pmh/tools/tools.php.

Orwell, G. & M. Bradbury, *Animal Farm* (Penguin Press, 2003).

Pannell, David, *278-Global Wealth Inequality* (2012), available at www.pannelldiscussions.net/2015/02/278-global-wealth-inequality/.

Peter K. Yu, *Peter Yu* (2014), available at www.peteryu.com/publications.htm

Philanthropy News Digest, *Ford Foundation Announces Open Licensing Policy for Grantees* (2015), available at http://philanthropynewsdigest.org/news/ford-foundation-announces-open-licensing-policy-for-grantees.

PLOS, *Open Access*, available at www.plos.org/about/open-access/.

PLOS, 'PLOS One Is a Peer-Reviewed, Open Access Journal' *PLOS One*.

Queensland University of Technology, *QUT ePrints*, available at http://eprints.qut.edu.au/.

Tom, G. Cochrane & Paula, A. Callan, Making a Difference: Implementing the eprint mandate at QUT. International Digital Library Perspectives' 23 (2007) *International Digital Library Perspectives*.

RCUK, *RCUK Policy on Open Access*, available at www.rcuk.ac.uk/research/Pages/outputs.aspx.

Reichman, Jerome H. & Ruth L. Okediji, 'When Copyright Law and Science Collide: Empowering Digitally Integrated Research Methods on a Global Scale' 96 (2012) *Minnesota Law Review*.

Rizk, Nagla & Lea Shaver (eds.) *Access to Knowledge in Egypt: New Research on Intellectual Property, Innovation and Development* (Bloomsbury Academic, London 2009).

ROARMAP, *Registry of Open Access Repositories*, available at http://roar.eprints.org/cgi/roar_search/advanced?location_country=&software=&type=institutional&order=-recordcount%2F-date.

ROARMAP, *Registry of Open Access Repositories Mandatory Archiving Policies*, available at http://roarmap.eprints.org/.

Sarah, Quin, *Open Access by IOP Publishing* (2013), available at http://australe.upmc.fr/access/content/group/fcMED_infoScient/seminaire_2012/UPMC_IOP_2012_11_anglais.pdf.

SHERPA/RoMEO, *Publisher Copyright Policies & Self-Archiving*, available at www.sherpa.ac.uk/romeo/PDFandIR.html.

Smith, Kevin, *Are Fair Use and Open Access Incompatible?* (Duke University, 2014), available at https://blogs.library.duke.edu/scholcomm/2014/09/25/fair-use-open-access-incompatible/.

Solomon, David & Bo-Christer Bjork, 'A Study of Open Access Journals Using Article Processing Charges' 63 (2012) *The Journal of the American Society for Information Science and Technology* 1485.

Suber, Peter, *Gratis and Libre Open Access*, available at http://legacy.earlham.edu/~peters/fos/newsletter/08-02-08.htm#gratis-libre.

Suber, Peter, *Green/Gold OA and Gratis/Libre OA* (2008), available at http://legacy.earlham.edu/~peters/fos/2008/08/greengold-oa-and-gratislibre-oa.html.

Suber, Peter, Knowledge as a Public Good, *SPARC* (2009), available at www.sparc.arl.org/resources/articles/knowledge#sthash.R1nBSlQF.dpuf.

Suber, Peter, *Open Access* (MIT Press, Cambridge MA 2012).

Suber, Peter, *Open Access Overview: Focusing on Open Access to Peer-Reviewed Research Articles and Their Preprints*, available at www.earlham.edu/~peters/fos/overview.htm (Peter Suber ed.).

Suber, Peter, 'Praising Progress, Preserving Precision' *SPARC Open Access Newsletter*, available at www.earlham.edu/~peters/fos/newsletter/09-02-04.htm#progress.

Swan, Alma & Sheridan Brown, *Open Access Self-Archiving: An Author Study* (Key Perspective Limited, 2005).

UNdata, *Nigeria*, available at https://data.un.org/CountryProfile.aspx?crName=NIGERIA.

UNESCO, Major Push for Adult and Youth Literacy in Nigeria, *UNESCO* (2012), available at www.unesco.org/new/en/dakar/about-this-office/single-view/news/major_push_for_adult_and_youth_literacy_in_nigeria/.

UNISA, *Unisa Institutional Repository*, available at http://uir.unisa.ac.za/.

United Nations UN, *The Millennium Development Goals Report 2014* (2014), available at www.un.org/millenniumgoals/2014%20MDG%20report/MDG%202014%20English%20web.pdf.

UN News Centre, *Literacy Vital for Beating Poverty and Disease and Reinforcing Stability – UN*, available at www.un.org/apps/news/story.asp?NewsID=39485&Cr=literacy&Cr1#.USQB_h1BP-Y.

U.S. Congress, *Declaration of Independence* (1776), available at www.archives.gov/exhibits/charters/declaration_transcript.html.

Vollmer, Timothy, *New Federal Education Fund Makes Available $2 Billion to Create OER Resources in Community Colleges* (2011), available at http://creativecommons.org/weblog/entry/26100.

WHO, *About HINARI* (2014), available at www.who.int/hinari/about/en/.

Williams, Tate, Why Big Foundations Ganging Up for Open Access Is Important, *Inside Philanthropy* (2015), available at www.insidephilanthropy.com/home/2015/2/6/why-big-foundations-ganging-up-for-open-access-is-important.html.

Wikipedia, *Delayed Open Access*, available at http://en.wikipedia.org/wiki/Delayed_open-access_journal.

Wikipedia, *Hybrid Open Access*, available at http://en.wikipedia.org/wiki/Hybrid_open-access_journal

The William and Flora Hewlett Foundation, *Commitment to Open Licensing*, available at www.hewlett.org/about-us/values-policies/commitment-open-licensing.

Willinsky, John, *The Access Principle: The Case for Open Access to Research and Scholarship* (MIT Press, Cambridge MA 2006).

WIPO Performances Phonograms Treaty, adopted in Geneva on 20 December 1996, www.wipo.int/treaties/en/ip/wppt/pdf/trtdocs_wo034.pdf WPPT.

The World Bank, *Open Knowledge Repository*, available at https://openknowledge.worldbank.org/.

The World Bank, *Poverty & Equity Data* (2015), available at http://povertydata.worldbank.org/poverty/home/.

The World Bank, *Poverty Overview* (2015), available at www.worldbank.org/en/topic/poverty/overview.

The World Bank, *World Bank Announces Open Access Policy for Research and Knowledge, Launches Open Knowledge Repository* (2012), available at www.worldbank.org/en/news/press-release/2012/04/10/world-bank-announces-open-access-policy-for-research-and-knowledge-launches-open-knowledge-repository.

2 Theory of open access

> One person gives freely, yet gains even more; another withholds unduly, but comes to poverty. A generous person will prosper; whoever refreshes others will be refreshed.[1]
>
> Proverbs 11: 24–25

1 Introduction

The Greek philosopher Aristotle told us over 2,300 years ago that "Man is a social animal. He who lives without a society is either a beast or a God."[2] We all exist as a result of a combined effort. Development has brought about an increase in man's standard of living but has also caused a strain on social values. Values such as dependency and inter-dependence, sharing, caring and helping have gradually gravitated towards a culture of self-aggrandizement, self-acquisition and self-dependency to the exclusion of others. The reality is that we are who we are because of who we all are.[3] No man is an island; we need each other. The wise book teaches that two are better than one, because they have a good reward for their labour;[4] how good and pleasant it is for brethren to dwell together in unity;[5] and that Iron sharpens Iron.[6] It is in sharing, giving, caring and helping that life finds its true expression, meaning and fulfilment. As aptly captured by Viktor Frankl in his book Man's Search for Meaning, "Ultimately, man should not ask what the meaning of his life is, but rather he must recognize that it is he who is asked."[7] Life is not about "me". It is not about "you". It is about "us".

It is this spirit of camaraderie that open access seeks amongst other things to build. It seeks to draw our focus away from the egocentric and self-centredness that have become the norm in the society and re-engineer a sharing structure that would bring about a balanced knowledge society. Open access is about a revolutionary change in how peer-reviewed literature and all other information is accessed, used, reused and generally exploited.[8] It seeks a shift in the publication process from *closed* to *open*, *restricted* to *unrestricted*, *payment* to *free*, *all rights reserved* to *some rights reserved*, or better still, *no rights reserved*. Open access is not merely putting any material up online, it is not vanity publishing, it does not honour fragrant disregard for the legal system; rather it is a revolution working within legitimate rules against structures that have permitted and enabled a business model which erects and facilitates legal, price and technical restrictions against users.

2 Knowledge development process

Information dissemination within the knowledge management framework falls within the exclusive right of copyright owners and is therefore restricted unless permission is granted or it falls under some form of limitation, exception or compulsory licensing system.[9] Knowledge/information development within the academic and research community have a practice of peer review for purposes of ascertaining and maintaining quality.[10] The practice is for academics to write and for publishers' to take care of the peer review, publication and marketing aspects. The practice of Journal publishing dates back to 1665, when the first journal *Le Journal des Scavan*, later renamed *Les Journal Savants*, was published by Jean Cusson, rue S. Jacques.[11] In the same year the first scientific journal printed in the English language and edited by Henry Oldenburg titled *Philosophical Transactions of the Royal Society of London* was also published.[12] Henry Oldenburg had the practice of sending out submitted manuscripts for independent evaluation by competent referees and has been recognized as the initiator of the peer-review process.[13]

2.1 The publishing industry

The duo of the printing press and peer-review process has developed into what today is the publishing industry and has become a major player in determining how knowledge, particularly peer-reviewed knowledge is disseminated. This influence by the publishing industry on knowledge dissemination can be traced to the strategic role of publishers as the doorway to the output of research and to the introduction of subscription payment: payments which users, mostly libraries, must pay before they can access published peer-reviewed information.

Publishers are responsible for the investments put into publishing the written works of authors and have a business model based on subscription payments by users to recoup their investments. Initially these fees were minimal, but with time, the consistent rise in subscription fees have turned the publishing industry into knowledge barricades instead of knowledge access gates. Even the wealthiest of universities are not able to keep up with the rising cost of journal subscriptions.[14] It has been reported that the rate of increase in journal subscription prices is second to none.[15] Increase in student loan indebtedness has also been reported and may not be unconnected to the high subscription rates which directly or indirectly affect students' ability to pay for the kind of education they desire.[16]

If all libraries and research institutions in the world can afford the cost of journal subscriptions and are therefore able to pay and subscribe continually to all journals, universal access to peer-reviewed literatures would be attained. If that was a dream or an expectation, it unfortunately is one that is unlikely to come true, considering the continued rise in subscription cost. Libraries and research institutions all over the world are cancelling subscriptions due to its ever-rising cost and worse still, most libraries and research institutions in developing countries are not able to maintain subscriptions with journals.[17] Where such subscriptions are maintained, they are usually not in the fields that are most relevant to their research needs, and this is directly connected to the inability of these institutions to keep up with the increase in subscription fees.[18]

The high cost of journal subscriptions, the frustrations experienced by users due to an inability to access information, the need to explore new business models for publishing, as well as the moral sensitivity of the human soul to share knowledge, has precipitated the emergence of the movement advocating for free unrestricted access to use and reuse peer-reviewed literature off the Internet. Other precipitating factors include the academic culture of publish or perish,[19] the eagerness to increase impact factor on the side of authors in respect of their works,[20] the goal of sharing the knowledge of the poor with the rich and that of the rich with the poor,[21] as well as the pursuit to provide available platforms for the visibility, impact and accessibility of works originating in developing countries. Also included is the need by governments to be seen to be providing access to knowledge,[22] education for all and freedom of information in compliance with international best practices, and probably one of the most compelling reasons is the desire to maximize the Internet as a platform for knowledge dissemination. Regardless of the thoughts underpinning the idea to promote an open culture, a culture where peer-reviewed literature is freely and immediately available upon publication and in the broadest and most effective way, free from price, legal and technical restrictions, such thoughts have a bearing on four factors which I have identified with the acronym "SELP" referring to *S* for social, *E* for economic, *L* for legal and *P* for political.

2.2 Guerrilla

The Guerrilla Open Access Manifesto noted the power of information and that those with access to information must do something about sharing this information to those who do not have access. The manifesto decried the greed of corporations and calls on everyone to oppose the privatization of knowledge. The manifesto noted that

> Information is power. But like all power, there are those who want to keep it for themselves. . . . There are those struggling to change this. The Open Access Movement has fought valiantly to ensure that scientists do not sign their copyrights away but instead ensure their work is published on the Internet, under terms that allow anyone to access it. . . . Those with access to these resources, students, librarians, scientists, you have been given a privilege. You have a duty to share it with the world.[23]

The fact that there are many supporters and drivers is an indication that different groups may approach the goal of free, immediate, broad and effective dissemination of knowledge to the public from different perspectives. The goal may be the same, but the rationale for the goal often differs, and therefore, the approach by the different groups to achieving the goal may also differ. Some supporters and drivers come to the table from an economic perspective,[24] others social reasons,[25] and yet others join the movement due to the frustrations of the current legal regime.[26] For some others, they come for political reasons.[27] Whatever the underpinnings of the supporters or drivers be it social, economic, legal or political, the end-user is happy to have immediate, broad, effective, free and unrestricted access to use and reuse peer-reviewed literature without the barriers of price, legal and technical restrictions.

This chapter examines these underpinnings in the minds of the varied supporters and drivers from a social, economic, legal and political perspective.

3 Social

3.1 Ubuntu

It is a South-African word that captures Mandela's greatest gift, his recognition that we are all bound together in ways that are invisible to the eye; that there is a oneness to humanity; that we achieve ourselves by sharing ourselves with others and caring for those around us.[28]

The word *Ubuntu* means "humanity to others". The more popular meaning is "I am what I am because of who we all are."[29] It depicts that "your pain is my pain, my wealth is your wealth, your salvation is my salvation."[30] We are all intertwined through our humanity and as the word Ubuntu depicts, humans are interdependent. We are who and what we are because of who we all are. The African culture although very diverse is community based and has celebrated mutuality and connectedness for centuries.[31] No man is an island: man thrives best when he works in cooperation with others.[32] The spirit of the Ubuntu ideology was aptly captured by David Cameron when he said

> It's time we admitted that there's more to life than money, and it's time we focused not just on GDP, but on GWB – general well-being, . . . Well-being can't be measured by money or traded in markets. It's about the beauty of our surroundings, the quality of our culture and, above all, the strength of our relationships. . . . Improving our society's sense of well-being is, I believe, the central political challenge of our times.[33]

The essence of Ubuntu is exemplified in Amy Biehl's story.[34] Amy was a promising lady who graduate from Stanford University and had extensive work experience in the different continents of the world. Amy was the winner of a 1993 Fulbright scholarship, which she dedicated to the establishment of a multiracial democracy in South Africa. She was an active member of the ANC and helped in registering voters for South Africa's first free elections. On 25 August 1993, Amy was killed in an act of political mob violence in Guguletu, a town outside of Cape

Town. Four young men were arrested and sentenced to 18 years imprisonment. In honour of Amy's values for peace and reconciliation and in the spirit of Ubuntu, Amy's parents supported the grant of amnesty to all four of the convicted killers. Today, two of the four young men (Ntobeko Peni and Easy Nofemela) work at the Amy Biehl Foundation, which was set up to address the challenges of violence. In the words of the Managing Director of the foundation "They are a living embodiment of values, such as forgiveness, reconciliation and tolerance, which we strive to teach the youth of Cape Town through our work."[35] The spirit of Ubuntu is not one that condones violence or fragrant disregard of the law, but rather it is one that is alive to the realities of violence and instead of responding to violence with violence or hatred, it stretches out the hand of forgiveness, love and sharing. It is this hand, open access seeks to stretch out in the information hemisphere, the hand that shares instead of keeps, that opens instead of closing.

3.2 Koinonia

Human flourishing is dependent in many ways on the quality of our relationships with one another. This is what the Greek word "Koinonia" connotes. It "is the selfless emersion into each other lives. . . . It means to be a sharer, a companion, one who is a partaker, a participant in communion."[36] Life is best lived when it is shared. That is why the open movement advocates a sharing culture. A culture of koinonia, where participants selflessly immerse themselves into each other as sharer, companion and partakers. The Android technology which is an open source project led by Google is a living proof of the benefits, efficiency and effectiveness of sharing.[37] Interestingly, knowledge is given a tangible form because man decides to reveal what was hitherto hidden in the mind. The whole essence of revealing the unseen ideas in the mind is for others to appreciate and benefit from it. It is for it to be shared; otherwise, it could and indeed should have been left hidden from all others, locked up in the mind.

3.3 Sharing: a social responsibility

Sharing the output of research findings can be the difference between life and death to somebody. Accessing a freely downloadable article or getting some open educational resources (OER) to help with a class assignment can be the difference between success and failure. Access to public sector information has the tendencies to bring about good governance, responsibility and accountability.[38] Sharing knowledge is paramount to development.[39] No other living being on Earth has the privilege that humans enjoy when it comes to knowledge creation and dissemination. We therefore owe it to ourselves as a social responsibility to share knowledge with one another, more so that knowledge is power,[40] and that people are destroyed for lack of knowledge.[41] Knowledge provides the requisite know-how and access is key to knowledge acquisition. Aaron Swartz captured this social responsibility succinctly in the Guerrilla open access manifesto when he said

> Those with access to these resources – students, librarians, scientists – you have been given a privilege. You get to feed at this banquet of knowledge

> while the rest of the world is locked out. But you need not – indeed, morally, you cannot – keep this privilege for yourselves. You have a duty to share it with the world.[42]

Aaron understood that we all have a duty, a responsibility to share knowledge because of the potential power it carries, because of its potency as a change agent and because of its revolutionary abilities. This was what motivated him to challenge everyone with access to that all important social responsibility to share it with the world.

Aristotle explaining the meaning and essence to life noted that "all men by nature desire knowledge"[43] and that the good life is what we all should aim for and that it is all about flourishing. He called it "Eudaimonia": a life that fulfils man's natural drive (a drive which he identified as the search for knowledge) and drives them to the highest end.[44] Aristotle advocates that we should live not just for ourselves, but we should live in pursuit of the common good and

> to speak of the common good is to recognise that there are numerous proper goals in life beyond our own private benefits. Responsible people look for opportunities to contribute to worthy causes and to improve society however possible, even when the benefits of this progress will go primarily to others. . . . Everyone has an obligation to promote the common good by making whatever contributions are necessary to improve the lives of all.[45]

This obligation may not be compellable or enforceable under the law but is a social responsibility which all well-meaning individuals must strive to meet. It must be focused on planning for the community and not for a limited class.[46] This is probably what was behind the minds of those gathered at the Bethesda meeting when they said

> Our organizations sponsor and nurture scientific research to promote the creation and dissemination of new ideas and knowledge for the public benefit. . . . This mission is only half-completed if the work is not made as widely available and as useful to society as possible. . . . We adopt these policies in the expectation that the publishers of scientific works share our desire to maximize public benefit from scientific knowledge and will view these new policies as they are intended – an opportunity to work together for the benefit of the scientific community and the public.[47]

3.4 Give and it shall be given unto you

Luke 6:38, "Give, and it shall be given unto you; good measure, pressed down, and shaken together, and running over, shall men give into your bosom. For with the same measure that ye mete withal it shall be measured to you again."[48] King Solomon in the book of Proverbs 11:24–25 emphasizes the wisdom of sharing freely above undue restrictions and says that "One person gives freely, yet gains even more; another withholds unduly, but comes to poverty. A generous person will prosper; whoever refreshes others will be refreshed."[49] It is in sharing that humanity finds true fulfilment and development. Margaret Wheatley corroborates this point in "The Paradox and Promise of Community", a chapter in her book *Finding Our Way, Leadership for an Uncertain Time.*[50]

The open access movement builds on the above principles by encouraging the sharing of scholarly works. The greater the works shared, the higher its visibility, citation and impact.[51] Therefore the author who gives out a work for free will definitely receive some form of reward. The work will come back, but this time it may have been reused, modified or adapted (*pressed down, shaken together and run over*). Ken Smith in *Free Is Cheaper* discusses the inhumanity of man to man but however notes that the "urge to co-operate freely is as old as the human race."[52] Isaac Newton appreciated the essence and importance of sharing and expressed it this way, "if I have seen further it is by standing on the shoulders of giants."[53] He could stand on their shoulders because they provided the needed access. The open access movement is advocating that this generation of giants provide the needed access and not hide their shoulders but should allow, permit, authorize and provide the needed platforms and opportunities for others to see further by sharing the use of their shoulders.

4 Economic

4.1 Global inequality/greed

The scale of global inequality is staggering. In 2014, it was reported that 48 percent of global wealth was owned by the richest 1 percent. $1.9 trillion wealth of 80 top billionaires is equal to the bottom 50 percent of the rest of the world. There has been a US$600bn increase in wealth for 80 top billionaires in four years, comprising a 50 percent rise, and there has been a US$750 billion drop in wealth for the poorest 50 percent of the world in four years.[54] The above reports reveal that the financial purchasing capacity of the average global citizen is on the decline, and this is affecting every kind of commodity inclusive of knowledge products which are vital to development. This global economic inequality is depriving many of a fundamental right, the right to access knowledge and as pointed out by the Guerrilla open access manifesto, "Only those blinded by greed would refuse to let a friend make a copy. . . . Large corporations, of course, are blinded by greed. The laws under which they operate require it, their shareholders would revolt at anything less."[55] The above words reflect the mind of certain proponents of open access who believe that greed is one of the underlying factors that have enabled the continued lock up of access to knowledge.

There is the capitalist argument that people need to be incentivized for hard work and individual initiative and that competition brings out the best in people.[56] This postulation has brought about great innovations, creativity, employment and great opportunities, but at the same time, it has widened the divided between the rich and poor, between those who have access and does who are unable to obtain access. It is not always about gain, about money, about how much one acquires.

If the meaning of life were tied to wealth, King Solomon with all his wealth would not have cried out meaningless, meaningless, life is meaningless. As noted earlier while discussing Ubuntu, meaning is found in sharing, and that is why the open community is making great strides through sharing and are yet able to find business models which run concurrently. The examples of Android,[57] Apache,[58] Ubuntu,[59] Linux,[60] SUSE,[61] and Creative Commons licences[62] are all examples of knowledge products that are developed based on communal cooperation and are shared freely yet the organization behind managing these products have been able to work out business models for the effective running of their organizations.

4.2 Adam Smith (1723–1790)

Adam Smith's book *Wealth of Nations* had postulated "the invisible hands"[63] and noted that individual self-interest constitutes a major motivating factor for the production and acquisition of goods and services. He referred to butchers and bakers who use their discretion in determining the amount to produce and points out that this power of discretion is made possible because of a free market economy which he relates to his classical economics theory.[64] The theory postulates that a "laissez-faire attitude by government toward the market place will allow the invisible hand to guide everyone in their economic endeavours, create the greatest good for the greatest number of people, and generate economic growth."[65] This capitalist theory is what prevails in the global economy today.

4.3 Karl Marx (1818–1883)

Karl Marx did not share Smith's theory on capitalism. Whereas Smith saw capitalism as a motivating agent in individuals, Marx saw it as exploitation. In his 1867 *Das Kapital*, he noted that capitalist's derive their gains from an exploitative system and explained that they underpaid workers for the value of work done.[66] Marx posited that capitalism breeds exploitation and leads to class struggle.[67] He predicted that this same struggle will lead to the demise of capitalism.[68] He noted that as business entities increase production capacity and profit margins rise, the rich get richer and poor poorer thus breeding dissatisfaction, oppression and exploitation. This underscores today's situation where 1 percent of the wealthiest control about 50 percent of the global wealth.

4.4 Economic realities versus imperatives for free

The publishing cycle costs money and entails multiple processes consisting of peer review by editors, typesetting, printing, distribution and marketing.[69] This process can be cost intensive, and most authors and researchers may not be in the position to fund the actual publication of their works.[70] When the practice of journal publication began, it served as the major avenue for disseminating literary scholarly works, and this system for knowledge dissemination has grown through the years.[71] Technological development has however enabled easier and faster publication of copyright protected content and the structure that has existed where authors write and publishers invest in publishing was effective until two issues began to raise their heads. The first was the continuous rise in journal subscription fees, and the other was the emergence of the Internet.[72]

The rise in journal subscription fees was and still is a cause of frustration within the research community. The Internet provided the platform for a change. However, an industry that had thrived for hundreds of years would not seat back and be sent to oblivion. It therefore is only reasonable to consider that, if this new technology can enable global online distribution of peer-reviewed literature free of charge and without any form of access restriction to the user public, how will this new initiative built on the shoulders of this new invention called the Internet affect the economic well-being of the traditional publishing industry? As can be imagined, the economic factor, the capitalist spirit, the invisible hand referred to by Adam Smith will rise to protect its territory and even annex more.

It is important to give some thoughts to these economic concerns, considering the high returns on investment that have been recorded in the publishing industry. These high financial returns imply that, there are interests to be protected. This is why the open access movement provides for article processing charges (APC) to cover the cost of publication production in the open access environment.[73] The CEO of Springers in an interview put it this way "our policy is very simple: as long as the cost of the value-added services provided by publishers is recognized and covered, Springer is happy to provide the research community with an open access publishing option."[74] The need to find a balance between the quest for profit and the provision of access to knowledge is the rationale for open access.

4.5 Open access will adversely affect traditional publishing

The fears however, that freedom to access peer-reviewed literature at no cost or restriction to the users would adversely affect the publishing industry has been proved wrong. It is now 23 years since Arxiv was established, and it has not adversely affected the revenues of journals publishing in the field of physics.[75]

4.6 Open access is not a viable publishing business model

The fears that open access publishing cannot be economically viable has been disproved by the successes of BioMed Central, its acquisition by the second largest commercial publishers Springer,[76] and the continued establishment of more open access publishing outfits. The concept of free, unrestricted and immediate access to the peer-review literature is not merely a socially oriented ideology, but also a new business model running on the possibilities enabled by the Internet and now asserted by the successes of several open access publishers.[77]

4.7 Rivalrous against non-rivalrous

In the pre-digital era, printed materials could only be used one at a time. It would be impossible for the same book to be in two places at the same time or for two persons to use it at the same time. In that sense, they were rivalrous goods, that is, goods that can only be consumed or enjoyed one at a time, or goods which when used reduces in value, quantity or quality. The digital era has altered this position and has enabled the simultaneous production, reproduction, usage and enjoyment of printed materials, thus moving such works into the category of non-rivalrous goods, which are goods which when simultaneously utilized do not diminish in value.[78] Examples of non-rivalrous goods are air, public roads, public libraries and water in the sea.

From an economic perspective, goods that are rivalrous in nature are depletable and therefore require replacement with cost implications and other cost effects. On the other-hand, non-rivalrous goods are generally non-depletable, and thus regardless of the number of users or the quantum of usage, the goods are still available. If regardless of the quantum of use of a good such goods are still available, and it is clear that such goods are important, it is not only a social responsibility to make such goods available but there is also an economic imperative to make it accessible at a zero cost or a cost closest to zero. The CEO of Springer noted, that as long as the costs associated with the added value on the goods have been taken care of, then open access can be provided to the general public.[79]

There is no doubt that there will be economic implications as a result of open access. The implications are just not that of the non-feasibility of an open access publishing model neither is it that open access will adversely affect the subscription base of journal articles. These fears have been addressed by the continued successes of BioMed Central and the parallel existence of Arxiv and other journals in the field of physics. Derk Haank captured it succinctly when he opined that

> Personally, I do not believe that open access will ever totally replace the subscription model, but I am more than happy to be proved wrong. I do believe, however, that STM publishers will continue to play a vital role as partners to the research community, as long as we make every effort to give the scientific community what it wants, rather than simply telling it what we are willing to provide.[80]

The effort he referred to is where the economic implication comes in, the implications associated with finding a new business model, and committing to human resource development to satisfy the scientific and research community rather than holding to old models which are now obsolete and non-desirable by the user publics.

5 Legal

> No society is static. . . . When the behaviour of people has moved away from the law with a sufficient degree of permanence, tensions arise with varying results. The law itself may be stretched to take account of the development, or it may be ignored until it becomes a dead letter, or it may be repealed, and a new law substituted. In these ways evolution gives direction to future development.[81]

Change is inevitable. The tools of communication available in this generation exemplified by social media platforms such as Skype, Facebook, WhatsApp, YouTube, Twitter, Instagram and many others have changed the landscape of society and has brought in new dimensions to human relationships. Technological changes appear to be way ahead of the law, and the law is not responding promptly to these change, thereby leaving gaps between the law and societally accepted practices.[82] Many of today's global citizens are not ready to sit back and wait for the legal system to change. They see some of the current laws as impracticable and unrealistic and as Littman observed,

> People don't obey laws that they don't believe in. It isn't necessarily that they behave lawlessly, or that they'll steal whatever they can steal if they think they can get away with it. Most people try to comply, at least substantially, with what they believe the law to say. If they don't believe the law says what it in fact says, though, they won't obey it – not because they are protesting its provisions, but because it doesn't stick in their heads. Governments stop enforcing laws that people don't believe in. Laws that people don't obey and that governments don't enforce get repealed, even if they are good laws in some other sense of the word.[83]

This section will consider the reactions of Aaron Swartz and Edward Snowden to the legal system and discuss other legal dimensions to the society in light of the open access movement.

5.1 Aaron Swartz

Aaron Swartz did not believe the law represented the interest of the ordinary people, he did not see any hope in sight through legislative channels, and therefore, he encouraged everyone to take the law into their hands by downloading as much information as they could and make it available to the world on the Internet. In his 2008 Guerrilla Open Access Manifesto, he noted that

> We need to take information, wherever it is stored, make our copies and share them with the world. We need to take stuff that's out of copyright and add it to the archive. We need to buy secret databases and put them on the Web. We need to download scientific journals and upload them to file sharing networks. We need to fight for Guerrilla Open Access.[84]

This is exactly what he eventually did through the MIT website when he downloaded copyright protected contents belonging to *JSTOR*, which lead to his prosecution and eventually to him committing suicide on the 11th of January 2013.[85]

5.2 Edward Snowden

In a similar action, we see Edward Snowden leaking out classified intelligence information to the entire world and basing his action on the failure of the system to respect the ordinary citizens' right to freedom of information and privacy. Snowden who himself worked as an intelligence officer had seen the scale of surveillance on the ordinary citizen, businesses and foreign governments, and had become agitated by the happenings. His hope for some form of reforms was not coming, and he like Aaron Swartz decided to take laws into his own hands. It was noted that

> He got hardened. In other words, the more information he saw about what he viewed as . . . mass surveillance, the more disillusioned he became. He says quite explicitly that he thought that (President Barack) Obama would roll back some of these programs when he came into the White House, and when this didn't happen, essentially Snowden decided he would take things into his own hands, and become a whistle-blower," the author said.[86]

In what has been described as US worst disclosure, he leaked out sensitive intelligence information causing political and diplomatic instabilities, and it is said that the worst is yet to come.[87]

Prominent figures like Dr King and Mahatma Ghandi have advocated that when the laws are unjust, disobedience is a social responsibility. Whilst they both did not advocate violence, they noted that unjust laws are themselves species of violence. On the contrary side were philosophers like Thomas Aquinas, Plato, Socrates, and Aristotle who all noted that laws may be unjust, but obedience is the best way to preserve and maintain an orderly society.[88]

5.3 The law is an ass[89]

When Mr Brumble was told that the court supposes his wife acts according to his instruction, he responded that if the law supposes so, then "the law is a ass – a idiot."[90] The above phrase in the popular book *Oliver Twist* by Charles Dickens points out the law has the propensity to exhibit some stupidity and rigidity.

The open movement is about responding to the need for greater access and were possible completely free access to knowledge, information, education, government and all things that should belong to the ordinary citizen. The open access movement recognizes the frustration of researchers and users in gaining access to peer-reviewed literature and identifies that some interest groups have utilized the current legal system as a tool for locking up access.

The crux of the challenge with the legal system is that laws are reactionary in that they are drafted to deal with current and past issues but not future issues. The dynamic and changing nature of society however leaves citizens in dilemma as a result of the gaps between the law and new societal norms. This is what Lessig referred to when he noted that the current copyright legal framework which is over 300 years old has criminalized today's generation (the Internet and social media generation) who see downloading and sharing of files (music, video and pictures) as a normal part of everyday life.[91]

As exemplified in Oliver Twist's story, the open access movement recognizes that the law can be an ass and notes that if the law is being deployed to serve the selfish interest of a few to the detriment of the generality, then the generality can also deploy the same law to work in their interest. This is exactly what the open access movement has chosen to do, and that is why Peter Suber has noted that while he supports the legally correct aspect of the Guerrilla open access manifesto, he is not in support of the illegal aspects, and this is because open access has not been structured to run and thrive on illegality. Open access respects the current legal framework that controls information and actually builds on that same framework to provide open access. Suber expressed it this way when he said,

> I support all the legal tactics recommended here (and then some) and none of the illegal tactics. It's legal to self-archive and it's legal to make public-domain texts OA. It's not legal to make copyrighted texts OA without the copyright holder's permission, even if you paid for your own copy.[92]

The laws could be frustrating, and compliance often constitutes a problem when these laws appear unreasonable and non-representative of the people. That appears to have been the dilemma of both Aaron and Edward, but frustration is no licence for conscientious disobedience, but rather it should stir a prompting for radical but positive change. Seeing that the law is an ass and is amenable to different situation, the law can be stirred in the direction of open. This is not an easy task as the stir towards open is a stir against the current legal system, and change is often not easily achieved. Nonetheless, progress is already being made in this direction with initiatives like open licensing. Although it has not changed the laws, it has stirred the law in its direction by turning around to positive, the erstwhile negative powers inherent in Copyright.

5.4 Law reforms?

Attempts to restructure copyright has only seen copyright laws being strengthened in favour of copyright owners. Trade-Related Aspects of Intellectual Property Rights (TRIPS) agreement and other bilateral agreements have only strengthened IP rights and have made it a necessity for criminal sanctions to be introduced into virtually every national intellectual property legislation, thereby criminalizing more and more the unapproved exploitation of content by the general public. This really should not come as a surprise and it is because the whole concept of copyright is esoteric and not very general public friendly.[93] Most people do not understand what it is all about and have generally accepted whatever is told to them. This system of general acceptance of what was passed down was acceptable when the exploitation of content (reproduction, distribution and marketing) was within the control of a few. But today, everyone with a laptop and an Internet-enabled mobile phone is involved in numerous acts of reproduction on a daily basis, and it is quite difficult to expect such number of persons' to merely accept a rule that requires them to go and seek permission from the copyright owner who they may not know and if they do, may not know where he is, and if they do know where he is, it may not be practicable for them to seek and obtain such permission.

Clamour for a change in the legal rules governing the use and reuse of content is continually been made, but the current legal provisions regulating the information system is still not adequately reflective of the current technological realities. In the November 2009 issue of the *SPARC* open access newsletter, Peter Suber opining on this issue noted that

> We possess a revolutionary technology for knowledge sharing but are often restrained from using it by laws which (in the relevant respects) have not changed for more than two centuries. It's not just that legal change is slower than technological change. The desire for legal change is either not sufficiently widespread or is dispersed among the comparatively powerless and opposed by the comparatively powerful. Some of us want to seize the opportunities created by digital media and lift the legal restrictions on new kinds of knowledge sharing. But many others want to keep the restrictions in place and force us to forego the full benefits of our revolutionary technology.[94]

Even if we had no problems to tackle with regards to accessing peer-reviewed literature, the thought of a technological invention that enables unprecedented ways for knowledge dissemination is another reason to explore the open culture as against the old toll publishing system. However, we have both the problems and the opportunities for resolving them.

5.5 Alternative to legal reform

Considering the difficulties encountered in the several processes of changing the laws from its default closed access model to an open access model,[95] the open community working within the current legal framework of copyright have deplored exclusive rights of copyright owners as enabling tools for empowering prospective users. It considers that if copyright owners have powers to restrict others from exploiting a work, such copyright-owners are equally empowered to grant consent for the use of such works. It considers that the hitherto restrictive (negative) powers can be turned into enabling (positive) powers.[96]

This can be achieved through the rules of contract.[97] By agreement through the rules of contract, the right of the copyright owner to license his or her work is deployed in making copyright an enabling tool for granting access to prospective users. The copyright owner by issuing an open licence to prospective users' both establishes his or her intention to enter a binding legal relationship and at the same time makes an offer which is open to the general public. Any interested member of the public is therefore free to accept the terms of the offer and, by using the content either through downloads, translation or any other form of reuse, confirms acceptance and at the same time furnishes consideration, thereby establishing that a contract has been entered into.

In practical terms, the author or copyright owner is able to provide access to peer-reviewed literatures through a two-tiered structure. The first tier is for copyright owners to place their works in a repository where anyone who has access to the Internet is able to access it and basically read such works. The permission granted in this respect must contain at least the right to use the work but may exclude the right to reuse the work. This is not to say that woks placed in repositories may not be licensed for reuse. At the level of the second tier, which involves publishing in an open access journal, the copyright owner makes available his work to prospective users through journals that provide immediate, free and permanent access for use and reuse of peer-reviewed literatures and via this platform clearly tells them what it is what they can do or may not do with such works. Most often reuse rights are granted in this tier and such grants could be restrictive or non-restrictive. Some permission to use and reuse would allow reproduction, distribution but would not allow adaptation and commercialization of the work. Others allow reproduction, distribution and adaptation, but not commercialization, and still others allow all the above activities. This is achieved via the licensing vehicle, using the laws of copyright and contract. The software industry has taken the lead in this initiative with open source licences,[98] for example the GNU GPL licence.[99] The content industry has followed suit with several content licences in use today, but the creative commons licences have made the greatest impact in this respect.[100]

6 Political

> We hold these truths to be self-evident, that all men are created equal, that they are endowed by their Creator with certain unalienable Rights, that among these are Life, Liberty and the pursuit of Happiness. . . . -That to secure these rights, Governments are instituted among Men, deriving their just powers from the consent of the governed,--That whenever any Form of Government becomes destructive of these ends, it is the Right of the People to alter or to abolish it, and to institute new Government, laying its foundation on such principles and organizing its powers in such form, as to them shall seem most likely to effect their Safety and Happiness.[101]

Philosophers argue that man by nature is a communal being and should not live in isolation. Aristotle postulated that the city–state exists by nature and that humans by nature are political animals.[102] Thomas Hobbes in his well-known aphorism notes that life is "solitary, poor, nasty, brutish and short", that man is intrinsically self-centred, and to ensure peace, law and order, a government is required.[103]

John Locke agrees with Hobbes on the role of government in the society but argues against Hobbes view that man is by nature bestial. Locke argues that man has rights to property and that God created the earth for man to enjoy and when man works the earth, he should be entitled to the revenues. Locke argues that man has rights and that when a government is unjust, the oppressed have a right to resist tyranny. In his opinion, a tyrant has no authority.[104]

Jean Jacques Rousseau[105] is somewhat more metaphysical than either Hobbes or Locke and argues that the general will is what controls society. He describes this general will as an agreement between the individual and the community and that the government represents this agreement. He argues that so long as the government represents this general will, it can do anything.[106] It appears in one breath that Rousseau advocates democracy by acknowledging the role of citizenry participation but in another breath acknowledges the ability of the state to do anything, thereby endorsing totalitarianism.

The role of government in maintaining law and order in the society is unquestionable. When however, this role is abused, and the people do not feel adequately represented or they feel misrepresented, tyranny sets in, and Locke has argued that in such instances, man has a right to challenge tyranny. The declaration of independence states that "whenever any Form of Government becomes destructive of these ends, it is the Right of the People to alter or to abolish it, and to institute new Government." The next section will show the exercise of these rights.

6.1 SOPA and PIPA

The reaction by the public to the two bills introduced at both houses of the United States' legislative arm, Stop Online Anti-piracy Act (SOPA) at the House of Representatives and Protect IP Act (PIPA) in the Senate is a vivid evidence of the power of the people through social media and the Internet. It was reported that as an aftermath of the online protest, "more than 162 million people saw the protest message on Wikipedia, 18 senators backed away from the proposed legislation, and 4.5 million people signed a petition against the acts."[107] The bills failed due to the voice of the people, and politicians listened to the people.

Politicians are also listening to the people who are speaking in favour of open access and have made decisions whether politically oriented or not, that favour the open cause and the generality of people would be better for it.

6.2 FASTR

Senators Cornyn and Wyden, as well as Reps Doyle, Yoder and Lofgren of the United States congress have in a bi-partisan move introduced the Fair Access to Science and Technology Research Act (FASTR) in both the House of Representatives and the Senate.[108] The Act requires federal agencies with annual research funding of $100 million or more to provide open access to the outputs of funded research no later than six months after publication.[109] If passed, the legislation will represent an improvement on the National Institutes of Health Policy by reducing the embargo period and would increase the usefulness of public access to research. It would particularly maximize the impact and utility of such researches by its focus on reuse rights as reflected in the main text of the act.[110]

The political imperatives for the open culture are not only linked to the need to score political points but is more about fulfilling the core purpose of representing the people. The open culture affords the opportunity for everyone to participate in governance and allows for the voice of the people to be heard. When SOPA and PIPA where being pushed in both houses, the people were able to speak up affirmatively although in a new and unprecedented way, and their voices were heard. The bills were not passed. The legislations giving effect to the National Institutes of Health's mandate are another example of legislations which are working in the interest of the ordinary people.[111] The legislation which makes it a requirement for research funded by NIH to be made available within 12 months in PubMed has given researchers a strong foot against publishers.[112] FASTR now seeks to reduce the 12 month embargo period to 6 months, thereby increasing the opportunities for availability and accessibility to these research findings and at the same time maximizing their useful and impact.[113] Use of political positions in the ways referred to above enables proper representation of the people and ensures that these kind of legislation do not end up on the shelves of some government department or within the exclusive access of a privileged few. It also assists young researchers from being confronted with the up-heel task of having to negotiate terms of agreement for self-archiving with publishers.

7 Knowledge is not an end in itself: it is a means to an end

With the advent of digital technology and the Internet, the production of knowledge has increased astronomically, and it continues to increase with endless avenues to create and disseminate such knowledge.[114] Considering the vast amount of knowledge available and accessible today (let us leave out the inaccessible knowledge), if knowledge strictly speaking was the key change factor, then definitely, the overwhelming amount of available and accessible knowledge would have solved all the world's problems already, but as we all know the world still has its large share of problems, and the ultimate solution is not in sight.[115] Several initiatives have been pushed to help solve global challenges through the eight Millennium Development Goals of the United Nations, but as we all know, these problems are not even nearly solved.[116] The efforts at addressing poverty, universal basic education, gender inequality, HIV/AIDS, infant mortality, maternal mortality, environmental sustainability and global partnership for development are indeed helping the world, especially developing countries, and this is most commendable.[117] However, the collation of information on the above-noted issues is not what solves the problems, but rather how the information gathered is utilized as an agent for change. Albert Einstein put it this way; he said, "any fool can know, the point is to understand."[118] Just like every flour is a potential loaf of bread, so is every knowledge a potential solution to a problem, but just as flour is not bread, knowledge is not "solution to a problem". The same way some effort and extra steps need to be taken to transform flour into bread, some effort and extra steps must be taken to transform knowledge into "solutions to problems", and that is what Einstein was referring to when he noted that the point is understanding.

It is therefore not the availability of knowledge alone that spurs change, but rather, it is the positive use of knowledge; in other words, it is not what you know that matters but what you do with what you know. However, you cannot do anything with knowledge if you don't first have it, and hence the movements for greater access to knowledge through the multiple platforms of open access, OER and public-sector information.

8 Conclusion

The open access movement is a movement for change, which some are pursuing within legally recognized limits, while others are more radical in their approach. As explained earlier, philosophers have postulated on the two sides of the divide that, firstly, change must be within the confines of the law, and secondly, where citizens are dissatisfied with a tyrannical government or the laws are unrepresentative of the people, the people are free to fight for change, and protest is in fact a social responsibility of the people.

The desire to see a world where access to peer-reviewed knowledge is free from the structural restrictions of price, the law and technology is now an international objective. The realities of today made possible by technological developments and innovation have altered the architecture of information dissemination and have enabled a group who before now were purely users and spectators to become themselves creators and stakeholders in the knowledge industry. However, the laws regulating information dissemination are still fundamentally what they used to be some 300 years ago. The gap between the written laws and today's reality has brought about a generation that abhors the law, not because they are miscreants or truants, but rather because they see that the laws are not reflective of today's reality and that those who are meant to ensure these reflections have failed and are continually failing the system. They have therefore taken laws into their hands, and the consequences have been severe.

Careful consideration on how the goals of open access, open educational resources (OER) and public-sector information can be achieved has brought about open access journals, institutional repositories and open licences, which are platforms and mechanisms that enable instant, free and unrestricted publishing and sharing of information in the research, educational and governmental realms. These platforms have brought about the development of mandates and policies which are addressing the negotiating imbalance between publishers and authors and have enabled greater successes for institutional repositories. They have also produced successes through the introduction of open licensing, a concept which utilizes the current laws governing information dissemination and deploys it to create a shift from an all rights reserved regime to some rights reserved and in certain instances no rights reserved. The products of these platforms have been able to address the fears in some minds about the viability of open access, OER and public-sector information as a business model and about its impact on the publishing industry. Today most of the major publishers have embraced open policies.

The underpinnings of the open movement are intrinsically linked to respect for the dignity of the human person which recognizes Aristotle's postulation that man is a social animal and recognizes the intrinsic value of each person. It is further inspired by the word Ubuntu, which teaches us that we are who we are because of who we all are and that we really cannot thrive alone. We owe ourselves a social responsibility to share. Each one of us must always remember: it's not about me, rather it is about us. It is an open world, and the best way to maximize the riches of the world is to leave it open, to leave the knowledge open, to leave the opportunities open and to open it up so we all can continue to build just like Isaac Newton who understood that his development was intrinsically connected to that which had been provided by his forerunners. The rationale for open access is diverse, encompassing socio-economic, legal and political aspects. In some ways they affect us, and it is therefore our responsibility to respond and bring about the goal of a world where everyone has not only the opportunity for access to knowledge, but actually has access to knowledge.

Notes

1 *The Holy Bible: New International Version (NIV)* (Tyndale House Publishers, 1978).
2 G. Catt, 'Man The Social Animal' 29 (1962) *The Western Socialist* 20. See also, Luntley Michael, *The Meaning of Socialism* (Open Court, 1990), 78. See also, Bharat Kumar, '1333 Words Essay on Man Is a Social Animal' *Preserve Articles*, available at www.preservearticles.com/201102184074/man-is-a-social-animal-essay.html.
3 Relando Thompkins, *Ubuntu: A Humanitarian Philosophy*, available at www.relandothompkins.com/philosophy/.
4 See, Ecclesiastes 4:9, *The Holy Bible: Authorized King James Version, Containing the Old and New Testaments* (Holman Bible Publishers Read-to-me ed., 1984).
5 See, Psalm 133:1 id. at.
6 See, Proverbs 27:17 id. at.
7 V. E. Frankl, *Man's Search for Meaning* (Beacon Press, 1992), 99.
8 He calls the commons "a new paradigm for creating value and organizing a community of shared interest". See David Bollier, *Viral Spiral: How the Commoners Built a Digital Republic of Their Own* (New Press, 2008), 6, "A commons arises whenever a given community decides that it wishes to manage a given resources in a collective manner with special regard for equitable access, use and sustainability."
9 Brian Fitzgerald et al., OAK LAW PROJECT NO.1: Creating a Legal Framework for Copyright Management of Open Access Within the Australian Academic and Research Sector (Report for the Department of Education and Science and Training (DEST) 21 (2006).
10 Richard Smith, 'Peer-Review: A Flawed Process at the Heart of Science and Journals' (2006) *Journal of the Royal Society of Medicine* 99.
11 *Le Journal des Sçavans* (1665), available at http://gallica.bnf.fr/ark:/12148/bpt6k56523g.
12 *Philosophical Transactions of the Royal Society of London (or Phil. Trans.)* (1665), available at http://gallica.bnf.fr/ark:/12148/bpt6k55806g.
13 World Health Organization (WHO), *About HINARI* (2014), available at www.who.int/hinari/about/en/.
14 Justin Norrie, 'Harvard Decries The High Cost of Journal Subscription' (2012) *The Conversation*, available at http://theconversation.edu.au/harvard-journal-subscription-fees-are-prohibitive-6659, 24 April.
15 University of Illinois at Urbana-Champaign University Library, *The Cost of Journals*, available at www.library.illinois.edu/scholcomm/journalcosts.html.
16 Greg Edwards, 'Fed: Student Loan Debt Surpasses Auto, Credit Card Debt', *St. Louis Business Journal*, available at www.bizjournals.com/stlouis/blog/2013/04/fed-student-loan-debt-surpasses-auto.html.
17 University Library.

18 John Willinsky, *The Access Principle: The Case for Open Access to Research and Scholarship* (MIT Press, 2006). See the introduction where he noted that "the final five subscriptions which they could barely afford, did not include the leading journals on the institute's principal research interest."
19 Phil Davis, Publish-or-Perish Culture Promotes Scientific Narcissism, *The Scholarly Kitchen*, available at http://scholarlykitchen.sspnet.org/2012/05/07/publish-or-perish-culture-promotes-scientific-narcissism/.
20 Stevan Harnad et al., 'The Access/Impact Problem and the Green and Gold Roads to Open Access' 30 (2004) *Serial Review* 310–314.
21 *Budapest Open Access Initiative*, available at www.opensocietyfoundations.org/openaccess/read.
22 See the following case studies which signify the effort of governments to enable access to knowledge in their respective countries. *Ireland: The Transition to Open Access* (2014), available at www.pasteur4oa.eu/sites/pasteur4oa/files/resource/Ireland%20Case%20Study.pdf; *Education, Research and Open Access in Norway* (2014), available at www.pasteur4oa.eu/sites/pasteur4oa/files/resource/Norway%20Case%20Study_0.pdf; *Hungary Open Access Case Study*, available at www.pasteur4oa.eu/sites/pasteur4oa/files/resource/Hungary%20Case%20Study.pdf (2014); *UK Open Access Case Study* (2014), available at www.pasteur4oa.eu/sites/pasteur4oa/files/resource/UK%20Case%20Study.pdf; *PASTEUR4OA/Case Study: Potugal Open Access Policy Landscape* (2014), available at www.pasteur4oa.eu/sites/pasteur4oa/files/resource/Portugal%20Case%20Study.pdf.
23 Aaron Swartz, 'Guerilla Open Access Manifesto' *Internet Archive* (2008), available at http://archive.org/stream/GuerillaOpenAccessManifesto/Goamjuly2008_djvu.txt.
24 John Willinsky, 'The Stratified Economics of Open Access' 39 (2009) *Economic Analysis & Policy* 53.
25 T. Massaro, *Living Justice: Catholic Social Teaching in Action* (Rowman & Littlefield Publishers, 2008), 79–119. See Chapter 5 on the nine key themes of Catholic Social Teachings and the table of the nine keys at page 80.
26 Jessica Litman, 'Copyright Non-Compliance (Or Why We Cant "Just Say Yes" to Licensing")' (1997) *New York University Journal of International Law & Politics* 29.
27 Cable Green, *British Columbia Government Lends Support to Open Textbooks*, available at http://creativecommons.org/weblog/entry/34566?utm_campaign=newsletter_1210&utm_medium=blog&utm_source=newsletter.
28 Edwin Rutsch, *Obama Speaks About Ubuntu & Empathy at Nelson Mandela Memo* (2013), available at www.youtube.com/watch?v=jiebOGRPPxg, accessed on 23/01/2014.
29 Ubuntu, *The Ubuntu Story*, available at www.ubuntu.com/about/about-ubuntu/.
30 Barbara Nussbaum, 'African Culture and Ubuntu: Reflections of a South African in America' 17 (2003) *World Business Academy, Perspectives* 1.
31 Kimmerle Heinz, 'Ubuntu and Communalism in African Philosophy and Art' *Rozenberg Quarterly Magazine*. See also, Barbara Nussbaum, 'Reflections of a South African on our Common Humanity' 4 (2003) *Reflections* 21.
32 See, Roy Jackson, 'Aristotle on What It Means to Be Happy' (2007) *Richmond Journal of Philosophy* 2.
33 Allegra Stratton, 'David Cameron Aims to Make Happiness the New GDP' *The Guardian*, available at www.theguardian.com/politics/2010/nov/14/david-cameron-wellbeing-inquiry.
34 Amy Biehl Foundation, *Amy's Life and Legacy*, available at www.amybiehl.org/amy.php.
35 Kevin Chaplin, *The Ubuntu Spirit in African Communities*, available at https://www.coursehero.com/file/24549908/BookCoE20-Chaplinpdf/
36 Dan Grubbs, 'More Than Fellowship: Understanding Koinonia' *Sermon Central* (2004), available at www.sermoncentral.com/sermons/more-than-fellowship-understanding-koinonia-dan-grubbs-sermon-on-discipleship-84103.asp.

37 Android, *Welcome to the Android Open Source Project*, available at http://source.android.com/.
38 Judge Elizabeth, 'Enabling Access to Public Sector Information in Canada' in Michael Geist ed., *From Radical Extremism to Balance Copyright: Canadian Copyright and the Digital Agenda* 598, 601 & 603 (Irwin Law, Canada, 2010). "Public sector information, which is information created by government in the course of governing, is essential for transparency, accountability, democratic participation, and citizen engagement."
39 See, Kunle Ola, 'Evolution and Future Trends of Copyright In Nigeria' 2 (2014) *Journal of Open Access to Law (JOAL)* 1, 30. "Acquiring knowledge is therefore imperative for development and the currency to acquiring knowledge is access. No knowledge no development, no access, no knowledge."
40 The World Bank, *World Bank Announces Open Access Policy for Research and Knowledge, Launches Open Knowledge Repository* (2012), available at www.worldbank.org/en/news/press-release/2012/04/10/world-bank-announces-open-access-policy-for-research-and-knowledge-launches-open-knowledge-repository.
41 Hosea Chapter 4 Verse 6 *The Holy Bible: Authorized King James Version, Containing the Old and New Testaments* (1984).
42 Swartz (2008).
43 Aristotle (384 BC–322 BC), available at www.quotationspage.com/subjects/knowledge/.
44 Jules Evans, *Aristotelians: What Is Aristotle's Theory of Human Nature?* available at http://philosophyforlife.org/philosophies-for-life/aristotelians/.
45 Thomas Massaro, *Living Justice: Catholic Social Teaching in Action* (Rowman & Littlefield, 2012), 84.
46 A. C. Pigou, *Socialism Versus Capitalism* (Palgrave Macmillan, 1937), 9.
47 *Bethesda Statement on Open Access Publishing* (2003), available www.earlham.edu/~peters/fos/bethesda.htm.
48 *The Holy Bible: King James Version* (Hendrickson Bibles, 2011).
49 *The Holy Bible: New International Version (NIV)* (1978).
50 M. J. Wheatley, *Finding Our Way: Leadership for an Uncertain Time (Large Print 16pt)* (ReadHowYouWant.com Limited, 2010).
51 Tim Brody et al., 'Incentivizing the Open Access Research Web. Publication-Archiving, Data Archiving and Scientometrics' 3 (2007) *CTWatch Quarterly* 42. "It has now been repeatedly demonstrated that making publications OA by self-archiving them in an OA IR dramatically enhances their research impact."
52 K. Smith, *Free Is Cheaper* (John Ball Press, 1988). See the Introduction to Chapter 1.
53 Isaac Newton, *From a Letter Written by Isaac Newton to Robert Hooke*, 5 February (1676).
54 BBC News Business, *Richest 1% to Won More Than Rest of the World, Oxfam Says* (2015), available at www.bbc.com/news/business-30875633.
55 Swartz (2008).
56 B. R. Scott, *Capitalism: Its Origins and Evolution as a System of Governance* (Springer, 2011).
57 Android, *The Android Source Code*, available at https://source.android.com/source/index.html.
58 Apache, *The Apache Software Foundation: Community-Led Development Since 1999*, available at www.apache.org/.
59 Ubuntu.
60 Linux, *Introduction to Linux, Free Software and Open Source*, available at http://linux.org.au/introduction-linux-free-software-and-open-source.
61 SUSE, *About SUSE*, available at www.suse.com/company/open-source/.
62 (CC) Creative Commons, *About the Licenses*, available at http://creativecommons.org/licenses/.

63 A. Smith, *Wealth of Nations* (Hayes Barton Press, 2001), 288.
64 Infoplease, *Overview of Economics*, available at www.infoplease.com/cig/economics/three-economists-their-theories.html.
65 T. Gorman, *The Complete Idiot's Guide to Economics* (Alpha, 2003), 58.
66 K. Marx et al., *Das Kapital: A Critique of Political Economy* (Regnery Gateway, 1996), 174, 178, and 190.
67 Woods Alan, 'The Ideas of Karl Marx' *International Marxist Tendency (IMT)*, available at www.marxist.com/karl-marx-130-years.htm.
68 Marx et al., (1996).
69 The STM Report, *An Overview of Scientific and Scholarly Publishing* (Mark Ware Consulting, 2012), 12, available at www.markwareconsulting.com/articles-reports/the-stm-report-an-overview-of-scientific-and-scholarly-journal-publishing-2/
70 University Library.
71 See, *Philosophical Transactions of the Royal Society of London (or Phil. Trans.)* (1665), available at http://gallica.bnf.fr/ark:/12148/bpt6k55806g. See also, Le Journal des Sçavans (1665). See also, *The History of Journal Publication*, available at www.journal.au.edu/au_techno/2008/jan08/journal113_editorial.pdf.
72 Brian Fitzgerald et al., *Internet And E-Commerce Law Business and Policy* (Thomson Reuters, 2011), 5.
73 BioMed Central, 'Article-Processing Charge' *BioMed Central*, available at www.biomedcentral.com/authors/apc.
74 Springer, *Interview with Derk Haank on Open Access*, available at www.springer.com/societies+%26+publishing+partners/society+%26+partner+zone?SGWID=0-173202-12-489299-0.
75 See John Willinsky, 'The Stratified Economics of Open Access' 39 (2009) *Economic Analysis & Policy* 59 noting that "the publishers of the relevant physics journals reports that after more than a decade of a substantial portion of their content being archived, they have no greater decline in journal subscriptions than they are experiencing more generally."
76 See Springer, *Springer Acquires BioMed Central Group*, available at www.springer.com/authors/author+zone?SGWID=0-168002-12-563100-0.
77 Willinsky (2009).
78 Peter Suber, 'Knowledge as a Public Good' *SPARC* (2009), available at www.sparc.arl.org/resources/articles/knowledge#sthash.R1nBSlQF.dpuf, where he noted that "a public good is non-rivalrous and non-excludable. . . . Knowledge is non-rivalrous. Your knowledge of a fact or idea does not block mine, and mine does not block yours."

See also, Bill Cope & Mary Kalantzis, *Signs of Epistemic Disruption: Transformations in the Knowledge System of the Academic Journal*, available at www.firstmonday.dk/ojs/index.php/fm/article/view/2309/2163.
79 Springer, Interview with Derk Haank on Open Access.
80 Id.
81 See Chapter 15 on Justice in adapting to change by, R. W. M. Dias, *Jurisprudence* (Butterworths, 1985), 305.
82 L. Lessig, *Free Culture: How Big Media Uses Technology and the Law to Lock Down Culture and Control Creativity* (Penguin Press, 2004), 199.

> Overregulation stifles creativity. It smothers innovation. . . . The war that is being waged today is a war of prohibition . . . it is targeted against the behaviour of a very large number of citizens. According to The New York Times, 43 million Americans downloaded music in May 2002. According to the RIAA, the behaviour of those 43 million Americans is a felony. We thus have a set of rules that transform 20 percent of America into criminals.

83 Jessica Litman, 'Copyright Non-Compliance (Or Why We Cant "Just Say Yes" to Licensing)' (1997) *New York University Journal of International Law & Politics* 29.

84 Aaron Swartz, 'Guerilla Open Access Manifesto' *Internet Archive* (2008), available at http://archive.org/stream/GuerillaOpenAccessManifesto/Goamjuly2008_djvu.txt.
85 Paul McGeough, 'Aaron Swartz: A Beautiful Mind' *The Sydney Morning Herald* (2014), available at www.smh.com.au/technology/technology-news/aaron-swartz-a-beautiful-mind-20140127-31hjr.html.
86 Mark Morgenstein, 'Edward Snowden: World's Most Wanted Man, Says New Book' *CNN* (2014), available at http://edition.cnn.com/2014/02/02/world/europe/uk-snowden-book/.
87 Wikipedia, *Edward Snowden*, available at http://en.wikipedia.org/wiki/Edward_Snowden.
88 Simona Vieru, 'Aristotle's Influence on the Natural Law Theory of St Thomas Aquinas' 1 (2010) *The Western Australian Jurist*.
89 The phrase has been attributed to an English dramtist,George Chapman in 1654 – Revenge for Honour. See Gary Martin, *The Law Is an Ass*, available at www.phrases.org.uk/meanings/the-law-is-an-ass.html.
90 C. Dickens, *Oliver Twist* (Richard Bentley, 1839), 279.
91 Lessig, 207 (2004). See where he noted that "When forty to sixty million Americans are considered 'criminals' under the law, and when the law could achieve the same objective – securing rights to authors – without these millions being considered 'criminals,' who is the villain? Americans or the law? Which is American, a constant war on our own people or a concerted effort through our democracy to change our law?"
92 Peter Suber, 'Guerilla OA' *Open Access News* (2008), available at http://legacy.earlham.edu/~peters/fos/2008/09/guerilla-oa.html.
93 Litman (1997).
94 Suber, Knowledge as a Public Good. 2009.
95 J. Litman, 'Revising Copyright Law for the Information Age' 75 (1996) *Oregon Law Review* 19, 20. She noted that "Our current copyright law is based on a model devised for print media, and expanded, with some difficulty to embrace a world that includes live, filmed and taped performances, broadcast media, and, most recently, digital media. That much is uncontroversial. The suitability of that model for new media is much more controversial. As one might expect, to the extent that current legal rules make some parties 'haves' and others 'have-nots,' the haves are fans of the current model, while today's have-nots suggest that some other model might be more appropriate for the future."
96 Brian Fitzgerald, *Open Content Licensing: Cultivating the Creative Commons* (Sydney University Press, 2007), 5, where it was noted that "The genius of Stallman was in understanding and implementing the ethic that if you want to create a community of information or creative commons you need to be able to control the way the information is used once it leaves your hands. The regulation of this downstream activity was achieved by claiming an intellectual property right (copyright in the code) at the source and then structuring its downstream usage through a licence (GNU GPL). This was not a simple 'giving away' of information but rather a strategic mechanism for ensuring the information stayed 'free' as in speech. It is on this foundation that we now see initiatives like the Creative Commons expanding that idea from open source code to open digital content."
97 Hugh Collins, *The Law of Contract* (Butterworths, 1993), 3.
98 Richard Stallman, 'Free Software' in Mark Perry & Brian Fitzgerald eds., *Knowledge Policy for the Twenty-First Century: A Legal Perspective* (Irwin Law, 2011).
99 Richard Stallman, *The GNU Project*, available at www.gnu.org/gnu/thegnuproject.html.
100 Kunle Ola, 'Evolution and Future Trends of Copyright In Nigeria' 2 (2014) *Journal of Open Access to Law (JOAL)*.
101 U.S. Congress, *Declaration of Independence* (1776), available at www.archives.gov/exhibits/charters/declaration_transcript.html.

102 Fred Miller, 'Political Naturalism' in *Standford Encylopedia of Philosophy*, available at http://plato.stanford.edu/entries/aristotle-politics/supplement3.html.
103 T. Hobbes & R. Tuck, *Hobbes: Leviathan: Revised Student Edition* (Cambridge University Press, 1996), 89.
104 J. Locke, *Two Treatises of Government* (C. and J. Rivington, 1824), 270.
105 J. J. Rousseau & G. D. H. Cole, *The Social Contract* (Cosimo Incorporated, 2008).
106 R. Wacks, *Understanding Jurisprudence: An Introduction to Legal Theory* (Oxford Univesity Press, Oxford, 2012), 24–25.
107 Paul Ian, 'Were SOPA/PIPA Protests a Success? The Results Are in' *PC World* (2012), available at https://www.pcworld.com/article/248401/were_sopa_pipa_protests_a_success_the_results_are_in.html.
108 U.S. Congress, 'Fair Access to Science and Technology Research Act of 2013' *Congress.gov*, available at www.congress.gov/bill/113th-congress/house-bill/708/text.
109 Timothy Vollmer, *FASTR Introduced in U.S. Congress to Drastically Expand Public Access to Federally Funded Research* (2013), available at http://creativecommons.org/weblog/entry/36699?utm_campaign=newsletter_1302&utm_medium=blog&utm_source=newsletter.
110 Congress, Fair Access to Science and Technology Research Act of (2013). See Preamble 2.3 and Provision 4.b.5: "the United States has a substantial interest in maximizing the impact and utility of the research it funds by enabling a wide range of reuses of the peer-reviewed literature."
111 National Institute of Health (NIH), *NIH Public Access Policy*, available at http://publicaccess.nih.gov/.
112 NIH, *Policy on Enhancing Public Access to Archived Publications Resulting from NIH Funded Research § NOT-OD-05–022* (Health and Human Services ed., 2005).
113 Peter Suber, 'United States Doubles Down on Open Access to Federally-Funded Research' *SPARC Open Access Newsletter*, available at http://legacy.earlham.edu/~peters/fos/newsletter/03-02-13.htm.
114 Rogers Paul et al., 'Infobesity: The Enemy of Good Decisions' *Insight*, available at www.bain.com/publications/articles/infobesity-the-enemy-of-good-decisions.aspx.
115 Jon Sobrino, 'Humanizing a Sick Civilization' in R. Ammicht-Quinn ed., *Evil Today and Struggles to Be Human* (Wiley-Blackwell, 2009). "The world's tragedy is plain to see, but as far as possible, it is ignored." See also, Annie Malknecht, *What the Millennium Development Goals Have Accomplished*, available at www.americanprogress.org/issues/security/news/2014/08/18/95805/what-the-millennium-development-goals-have-accomplished/.
116 Ana Jesus Lopez Menendez & Rigoberto Perez Suarez, *Measuring Progress Towards the Millennium Development Goals. A Regional Approach*, available at www.academia.edu/999515/Measuring_Progress_towards_the_Millennium_Development_Goals._A_Regional_Approach.
117 United Nations, *Millennium Development Goals and Beyond 2015*, available at www.un.org/millenniumgoals/.
118 Robert Mills, *Knowing vs Understanding* (2012), available at www.robertmills.me/knowing-vs-understanding-2/.

Bibliography

Alan, Woods, *The Ideas of Karl Marx*, International Marxist Tendency (IMT), available at www.marxist.com/karl-marx-130-years.htm.

Amy Biehl Foundation, *Amy's Life and Legacy*, available at www.amybiehl.org/amy.php.

Android, *The Android Source Code*, available at https://source.android.com/source/index.html.

Android, *Welcome to the Android Open Source Project*, available at http://source.android.com/.

Apache, *The Apache Software Foundation: Community-Led Development Since 1999*, available at www.apache.org/.

Aristotle ((384 BC–322 BC)), available at www.quotationspage.com/subjects/knowledge/.

BBC News Business, *Richest 1% to Won More Than Rest of the World, Oxfam Says* (2015), available at www.bbc.com/news/business-30875633.

Berlin Declaration on Open Access to Knowledge in the Sciences and Humanities (2003), available at http://oa.mpg.de/files/2010/04/berlin_declaration.pdf.

Bethesda Statement on Open Access Publishing (2003), available at www.earlham.edu/~peters/fos/bethesda.htm.

BioMed Central, Article-Processing Charge, *BioMed Central*, available at www.biomedcentral.com/authors/apc.

Bollier, David, *Viral Spiral: How the Commoners Built a Digital Republic of Their Own* (New Press, 2008).

Brody, Tim, et al., 'Incentivizing the Open Access Research Web Publication-Archiving, Data Archiving and Scientometrics' 3 (2007) *CTWatch Quarterly* 42.

Budapest Open Access Initiative, available at www.opensocietyfoundations.org/openaccess/read.

Catt, G., 'Man the Social Animal' 29 (1962) *The Western Socialist* 20.

(CC) Creative Commons, *About the Licenses*, available at http://creativecommons.org/licenses/.

Chaplin, Kevin, *The Ubuntu Spirit in African Communities*, available at https://www.coursehero.com/file/24549908/BookCoE20-Chaplinpdf/

Collins, Hugh, *The Law of Contract* (Butterworths, 1993).

Cope, Bill & Mary Kalantzis, *Signs of Epistemic Disruption: Transformations in the Knowledge System of the Academic Journal*, available at www.firstmonday.dk/ojs/index.php/fm/article/view/2309/2163.

Cornell University Library, *arXiv.org*, available at http://arxiv.org/.

Davis, Phil, Publish-or-Perish Culture Promotes Scientific Narcissism, *The Scholarly Kitchen*, available at http://scholarlykitchen.sspnet.org/2012/05/07/publish-or-perish-culture-promotes-scientific-narcissism/.

Dias, R. W. M., *Jurisprudence* (Butterworths, 1985).

Dickens, C., *Oliver Twist* (Richard Bentley, 1839).

Education Policy Analysis Archive, University of Arizona, available at http://asu.academia.edu/EPAAAAPE.

Education, Research and Open Access in Norway (2014), available at www.pasteur4oa.eu/sites/pasteur4oa/files/resource/Norway%20Case%20Study_0.pdf.

Edwards, Greg, 'Fed: Student Loan Debt Surpasses Auto, Credit Card Debt' *St. Louis Business Journal*, available at www.bizjournals.com/stlouis/blog/2013/04/fed-student-loan-debt-surpasses-auto.html.

Elizabeth, Judge, '*Enabling Access to Public Sector Information in Canada*' in Michael Geist ed., *From Radical Extremism to Balance Copyright: Canadian Copyright and the Digital Agenda* (Irwin, Canada, 2010).

Evans, Jules, *ARISTOTELIANS: What Is Aristotle's Theory of Human Nature?* available at http://philosophyforlife.org/philosophies-for-life/aristotelians/.

Fitzgerald, Brian, *Open Content Licensing: Cultivating the Creative Commons* (Sydney University Press, Sydney 2007).

Fitzgerald, Brian, et al., *Internet and E-Commerce Law Business and Policy* (Thomson Reuters, 2011).

Fitzgerald, Brian, et al., OAK LAW PROJECT NO.1: Creating a Legal Framework for Copyright Management of Open Access Within the Australian Academic and

Research Sector (Report for the Department of Education and Science and Training (DEST) (2006).

Frankl, V. E., *Man's Search for Meaning* (Beacon Press, 1992).

Gorman, T., *The Complete Idiot's Guide to Economics* (Alpha, 2003).

Green, Cable, *British Columbia Government Lends Support to Open Textbooks*, available at http://creativecommons.org/weblog/entry/34566?utm_campaign=newsletter_1210&utm_medium=blog&utm_source=newsletter.

Greenwald, Glenn, et al., 'Edward Snowden: The whistleblower behind the NSA Surveillance Revelations' (2013) *The Guardian*, available at www.theguardian.com/world/2013/jun/09/edward-snowden-nsa-whistleblower-surveillance.

Grubbs, Dan, More Than Fellowship: Understanding Koinonia, *SermonCentral* (2004), available at www.sermoncentral.com/sermons/more-than-fellowship-understanding-koinonia-dan-grubbs-sermon-on-discipleship-84103.asp.

Gutterman, Brian, 'Internet as a Catalyst for Change: Access, Development, Freedoms and Innovation' *Internet Governance Forum (IGF) 2011*, available at www.intgovforum.org/cms/documents/publications/176-internet-as-a-catalyst-for-change-access-development-freedoms-and-innovations

Harmon, Elliot, *U.S. News and World Report Examines the Growth of Open Education* (2013), available at http://creativecommons.org/weblog/entry/36366?utm_campaign=newsletter_1301&utm_medium=blog&utm_source=newsletter.

Harnad, Stevan, et al., 'The Access/Impact Problem and the Green and Gold Roads to Open Access' 30 (2004) *Serial Review, 310–314*

Hebdo, Livres, *The Global Ranking of the Publishing Industry 2014*, Rüdiger Wischenbart Content and Consulting (2014), available at http://wischenbart.com/upload/Global-Ranking-of-the-Publishing-Industry_2014_Analysis.pdf.

Heinz, Kimmerle, 'Ubuntu and Communalism in African Philosophy and Art' (2011) *Rozenberg Quarterly Magazine*.

The History of Journal Publication, available at www.journal.au.edu/au_techno/2008/jan08/journal113_editorial.pdf.

Hobbes, T. & R. Tuck, *Hobbes: Leviathan: Revised Student Edition* (Cambridge University Press, 1996).

The Holy Bible: Authorized King James Version, Containing the Old and New Testaments (Holman Bible Publishers Read-to-me ed., 1984).

The Holy Bible: King James Version (Hendrickson Bibles, 2011).

The Holy Bible: New International Version (NIV) (Tyndale House Publishers, 1978).

Hungary Open Access Case Study (2014), available at www.pasteur4oa.eu/sites/pasteur4oa/files/resource/Hungary%20Case%20Study.pdf.

Ian, Paul, *Were SOPA/PIPA Protests a Success? The Results Are in* (PC World, 2012), available at https://www.pcworld.com/article/248401/were_sopa_pipa_protests_a_success_the_results_are_in.html.

Infoplease, *Overview of Economics*, available at www.infoplease.com/cig/economics/three-economists-their-theories.html.

International Publishers Association IPA, *Annual Report October 2013|October 2014* (2014), available at www.internationalpublishers.org/images/reports/2014/IPA-annual-report-2014.pdf.

Ireland: The Transition to Open Access (2014), available at www.pasteur4oa.eu/sites/pasteur4oa/files/resource/Ireland%20Case%20Study.pdf.

Jackson, Roy, 'Aristotle on What It Means to Be Happy' 16 (2007) *Richmond Journal of Philosophy. 1, 1–8*.

Kumar, Bharat, 1333 Words Essay on Man Is a Social Animal, *Preserve Articles*, available at www.preservearticles.com/201102184074/man-is-a-social-animal-essay.html.

Lawrence, Lessig, 'The Vision for the Creative Commons. What Are We and Where Are We Headed? Free Culture' in Fitzgerald Brian ed., *Open Content Licensing: Cultivating the Creative Commons* (Sydney University Press, Sydney, 2007).

Le Journal des Sçavans (1665), available at http://gallica.bnf.fr/ark:/12148/bpt6k56523g.

Lessig, L., *Free Culture: How Big Media Uses Technology and the Law to Lock Down Culture and Control Creativity* (Penguin Press, New York, 2004).

Linux, *Introduction to Linux, Free Software and Open Source*, available at http://linux.org.au/introduction-linux-free-software-and-open-source.

Litman, J., 'Copyright Non-Compliance (Or Why We Can't "Just Say Yes" to Licensing")' 29 (1997) *New York University Journal of International Law and Politics*.

Litman, J., *Digital Copyright: Protecting Intellectual Property on the Internet* (Prometheus Books, Amherst, New York 2006).

Litman, J., 'Revising Copyright Law for the Information Age' 75 (1996) *Oregon Law Review* 19.

Locke, J., *Two Treatises of Government* (C. and J. Rivington, 1824).

Lopez Menendez, Ana Jesus & Rigoberto Perez Suarez, *Measuring Progress Towards the Millennium Development Goals: A Regional Approach*, available at www.academia.edu/999515/Measuring_Progress_towards_the_Millennium_Development_Goals._A_Regional_Approach.

Malknecht, Annie, *What the Millennium Development Goals Have Accomplished*, available at www.americanprogress.org/issues/security/news/2014/08/18/95805/what-the-millennium-development-goals-have-accomplished/.

Martin, Gary, *The Law Is an Ass*, available at www.phrases.org.uk/meanings/the-law-is-an-ass.html.

Marx, K., et al., *Das Kapital: A Critique of Political Economy* (Regnery Gateway, 1996).

Massaro, T., *Living Justice: Catholic Social Teaching in Action* (Rowman & Littlefield Publishers, 2011).

McGeough, Paul, 'Aaron Swartz: A Beautiful Mind' (2014) *The Sydney Morning Herald*, available at www.smh.com.au/technology/technology-news/aaron-swartz-a-beautiful-mind-20140127-31hjr.html.

Michael, Luntley, *The Meaning of Socialism* (Open Court, 1990).

Miller, Barbara, 'Fugitive Edward Snowden Meets with Human Rights Groups at Moscow Airport' (2013) *ABC News*, available at www.abc.net.au/news/2013-07-12/snowden-meets-with-human-rights-groups/4817674.

Miller, Fred, 'Politcal Naturalism' *Standford Encyclopedia of Philosophy*, available at http://plato.stanford.edu/entries/aristotle-politics/supplement3.html.

Mills, Robert, *Knowing Vs Understanding* (2012), available at www.robertmills.me/knowing-vs-understanding-2/.

Morgenstein, Mark, *Edward Snowden: World's Most Wanted Man, Says New Book* CNN (2014), available at http://edition.cnn.com/2014/02/02/world/europe/uk-snowden-book/

National Institute of Health (NIH), *Policy on Enhancing Public Access to Archived Publications Resulting from NIH Funded Research § NOT-OD-05–022* (Health and Human Services ed., 2005)

Newton, Isaac, *From a Letter Written by Isaac Newton to Robert Hooke*, 5 February (1676).

NIH, *NIH Public Access Policy*, available at http://publicaccess.nih.gov/.

Norrie, Justin, Harvard Decries the High Cost of Journal Subscription, *The Conversation* (2012), available at http://theconversation.edu.au/harvard-journal-subscription-fees-are-prohibitive-6659, 24 April.

Nussbaum, Barbara, 'African Culture and Ubuntu: Reflections of a South African in America' 17 (2003) *World Business Academy, Perspectives* 1.

Nussbaum, Barbara, 'Reflections of a South African on our Common Humanity' 4 (2013) *Reflections* 21.

Ola, Kunle, 'Evolution and Future Trends of Copyright in Nigeria' 2 (2014) *Journal of Open Access to Law (JOAL)* 1.

Ola, Kunle, 'Fundamentals of Open Access' 36 (2) (2014) *European Intellectual Property Review* 112.

PASTEUR4OA/Case Study: Portugal Open Access Policy Landscape (2014), available at www.pasteur4oa.eu/sites/pasteur4oa/files/resource/Portugal%20Case%20Study.pdf.

Paul, Rogers, et al., Infobesity: The Enemy of Good Decisions, *Insight*, available at www.bain.com/publications/articles/infobesity-the-enemy-of-good-decisions.aspx.

Philosophical Transactions of the Royal Society of London (or Phil. Trans.) (1665), available at http://gallica.bnf.fr/ark:/12148/bpt6k55806g.

Pigou, A. C., *Socialism Versus Capitalism* (Palgrave Macmillan, 1937).

Renoux, Christian, *The Origin of the Peace Prayer of St Francis by Dr. C. Renous, Associate Professor of the University of Orleans, Frances* (2001), available at www.franciscan-archive.org/franciscana/peace.html.

Rousseau, J. J. & G. D. H. Cole, *The Social Contract* (Cosimo Incorporated, 2008).

Rutsch, Edwin, *Obama Speaks About Ubuntu & Empathy at Nelson Mandela Memo* (2013), available at www.youtube.com/watch?v=jiebOGRPPxg.

Scott, B. R., *Capitalism: Its Origins and Evolution as a System of Governance* (Springer, 2011).

Smith, A., *Wealth of Nations* (Hayes Barton Press, 2001).

Smith, K., *Free Is Cheaper* (John Ball Press, 1988).

Smith, R., 'Peer-Review: A Flawed Process at the Heart of Science and Journals' 99 (2006) *Journal of the Royal Society of Medicine*.

Sobrino, Jon, 'Humanizing a Sick Civilization' in R. Ammicht-Quinn ed., *Evil Today and Struggles to Be Human* (Wiley-Blackwell, 2009).

Solomon, David, 'The Role of Peer Review for Scholarly Journals in the Information Age' 10 (2007) *The Journal of Electronic Publishing (JEP)*.

Springer, *Interview with Derk Haank on Open Access*, available at www.springer.com/societies+%26+publishing+partners/society+%26+partner+zone?SGWID=0-173202-12-489299-0.

Springer, *Springer Acquires BioMed Central Group*, available at www.springer.com/authors/author+zone?SGWID=0-168002-12-563100-0.

Stallman, Richard, 'Free Software' in Mark Perry & Brian Fitzgerald eds., *Knowledge Policy for the Twenty-First Century: A Legal Perspective* (Irwin Law, 2011).

Stallman, Richard, *The GNU Project*, available at www.gnu.org/gnu/thegnuproject.html.

The STM Report, *An Overview of Scientific and Scholarly Publishing* (Mark Ware Consulting, 2012), available at www.markwareconsulting.com/articles-reports/the-stm-report-an-overview-of-scientific-and-scholarly-journal-publishing-2/

Statute of Anne, 8 Anne c. 19 (1710).

Stratton, Allegra, 'David Cameron Aims to Make Happiness the New GDP' *The Guardian*, available at www.theguardian.com/politics/2010/nov/14/david-cameron-wellbeing-inquiry.

Suber, Peter, 'Guerilla OA' *Open Access News* (2008), available at http://legacy.earlham.edu/~peters/fos/2008/09/guerilla-oa.html.

Suber, Peter, Knowledge as a Public Good, *SPARC* (2009), available at www.sparc.arl.org/resources/articles/knowledge#sthash.R1nBSlQF.dpuf.

Suber, Peter, *Open Access* (MIT Press, Cambridge, MA 2012).

Suber, Peter, 'United States Doubles Down on Open Access to Federally-Funded Research' *SPARC Open Access Newsletter*, available at http://legacy.earlham.edu/~peters/fos/newsletter/03-02-13.htm.

SUSE, *About SUSE*, available at www.suse.com/company/open-source/.

Swartz, Aaron, Guerilla Open Access Manifesto, *Internet Archive* (2008), available at http://archive.org/stream/GuerillaOpenAccessManifesto/Goamjuly2008_djvu.txt.

Thompkins, Relando, *Ubuntu: A Humanitarian Philosophy*, available at www.relandothompkins.com/philosophy/.

Ubuntu, *The Ubuntu Story*, available at www.ubuntu.com/about/about-ubuntu/.

UK Open Access Case Study (2014), available at www.pasteur4oa.eu/sites/pasteur4oa/files/resource/UK%20Case%20Study.pdf.

United Nations UN, *Millennium Development Goals and Beyond 2015*, available at www.un.org/millenniumgoals/.

University of Illinois at Urbana-Champaign University Library, *The Cost of Journals*, available at www.library.illinois.edu/scholcomm/journalcosts.html.

U.S. Congress, *Declaration of Independence* (1776), available at www.archives.gov/exhibits/charters/declaration_transcript.html.

U.S. Congress, 'Fair Access to Science and Technology Research Act of 2013' *Congress.gov*, available at www.congress.gov/bill/113th-congress/house-bill/708/text.

Vieru, Simona, 'Aristotle's Influence on the Natural Law Theory of St Thomas Aquinas' (2010) *The Western Australian Jurist* 1.

Vollmer, Timothy, *FASTR Introduced in U.S. Congress to Drastically Expand Public Access to Federally Funded Research* (2013), available at http://creativecommons.org/weblog/entry/36699?utm_campaign=newsletter_1302&utm_medium=blog&utm_source=newsletter.

Wacks, R., *Understanding Jurisprudence: An Introduction to Legal Theory* (Oxford University Press, Oxford, 2012).

Wheatley, M. J., *Finding Our Way: Leadership for an Uncertain Time (Large Print 16pt)* (ReadHowYouWant.com Limited, 2010).

WHO, *About HINARI* (2014), available at www.who.int/hinari/about/en/.

Wikipedia, *Edward Snowden*, available at http://en.wikipedia.org/wiki/Edward_Snowden.

Willinsky, John, *The Access Principle: The Case for Open Access to Research and Scholarship* (MIT Press, Cambridge MA, 2006).

Willinsky, John, 'The Stratified Economics of Open Access' 39 (2009) *Economic Analysis & Policy* 53.

WIPO, *WIPO Internet Treaties*, available at www.wipo.int/copyright/en/activities/wct_wppt/wct_wppt.html.

World Bank, *World Bank Announces Open Access Policy for Research and Knowledge, Launches Open Knowledge Repository* (2012), available at www.worldbank.org/en/news/press-release/2012/04/10/world-bank-announces-open-access-policy-for-research-and-knowledge-launches-open-knowledge-repository.

3 Framework for open access in Nigeria

1 Introduction

The overarching goal of the open access movement is to provide platforms that enable freedom of access to knowledge. The dynamics of information dissemination is spreading across virtually every field of the endeavour, thereby making the management and regulation of the creation, dissemination and exploitation of information an important issue. Information management recognizes the right of copyright owners to exclude all others from exploiting their creativity, unless appropriate consent or exemptions apply.[1] In the pursuit of development, Nigeria recognizes the role of creativity and innovation as tools for development and encourages research in different fields through its different ministries, departments and agencies. For example, the national development strategy of Nigeria, Nigeria–Vision 20:2020, has a vision where by 2020, Nigeria will have a large, strong, diversified and sustainable economy that effectively harnesses the talents and energies of its people and responsibly exploits its natural endowments to guarantee a high standard of living and quality of life to its citizens. One of the ways it aspires to achieve this is by strengthening the national health information systems and integrating them into a comprehensive national database to improve health data and promote research.[2] The mechanism that would enable the free dissemination of the output of these creative endeavours is at the heart of this chapter.

PART I[3]

2 Nigeria

Nigeria is a country with over 160 million people, 500 ethnic groups, 250 local languages (however, English is the official language), 36 states, a Federal Capital Territory (Abuja) and 774 local government councils. It is the most populous African nation and the 7th most populous nation in the world.[4] It has a dual mixed culture, one from its traditional background and the other from its British colonial heritage. Its people are distinct in culture, tradition, belief and religion, and it is these differences that bring about an enriched cultural diversity and a uniqueness in the expression of Nigeria's creativity.

Nigeria's rich cultural diversity plays a key role in the creative expressions of its people and has a strong influence on the copyright-based works created by Nigerians. The rise in the Nigerian entertainment industry, popularly known as Nollywood, has put Nigeria on the limelight both in the music and film industries. It is therefore not surprising that Nigeria's film industry has been rated as the third largest in the world after Hollywood in the United States and Bollywood of India.[5] These creative works continue to lay credence to the creative capabilities of Nigerians and underscore the need to encourage further creativity by putting in place a strong and viable copyright system.

Creativity is the bedrock of every civilization, and it encourages the transformation of ideas into tangible products. Appreciation of the value of these tangibly expressed ideas often leads to commercialization of the products. This was the situation that occurred in the United Kingdom when printers were enabled by the invention of the printing press to commercialize the writings of popular authors.[6] This practice gave rise to complaints and agitations which brought about the introduction of the first copyright law to protect the rights of authors to their literary works by the grant of exclusive rights to the work, for a specified period of time.[7]

Since the passage to law of the first copyright legislation, the Statute of Anne,[8] many copyright legislations have been passed by national governments and the international community.[9] These legislations underscore the importance of copyright. Nigeria is one of the nations with a copyright legislation[10] and plays its role within the international copyright system.

3 English Copyright Act 1911

Nigeria's copyright history is connected to the United Kingdom through colonialization, and it can be traced from two perspectives. The first perspective is the introduction of the English Copyright Law. A new copyright legislation replacing the Statute of Anne was passed, and by virtue of the extension order in council of 1912 of the English Copyright Act of 1911, the English Copyright Law became applicable in the Southern Protectorate of Nigeria. The second perspective is that copyright has been and is an intrinsic part of the customs and traditions of Nigerians. This view points to the practice where dancers and singers pay homage to their ancestors and predecessors in the trade before they commence their performances. The intent for acknowledgement is the traditional belief that if the current performer wants to succeed, homage must be paid to their ancestors and predecessors in the trade, and such homage will attract the requisite blessings. They also point to the practice where money, gifts, refreshment and other forms of remuneration are given to the performers in appreciation and recognition of their performances.[11] All these practices go to the root of the modern copyright concepts of moral and economic rights. Both perspectives support the importance of respect, appreciation and some form of remuneration for the efforts of those who have produced creative works. It is without contention, however, that the extension of the English Copyright Act of 1911 to Nigeria in 1912 introduced a copyright legal framework into Nigeria's legal system.

The introduction of the English Copyright Act of 1911 (hereinafter referred to as CA 1911) in Nigeria made very little impact on the ordinary Nigerian's daily life, and this was probably due to cultural differences between the people that originated the CA of 1911 and those to whom it was now being applied in Nigeria. At the time of the enactment of the CA 1911, writing had become a way of life in the United Kingdom; expressing ideas, be they original or non-original, in fixed tangible forms had become the general mode of communication and it constituted important elements in the "fixation and originality" requirements for what would qualify as a copyright work.[12] In Nigeria however, the predominant mode of communication at the time was through verbal and non-written modes. Information was passed down from one generation to the other verbally, that is, by word of mouth.[13]

Furthermore, the Nigerian tradition that favours communal ownership and encourages the spirit of camaraderie and free sharing was at variance with the individualistic and proprietary nature of the modern concepts of copyright. In the eyes of the ordinary person, the laws did not exist and would have been regarded as just another administrative process introduced by the colonial masters. The Act however provided the first legislative framework for Nigeria's administration of a copyright system and provided the basis for further development of copyright laws in Nigeria. This Act continued to be in force through independence in 1960 until 1970, when the first indigenous Copyright Act was promulgated.

4 The 1970 Copyright Act

The 1970 Act was passed as a decree on 24 December 1970. It provided for eligibility and conferment of copyright, nature of copyright in certain works, first ownership, assignment and licensing, duration, infringement, actions for infringement and the appointment of a competent authority to resolve copyright licensing conflicts.[14]

Concerns about the lacuna in the 1970 act led to agitations in the copyright-based industries, which eventually led to the 1988 Copyright Act. The legislation has been described as a lame duck due to its inability to support the growing Nigerian copyright industry. Okoroji captured the frustration succinctly when he said:

> The very weak provisions of Decree No 61 of 1970, the copyright law then in force, was identified as the major obstacle to effective confrontation of the copyright problem. The civil provisions were cumbersome and had many loop holes. . . . The criminal sanctions . . . were laughable. There was no provision for any imprisonment. There was therefore very little legal deterrent against piracy. . . . It became very clear that the most important and urgent task . . . was to get an effective copyright law promulgated in Nigeria.[15]

5 The 1988 Copyright Act

The 1988 Copyright Act was promulgated under a military administration and was passed as a decree. The Act has been amended twice, in 1992 and 1999. In

2004, the laws were re-codified under the laws of the federation of Nigeria and have four parts and five schedules.

5.1 Works eligible for copyright under the act

Under the Nigerian Copyright Act, there are six works eligible for copyright. They are *literary, musical and artistic works; cinematograph films, sound recordings and broadcasts.*[16]

For a work to be eligible for copyright under the act, sufficient effort must have been expended on the work to give it an original character, and it must have been fixed in a definite medium directly perceivable or perceivable with the aid of any device or machine.[17] The fact that the making of a work involved some form of copyright infringement would not alone constitute grounds for ineligibility.[18]

5.2 Conferment of copyright

Once a work is eligible for copyright, copyright may be conferred on such a work through a number of channels.

1 *By virtue of nationality or domicile:* The author(s) is a citizen of or is domiciled in Nigeria or an organization/company duly registered under the laws of Nigeria.[19]
2 *By reference to country of origin:* The work was first published or made in Nigeria.[20]
3 *In works of government, State authorities and international bodies:* The work is made under the direction of the government, a state authority or an international body.[21]
4 *Reference to international agreements:* The work is made by a person who on the date of the first publication of the work, such person was a citizen of a country or domiciled in a country to which Nigeria is a party to an obligation in a treaty or other international agreement; or where the work was first published in a country where Nigeria has treaty obligations, or where it was first published in either of the following organizations, the United Nations or any of its specialized agencies, the African Union or the Economic Communities of West African States.[22]

5.3 Powers of a copyright owner

The author of a copyright work or the owner of copyright enjoys certain exclusive rights. These rights operate as restrictive rights in that the author is empowered by copyright to control the performance of certain actions, and without his or her consent or authorization, such works may not be carried out. The performance of any of such works amount to an infringement of the right of the author or the copyright owner. Sections 6–9 of the Act provide for the general nature of copyright and provide for the exclusive actions that the author/copyright owner controls.

These exclusive actions include reproducing, publishing, performing, translating, making any cinematograph film or a record in respect of the work, distributing to the public for hire or for commercial purpose copies of the work, communicating to the public and making an adaptation of the work. Any of the aforementioned actions without due authorization amounts to copyright infringement, which carries consequences both in the civil and criminal realms.

5.4 Infringement of copyright

An important part of the legislation are the infringement provisions of the Act that provide for both civil and criminal actions, which may be instituted simultaneously.[23] The Act specifically states amongst other things when prescribing copyright infringement that copyright is infringed by any person who without the licence or authorization of the owner of the copyright

(a) does or causes any other person to do an act, the doing of which is controlled by copyright;
(b) imports or causes to be imported into Nigeria any copy of a work which, if it had been made in Nigeria would be an infringing copy under this section of this Act.[24]

In the event of an infringement, the copyright owner, assignee or exclusive licensee may bring an action before the Federal High Court and may claim for damages, injunctions and/or accounts. Ignorance is a defence to copyright infringement, but it must be proven that at the time of the infringement, the defendant was actually unaware and had no reasonable grounds to suspect that copyright subsisted in the work. In such situations plaintiffs are not entitled to damages, but rather account for profits in respect of the infringement.[25]

6 Nigerian copyright commission

6.1 Establishment

The 1999 amendment to the Act amongst other things established a body responsible for all matters affecting copyright in Nigeria, known as the Nigerian Copyright Commission.[26]

6.2 Strategies

In 2005, the Commission launched the Strategic Action Against Piracy (STRAP), which had three core components, namely, mass enlightenment, rights administration and enforcement. This strategy also entailed an alternative dispute resolution (ADR) component tagged Copyright Litigation and Mediation Programme (CLAMP), which enable out-of-court settlements in the event of misunderstandings.[27] The focus of STRAP when launched was to reduce the menace caused by piracy through strategic engagement with the general public and with stakeholders through targeted enlightenment programs, effective rights administration and, where necessary, through enforcement. The current administration of the Commission has re-adapted STRAP into what is now called a Medium Term Corporate Plan and Strategy (MTCPS).

6.3 Public enlightenment

Article 34 (2) d of the Nigerian Copyright Act requires the Commission to "enlighten and inform the public on matters relating to copyright". Enlightenment in any society is crucial because it provides requisite information and empowers ordinary citizens with the knowledge required to interact in the society. The esoteric nature of copyright makes it somewhat difficult for the ordinary person to comprehend or appreciate its complexity.

Under STRAP and now vigorously pursued under the MTCPS, the Commission disseminates copyright information. It has the training arm of the Commission called the Nigerian Copyright Institute, which is responsible for training members of staff and the public on copyright issues.[28]

6.4 Rights administration

The Commission administers a number of schemes. These schemes include administration of the following:

1 Copyright (Reciprocal Extension) Regulation 1972[29]
2 Copyright (Security Devices) Regulation 1999[30]
3 Copyright (Video Rental) Regulations 1999[31]
4 Copyright Notification Scheme[32]
5 Copyright (Optical Disc) Regulation 2006[33]
6 Copyright (Collective Management Organisation) Regulations 2007[34]
7 Copyright (Levy on Materials) Order 2012[35]

6.5 Enforcement

In addition to public enlightenment and rights administration, the Commission uses enforcement mechanisms in tackling the challenges in the industry. It does this in collaboration with the traditional enforcement agencies in the country such as the Nigerian Police Force (NPF), the Nigerian Customs Services (NCS), the Economic and Financial Corruptions Commission (EFCC) and other non-enforcement sister agencies. The Commission shares information with other agencies and maximizes available platforms. The Commission embarks on regular anti-piracy raids, arrests and prosecution of pirates. These raids are conducted in conjunction with sister organizations and cover notorious areas such as well-known markets where the products are usually trafficked and the borders through which the products are known to be brought in or taken out.

In the discharge of the Commission's enforcement mandate, the Commission carries out its operations through Copyright Inspectors who are empowered by Section 38 of the Act to enter, inspect and examine any premises they reasonably believe are being used for infringing activities. They are also empowered to seize items which they reasonably suspect to be infringing items as well as to arrest any person who they reasonably believe has committed an offence, as stipulated by the Act. See the Commission's 2012 annual report for some successful enforcement activities.[36]

The legal framework for copyright in Nigeria covers administrative, enforcement and regulatory issues. The pro-enforcement and pro-copyright owner slant of the legislation has been a veritable tool in tackling piracy in Nigeria. The digital age has however introduced new challenges to copyright which exceptions from copyright control as provided in the second schedule to the act cannot adequately cater for, and there is therefore the need for Nigeria's copyright law to adequately respond to these issues.[37] The next section on the future of copyright in Nigeria looks at how Nigeria can address these issues.

7 The future of copyright in Nigeria

As noted at the beginning of this chapter, Nigeria is a nation rich in creativity. The pre-colonial era provides evidence of this in the artistic works seating in the museum in the western parts of the world. Today, Nigeria's Nollywood, the third largest film industry in the world is also evidence of Nigeria's rich and ingenious creativity. Nigeria's collective management organization in music, copyright society of Nigeria (COSON), distributed royalties of 25 million naira in 2011 and 100 million naira in 2012 to members of the society.[38] The legal framework covering copyright in Nigeria has been instrumental to these developments. The future of Nigeria like any other country is intrinsically tied to its ability to harness the potentials in its people as the world has since moved from industrial-based economies to knowledge-based economies with structural frameworks protected under the laws of intellectual property of which copyright is a core component. If Nigeria must play a significant role in this new frontier, there is the urgent need for strategic repositioning to ensure maximal benefits in today's global knowledge-based economy and tomorrow's dynamic technologically driven market.

7.1 TRIPS and flexibilities

The Uruguay round negotiations that in 1996 produced the agreements on Trade-Related Aspects of Intellectual Property (TRIPS) upgraded international copyright protection and placed on all parties to the agreement obligations to provide certain minimum standard of protection to copyright works. Nigeria as a developing country has complied with most of these requirements, but it is important to note that these requirements are mainly in the interest of developed and not developing countries. Articles 7 and 8 of the agreement provide some flexibilities to developing countries. Understanding these flexibilities and maximizing them in the interest of Nigeria's creative industry and copyright legislation will enable it to play a stronger role in the present and upcoming economies. Nigeria's copyright future must therefore be one of strategic engagement for the development of the Nigerian creative industry through appropriate legislative reforms, strengthening international negotiation in the interest of Nigeria's creative industry and encouraging further development of creativity from the cradle to the grave.

8 Open access and the future of copyright law

8.1 Copyright and open access

In situating copyright in today's technologically enabled and driven society, balancing the interest of copyright owners and users is key. In achieving this, there is the need to create some kind of synergy between copyright as a system and the open culture that favours free, online, unrestricted and immediate dissemination of information (open access). Whereas the current copyright system is restrictive by default, the open culture seeks ways to change that default. The underpinning for this change is the inability to access requisite information due to certain factors hindering access: factors which as explained in Chapter 1 have been identified as "price, permission and technical".[39] The price is understood as subscription costs by publishers, as well as pay-per-view by specialized vendors. The obstacle created by permission is directly connected to the exclusive rights granted to copyright owners who restrict the access to copyright materials unless a permission has been obtained.[40] Technology provides the opportunity for right owners to place technologically enabled measures for protection on devices carrying their copyrighted contents, as well as to monitor the use of such contents. By means of these measures, right owners are able to block access to their copyrighted materials and are also able to manage the use of their copyrighted content. These technical possibilities may actually prove to be beneficial to right-owners, but at the same time, they constitute a hindrance to access: access to knowledge, access to information and access to peer-reviewed literature. In a global context, access restriction constitutes hindrance to knowledge whether it is peer reviewed, educational, public sector information or purely entertainment information. For the purpose of this chapter, access to information intended purely for entertainment purposes, such as music, films and novels, is the focus, because this type of information can be considered as luxury, not necessary for fundamental development. On the other hand, access to peer-reviewed literature, educational resources and public-sector information is cardinal for the development of any society.

8.2 Changing the default from closed to open

Whereas the default for protecting knowledge under the current copyright regime is closed (no access without permission), the open access movement seeks to change this default from closed to open for the purpose of empowering the general public with access to peer-reviewed literature, access to educational resources, and access to public sector information to the end that the general public will be properly equipped to make the best from available knowledge. As Nelson

Mandela noted, education is the greatest tool for changing lives.[41] But what is the value of education when the knowledge required to gain education cannot be accessed? It is now commonly known that knowledge is power and that we live in a knowledge-based economy.[42]

In recognition of the importance of the current copyright system, which empowers the copyright owner to restrict all others (except those falling under some form of limitation or exception) from exploiting copyright-protected works without prior consenting having first been obtained, the movement relies on this right of the copyright owner, but this time not in a restrictive manner, but rather in an enabling manner. It achieves this through *open licensing systems*, which grant prior consent to prospective users. This system has been very successful in the software industry through the free open source software licences such as GNU GPL.[43] In the content industry, there are several licences, but the creative commons licences appear to be the most popular.[44]

In Nigeria's copyright future, embracing the open culture will be instrumental to its development. However, in adopting this culture, there is the need for proper understanding of the concepts through enlightenment and also the need to adopt policies that would encourage further creativity within the Nigerian creative industry. This is important because the open culture has the tendency of opening developing countries to become mere consumers and non-contributors to the world library. To benefit from the open access movement, Nigeria needs to strategically engage with the open culture for purposes of empowerment and not mere consumption. A mentality or attitude of mere consumption may seem to provide an easy win at the beginning but will eventually kill creativity and could no doubt bring about the eradication of the Nigerian culture and may produce the next dispensation of colonization.[45] Proper engagement with the open culture will afford the opportunity to share the knowledge of the poor with the rich and the rich with the poor; it will also afford the highest level of visibility to works by Nigerian authors and allow for the possibility of global impact on locally generated works. The sharing culture typified by "open" is the now and future for all forms of content. If the open culture is not embraced, copyright may be suffocated and relegated to a place of insignificance.

PART II

The second part of this chapter examines the framework that exists within some of Nigeria's ministries, departments and agencies to ascertain the level of appreciation of the open culture.

9 The current legal, regulatory and policy frameworks for open access in Nigeria

Part I discussed Nigeria's copyright laws. Copyright is critical to research because it controls information management. The legal, regulatory and policy frameworks discussed hereunder all have intellectual property/copyright components, and this is because the output of research is often expressed as literary works and is therefore covered under copyright laws. Part II examines four federal ministries under the Federal Republic of Nigeria and analyzes their institutional framework in light of the open culture.

Research in Nigeria is administered from a multi-ministerial and multi-departmental perspective.[46] The Federal Ministries of

1 Health[47]
2 Agriculture and Rural Development[48]
3 Education[49]
4 Science and Technology[50]

all play key roles in the development of research as well as in the dissemination of the output of such research. These ministries put in place policies and legislations which enable the establishment of regulatory bodies to administer, regulate and manage research issues. They are also saddled with the responsibility to oversee several agencies which have specific mandates covering different research interests. In the pursuit of development, creativity and innovation has been recognized as pillars for development, and the encouragement of research has been enshrined in most of the government ministries, departments and agencies.[51] This development is commendable and worthy of praise. However, the focus should not be limited to merely encouraging research and development, but in addition, on freedom to accessing the output of such research.[52] What value is the research when the output is simply compiled and locked up in some official cabinet or is made available to only the members of an elite group or produced as articles or series of articles by journal publishers who subsequently lock up the output of such research behind their paywalls?

In the draft of the framework for Nigeria's National Innovation System, it was noted that a resilient and effective innovation system is key to overcoming the great challenges of "poverty, wealth creation, insecurity, environmental issues, sustainable and productive industries, curing diseases, affordable and robust education" in Nigeria.[53] It also pointed out that in an attempt to deploying innovation as a tool for development, it is crucial to understand that this

> system is about people: the knowledge, technology, infrastructure and cultures they have created or adopted, who they work with, and what new ideas they are experimenting with. An innovation system is an open network of organizations both interacting with each other . . . and it is an open system, which interacts with its environment.[54]

Open access seeks to provide an enabling environment where similar interactions as referred to above can take place without restrictions. It seeks to ensure that the output of research is readily available and accessible to all willing minds who are desirous of investigating further and adding to the development and betterment of the society howbeit by building on the ideas and knowledge which others have developed and interacted with.[55]

This section of the chapter will therefore examine the institutional frameworks of the Ministries of Health, Agriculture and Rural Development, Education, and Science and Technology with a view to determining their relevance, applicability and compliance with the overarching goals of the open access movement.

10 Federal Ministry of Health

This ministry is responsible for ensuring quality health care for Nigerian's and has the vision "to develop and implement policies that strengthen the national health system for effective, efficient, accessible and affordable delivery of health services in partnership with other stakeholders".[56] The ministry has four departments, namely, Departments for Health Planning, Research and Statistic (P.R.S), Public Health, and Family Health and Procurement, and it is saddled with oversight functions covering 55 parastatals[57] including eight federal specialty hospitals, three national orthopaedic hospitals, one national eye centre, one national ear care centre, 22 federal medical centres, 20 federal teaching hospitals and five agencies.[58] Virtually all of these departments, parastatals and agencies encourage and carry out research and in turn produce research outcomes.

In a National Health Policy of the Federal Republic of Nigeria, it has been identified that "most of Nigeria's disease burden is due to preventable diseases and poverty is a major cause of these problems."[59] In a similar release by the United Nations Press, the Secretary General of the United Nation took cognizance of the role illiteracy plays in poor health when he noted that "[i]lliteracy exacerbates cycles of poverty, ill-health and deprivation. It weakens communities and undermines democratic processes through marginalization and exclusion. These and other impacts can combine to destabilize societies."[60] If these diseases are preventable, what is being done to prevent them? Strategic engagement in inquiry, interrogation, research and development is more often than not central to addressing these questions, and access to knowledge is crucial for effective inquiry and interrogation as well as for the maximization of the output of research and development.[61]

Nigeria's national health strategies are currently guided by the National Strategic Health Development Plan (NSHDP 2010–2015), which was endorsed by the National Council on Health (the highest health policy advisory body in Nigeria) on the 16th of March 2010 and approved by the Federal Executive Council on the 10th of November 2010. This policy was preceded by the revised National Health Policy of 2004 which had seven major thrusts.[62] The current NSHDP has eight, namely, the NSHDP Leadership and Governance for Health; Health Service Delivery; Human Resources for Health; Financing for Health; National Health Management Information System; Partnerships for Health; Community Participation and Ownership; and Research for Health. Common to both policies is the recognition of the importance of research and the inclusion of information management in the national policy for health.

Paragraph 8.3 of NSHDC provides for a comprehensive repository and states that it shall "develop a comprehensive repository for health research at all levels (including both public and non-public sectors)".[63] From Paragraphs 8.3.1–8.4.2, the policy document discusses developing strategies for getting research into strategies and practices, enshrining mechanisms that would ensure that funded research produces new knowledge, creating a framework for sharing the output of research, establishing channels for sharing research outputs between researchers, policy makers and development practitioners. At Paragraph 8.4.2, it was noted that

> governments and donors will support; the publication of high quality national journals, following a review of editorial boards, establishing appropriate linkages between editors of national journals and reputable publishers (especially online, free web-based access publishers) and international collaborators, to improve the quality of national journals.

It would also vigorously pursue "wide dissemination of selected national journals to all stakeholders at federal, state and LGA levels."[64]

High Points: The high points of the policy document are that the above provisions reveal an awareness of the importance of access to knowledge and at the same time some form of willingness on the part of policy makers to create an environment for knowledge dissemination. The mention of the development of a comprehensive repository for health research at all levels, as well as the intention of government to support high-quality journal publication particularly those that are online and that have free web-based access publishers are indications that access to knowledge appears to be relevant to Nigeria's policy makers.

Downside: The downside of the policy document is that an attempt to locate the comprehensive repository referred to in the national policy document via a careful analysis of the website of the ministry revealed that no such repository exists. The mention however of the term *repository* is an indicator that policy makers may be aware of a global trend to disseminate information through repositories or databanks. Another issue is the absence of the freedom to use and reuse information, a crucial element for open access publishing. In addition to the above is the failure to provide the infrastructures that would enable the dissemination of the output of research (peer-reviewed literatures) in a way that is free, available, online, immediate and where possible open for reuse.

The fact that repositories are mentioned is commendable, but merely mentioning them will not provide the desired result. The policy clearly attempts to address dissemination and sharing of research findings by addressing online publication; it however leaves out the practical mechanism of obtaining access, use and reuse of the research output unaddressed. Addressing the gaps between the current positions by the introduction of practical open access publishing mechanisms will be imperative.[65] Most of the research outputs are generated by the work undertaken by agencies under the supervision of the Federal Ministry of Health. The National Institute for Medical Research (NIMR) is an example.[66]

10.1 National Institute for Medical Research

NIMR was established in 1977, pursuant to the National Science and Technology Development Agency Decree (No 5) of 1977,[67] and is responsible for research into human medicine. Medical research in Nigeria dates back to 1920 when the Rockefeller Foundation, Yellow Fever Commission to the West Coast of Africa arrived in Nigeria. In 1925, the West African Yellow Fever Commission arrived and built a research unit in Yaba, Lagos.[68] The West African Council for Medical Research was later established in 1954. The predecessor to the current NIMR was the Medical Research Council of Nigeria established pursuant to Decree No.1 of 1972.[69] NIMR lists out very important areas as her priority research focus and they include malaria, onchocerciasis, schistosomiasis, diarrhoeal diseases, tuberculosis, HIV infections, maemoglobinopathies, nutrition, special childhood communicable diseases, strategic research, biotechnology research and leprosy research.[70] It is expected that some level of considerable research has been carried out in the above-mentioned areas. An attempt to locate published research output on the above-mentioned priority areas revealed a list of publications with no access to the actual publications. The implication is that the output of these priority researches is inaccessible.[71] This not only limits accessibility to the information but also reduces the possible utility the work can achieve.

10.2 National Agency for Control of AIDS

Another agency under the Federal Ministry of Health is the National Agency for Control of AIDS, formerly known as the National Action Committee for AIDS, which has the vision "to make Nigeria a nation of people with functional knowledge of HIV/AIDS who provide care and support to individuals, families and communities confronted with the epidemic".[72] This vision of imparting functional knowledge is at the heart of the organization, and indeed several public enlightenment campaigns have been carried out by NACA.[73] However, a careful search of the organization's website provides some information in the frequently asked question (FAQ) section, but when it comes to reports and publications which constitute an integral part of research output, that section is mainly empty, and the expected reports and publications are not available.

11 Federal Ministry of Agriculture

This Ministry which was established in 1966 regulates agricultural research, agriculture and natural resources, forestry and veterinary research all over Nigeria. It has the responsibility amongst many other things to address Nigeria's food and agricultural problems, thereby reducing the poverty level in Nigeria.[74] One of the agricultural policies of the ministry is to transform the Agricultural Research Council which was established pursuant to Agricultural Research Council Act.[75] The Act in Section 5 provide for the functions of the council and narrows down at sub-sections (f–j) on encouraging research and ensuring the greatest utility for such research as follows:

(f) maintain an up-to-date record of all existing facilities for research, training and extension in the agricultural sciences in Nigeria and advise the Federal Government on their adequacy and efficient utilization;

(g) advise the Federal Government on the re-organization of existing institutes, including the creation of new ones, as are required to implement or further the efficiency of research, training and extension in the agricultural sciences;
(h) promote collaboration between scientists engaged in research in the agricultural sciences in Nigeria and their counterparts in other countries or international bodies;
(i) establish and maintain a National Agricultural Science Library and Documentation Centre and publish or sponsor the publication of the research results in the agricultural sciences; and
(j) carry out such activities as may, in the opinion of the Council, further the advancement of research, training and extension in the agricultural sciences.[76]

Nigeria is the country with the highest population in Africa. It has vast expanse of cultivatable lands, but ironically, it faces food and poverty challenges.[77] These challenges make the issue of agricultural research of paramount importance. The act as quoted above provides at S. 5(f) for the maintenance of records on research facilities for purposes of facilitating agricultural research, thus recognizing the importance of research. S.5(g) addresses the provision of structures to support efficient and effective research, S.5(h) focuses on promoting local and international collaboration between researchers in the agricultural sciences and S.5(i) provides for a library/documentation centre which would publish or sponsor the publication of the output of research. The above provisions are a manifest demonstration of the agencies acknowledgement that research plays a key role in development.

S.5(g) particularly provides for the reorganization of existing research institutes or the establishment of new ones. The purpose of reorganizing or establishing these research institutes is amongst other things to encourage research that would produce useful knowledge able to transform the agricultural sector and positively address the food and poverty challenges in Nigeria. Access by interested researchers and curious minds to the output of these researches becomes imperative to achieve agricultural development.

In an attempt to search for the output of agricultural research generated by the research institutes in Nigeria, a careful analysis of the library and documentation centre (National Agricultural Science Library and Documentation Centre)[78] revealed an exact match, but the centre was that of Hungary,[79] and it did not reveal any result for Nigeria. It appears that the said library and documentation centre has either not been established and if established, it is yet to come online. A further search of the publication section of the ministry's website reveals a file library which has 11 available and downloadable documents. It would also be noted that although Section 5 of the Act provides for advising government on adequate and efficient utilization of research, as well as encouraging research collaboration between researchers, the Act makes no clear provision for the management of research output. It is silent as to online access, use and reuse rights with regards to the output of research. Online availability and accessibility to the output of research is one of the pillars upon which open access stands and this no doubt should be an important aspect of agricultural research considering the many agricultural institutes in Nigeria covering agricultural produce including cocoa, oil, rubber, fisheries and animals.[80] Easy access to the output of research from all these research institutes has the capacity of enhancing agricultural research in Nigeria, reducing poverty and addressing the food challenge in Nigeria.

12 Federal Ministry of Education

This ministry has the vision of delivering sound education for public good and seeks to deplore education as a tool for fostering national development. It is responsible for formulating, coordinating, harmonizing and supervising the implementation of Nigeria's education policies.[81] It has oversight functions over 24 parastatals/agencies including the Universal Basic Education Commission (UBEC), National Library of Nigeria (NLN), National Open University of Nigeria (NOUN), National Universities Commission (NUC), and Nigeria Educational Research and Development Council (NERDC). Common to all of these agencies is that they promote education and research. For example, the policy of the nation in furtherance of universal basic education is implemented under the auspices of the *Universal Basic Education Act*, which provides at Section 2 for the right to compulsory, free, universal basic education for children in their primary and junior secondary school stages.[82] One major issue with the ministry is the absence of a dedicated website.[83] A Wikipedia[84] and Facebook page[85] is what is found when a search is conducted for the ministry. The implication is that the Federal Ministry of Education has no online presence, and any information that would be obtained on the ministry can only be obtained offline. People desirous of obtaining relevant information are cut off. This is something that must be addressed urgently. Most of the agencies under the parent ministry however have functional websites. The Nigerian Educational Research Development Council and the National Universities Commission are examined hereunder.

12.1 Nigerian Educational Research Development Council

Another agency involved in educational research is the Nigerian Educational Research Development Council established pursuant to the Nigerian Education Research Development Council Act No. 53. The Council's core objective is "educational research and development in Africa".[86] It is responsible amongst other things for compiling relevant publications, sponsoring the publication of education research and making such publications available.[87] These publications are meant to be made available and accessible through the agency's "library and informatic centre".[88] It is the responsibility of the centre to serve as a point of exchange for information, provide information on completed research and to promote the dissemination of such research as e-resources; the Council's library and informatics centre provide links to the abstract of the output of research. The two links on the e-resource page "Nigerian Education Abstracts Volume II and Family Life HIV/AIDS Education (FLHE) Manual do not provide download opportunities."[89]

Whereas the first provides abstracts of different thesis, the second is merely a link to another webpage.

12.2 National Universities Commission

The National Universities Commission (NUC) is probably one of the most important agencies under the Federal Ministry of Education.[90] The agency is responsible for regulating the activities of all universities in Nigeria, which is currently 147, that is 46 federal, 40 state and 61 private universities.[91] The agency has 11 departments.[92] Five of the departments are mentioned hereunder.

The vision of the *Department of Research and Innovation* is to be "the catalyst for quality research and development outputs and outcomes delivery by Nigerian universities that impact positively on the socio-economic sectors of Nigeria". It seeks to "deliver desired, relevant, innovative, and quality-driven interventions in Nigerian universities in partnerships with other stakeholders to enhance the infrastructure and capacity of Nigerian universities to better execute their research and development mandates".[93]

The Department of Inspection and Monitoring is responsible for monitoring the level of compliance of Nigerian Universities with the provisions of the Benchmark Minimum Academic Standards (BMAS) and other quality assurance guidelines laid down by government. It undertakes regular visits to universities and prepares periodic reports on the state of university education in Nigeria[94]

Department of Students' Support Services (DSSS) has a vision "to be a catalyst in the Commission's drive to deploy strategies for improving Nigerian University students' career opportunities and sense of social responsibility".[95]

The Department of Information and Communication Technology seeks to facilitate the utilization of ICT for teaching, research, planning management and effective evaluation through decision-making package in the Nigeria university system.[96]

Department of Open and Distance Education was established on the 26th of July 2011 to tackle the challenges of inadequate access in the Nigerian University system using the Open Distance Learning (ODL) mode.[97]

The laudable visions and missions of the departments are evident in the administration of Nigerian Universities. Monitoring quality, tackling the challenges of inadequate access, deploying information communication technology as a tool for integration and cooperation as well as encouraging and facilitating research and development are fundamental issues that guarantee quality education and that enhance the culture of research.

Universities are known for not just educating students, but also for research and for providing peer-reviewed literature with ground-breaking ideas.[98] This practice is inspired by the research culture which has become part and parcel of the university system. Universities account for most of the knowledge published as peer-reviewed literature, and quality research thrives on accessibility to this knowledge. It is generally agreed that the global academic community have a culture of sharing research output for free and that they are more concerned about the impact of their work: therefore accessibility, visibility, impact and maximal utilization of these works are what is paramount to academics.[99]

Two of the cardinal issues with Nigerian Universities are the problem of inaccessibility to peer-reviewed literature and poor visibility of research generated in Nigeria. The visibility problem is both local and international. It is local in the sense that fellow researchers within Nigeria are unable to access the work, as well as fellow researchers within the wider global community. How to ensure visibility to research generated in Nigeria as well as accessing the output of research generated in other parts of the world have been the preoccupation of several writings all of which are united in the view that open access provides the platform for actualizing these objectives.[100]

The adoption of open access by Nigerian universities has been slow as only 8 of the 140 universities have repositories.[101] The National University Commission in its role as regulator can influence the policy direction of access to knowledge in Nigeria by encouraging all Nigerian Universities to develop open access mandates and develop institutional repositories.

13 The Federal Ministry of Science and Technology

This ministry is "saddled with the responsibility of facilitating the development and deployment of Science, Technology and Innovation to enhance the pace of socio-economic development of the country".[102] The ministry deplores specialized research and development projects using the platform of parastatals and agencies under its charge to distil the vision and mission of the ministry. The ministry works with a number of strategies to further the goal of strengthening innovation in Nigeria through research and development. The strategies include the following:

1 The Science, Technology and Innovation (STI) Policy[103]
2 The Framework for the Nigerian National System of Innovation[104]
3 The National ICT Policy[105]
4 The National Information Technology Development Act[106]

These strategy documents contain the legislative, regulatory and policies frameworks that have been put in place by the Nigerian government and are geared towards entrenching a culture of research and development aimed at strengthening the innovation capacity of Nigeria and Nigerians. At the 17th session of the Commission on Science and Technology for Development (CSTD) organized by the United Nations conference on Trade and Development (UNCTAD), the supervising minister for the ministry of science and technology for Nigeria noted that Nigeria had successfully revised its Science, Technology and Innovation (STI) policy and that "the revised STI policy articulates the establishment of a National Research and Innovation Council to facilitate the transformation of Nigeria into a knowledge based economy with strong capabilities in STI."[107]

13.1 Nigeria's Science, Technology and Innovation policy

The STI policy contains eight broad provisos with a total subdivision of 20 provisos. The preamble, national STI policy, vision, mission, general and specific objectives are all covered under provisos 1.0, 2.0, 2.1, 2.2, 2.3 and 2.4, respectively.[108] Proviso 3 is the key provision in the policy document, and it contains the core of the policy strategies addressing the issues of human resources development, research and development, intellectual property rights, technology transfer and diffusion, standardization and quality assurance, STI information management system, and finally, women and STI. The last section of the document covers funding, partnership, governance, institutional and legal framework, and appreciation under proviso's 4.0, 5.0, 6.0, 7.0 and 8.0, respectively.[109]

The STI policy seeks to accelerate development, competitiveness and creation of wealth for all Nigerians in line with Nigeria's vision 20:2020 Economic Transformation Blueprint (NV20:2020)[110] and therefore has the mission of "evolving a nation that harnesses, develops and utilizes STI to build a large, strong, diversified, sustainable and competitive economy that guarantees a high standard of living and quality of life to its citizens."[111]

Both the general and specific objectives of the STI policy focus on capacity development and underscore the importance of access to knowledge. The policy identifies the importance of not just access to the use of knowledge but also reuse. It notes that the STI seeks to "facilitate the acquisition of knowledge to adapt, utilize, replicate and diffuse technologies for the growth of SMEs, agricultural development, food security, power generation and poverty reduction".[112] The STI policy document is evidence of one of Nigeria's institutional recognitions that the task of development is best achieved under a collaborative atmosphere. The more works open for utilization and replication (use), adaptation and diffusion (reuse), the greater the possibilities for development. It is based on the above that Proviso 3 sets out a policy strategy that seeks to create awareness and build a sharing culture that would foster development. The document employs multiple strategies in addressing the problems. For instance, at 3.1.3, it employs the approach of creating awareness through primary, secondary and technical schools. In this way, it adopts the grassroot approach by going to early learners to inculcate the concepts into the academic curricula of schools and thereby stir an interest for STI in youths. At 3.3, it emphasizes the need to prioritize research and development for purposes of "generation, acquisition, storage, application and diffusion of S&T knowledge for national development".[113] The focus of this research and development encompass different sectors ranging from agriculture, water resources, biotechnology, health, energy, environmental science and technology, mines and materials development, ICT, transport system, space research, industrial research, youths, sports and tourism development, works, land, housing and urban development, defence and national security, word resources, science laboratory technology, raw materials, as well as new and emerging technologies.

The Act recognizes the need to respect intellectual property rights and notes that creativity and innovation are easily advanced where a system that ensures the management, harmonization and coordination of IPRs are in place.[114]

The policy directly addresses the issue of access to use and reuse of knowledge at 3.7 where it seeks to "establish an effective information management system designed to provide real-time access to functional and updated database on STI activities in order to provide a platform for accessing, sharing and exchanging information".[115] It further outlines seven strategies to achieve its information management goal:

1 Developing national STI indicators that will be revised periodically in line with international standards
2 Establishing and maintaining a national database on STI input/outputs within an agency of FMST and strengthening the existing information management system on R&D in all sectors
3 Creating active networks for interaction, cooperation and exchange of ideas among STI actors and stakeholders within and outside the country.
4 Establishing a mechanism within the FMST to coordinate the management of STI Information system
5 Establishing information system nodes in all agencies of FMST and other cognate ministries
6 Linking the National STI information system with the National Bureau of Statistics for local and international usage
7 Facilitating ICT infrastructure deployment to all S&T institutions[116]

So far, the activities of this ministry have proved very positive on Nigerians and Nigeria as a whole. The provision of better Internet access has made it possible for the ordinary Nigerian to gain better access to the Internet. Recently, the Alliance for Affordable Internet (A4AI) ranked Nigeria as the 2nd among emerging economies.[117] Building on these improvements, Nigerians are able to build and develop initiatives to enhance communication, trade and commerce and for effective participation in eGovernment.[118] Recently, the United Nations noted Nigeria's rise on the eGovernment Development ranking from 193 to 141, a 21-point rise.[119] These developments are positive indicators that needed infrastructures are being put in place to enable effective and efficient creation, storage, dissemination and adaptation of knowledge resource. The policy document's aspiration at 3.7.3 (vi) to create a platform for information linkage to the National Bureau of Statistics for purposes of enabling use and reuse of information locally and internationally appears to be ongoing. A search of the National Bureau of Statistics website revealed links to a number of downloadable resources and reports.[120] The website particularly has an NBS data portal which has different tabs including those for data, maps, data analysis, state profiles, dashboards, resource centre, tutorial and user guides.[121] A very significant part of the NBS is its data archive called the Nigerian National Data Archive (NADA) centre. Through this archive, the agency seeks to promote equitable access to microdata in the interest of all citizens. The agency particularly notes that "Survey and census microdata are invaluable resources for statisticians, researchers and analysts because they constitute important and irreplaceable assets which need to be managed in a way that encourages their use and reuse, while protecting the privacy of respondents."[122] No doubt the Ministry of Science and Technology is moving in the right direction when it comes to access to knowledge. The fact that the STI policy document recognizes that the creation, use and reuse of knowledge resources play a dominant role in social, economic and political development is an indicator that Nigeria is beginning to appreciate the importance of access to knowledge.

14 Conclusion

The legal, regulatory and policy frameworks discussed above all indicate that there is growing awareness about open access in Nigeria and that some of the frameworks have even began to build structures that are able to implement the goals of open access. However, it is unthinkable and inexcusable that in this digital age, a Federal Ministry of Education would not have an official website. The analysis has also shown that a lot of the institutional infrastructures are inherently defective and reveal a dearth of understanding about the concept and culture of open access. Nigeria's legal, regulatory and policy structures provide for the establishment of digital libraries, documentation and informatics centres, but most of these institutions do not even have any such platform, and where they exist, they do not provide free, online, unrestricted, immediate access to the actual output of their research.

The websites of some of these agencies are able to provide abstracts of papers, some provide the list of some research, while others provide information on frequently asked questions, but the actual output of research is often not available online, thereby constituting barriers to access. Removing these barriers on the legal, regulatory and policy framework front is imperative because without their removal, advancing open access, OER and public-sector information in Nigeria would be an uphill task. The good news is that the open culture is gradually being introduced into Nigeria through initiatives like the National Data Archive Centre under the National Bureau of Statistics. This gradual introduction will form important building blocks in constructing a sustainable framework for the development and implementation of open access to knowledge in Nigeria. The next chapter will amongst other things consider how open access was introduced into Nigeria and will evaluate how the two strategies of open access – self-archiving and open access journals – are being implemented in Nigeria. Finally, it will discuss the advantages of open access to Nigerians.

Notes

1 D. J. Gervais, *Collective Management of Copyright and Related Rights* (Kluwer Law International, 2010), 1–2. See where the author noted that "The apparent paradox of copyright is that . . . it provides copyright owners with a right to exclude others from copying, performing and communicating those new works."

2 National Planning Commission, *Nigeria Vision 20:2020* (NPC ed., 2009).

3 Part I is largely based on an article by the author, titled "Evolution and Future Trends of Copyright in Nigeria", published in the *Journal of Open Access to Law (JOAL)* in

2 (1) (2014), available at https://ojs.law.cornell.edu/index.php/joal/article/view/26 under a CC BY licence.

4 Federal Republic of Nigeria, *About Nigeria*, available at www.nigeria.gov.ng/2012-10-29-11-05-46.

5 *Assessing the Participation of Domestic SMEs in the International Production Chain: The Case of Nu Metro in Nigeria* (2010), available at http://unctad.org/en/Docs/diaeed20095_en.pdf.

6 Chris Butler, *FC74: The Invention of the Printing Press and Its Effects*, available at www.flowofhistory.com/units/west/11/FC74.

7 Olukunle OLA, *Copyright Collective Administration in Nigeria Lessons for Africa* (Springer, 2013), 6–7.

8 Statute of Anne, 8 Anne c. 19 (1710).

9 World Intellectual Property Organization (WIPO), *WIPO Administered Treaties*, available at www.wipo.int/treaties/en/. WIPO provides a comprehensive list of all national and international copyright legislations.

10 Nigerian Copyright Act, Cap C28 (2004).

11 Adebambo Adewopo, *Nigerian Copyright System: Principles and Perspectives* (Odade Publishers, 2012).

12 Jennifer Davis, *Intellectual Property Law* (Oxford University Press Third ed., 2008), particularly at 2.12, 2.14 and 2.15.

13 John Asein, *Nigerian Copyright Law and Practice* (Books and Gavel Limited, 2nd ed., 2012).

14 OLA, 28 (2013).

15 Tony Okoroji, *Copyright Neighbouring Rights & the New Millionaires (The Twists and Turns in Nigeria)* (Tops Limited, 2008).

16 Section 1 (1) (a)-(f) Cap C28 (2004).

17 Ibid., Section 1 (2) (a) & (b)

18 Ibid., Section 1 (4).

19 Ibid., Section 2.

20 Ibid., Section 3.

21 Ibid., Section 4.

22 Ibid., Section 5.

23 Ibid., Section 24.

24 Ibid., Section 15 (1).

25 Ibid., Section 16 (3).

26 Ibid., Section 34.

27 'Nigerian Copyright Commission NCC, STRAP and CLAMP – Nigeria Copyright Commission in Action' (2008) *WIPO Magazine*, September.

28 Nigerian Copyright Commission (NCC), *Nigerian Copyright Institute*, available at www.copyright.gov.ng/index.php/2013-02-10-16-11-10/nigerain-copyright-institute-nci.

29 NCC, *Copyright (Reciprocal Extension) Regulation 1972* (1972), available at www.copyright.gov.ng/images/downloads/Copyright%20Reciprocal%20Extension%20Order%201972.pdf.

30 NCC, *Copyright (Security Devices) Regulation 1999* (1999), available at www.copyright.gov.ng/images/downloads/Copyright%20Security%20devices%20regulation%201999.pdf.

31 NCC, *Copyright (Video Rental) Regulation 1999* (1999), available at www.copyright.gov.ng/images/downloads/Copyright%20Video%20rental%20regulation%201999.pdf.

32 NCC, *Copyright Notification Scheme* (2005), available at www.copyright.gov.ng/index.php/regulatory-schemes/copyright-notification.

33 NCC, *Copyright (Optical Discs Plants) Regulation 2006*. B 697–711 (2006), available at www.copyright.gov.ng/images/downloads/Optical%20Disc%20Regulation.pdf.

34 NCC, *Copyright (Collective Management Organisation) Regulation 2007* (2007), available at www.copyright.gov.ng/images/downloads/CMO%20Regulation%202007.pdf. The earlier regulation was called Copyright (Collecting Societies) Regulation 1993.
35 NCC, *Copyright (Levy on Materials) Order 2012* (2012), available at www.copyright.gov.ng/images/downloads/REVISED%20DRAFT%20LEVY%20ON%20COPYRIGHT%20MATERIALS%20ORDER.pdf.
36 NCC 2012 Annual Report. (2012). See pages 6–9.
37 Nigerian Copyright Act, Cap C28, Laws of the Federation of Nigeria, 2004 Cap C28 (2004). See the Second Schedule to the Act, which provides for fair dealing.
38 Kunle Ola, *Copyright Collective Administration in Nigeria Lessons for Africa* (Springer, 2013).
39 Peter Suber, *Open Access* (MIT Press, 2012), 4–5. See also, Budapest Open Access Initiative, *Ten Years on from the Budapest Open Access Initiative: Setting the Default to Open*, available at www.opensocietyfoundations.org/openaccess/boai-10-recommendations.
40 OLA, 4 (2013).
41 Valerie Strauss, 'Nelson Mandela's Famous Quote on Education' (2013) *The Washington Post*.
42 World Bank, World Bank Announces Open Access Policy for Research and Knowledge, Launches Open Knowledge Repository, Press-Release No. 2012/379/EXTOP (2012), where the World Bank Group President Robert Zoellick said, "knowledge is power."
43 Richard Stallman, *The GNU Project*, available at www.gnu.org/gnu/thegnuproject.html
44 Brian Fitzgerald, *A Short Overview of Creative Commons* (Sydney University Press, 2007).
45 Kunle Ola, 'Scholarly Publication in Nigeria: Implications of Open Access' 6 (2015) *The WIPO Journal* 117, 130–132.
46 Federal Ministry of Health, *Revised National Health Policy* (2004), available at http://osgf.dammy.net/payload?id=19d51d38-c75f-4461-91ce-f6a6d2298b87. See where it was noted that "Priorities for health service and biomedical research shall be set and reviewed in collaboration with the Federal Ministry of Education and the Federal Ministry of Science and Technology and the Federal Ministry of Justice."
47 Federal Ministry of Health, *Home*, available at www.health.gov.ng/?view=featured.
48 Federal Ministry of Agriculture and Rural Development, *About Us*, available at www.fmard.gov.ng/About-us-new.
49 Federal Republic of Nigeria, *Federal Ministry of Education*, available at www.nigeria.gov.ng/2012-10-29-11-06-51/executive-branch/93-federal-ministry-of-education/116-federal-ministry-of-education.
50 Federal Ministry of Science and Technology (FMST), *Harnessing Technology for Nigeria's Social and Economic Development*, available at http://fmst.gov.ng/.
51 Federal Republic of Nigeria FMST, *Science, Technology and Innovation (STI) Policy*, available at http://workspace.unpan.org/sites/internet/Documents/UNPAN048879.pdf (Federal Ministry of Science and Technology ed., Federal Government of Nigeria 2011). See where it was noted that the policy was designed to foster the pursuit of knowledge through providing an enabling environment for the research and development. See also, UNESCO, *Nigerian President Pledges US$5 billion Towards National Science Foundation*, available at www.unesco.org/new/en/natural-sciences/science-technology/sti-policy/country-studies/nigeria/nigerian-president-pledges-us5-billion-towards-national-science-foundation/. "Its main functions would be the provision of grants to research bodies, universities, enterprises and individuals on a competitive basis; the equipping and capitalization of research groups and; the establishment of research universities."
52 Leni Wild, 'Information Alone is Not Enough: It's All About Who Uses It, and Why' *World Bank* (2014), available at http://blogs.worldbank.org/publicsphere/information-alone-not-enough-it-s-all-about-who-uses-it-and-why.

53 FMST, *Framework for the Nigerian National System of Innovation*, available at http://fmst.gov.ng/downloadable/NATIONAL%20SYSTEM%20OF%20INNOVATION%20-%20Draft.pdf. See page 1 of the policy document.

54 Ibid., 3 of the policy document.

55 Isaac Newton, *From a letter written by Isaac Newton to Robert Hooke*, 5 February 1676.

56 Federal Ministry of Health, *Mission and Vision*, available at www.health.gov.ng/index.php/about-us/mission-and-vission.

57 Federal Ministry of Health, *Parastatals*, available at www.health.gov.ng/index.php/parastatals.

58 Federal Ministry of Health, *Agencies Under FMOH*, available at www.health.gov.ng/index.php/about-us.National Primary Health Development Agency, National Agency for Food & Drugs Administration Control, National Health Insurance Scheme, National Institute of Medical Research, National Institute of Pharmaceutical Research & Development and National Agency for the Control of AIDS (NACA).

59 Health (2004). See Health Status at page 3.

60 UN News Centre, *Literacy Vital for Beating Poverty and Disease and Reinforcing Stability – UN*, available at www.un.org/apps/news/story.asp?NewsID=39485&Cr=literacy&Cr1#.USQB_h1BP-Y.

61 Bill and Melinda Gate, *2015 Gates Annual Letter: Our big Bet For the Future* (2015), available at www.gatesnotes.com/2015-annual-letter?page=0&lang=en&WT.mc_id=01_21_2015_AL2015-GF_GFO_domain_Top_21. Where they discuss about "Finding the secret to the destruction of Malaria" and "Forcing HIV to a tipping point".

62 Health (2004). The seven thrusts were the National Health System and Management, National Health Care Resources, National Health Interventions, National Health Information System, Partnerships for Health Development, Health Research, and National Health Care Laws.

63 Federal Ministry of Health, *National Strategic Health Development Plan (NSHDP 2010–2015)*, available at www.health.gov.ng/doc/NSHDP.pdf.

64 Ibid.

65 See generally, EIFL, '22 Open Access Policies Adopted in 2014' *EIFL* (2014), available at www.eifl.net/news/22-open-access-policies-adopted-2014?utm_source=EIFL all&utm_medium=email&utm_campaign=newsletter72.

66 *National Institute for Medical Research, Research for National Health*, available at www.nimr-ng.org/.

67 National Science and Technology Development Agency Decree (NSTDA) (1977).

68 *National Institute for Medical Research, History*, available at www.nimr-ng.org/NIMR-history.htm.

69 Aminu Yakubu & Clement A. Adebamowo, 'Implementing National System of Health Research Ethics Regulations: The Nigerian Experience' 1 (2012) *BEOnline: Journal of the West African Bioethics Training Program.*

70 *National Institute for Medical Research, Research Priorities*, available at www.nimr-ng.org/NIMR-research-priorities.htm.

71 *National Institute for Medical Research, List of Publications*, available at www.nimr-ng.org/NIMR-publications.htm.

72 NACA, *National Agency for the Control of AIDS*, available at www.naca.gov.ng/history-naca.

73 NACA, *PMTCT Advert NACA Nigeria* (2013), available at http://vimeo.com/66643571. See also, NACA, *HIV Prevalence Advert NACA Nigeria on vimeo* (2013), available at http://vimeo.com/66643577.

74 FMARD, *Federal Ministry of Agriculture and Rural Development*, available at www.fmard.gov.ng/About-us-new.

75 *Agricultural Research Council Act* (2004), available at http://placng.org/lawsofnigeria/node/17 Cap L5.

76 Ibid.

77 A. A. Enete & T. A. Amusa, *Challenges of Agricultural Adaptation to Climate Change in Nigeria: A Synthesis from the Literature The Journal of field Actions: Field Actions Science Reports*, available at http://factsreports.revues.org/678#quotation. See also, Nigeria, About Nigeria, where it was noted that "Nigeria is the most populous country in Africa and the eighth most populous country in the world with a population of over 150 million, therefore making it the most populous 'black' country in the world." See also, Wikipedia, *Demographics of Nigeria*, available at http://en.wikipedia.org/wiki/Nigeria#Demographics, where it noted that "Nigeria, known as 'the Giant of Africa', is the most populous country in Africa and the seventh most populous country in the world."

78 See Section 5(i), Cap L5 (2004).

79 AgriVIVO, *National Agricultural Science Library and Documentation Centre*, available at www.agrivivo.net/organization/national-agricultural-library-and-documentation-centre.

80 FMARD, *Parastatals*, available at www.fmard.gov.ng/parastals.php?0=0&limit=6&pno=8. There are over 15 research institutes in the Nigerian Agricultural sector inclusive of 1. National Cereals Research Institute, Badeggi; 2. National Veterinary Research Institute, Vom; 3. National Root Crops Research Institute, Umudike; 4. National Institute for Oil Palm Research, Benin; 5. Lake Chad Research Institute, Maiduguri; 6. National Institute of Oceanography & Marine Research; 7. Cocoa Research Institute, Ibadan; 8. National Institute for Fresh Water Fisheries Research; 9. Nigeria Stored Product Research Institute, Ilorin; 10. National Horticultural Research Institute, Ibadan; 11. Rubber Research Institute, Benin; 12. National Agricultural Extension and Research Liaison; 13. National Animal Production Research Institute, Zaria; 14. Nigerian Institute of Animal Sciences, Abuja.

81 See, Nigeria, Federal Ministry of Education.

82 See Section 2 of the Compulsory, *Free Universal Basic Education Act* (2004), available at www.placng.org/lawsofnigeria/node/121 UBE. See also, UBEC, Universal Basic Education Commission, available at http://ubeconline.com/about_ubec.html.

83 Nairaland, *Where Is the Official Website to the Ministry of Education? – Education – Nairaland* (2013), available at https://www.nairaland.com/1350161/gbagaun-where-official-website-ministry

84 Wikipedia, *Nigerian Federal Ministry of Education*, available at http://en.wikipedia.org/wiki/Nigerian_Federal_Ministry_of_Education.

85 Facebook, *Federal Ministry of Education, Federal Scholarship Board Nigeria* (2013), available at https://www.facebook.com/FSBNigeria/posts/federal-ministry-of-educationfederal-scholarship-board-abujaplot-245-samuel-adem/216251851847903/

86 NERDC, *Nigerian Educational Research and Development Council (NERDC)*, available at http://nerdc.ng/about-nerdc.

87 Ibid. See "Responsibility of the Council".

88 NERDC, *Library and Informatics Centre*, available at http://nerdc.ng/academic-centres/library-and-informatics-centre.

89 NERDC, *Resource*, available at www.nerdc.gov.ng/i/contents/eresources.html.

90 National Universities Commission Act, Cap N.81, Laws of the Federation of Nigeria (LFN), available at www.placng.org/lawsofnigeria/node/507 Cap N.81 LFN (2004). See Section 4 where it provides for the functions of the Commission.

91 National Universities Commission, *List of Nigerian Universities and Years Founded*, available at www.nuc.edu.ng/pages/universities.asp?ty=1&order=inst_name.

92 Executive Secretary's Office, Academic Standards Department, Management Support Services Department, Research and Innovation Department, Inspection and Monitoring Department, Student Support Services Department, Information and Communication Technology Department, Finance and Accounts Department, Quality Assurance Department, Physical Planning and Development Department, Open and Distance Education Department, Liason Office Department, Department of Protocol and Special Duties.

93 National Universities Commission (NUC), *Department of Research and Innovation*, available at www.nuc.edu.ng/pages/pages.asp?id=25.
94 NUC, *Department of Inspection and Monitoring*, available at www.nuc.edu.ng/pages/pages.asp?id=51.
95 NUC, *Department of Students' Support Services (DSSS)*, available at www.nuc.edu.ng/pages/pages.asp?id=08.
96 NUC, *Department of Information and Communication Technology*, available at www.nuc.edu.ng/pages/pages.asp?id=75.
97 National Universities Commission NUC, *Department of Open and Distance Education*, available at www.nuc.edu.ng/pages/pages.asp?id=182.
98 See Sotunde Oluwabusayo, *World Bank Approves $150m Grant for Education in Africa*, available at www.ventures-africa.com/2014/04/world-bank-grants-150m-for-stem-education-in-africa/?utm_source=Friday%2C+25th+April+2014&utm_campaign=PR%2C+Africa+Business%2C+Africa+Economy%2C+Africa+Entrepreneur%2C+Ventures+Africa&utm_medium=email, where it noted that "The continent also needs its local research and innovative solutions to tackle its peculiar developmental challenges including climate change, political stability, and infectious diseases amongst others."
99 Initiative. See also, Peter Suber, *Open Access Overview: Focusing on Open Access to Peer-Reviewed Research Articles and Their Preprints*, available at www.earlham.edu/~peters/fos/overview.htm (Peter Suber ed.). See also, Stevan Harnad et al., 'The Access/Impact Problem and the Green and Gold Roads to Open Access' 30 (2004) *Serial Review 310–314*. See also, Leslie Chan et al., *Open Access and Development: Journals and Beyond* (Institute of Development Studies (IDS), 2012). See also, Barbara Kirsop et al., 'Access to Scientific Knowledge for Sustainable Development: Options for Developing Countries' *ARIADNE*, available at www.ariadne.ac.uk/issue52/kirsop-et-al. See also, John Willinsky, 'The Stratified Economics of Open Access' 39 (2009) *Economic Analysis & Policy* 53 Charles W. Bailey, *What is Open Access, in Open Access: Key Strategic, Technical and Economic Aspects* (N. Jacobs ed., 2006). See also, Kunle Ola, 'Fundamentals of Open Access' 36 (2) (2014) *European Intellectual Property Review* 112.
100 Samuel Utulu & Omolara Bolarinwa, 'Open Access Initiatives: Adoption by Nigerian Academics' 58 (2009) *Emerald Law Review* See also, E. S. Gbaje, *Open Access Journal Publishing in Ahmadu Bello University, Zaria, Nigeria*, 76th IFLA: World Library and Information Congress, available at http://conference.ifla.org/past-wlic/2010/138-gbaje-en.pdf. See also, O. Ivwighreghweta & O. K. Onoriode, 'Open Access and Scholarly Publishing: Opportunities and Challenges to Nigerian Researchers' 33 (2012) CLIEJ 4 www.iclc.us/cliej/cl33IO.pdf. See also, Okoye, M. O. & Ejikeme, A. N., 'Open Access, Institutional Repositories, and Scholarly Publishing: The Role of Librarians in South Eastern Nigeria' 2 (2011) *Library Philosophy and Practice (e-Journal)* 1–9. See also, G. E. Christian, *Issues and Challenges to the Development of Open Access Institutional Repositories in Academic and Research Institutions in Nigeria* (2008), International Development Research Centre (IDRC), available at https://idl-bnc.idrc.ca/dspace/bitstream/10625/36986/1/127792.pdf.
101 OpenDOAR, *Directory of Open Access Repositories*, available at www.opendoar.org/countrylist.php. See also, ROARMAP, *Registry of Open Access Repositories Mandatory Archiving Policies*, available at http://roarmap.eprints.org/.
102 FMST (2011).
103 Ibid.
104 FMST, *Framework for the Nigerian National System of Innovation*, available at http://fmst.gov.ng/downloadable/NATIONAL%20SYSTEM%20OF%20INNOVATION%20-%20Draft.pdf.
105 Federal Ministry of Information and Communication Technology (MICT), *National ICT Policy* (2012), available at www.nitda.gov.ng/downloads/NEW_ICT_Policy.pdf.

106 *National Information Technology Development Agency Act* (2007), available at www.placng.org/lawsofnigeria/node/342.
107 UNCTAD, 'Ministerial Round Table on "Science, Technology and Innovation for the Post-2015 Development Agenda"' E/2014/31-E/CN.16/2014/4, *UNCTAD* (2014), available at http://unctad.org/meetings/en/Presentation/CSTD_2014_STMT_Nigeria_Minister.pdf.
108 FMST (2011).
109 Ibid.
110 Commission (2009).
111 See Proviso 2.2 National STI Policy Mission, FMST (2011).
112 See Provisos 2.3 and 2.4 on General Policy Objective and Specific Policy Objectives, ibid.
113 Ibid. See Proviso 3.3 on Research and Development.
114 Ibid. See Proviso 3.4 on Intellectual Property Rights.
115 Ibid. See Proviso 3.7 on STI Information Management System.
116 Ibid. See 3.7.3 on Strategies.
117 Alliance For Affordable Internet (A4AI), *Alliance For Affordable Internet's 2014 Affordability Report* (2014), available at http://a4ai.org/affordability-report/report/. See also, FMCT, *Nigeria's Internet Ranks 2nd Among Emerging Economies* (2014), available at http://commtech.gov.ng/index.php/videos/daily-press-release/298-nig-internet-ranked-2nd.
118 United Nations, *Nigeria Makes Mild Stride in eGovernment Development Ranking* (2014), available at www.unpan.org/PublicAdministrationNews/tabid/651/mctl/ArticleView/ModuleID/1555/articleId/42587/Default.aspx.
119 FMCT, *Nigeria improves in United Nations eGovernment Development Ranking* (2014), available at http://commtech.gov.ng/index.php/videos/news-event/176-nig-improves-un-egov-dev.
120 NBS, *National Bureau of Statistics* (2015), available at www.nigerianstat.gov.ng/.
121 NBS, *Nigeria Statistical Data Portal* (2015), available at http://nigeria.prognoz.com/.
122 NBS, *Nigeria National Data Archive (NADA) Centre* (2015), available at www.nigerianstat.gov.ng/nada/index.php/home.

Bibliography

Adewopo, Adebambo, *Nigerian Copyright System: Principles and Perspectives* (Odade Publishers, Lagos 2012).

Agricultural Research Council Act, available at http://placng.org/lawsofnigeria/node/17 Cap L5 (2004).

AgriVIVO, *National Agricultural Science Library and Documentation Centre*, available at www.agrivivo.net/organization/national-agricultural-library-and-documentation-centre.

Alliance for Affordable Internet (A4AI), *Alliance for Affordable Internet's 2014 Affordability Report* (2014), available at http://a4ai.org/affordability-report/report/.

Asein, John, *Nigerian Copyright Law and Practice* (Books and Gavel Limited, 2nd ed., Abuja 2012).

Kunle Ola, Assessing the Participation of Domestic SMEs in the International Production Chain: The Case of Nu Metro in Nigeria in Integrating Developing Countries SMEs into Global Value Chains (UNCTAD, 2010), available at http://unctad.org/en/Docs/diaeed20095_en.pdf

Bailey, Charles W., 'What Is Open Access' in N. Jacobs ed., *Open Access: Key Strategic, Technical and Economic Aspects* (Chandos Publishing, 2006).

Bill and Melinda Gate, *2015 Gates Annual Letter: Our big Bet for the Future* (2015), available at www.gatesnotes.com/2015-annual-letter?page=0&lang=en&WT.mc_id=01_21_2015_AL2015-GF_GFO_domain_Top_21.

Budapest Open Access Initiative, *Ten Years on from the Budapest Open Access Initiative: Setting the Default to Open*, available at www.opensocietyfoundations.org/openaccess/boai-10-recommendations.

Butler, Chris, *FC74: The Invention of the Printing Press and Its Effects*, available at www.flowofhistory.com/units/west/11/FC74.

Chan, Leslie, et al., 'Open Access and Development: Journals and Beyond' (Institute of Development Studies (IDS), 2012), available at https://www.ids.ac.uk/files/dmfile/openaccessanddevelopmentjournalsandbeyond_nov2012_gray_et_al.pdf

Christian, G. E., *Issues and Challenges to the Development of Open Access Institutional Repositories in Academic and Research Institutions in Nigeria* (2008), International Development Research Centre (IDRC), available at https://idl-bnc.idrc.ca/dspace/bitstream/10625/36986/1/127792.pdf.

Compulsory, Free Universal Basic Education Act (2004), available at www.placng.org/lawsofnigeria/node/121 UBE.

Davis, Jennifer, *Intellectual Property Law* (Oxford University Press, 3rd ed., 2008).

EIFL, 22 Open Access Policies Adopted in 2014, *EIFL* (2014), available at www.eifl.net/news/22-open-access-policies-adopted-2014?utm_source=EIFLall&utm_medium=email&utm_campaign=newsletter72.

Enete, A. A. & T. A. Amusa, 'Challenges of Agricultural Adaptation to Climate Change in Nigeria: a Synthesis from the Literature' *The Journal of field actions: Field Actions Science Reports* [Online], available at http://factsreports.revues.org/678#quotation.

Facebook, *Federal Ministry of Education, Federal Scholarship Board Nigeria* (2013), available at https://www.facebook.com/FSBNigeria/posts/federal-ministry-of-education federal-scholarship-board-abujaplot-245-samuel-adem/216251851847903/

Federal Ministry of Agriculture and Rural Development, *About Us*, available at www.fmard.gov.ng/About-us-new.

Federal Ministry of Health, *Agencies Under FMOH*, available at www.health.gov.ng/index.php/about-us.

Federal Ministry of Health, *Home*, available at www.health.gov.ng/?view=featured.

Federal Ministry of Health, *Mission and Vision*, available at www.health.gov.ng/index.php/about-us/mission-and-vission.

Federal Ministry of Health, *National Strategic Health Development Plan (NSHDP 2010–2015)*, available at www.health.gov.ng/doc/NSHDP.pdf.

Federal Ministry of Health, *Parastatals*, available at www.health.gov.ng/index.php/parastatals.

Federal Ministry of Health, *Revised National Health Policy* (2004), available at http://osgf.dammy.net/payload?id=19d51d38-c75f-4461-91ce-f6a6d2298b87.

Federal Ministry of Information, *About Us*, available at http://fmi.gov.ng/.

Federal Ministry of Information and Communication Technology MICT, *National ICT Policy* (2012), available at www.nitda.gov.ng/downloads/NEW_ICT_Policy.pdf.

Federal Ministry of Science and Technology FMST, *Framework for the Nigerian National System of Innovation*, available at http://fmst.gov.ng/downloadable/NATIONAL%20SYSTEM%20OF%20INNOVATION%20-%20Draft.pdf.

Federal Ministry of Science and Technology FMST, *Harnessing Technology for Nigeria's Social and Economic Development*, available at http://fmst.gov.ng/.

Federal Republic of Nigeria, *About Nigeria*, available at www.nigeria.gov.ng/2012-10-29-11-05-46.

Federal Republic of Nigeria, *Federal Ministry of Education*, available at www.nigeria.gov.ng/2012-10-29-11-06-51/executive-branch/93-federal-ministry-of-education/116-federal-ministry-of-education.

Federal Republic of Nigeria FMST, *Science, Technology and Innovation (STI) Policy* (2011), Federal Ministry of Science and Technology ed., Federal Government of Nigeria, available at http://workspace.unpan.org/sites/internet/Documents/UNPAN048879.pdf.

Fitzgerald, Brian, *A Short Overview of Creative Commons* (Sydney University Press, 2007).

FMARD, *Federal Ministry of Agriculture and Rural Development*, available at www.fmard.gov.ng/About-us-new.

FMARD, *Parastatals*, available at www.fmard.gov.ng/parastals.php?0=0&limit=6&pno=8.

FMCT, *Nigeria improves in United Nations eGovernment Development Ranking* (2014), available at http://commtech.gov.ng/index.php/videos/news-event/176-nig-improves-un-egov-dev.

FMCT, *Nigeria's Internet Ranks 2nd Among Emerging Economies* (2014), available at http://commtech.gov.ng/index.php/videos/daily-press-release/298-nig-internet-ranked-2nd.

Gbaje, E. S., *Open Access Journal Publishing in Ahmadu Bello University, Zaria, Nigeria*, 76th IFLA: World Library and Information Congress, available at http://conference.ifla.org/past-wlic/2010/138-gbaje-en.pdf.

Gervais, D. J., *Collective Management of Copyright and Related Rights* (Kluwer Law International, 2010).

Harnad, Stevan, et al., 'The Access/Impact Problem and the Green and Gold Roads to Open Access' 30 (2004) *Serial Review, 310–314*

Ivwighreghweta, O. & O. K. Onoriode, 'Open Access and Scholarly Publishing: Opportunities and Challenges to Nigerian Researchers' 33 (2012) *Chinese Librarianship: An International Electronic Journal*. 1–13.

Kirsop, Barbara, et al., Access to Scientific Knowledge for Sustainable Development: Options for Developing Countries, *ARIADNE*, available at www.ariadne.ac.uk/issue52/kirsop-et-al.

NACA, *HIV Prevalence Advert NACA Nigeria on Vimeo* (2013), available at http://vimeo.com/66643577.

NACA, *National Agency for the Control of AIDS*, available at www.naca.gov.ng/history-naca.

NACA, *PMTCT Advert NACA Nigeria* (2013), available at http://vimeo.com/66643571.

Nairaland, *Where Is the Official Website to the Ministry of Education? – Education – Nairaland* (2013), available at https://www.nairaland.com/1350161/gbagaun-where-official-website-ministry.

National Information Technology Development Agency Act (2007), available at www.placng.org/lawsofnigeria/node/342.

National Institute for Medical Research, *History*, available at www.nimr-ng.org/NIMR-history.htm.

National Institute for Medical Research, *List of Publications*, available at www.nimr-ng.org/NIMR-publications.htm.

National Institute for Medical Research, *Research for National Health*, available at www.nimr-ng.org/.

National Institute for Medical Research, *Research Priorities*, available at www.nimr-ng.org/NIMR-research-priorities.htm.

National Planning Commission, *Nigeria Vision 20:2020* (NPC ed., 2009).

National Science and Technology Development Agency Decree NSTDA (1977).

National Universities Commission NUC Act, Cap N.81, Laws of the Federation of Nigeria (LFN) available at www.placng.org/lawsofnigeria/node/507 Cap N.81 Laws of the Federation of Nigeria (LFN) (2004).

National Universities Commission NUC, *Department of Information and Communication Technology*, available at www.nuc.edu.ng/pages/pages.asp?id=75.
National Universities Commission NUC, *Department of Inspection and Monitoring*, available at www.nuc.edu.ng/pages/pages.asp?id=51.
National Universities Commission NUC, *Department of Open and Distance Education*, available at www.nuc.edu.ng/pages/pages.asp?id=182.
National Universities Commission NUC, *Department of Research and Innovation*, available at www.nuc.edu.ng/pages/pages.asp?id=25.
National Universities Commission NUC, *Department of Students' Support Services (DSSS)*, available at www.nuc.edu.ng/pages/pages.asp?id=08.
National Universities Commission NUC, *List of Nigerian Universities and Years Founded*, available at www.nuc.edu.ng/pages/universities.asp?ty=1&order=inst_name.
NBS, *National Bureau of Statistics* (2015), available at www.nigerianstat.gov.ng/.
NBS, *Nigeria National Data Archive (NADA) Centre* (2015), available at www.nigerianstat.gov.ng/nada/index.php/home.
NBS, *Nigeria Statistical Data Portal* (2015), available at http://nigeria.prognoz.com/.
NCC 2012 Annual Report (2012).
NERDC, *Library and Informatics Centre*, available at http://nerdc.ng/academic-centres/library-and-informatics-centre.
NERDC, *Nigerian Educational Research and Development Council (NERDC)*, available at http://nerdc.ng/about-nerdc.
NERDC, *Resource*, available at www.nerdc.gov.ng/i/contents/cresources.html.
Newton, Isaac, *From a Letter Written by Isaac Newton to Robert Hooke*, 5 February (1676).
Nigerian Copyright Act NCC, Cap C28 (2004).
Nigerian Copyright Act NCC, Cap C28, Laws of the Federation of Nigeria, 2004 Cap C28 (2004).
Nigerian Copyright Commission NCC, *Copyright (Collective Management Organisation) Regulation 2007* (2007), available at www.copyright.gov.ng/images/downloads/CMO%20Regulation%202007.pdf.
Nigerian Copyright Commission NCC, *Copyright (Levy on Materials) Order 2012* (2012), available at www.copyright.gov.ng/images/downloads/REVISED%20DRAFT%20LEVY%20ON%20COPYRIGHT%20MATERIALS%20ORDER.pdf.
Nigerian Copyright Commission NCC, *Copyright Notification Scheme* (2005), available at www.copyright.gov.ng/index.php/regulatory-schemes/copyright-notification.
Nigerian Copyright Commission NCC, *Copyright (Optical Discs Plants) Regulation 2006*. B 697–711 (2006), available at www.copyright.gov.ng/images/downloads/Optical%20Disc%20Regulation.pdf.
Nigerian Copyright Commission NCC, *Copyright (Reciprocal Extension) Regulation 1972* (1972), available at www.copyright.gov.ng/images/downloads/Copyright%20Reciprocal%20Extension%20Order%201972.pdf.
Nigerian Copyright Commission NCC, *Copyright (Security Devices) Regulation 1999* (1999), available at www.copyright.gov.ng/images/downloads/Copyright%20Security%20devices%20regulation%201999.pdf.
Nigerian Copyright Commission NCC, *Copyright (Video Rental) Regulation 1999* (1999), available at www.copyright.gov.ng/images/downloads/Copyright%20Video%20rental%20regulation%201999.pdf.
Nigerian Copyright Commission NCC, *Nigerian Copyright Institute*, available at www.copyright.gov.ng/index.php/2013-02-10-16-11-10/nigerain-copyright-institute-nci.
Nigerian Copyright Commission NCC, 'STRAP and CLAMP – Nigeria Copyright Commission in Action' (2008) *WIPO Magazine*, September.

Okoroji, Tony, *Copyright Neighbouring Rights & the New Millionaires (The Twists and Turns in Nigeria)* (Tops Limited, 2008).

Okoye, M. O. & Ejikeme, A. N., 'Open Access, Institutional Repositories, and Scholarly Publishing: The Role of Librarians in South Eastern Nigeria' 2 (2011) *Library Philosophy and Practice (e-Journal)* 1–9.

Ola, Kunle, *Copyright Collective Administration in Nigeria Lessons for Africa* (Springer, 2013).

Ola, Kunle, 'Fundamentals of Open Access' 36 (2) (2014) *European Intellectual Property Review* 112.

Ola, Kunle, 'Scholarly Publication in Nigeria: Implications of Open Access' 6 (2015) *The WIPO Journal* 117.

OpenDOAR, *Directory of Open Access Repositories*, available at www.opendoar.org/countrylist.php.

ROARMAP, *Registry of Open Access Repositories Mandatory Archiving Policies*, available at http://roarmap.eprints.org/.

Sotunde, Oluwabusayo, *World Bank Approves $150m Grant for Education in Africa*, available at www.ventures-africa.com/2014/04/world-bank-grants-150m-for-stem-education-in-africa/?utm_source=Friday%2C+25th+April+2014&utm_campaign=PR%2C+Africa+Business%2C+Africa+Economy%2C+Africa+Entrepreneur%2C+Ventures+Africa&utm_medium=email.

Stallman, Richard, *The GNU Project*, available at www.gnu.org/gnu/thegnuproject.html.

Statute of Anne, 8 Anne c. 19 (1710).

Strauss, Valerie, 'Nelson Mandela's Famous Quote on Education' (2013) *The Washington Post*.

Suber, Peter, *Open Access* (MIT Press, Cambridge MA 2012).

Suber, Peter, *Open Access Overview: Focusing on Open Access to Peer-Reviewed Research Articles and Their Preprints*, available at www.earlham.edu/~peters/fos/overview.htm (Peter Suber ed.).

UBEC, *Universal Basic Education Commission*, available at http://ubeconline.com/about_ubec.html.

UNCTAD, Ministerial Round Table on "Science, Technology and Innovation for the Post-2015 Development Agenda" E/2014/31-E/CN.16/2014/4, *UNCTAD* (2014), available at http://unctad.org/meetings/en/Presentation/CSTD_2014_STMT_Nigeria_Minister.pdf.

UNESCO, *Nigerian President Pledges US$5 Billion Towards National Science Foundation*, available at www.unesco.org/new/en/natural-sciences/science-technology/sti-policy/country-studies/nigeria/nigerian-president-pledges-us5-billion-towards-national-science-foundation/.

United Nations UN, *Nigeria Makes Mild Stride in eGovernment Development Ranking* (2014), available at www.unpan.org/PublicAdministrationNews/tabid/651/mctl/ArticleView/ModuleID/1555/articleId/42587/Default.aspx.

UN News Centre, *Literacy Vital for Beating Poverty and Disease and Reinforcing Stability – UN*, available at www.un.org/apps/news/story.asp?NewsID=39485&Cr=literacy&Cr1#.USQB_h1BP-Y.

Utulu, Samuel & Omolara Bolarinwa, 'Open Access Initiatives: Adoption by Nigerian Academics' 58 (2009) *Emerald Law Review*.

Wikipedia, *Demographics of Nigeria*, available at http://en.wikipedia.org/wiki/Nigeria#Demographics.

Wikipedia, *Nigerian Federal Ministry of Education*, available at http://en.wikipedia.org/wiki/Nigerian_Federal_Ministry_of_Education.

Wild, Leni, *Information Alone Is Not Enough: It's All About Who Uses It, and Why* (2014), World Bank, available at http://blogs.worldbank.org/publicsphere/information-alone-not-enough-it-s-all-about-who-uses-it-and-why.

Willinsky, John, 'The Stratified Economics of Open Access' 39 (2009) *Economic Analysis & Policy* 53.

WIPO, *WIPO Administered Treaties*, available at www.wipo.int/treaties/en/.

The World Bank, World Bank Announces Open Access Policy for Research and Knowledge, Launches Open Knowledge Repository, Press Release No. 2012/379/EXTOP (2012).

Yakubu, Aminu & Clement A. Adebamowo, 'Implementing National System of Health Research Ethics Regulations: The Nigerian Experience' 1 (2012) *BEOnline: Journal of the West African Bioethics Training Program*.

4 Open access journal articles

1 Introduction

The open movement has made considerable progress since the Budapest meeting. The number of open access repositories, open access journals and open access mandates/policies has increased greatly. Many publishers that were sceptical about the viability of open access have now developed or bought over open access journals and are supporting the open access movement. A high percentage of scholarly publications are now open access, and a number of institutions recognize open access journals for purposes of academic assessment and promotions. There is virtually no country in the world without an open access presence. In some countries the presence may be low, but it exists.

2 Adoption of open access policies: national, international and funding organizations

2.1 United States

The United States was one of the early adopters of open access. The National Institutes of Health (NIH) is the world's largest research institute with 27 institutes and centres. The volume of research data and publication it generates annually is staggering.[1] On 26 February 2003, the NIH Statement on Sharing Research Data was issued. It noted that data sharing is essential for expedited translation of research results into knowledge, products and procedures to improve human health. It became effective on 1 October 2003.[2] Although this document encourages sharing of information, it was not focused on peer-reviewed documents.

In 2008, the NIH Public Access Policy was issued pursuant to the Consolidated Appropriations Act, 2008, making the United States the first national government to adopt a national open access mandate. Brazil was the first country however to put forward a bill in this regard, but the bill is yet to be passed. The NIH Public Access Policy states that the

> Director of the National Institutes of Health shall require that all investigators funded by the NIH submit or have submitted for them to the National

> Library of Medicine's PubMed Central an electronic version of their final peer-reviewed manuscripts upon acceptance for publication, to be made publicly available no later than 12 months after the official date of publication: Provided, that the NIH shall implement the public access policy in a manner consistent with copyright law.

NIH archives its papers in the PubMed Central, an archive of full text biomedical journal papers freely available online.[3] The archive is linked to other databases such as GenBank[4] and PubChem.[5] The materials in this archive help millions of people.

2.2 United Kingdom

The United Kingdom has been very strategic in the development of open access. The United Kingdom has empanelled a number of national inquiry on open access and has taken active steps to enable access to the output of scientific publications in the United Kingdom.

In 2004, the House of Commons published a report titled *Scientific Publications: Free for All?* The report was a reaction to the high pricing policies by publishers and the dwindling funds available to libraries. The report recommended that the UK government should take steps that would enable access to scientific publications, that Higher Education Institutions (HEIs) develop institutional repositories and that the government should develop a network that links these institutional repositories.[6] In response to the report, the Research Council United Kingdom in 2005 noted that "e-print repositories and open access journals can help improve access to the results of publicly funded research."[7] In 2006 six of the UK Research Councils namely, Arts and Humanities Research Council (AHRC), Biotechnology and Biological Sciences Research Council (BBSRC), Medical Research Council (MRC), Economic and Social Research Council (ESRC), Natural Environment Research Council (NERC) and Science and Technology Facilities Council (STFC) issued open access mandates for the first time, requiring peer-reviewed publications to be deposited in open access repositories.[8]

In 2011, a working group led by Dame Janet Finch was set up as a result of a round table discussion on transparency organized by the Department for Business, Innovation and Skills with representatives of the scholarly publishing industry.[9] In 2012, the working group submitted and published a report titled 'Accessibility, Sustainability, Excellence: How to Expand Access to Research Publication'.[10] The report favoured the Gold route to open access and recommended that "a clear policy direction be set towards support for publication in open access or hybrid journals funded by APCs as the main vehicle for the publication of research, especially when it is publicly funded". In July 2012, the UK government formally accepted and supported the recommendations in the Finch Report.[11] This prompted Research Councils United Kingdom (RCUK) to announce a new open access policy to the effect that research funded by RCUK must be published in open access or hybrid journals.[12]

In 2013, Science and Technology Select Committee of the House of Lords published a report titled *Implementation of Open Access*. The report was in response to the Finch Report and RCUK open access policy. The report recommended that RCUK provide clarification on certain areas of the policy, namely, incremental approach to compliance, embargo periods and also recommended that international best practices be observed to ascertain the preferred policy routes.[13] RCUK revised its open access policy in March of 2013 to clarify the issues raised by the House of Lords on the incremental approach to compliance during the five-year transition plan and on embargo periods.[14]

In September of 2013, the House of Commons published an Open Access report, criticizing the Finch Report and the RCUK open access policy. The report criticized the newly adopted open access policies, the choice of Gold over Green, the embargo periods, the CC-BY Licensing, APC costs and the capacity for UK educational institutions to remain globally competitive under the new publishing model. It recommended that since most HEIs already had Green open access in place and government had invested extensively in this area to develop repositories, authors should be allowed the freedom to choose between Green and Gold open access. It further recommended that HEFCE develop a policy mandating immediate deposit and that this be made a requirement for eligibility.[15] Government responded to these issues noting that market forces will play a major role in deciding the prime route. However, government noted its preference for the Gold route.[16]

In November 2013, the Review of Progress in Recommendations of the Finch Report was published. It was noted that most HEIs favoured Green above Gold. The choice of Green above Gold appears obvious when thought is given to the cost associated with APC. It has been noted that not all Gold requires APC, but if Green can be made available immediately without the issues of cost, and open access is about the removal of barriers, it only makes sense to pursue the route that achieves the goal easily and fastest. The report also emphasized the need to improve interoperability and recommended support for a mixed economy where both Gold and Green co-exist but with preference given to Gold open access.[17] This preference appears to be the position of the UK government as evidenced by the statement of Minister David Willetts, who noted that the preference is for Gold, but Green is also accepted.[18]

2.3 Brazil

The Scientific Electronic Library Online (SciELO) is a Brazilian open access initiative. It is one of the open initiatives providing visibility and accessibility to the output of research conducted in and by members of developing countries. It is an integral part of a project being developed by PAPESP-Fundacao de Amparo a Pesquisa do Estado de Sao Paulo, in partnership with BIREME, The Latin American and Caribbean Centre on Health Sciences Information. SciELO is both an electronic publisher and a repository. South Africa is currently the only African member country. It holds over 400,000 articles in 1,057 journals.[19] Brazil introduced a bill (PL 1120/2007) with a view to requiring all public institutions of higher education and research units to establish institutional repositories. The bill has not been passed, but it is a right step in the right direction. Brazil has been highly rated on the open access tipping point.[20] The positive disposition of Brazil to open access and the impact SciELO has made on Latin American and Caribbean countries can be useful in guiding Nigeria's development of a framework for open access to knowledge.[21]

2.4 Canada

In 2008, the National Research Council (NRC) Canada under its NRC Publication Archive Statement of Responsibility has made it mandatory starting January 2009, for all NRC institutes to deposit copies of all peer-reviewed publications in the NRC Publication Archive. The "NRC publication archive is a web-based repository that improves accessibility to, and increases the citation impact of, NRC publications, as well as facilitates multi-disciplinary and horizontal collaboration amongst NRC researchers."[22]

In February 2015, CIHR, NSERC and SSHRC in what has been described as a Tri-Agency Open Access Policy unveiled a harmonized open access policy.[23] This policy requires researchers who have been awarded funding from 1 January 2008, and onward to freely make available all research papers through the publisher's website or an online repository within 12 months of publication; to deposit data into the appropriate public database immediately upon publication of research results; to retain original datasets for a minimum of five years (or longer if other policies apply).[24]

2.5 European Union

The European Union (EU) is actively involved in advocating, encouraging and implementing open access. It notes that "open access provides researchers, businesses and citizens with improved and free of charge online access to EU-funded research results, including scientific publications and research data."[25] The EU implements its open access objectives through FP7[26] and Horizon 2020[27] and at the member state levels. The EU adopts both Green open access and Gold open access. It encourages member states to develop national initiatives and contributes to strategic co-ordination where the need arises.

In July of 2012, the EU adopted a scientific information communication package through which it seeks to move "towards better access to scientific information: Boosting the benefits of public investments in research."[28] The Commission's position on open access was made explicit in the recommendation on access to and preservation of scientific information. The recommendation (*Brussels, 17.7.2012 C[2012] 4890 final*) on access to and preservation of scientific information noted that

> publicly funded research should be widely disseminated through open access publication of scientific data and papers. The 'Innovation Union' initiative

calls for a European Research Area (ERA) framework to be set up to help remove obstacles to mobility and cross-border cooperation. It states that open access to publications and data from publicly funded research should be promoted and access to publications made the general principle for projects funded by the EU research Framework Programmes.

2.6 United Nations

The United Nations (UN) through several of its agencies have demonstrated commitment to open access. The United Nations Educational, Scientific and Cultural Organization (UNESCO) and the World Bank have been at the vanguard and have developed initiatives that maximize the utility of the output of funded research. UNESCO for example developed the Global Open Access Portal which provides information about the state of open access globally. "The Global Open Access Portal is designed to provide the necessary information for policy-makers to learn about the global open access environment and to view their countries status and understand where and why Open Access has been most successful."[29]

The World Bank in support of the open access movement has licensed most of its knowledge products under a CC–BY licence, thereby permitting use and reuse of such works.[30] In the same vein, the Bank now hosts the World Bank Knowledge Repository, which provides access to most of the research outputs of the World Bank.[31]

2.7 Organisation for Economic Co-operation and Development

In 2004, the Minister for Science and Technology cognizant of the fact that access to research data increases the returns on public investment, reinforces open scientific inquiry, encourages diversity of studies and opinion, and promotes new areas of work and enables the exploration of topics not envisioned by the initial investigators called on the Organisation for Economic Co-operation Development (OECD) to develop a set of guidelines based on commonly agreed principles to facilitate cost-effective access to digital research data from public funding.[32] In 2007, the *Principles and Guidelines for Access to Research Data from Public Funding* was published to assist in the sharing of, and access to research data.[33]

Although Brazil is not a developed country, the culture of sharing academic publications is one they had developed prior to the open access movement. Due to this culture, they have been able to strengthen the visibility of their journals. The analyses of open access in the four countries mentioned above shows that open access enables accessibility, visibility, and impact and maximizes the utility of peer-reviewed scholarly literatures. The role of policies and initiatives in the open access movement has been important. The choice of whether Gold, Green or a fine blend of both has raised arguments but the growth in the adoption and acceptance of open access globally is an indication that open access is the new model for publishing.

2.8 Funding organizations – governmental and non-governmental

Outside international and national governments, some of the most impacting stakeholders in the open access movement have been funding agencies. They include governmental and non-governmental funding agencies. The governmental funding agencies include NIH, ERC, ARC, RCUK and NRC, while the non-governmental funding agencies include Wellcome Trust, Ford Foundation, Bill & Melinda Gates Foundation, and William and Flora Hewlett Foundation. One important role these funding agencies have played outside that of mandating or requiring self-archiving or depositing in a repository is that of standing beside authors in the newly evolving publication mechanism. Most authors do not have the equivalent ability to compete with publishers when it comes to negotiation, but the involvement of funding agencies that are now either mandating or requiring archival deposits have made it imperative for publishers to come to the negotiating table and review not just the terms, but the entire publication circle and mechanism. In simple terms, publishers have met their match and have had to bend their knees. This section will discuss the role of funding agencies in the open access movement.

2.9 National Institutes of Health

National Institutes of Health (NIH) funds more than 300,000 research personnel who all generate data and are mandated to publish the output of their research with PubMed Central. PubMed Central is a free full-text archive of biomedical and life sciences journal literatures at the NIH. It currently holds over 3.5 million articles.[34] The goal of the institute is to strengthen the nation's research capacity, broaden the research base and inspire a passion for science in current and future generations of researchers. NIH seeks to expand the knowledge base in medical and associated sciences to enhance the Nation's economic well-being and ensure a continued return on the public investment in research. In realizing these goals, NIH embraces the open access movement by collating and sharing information and by supporting the development of medical libraries.[35]It is in response to the open access movement and in furtherance of the goal to collate and share information for the development of research that the NIH Public Access Policy has been issued.

The NIH 2008 Public Access Policy provides a strong policy framework by going further than requiring deposits to mandating deposits. However, the policy imposes two new compliance mandates. The first is related to the submission of manuscripts "final, peer-reviewed manuscript upon acceptance", and the second refers to copyright compliance. The policy "provided, that the NIH shall implement the public access policy in a manner consistent with copyright law".

Complying with copyright law requires that the author still holds the requisite rights when depositing the final manuscript with PubMed Central (PMC). Six different compliance options have been suggested for grantees and principal investigators working in collaboration with authors. They are

Option 1. Rely on individual authors to satisfy grantee's obligation under the award.
Option 2. Assist authors with copyright management
Option 3. The grantee license
Option 4. The grantee license – plus
Option 5. Negotiate directly with publishers.
Option 6. Pre-clear journals.[36]

2.10 European Research Council

The central focus of the European Research Council (ERC) is to encourage high-quality research in Europe through competitive funding. The ERC which was established in 2007 under the EU's Seventh Framework Programme for Research (FP7) seeks to promote bottom-up curiosity driven frontier research and boosting the careers of excellent researchers from anywhere in the world. The ERC supports open access as a fundamental part of its mission. It considers that open access provides the most effective way of ensuring that the output of ERC funded research can be accessed, read and used as the basis for further research.[37]

The idea for establishing the Council arose from widespread discussions between European scientists, scholars and research umbrella organizations at a time when there was no clear roadmap and central platform to support research around the European region.[38]

ERC provides funding for research. In 2014, it had a total annual budget of 1.7 billion Euros. Since 2007 when it was established, some 4,500 projects have been selected for funding from more than 43,000 applications. Over 20,000 articles have acknowledged ERC funding in their peer-reviewed high impact journals between 2008 and 2013. Under the new funding program Horizon 2020, it is estimated that around 7,000 grantees will be funded, and 42,000 team members supported.[39]

2.11 Research Council United Kingdom

RCUK are saddled with the responsibility of funding research in the UK for purposes of advancing knowledge and generating new ideas. The seven UK Research Councils are funded from government's science budget under the Department for Business, Innovation and Skills.[40] RCUK seeks to enhance the performance and impact of UK research, training and knowledge transfer. The RCUK's overall aim is "for the Research Councils to be recognized as the benchmark around the world in terms of the impact they have and the ways they work."[41]

RCUK recognizes that there are many benefits associated with publicly funded research and in line with the government's commitment to transparency and open data, RCUK is fully committed to ensuring that the output of public funded research is made freely available "not just to other researchers, but also to potential users in business, charitable and public sectors and to the general public"[42]

RCUK's commitment to open access is supported by the RCUK Policy on Open Access and the 2014 Independent Review of the implementation of the RCUK Policy on Open Access. Both documents provide the policy framework for RCUK's commitment to open access.[43] Open access under the RCUK policy framework applies only to peer-reviewed research articles, but this includes review articles not commissioned by publishers, and conference proceedings that acknowledge RCUK's funding but does not include books, monographs, critical editions, volumes and catalogues, or forms of non-peer reviewed material. The Council however encourages that authors of such works may wish to consider making these works open access (freely available).

RCUK supports both Gold and Green open access but prefers the Gold route to open access.

2.12 Australian Research Council

The Australian Research Council (ARC) was established in 2001 and seeks to advance Australian research and innovation globally and benefit the community. It provides funding for research through its National Competitive Grants Program and its Excellence in Research for Australia (ERA), and it is the primary source of advice to the Government on research investment issues.[44] ARC recognizes that the outcome of ARC-funded research delivers cultural, economic, social and environmental benefits to all Australians and "is committed to ensuring the widest possible dissemination of the research supported by ARC funding, in the most effective manner and at the earliest opportunity, taking into account any restrictions relation to intellectual property or culturally sensitive data".[45] In furtherance of this recognition and commitment, ARC has issued the ARC Open Access Policy, which took effect on 1 January 2013 and is to the effect that "Any publications arising from an ARC supported research Project must be deposited into an open access institutional repository within a twelve (12) month period from the date of publication."[46]

The issuance of this policy provides an institutional platform for strengthening open access. The policy is not optional but mandatory, therefore the output of any research (full-text copy of the publication) funded by ARC will enjoy the advantage of global accessibility and visibility and also the opportunity for maximal impact as such works must be deposited in an institutional repository.

2.13 Wellcome Trust

The Wellcome Trust is the brain child of Sir Henry Wellcome. It is a non-governmental charitable organization that champions science, funds research and influences health policies globally.[47]The Trust aims at improving health by supporting bright minds in learning, discovery, creativity and innovation through science, the humanities, social sciences and public engagement and provides more than £700 million annually to support the organization's vision.[48]It supports this vision through the instrumentality of a 10-year strategic plan (2010–2010) which is reviewed bi-annually.[49]

A fundamental part of the Trust's mission is to ensure that the output of funded research is given the opportunity of maximal availability, accessibility, utility and impact. The Trust supports this mission by an open access policy, which extends to all research articles, scholarly monographs and book chapters.[50] The Wellcome Trust's open access policy is predicated on the belief that "maximising the distribution of these publications by providing free, online access- is the most effective way of ensuring that the research we fund can be accessed, read and built upon. In turn, this will foster a richer research culture."[51] The policy specifically requires that electronic copies of any research papers that are accepted for publication in a peer-reviewed journal and are supported in whole or in part by trust funds to be made available through Pub Med Central or through Europe PMC as soon as possible, but within six months of the journal publisher's official date of final publication. The policy expects fund recipients to choose publishing options that provide immediate availability of publications. The policy encourages the use of the Creative Commons Attribution licence (CC-BY), and where it pays for open access fee, it is a requirement on authors and publisher. This will enable the work to be freely copied and reused.

2.14 Gates Foundation

Bill & Melinda Gates Foundation is a philanthropic organization set up to support education, world health and population. It is dedicated to bridging the digital divide by providing ICT access to less-advantaged communities. The Foundation is of the view that progress can be accelerated, and big impacts made around the world through research, creativity and innovation in technology.

The Foundation is committed to open access and supports immediate unrestricted online access to the output of research funded by their organization. However, a transition period of up to two years has been provided expiring on the 1st of January 2017. During the transitory period, publications in journals that provide up to a 12-month embargo period will be allowed. After this transition period however, all publications shall be available immediately without any embargo period. Publications are expected to be deposited in a specified repository with proper metadata tagging. All publications must be licensed under the Creative Commons Attribution 4.0 Generic Licence (CC BY 4.0) or an equivalent licence. The open access policy adopted by the organization "enables the unrestricted access and reuse of all peer-reviewed published research funded, in whole or in part, by the foundation, including any underlying data sets."[52]

2.15 Ford Foundation

The Ford Foundation is a not-for-profit organization founded by Edsel and Henry Ford in 1936 with the mission of advancing human welfare, strengthening democratic values, reducing poverty and injustice, promoting international cooperation and advancing human achievement.[53] The foundation supports visionary leaders and organizations on the frontlines of social change. This is done mainly by "making grants or loans that build knowledge and strengthen organizations and networks. Since our financial resources are modest compared with societal needs, we focus on key problem areas and program strategies".[54]

The Foundation has always been committed to transparency, and it supports the dissemination of the output of research funded in whole or in part by the foundation. In line with the foundations policy on openness, it has adopted an open licensing policy which requires all grant-funded projects and research to be made available subject to a Creative Commons licence allowing for immediate online access and the requisite use and reuse of rights provided appropriate credit is given to the original author.[55]

2.16 William and Flora Hewlett Foundation

The William and Flora Hewlett Foundation is popularly known for its support of the open movement, in particular, open educational resources (OER). Since 2001, the foundation has been at the forefront of providing funding for OER.[56] The foundation helps people build measurably better lives through their Education, Environmental, Global Development and Population, Performing Arts Programs and the Effective Philanthropy Group. The foundation provides grants in line with the above programs but also reserves funding to support special projects which may not align directly with the above-mentioned strategic areas.[57]

The Foundation is committed to openness and transparency and supports open licensing which provides a platform for unrestricted dissemination of information, thereby providing opportunities for good ideas to be read, used, reused and further developed. This further leads to an opportunity for greatest impact. The Foundations policy requires grant recipients to openly licence the final materials created under the most recent Creative Commons Attribution licence. Grantees are expected to post such materials on their websites. The choice of the CC-BY licence is meant to provide the widest opportunity for use and reuse of such materials. The Foundation has however noted that

> we will not enforce this new requirement thoughtlessly. If our default open license does not make sense for particular project-such as if the work contains sensitive information or if revenue generated by its sale is critical to an organization's financial well-being-we will work with the grantee to determine the most appropriate license. Our commitment to open licensing is meant to help, not harm, grantees, and we will administer it accordingly.[58]

All the governmental and non-governmental agencies discussed above have all issued open access policies. Whereas some of the policies are mandatory, others merely encourage deposits in some form of repositories be it in PubMed Central, Europe PMC, a personal, departmental or institutional repository. The aim is to enable immediate, unrestricted online access for use and reuse. Not all agencies are able to offer immediate access due to embargo periods, which range between six months and two years, but the willingness of these agencies to address the access problem and set timelines for unrestricted immediate online access is in the right direction. The policies by the non-governmental organizations is a testimony of the impact the private sector can make on national and international policies and should serve as an impetus to the private sector in Nigeria. If the public sector in Nigeria is bedevilled with corruption and unable to operate due to bureaucratic bottlenecks, the examples demonstrated by the non-governmental organizations above can serve as important indicators for Nigeria and possibly other developing countries.

2.17 Universities, publishers and libraries

Universities, publishers and libraries are three other important stakeholders in the open access movement.

Universities are institutions of learning, centres of research, and the rallying point for the incubation, birth, development and production of knowledge. They nurture authors, provide experts for peer review, encourage and fund research and train the next generation.[59] They play a major role in the open access movement as they serve as the nerve point that generates and ensures the integrity and quality of published materials. This is achieved through active participation in the peer-review process of journal articles.[60]

Publishers are the major commercial entity involved in the publication cycle. They are responsible for receiving manuscripts from authors, vetting and sending them for peer review, notifying authors of acceptance or rejection, preparing manuscripts for final prints, financing publication and marketing the published work as hard and soft copies.[61] Some publishers now publish solely online versions.[62] See the publishing cycle diagram below.

Libraries serve as the warehouse and middleman between publishers (the commercial entity) and users. These users include the university and research communities, other higher educational institutions and the general public. Libraries provide a platform for access to knowledge, archival of important and rare materials, preservation of documents in both hard and digital copies, but now mostly as digital copies, and they provide guidance to authors and users in multiple ways.[63] Libraries play a major role in the open access movement. The International Federation of Library Associations (IFLA), one of the major open access advocacy organizations, continues to work in collaboration with other open access advocates for the progress and expansion of access to knowledge.[64]

The interesting link between universities and libraries is that most libraries are associated with and funded by universities due to the institutional framework of university systems. Universities and publishers also have an interesting link in that a large number of authors, particularly those concerned with academic publishing, are from the university community and even more interesting is that those responsible for the peer-review process are also majorly from the university community. The publishing industry's continual increase in subscription costs coupled with declining or stagnated funds for libraries and universities brought about the "serials crisis", which led many libraries and universities back to the drawing board. The aim was to find a more realistic way to achieve access to knowledge in an affordable way and at an affordable price. The publishing industry came up with a new product known as "big deal or bundling", a strategy which give libraries access to a vast amount of published materials mostly in electronic format at discounted amounts for a period of three to five years. These deals are secured by way of contract through publishing agreements entered into between publishers and libraries. These agreements are often negotiated by a consortium of libraries to secure lower prices. The problem is that quite an amount of the published materials may be irrelevant to some of the libraries. The deal however is that access to a vast number of published materials is granted at a highly discounted price.[65]

3 Publishing agreement

Agreements play a critical role in information management. They determine the semantics of interacting with information including ownership, price, duration and what rights are available for use and reuse. Publishing agreements are one of the prominent agreements in the information management scheme.[66]

Most publishers have standard publishing agreements which most authors do not bother to read.[67] Most authors are more concerned with getting their work published than retaining their rights in the work (copyright). The implication of signing off on such documents must be understood and where necessary negotiated. Knowledge that authors can negotiate with publishers is important.[68] Although the negotiation table may be tilted in favour of publishers, it does not deny authors their right to negotiate. The difficulties associated with negotiating is part of what the open access movement is systemically addressing through open access policies. Funding agencies are major commercial stakeholders in the publishing industry because they fund research and in-turn the publication of such research. For this reason, publishers pay attention to their policy initiatives and will not ignore policies they make that concern publication. These policies which either mandate or require deposit of the output of published research in a repository form a strong basis for negotiating the terms of standard publishing agreements. Most of these standard agreements now contain clauses allowing for the deposit of pre-prints and post-prints.[69]

The dynamics of publishing agreements involves the law of contract and the principles of copyright.[70] They determine rights and obligations between authors and publishers. Once an original work has been created, authors of such works are automatically conferred with copyright ownership.[71] The agreements /contracts entered into between publishers and authors has the effect of either assigning or licensing author's copyright to publisher. An assignment effectively transfers, that is, moves all rights and privileges in the work from the author–assignor/transferor to the publisher–assignee/transferee. A licence is an authorization given by the licensor to the licensee to carry out certain acts. Licences may be exclusive or non-exclusive. An exclusive licence is similar to an assignment, but the right in the work reverts back to the author at the expiration of the agreed term. A non-exclusive licence allows that authorization be given to multiple parties simultaneously.[72]

Authors are confronted with a challenge of uncertainty and confusion in the exercise of their right to grant an exclusive licence. This challenge comes to the fore when there are multiple authors and with the increased ease of creating digital content, contents by multiple authors have become common. Where a work has been authored by more than one party, any of the authors may issue an exclusive licence in respect of the work to a third party. The other parties are entitled to profit that arise from the transaction. The challenge stems from the fact that the grant of an exclusive right can only be truly effective when he who grants the right has all the right but since the right in works created by multiple parties reside in all the parties, it is illogical for one party to grant an exclusive licence without the authorization of the other parties. This was the position of the court in *Sybersound v UAV*,[73] where the Ninth Circuit Court of Appeals held that a co-owner of a copyright could never give an exclusive licence. On a similar question, the district court in Wisconsin declined to follow the decision in Brownmark Case[74]on the grounds that the intention of congress expressed in Section 501(b) of the Copyright Act is to the effect that "the legal or beneficial owner of an exclusive right under a copyright is entitled . . . to institute an action for any infringement of that particular right committed while he or she is the owner of it." The court held that the grant of interest in WWITB by Ciraldo and Swaint's to Brownmark was a complete assignment of rights to Brownmark, and therefore Brownmark has the locus standi to sue for infringement of the underlying copyright.

The next section of this chapter looks at open access in Nigeria and at the entrance of open access to the Nigerian system. It explores scholarly publishing in Nigeria and identifies several initiatives that have been introduced for purposes of granting access to developing countries. It highlights the progress made so far towards enabling open access in Nigeria and discusses the implications of open access to Nigeria and other developing countries.

4 Open access in Nigeria

"Nigeria does not lack literary talent, but still, books written by native authors and published by Nigerian publishers are incredibly rare."[75] According to Nigerian poet and novelist Ben Okri, "The best writing is not about the writer, the best writing is absolutely not about the writer, it's about us, it's about the reader."[76]

The African writer and reader are however confronted with the challenge of getting his work out to both a local and global audience and faces the challenge of accessing works by fellow Africans. A lack of proper infrastructure to facility visibility and accessibility of Nigerian scholarly publication can be held accountable for the problem.

Nigeria has a large number of higher educational institutions.[77] Considering the high numbers, it is expected that a large amount of information and data ought to be generated and published in journal articles. Publishing the output of Nigerian-based research could be achieved in two ways; in a local journal and in an international/foreign journal. The choice of where you publish often determines accessibility, visibility, impact and utility of the work. Most works published in Nigeria suffer poor global and local visibility.[78] On the other hand, works published in foreign journals are globally visible but most often inaccessible to Africans and those in developing countries due to the high costs of subscription and pay-per-view fees. Most people in the global north have access to most peer-reviewed journal articles through their institutions which are able to afford subscription fees; but for those within the global south, the inability of virtually all universities and research institutions to keep up with the high subscription fees have necessitated cancellations and therefore they are unable to access peer-reviewed journal articles.[79]

There are Africans who publish in foreign journals and since these works are inaccessible to the average African, could the answer be to stop publishing in foreign journals? The promotion and assessment mechanism in the academic field has evolved a culture of "publish or perish", and it places high premium on works published within certain journals, most of which are foreign journals.[80] This being the case, how then will an author be convinced not to publish in foreign journals when that is the pathway to promotion? To worsen matters is the fact that works published with local journals mostly lack visibility and accessibility and are only seen, used and known by members of a particular association.[81]

Those who are actually meant to read and put the knowledge to use are unable to see the journals due to weak distribution infrastructures and due to the fact that most local publishers are not linked to the global publishing network. Most of these works are still largely un-digitized and sat in some shelves where the knowledge, although useful, is not visible and, therefore, will not make the impact it should. Nigerians are therefore technically cut out from this all-important intellectual discussion and from important information about issues and events. Even worse is that this inaccessibility is a deprivation of one's fundamental right, that is, the right of access to knowledge.[82]

The issue is then to identify for purposes of those in the global south and probably the few in the global north who are unable to access needed information due to some form of restriction, how to address the problem of visibility and inaccessibility to knowledge. Open access to knowledge provides a way.

5 Scholarly publishing in Nigeria

Journal publishing has existed in Nigeria for a long time. The *West African Medical Journal* was established in Nigeria during the colonial era in the 1920s.[83] The journal of the Nigerian Field Society, the *Nigerian Field*, was first published in 1931 and is still being published.[84] The establishment of the University College, Ibadan, in 1948 has been noted as what spiralled academic publishing in Nigeria. "From then till the late 1970s, Ibadan was the fountain of academic research, particularly in humanities."[85] As at 2015, records from African Journal Online (AJOL), the largest collection of African journals, show that it hosts 209 Nigerian journals.[86]

In the early days of scholarly publishing in Nigeria, the publishing cycle with authors responsible for writing intellectual thoughts, publishers responsible for organizing the logistics and financial components of the peer-review process, publication and marketing, and libraries through subscription providing access was strictly adhered to.[87] However, the decline in the Nigerian economy and the education sector led to the "brain drain syndrome",[88] low quality and irregularity of journal articles, inability of Nigerian university libraries to afford journal subscriptions, as well as a general dissatisfaction in the Nigerian academic community leading to endless strike actions by academic staff unions.[89] All of these brought about a gradual decay and a virtual collapse of scholarly publications in Nigeria.[90] The folding up of reputable journals and academic publisher such as the Journal of the Historical Society of Nigeria, a journal published by the oldest professional society in Nigeria were further indicators of the collapse in the industry.

Ever since this crisis, scholarly publication in Nigeria has been a survival of the fittest. The "publish or perish culture" have made it imperative for Nigerian academics to continue to publish.[91] Howbeit, quality has been sacrificed to satisfy the drive for publication at all cost. Many academics in Nigeria and most parts of Africa run the entire publication process from start to finish on their own and publications are sometimes made without going through any form of peer review.[92] It should therefore not be surprising that the output from these journals would be questionable. This is further buttressed by the fact that most Nigerian authors have no access to research materials because University libraries are unable to afford Journal subscription fees to the major international Journal Publishers.[93]

The decay in the system culminated in the creation of a multi-dimensional access problem. Nigerian Academics could not access current research from the West and the research findings that managed to be published by Nigerians not having been indexed remained localized and were therefore not accessible and visible to the international community. As a result of this, these works no matter how brilliantly researched made little or no impact.

Journal publication that survived the decay adopted one of the under-listed three options:

1. Levied members with annual dues to sustain the journals
2. Charged publication fees on every accepted manuscript before such papers were published
3. Charged assessment fees on every manuscript even before assessment

As would be expected, the third option was not very popular with prospective authors because of the risk of losing their money if the article was rejected. As a result, not many journals adopted that option.[94]

Using either of these options, journals were published, but a major challenge was that after publication, these works were not accessible, neither were they visible. Their impact and utility were very low, partly because the works could not be located on the major indexing services such as Medline, PubMed, ISI Web of Science or Google. The implication was that both the local and international community could not discover such publications, particularly considering the fact that majority of journals in developing countries are not indexed.[95] Therefore, many of the journals in Nigeria are being encouraged to get indexed and to embrace the possibilities enabled by technological development and particularly the open access movement which strives to remove restrictions to access.[96]

6 Nigeria introduced to open access

This movement, which started in the global north in 2002, has now found its way to Nigeria. In 2008, the first programme to sensitize Nigerians on open access took place in Nigeria.[97] The programme which was sponsored by the Electronic Information for Libraries Network (EIFL), the Department of Library and Information Sciences, Ahmadu Bello University and the Nigerian Universities Libraries Consortium (NULIB) was titled "Open Access Repositories: New Model for Scholarly Communication", and it had 89 participants inclusive of policy makers from the academic and research field.[98] Others included experts in the Libraries and Information Sciences as well as Information Communication Technology (ICT) experts working within the knowledge development sector. In all, 45 different institutions were present. The meeting addressed the importance of open access noting that "Communicating scholarly information through open access repositories provide the added advantages of faster publishing opportunities, greater visibility for authors and institutions and cheaper access"[99] and further noted the need for an open access policy for the nation. In 2009, another programme was held following-up on the earlier one with the theme "Open Access: Maximizing Research Quality and Impact", and it has been reported that as a result of these two workshops

> two institutions: University of Jos and Ahmadu Bello University, Zaria have developed institutional repositories. (University of Jos institutional repository and Ahmadu Bello University's institutional repository). In the Ahmadu Bello University, one of the Department's has converted two of its journals from toll access journals to OA: The Samaru Journal of Information Studies and The Information Manager.[100]

These are not the only journals providing open access in Nigeria. A number of universities are beginning to appreciate the importance of providing access to their research outputs and are developing institutional repositories, while publishers are beginning to embrace open access publishing. The next section of this paper will look at institutional repositories and open access journals in Nigeria.

7 Institutional repositories in Nigeria

A number of institutional repositories in Nigeria have begun a gradual but slow climb since 2009. The websites which track and register all open access repositories, the Registry of Open Access Repositories[101] (ROAR), as well as the Directory of Open Access Repositories[102] (DOAJ), provide information on the status of repositories in Nigeria. The first institutional repository in Nigeria was set up by the university of Jos in 2009 and by the next year, two other institutional repositories had been set up by the University of Nigeria and Covenant University on the 29th of August 2010 and 24th of November 2010 respectively. A search of the ROAR website indicates that there are nine repositories, eight of which use the Dspace software,[103] and one uses the Eprint software.[104] Both the DSpace and Eprint software are open source software developed to support the setting up and running of institutional repositories. The two open pieces of software are both built in compliance with the interoperable standards prescribed by the Open Archive Initiative, which aims to ensure interoperability by standardizing the method for inputting information and thereby facilitating efficient distribution of content.[105] Although the website lists nine repositories, these repositories represent six organizations. In addition to the repositories mentioned in ROAR, DOAR lists amongst others the Kashim Ibrahim Library of the Ahmadu Bello University as having a repository which uses a Dspace software. Table 4.1 provides information on the status of repositories in Nigeria using the information from the ROAR and DOAR websites.

The quest to investigate the issues and challenges to the development of open access in Nigeria, particularly through the self-archiving strategy, has led to a few publications.[106] Literature with regard to this is still somewhat scanty, and it is the hope of the author that this work will provide more information to what is currently available. The research paper prepared for the International Development Centre (IDRC) in Canada in 2008 examined the impact of the development

Table 4.1 Status of repositories in Nigeria

S/N	*Name*	*Date*	*Software*	*Comment*	*Website*
1	University of Jos (UNIJOS)	19/05/2009	DSpace	421	ROAR
2	University of Nigeria Nsukka (UNN)	29/08/2010		2989	ROAR
3	Covenant University	24/11/2010	Eprint	3307	ROAR
4	Federal University of Technology Akure (FUTA)	22/04/2012	DSpace	5130	ROAR
5	University of Jos (UNIJOS)	12/07/2012	Dspace	5649	ROAR
6	University of Nigeria	14/08/2012		5803	ROAR
7	Federal University Oye Ekiti	23/02/2013	DSpace	6543	ROAR
8	Michael Okpara University of Agriculture	25/07/2013	DSpace	7145	ROAR
9	CU Repository	27/01/2014	DSpace	7818	ROAR
10	Kashim Ibrahim Library, Ahmed Bello University	-	Dspace	-	DOAR

of information and communication technology on how knowledge is shared in Nigeria and South Africa. Christian who authored the paper noted the role institutional repositories can play in the dissemination of knowledge and identified issues militating against the maximization of the opportunities provided by institutional repositories.[107] Ivwighreghweta and Onoriode noted that the low profile of scientists in Africa can be attributed to poor access to scientific publications and that what is required is a platform providing unrestricted, worldwide, web-wide and free access to scientific publication.[108] Maximizing the opportunities provided by institutional repositories have been identified as tools for development capable of contributing to the attainment of the Millennium Development Goals (MDGs) particularly in Africa. He illustrated how institutional repositories provide the platform of information dissemination, which under the MDGs is a vital tool for development. The research calls for the adoption of policies for the establishment of institutional repositories by concerned institutions and possibly on a continental level.[109] Nigeria does not have any national open access policy, and it is the objective of this research to develop a guide that would aid in the development of such a policy. It has been noted however that Covenant University has adopted a university wide open access mandate.[110]

When Queensland University of Technology adopted the first ever university wide open access mandate, Tom Cochrane noted the impact it had on authors and the increase in the number of deposits in the University's Institutional repository "QUT Eprint".[111] The adoption of open access mandates has increased since then and so have deposits in Institutional repositories.[112]

There is a slow but growing realization and appreciation of the importance and value of open access in Nigeria, particularly in the academic sphere. The need for stronger advocacy and strategic engagement with the strategies that enable open access is imperative if the research community in Nigeria will maximize the opportunities made available through open access and particularly through self-archiving.

8 Open access journals in Nigeria

Journals that avail users the opportunity and freedom to use and reuse peer-reviewed literatures are often indexed in the DOAJ. This website provides an index of most open access journals and currently lists 38 journals and 1,167 articles published in Nigeria which provide open access. Amongst these journals are African Journal Online (AJOL),[113] Bioline International,[114] Academic Online,[115] Academia Publishing.[116] Some of these journals are listed as journals and providers, which means that they actually serve as both journals and hosts to several journals. The AJOL for instance "is the world's largest and pre-eminent collection of peer-reviewed, African-published scholarly journals". It is based in South Africa and currently hosts 496 journals, 9,247 issues, 105,655 abstracts and 100,430 full texts. Of the 496 journals, 186 are open access. Nigeria has 214 of the 496 journals spanning through virtually all the academic fields.[117] These journals are a mix of hybrid and delayed open access journals.

8.1 Open access and cost implications

Open access journals provide access to peer-reviewed literature at no charge, that is, free of charge to users. It is however without dispute that the cost of producing peer-reviewed journals is not free. The cost of peer review, editing, printing, marketing and other sundry costs are involved. This cost under the open access model is covered by the adoption of different business models. Some journals charge an article processing charge (APC) to cover the cost of production (BioMed Central uses this business model).[118] BioMed Central, one of the world's leading open access commercial publishers with over 258 peer-reviewed open access journals, 482 members in 52 countries charges an APC for each paper to cover the entire publication process. Other open access journals do not charge article processing fees but deploy other strategies for purposes of cost and production. The Murdoch University Law Review is an example.[119] This journal operates on the open journal system, an open source software freely available to journals worldwide.[120] The DOAJ indicates that there are 1,054 journals registered to Nigeria and of that number, 32 of them have indicated that they charge APC, while 6 do not charge any APC.[121]

In acknowledging the inequalities between the global north and the global south, a fund wavier scheme called "open access waiver fund" was instituted in favour of certain least developed and developing countries by BioMed Central. Nigeria is however not on the list of such countries and may not draw on such privilege. Another strategy to ease the payment of the APC is that authors who are part of the BioMed Central Membership program do not need to pay the APC as such fees are covered by their institutions.[122] Currently, there are two Nigerian institutions listed as members, namely Obafemi Awolowo University[123] and the University of Benin.[124]

9 Opening access to developing countries

Africa and most of the other developing countries are starving for knowledge.[125] Not because knowledge is not available, but because it has been inaccessible due amongst other things to the high cost of subscription, which virtually no developing country is able to afford.[126] Open access therefore comes as a much-needed panacea to people in developing countries and the wider the access gate is opened, the more information is made available to the public. Whereas the goal is free, immediate and unrestricted online access to all peer-reviewed literature, several initiatives have been put in place in Africa and other developing countries that have enabled greater access to knowledge. It may not have fully opened up the access gate, but it definitely has shifted from an entirely closed gate.[127] This section of the chapter will explore the initiatives that have enabled such opening up of access to knowledge.

9.1 Health Inter Network Access to Research Initiative

The need to improve the state of health in the developing world as well as the growing gap between academics and researchers in the developed and developing countries to access important scientific peer-reviewed articles prompted both the then Secretary General of the United Nations Kofi Annan and the Director General of the World Health Organization to make a call for the building of partnerships that would facilitate the improvement of health in the developing world.[128] It was to this call that the six major publishers, namely, Elsevier, Springer, Blackwell, Harcourt Worldwide STM Group, Wolters Kluwer and John Wiley responded to on the 9th of July 2001 in London and set up the Health Inter Network Access to Research Initiative (HINARI) with the aim of providing free or very-low-cost online access to the major journals in biomedical and health sciences to local, not-for-profit institutions in developing countries. Today, the partnering publishers have grown from 6 to about 160, and they supply in excess of about 42,000 information materials.[129]

The publishers in implementing this initiative put in place a structure that would identify bonafide academic and research institutions. This had to be done because the idea was not to provide global access, neither was it to provide free access, but rather it was to open up access by providing low-cost access and where it deems fit to provide free access.[130] The metrics used in determining countries that would fall within the two tiered access systems of either free or low-cost access was whether such countries were listed by the World Bank as low- or lower-middle-income countries.[131] The access granted was to be restricted to only biomedical and health information. Access authentication was also put into the HINARI access structure. Nigeria feel into the free access stream within the HINARI access structure.[132]

Beneficiaries of this initiative were expected to have computers with high-speed Internet connections of at least 56 bandwidths. They were also expected to comply with registration formalities.[133]

At the time, this initiative was an opening to the closed door. It surely did not provide clear-cut open access as we have it today, but it at least provided some form of opening to the prior toll and closed access. The challenges with the initiative was that access was provided to only specific institutions, and even within the institutions, it was highly restricted and thus not open to everyone. Even worse was the fact that it could only be accessed at specific locations and thus ease of working from different locations was not available. The access provided was highly restricted in that it was narrowed down to only biomedical and health information. The other fields were excluded. The Internet and computer requirements were other challenges, particularly when considering the poor Internet infrastructure in Africa and the bad power situation. Nonetheless, it was a step out of the dark room where the access doors were entirely closed.

9.2 International Network for the Availability of Scientific Publication

International Network for the Availability of Scientific Publication (INASP) is a charity organization set up in the United Kingdom in 1992 with the goal that developing countries should be able to access the world's wealth of scientific information. It works with a global network of partners to improve access, production and use of research information and knowledge.[134] INASP currently operates within over 70 countries and has over 1,800 partners. It supports librarians, IT staff, editors and policymakers, and it works closely with the different country partners to provide online scholarly literature to countries across Africa, Asia and Latin America. In the area of furthering the cause of open access, INASP works closely with libraries to provide them with access to millions of journal articles.[135] INASP also focuses on interpersonal development of authors by providing AuthorAids, an initiative which provides capacity building to authors and which assists them in the process of publication.[136] This initiative affords beneficiary authors the opportunity for visibility and high impact on their work. The 2012/2013 report of the organization tells the success story of two AuthorAids recipients who successfully published their research findings in reputable journals through the help of AuthorAids.[137] One of the landmark successes of INASP was the launch of the African Journal Online in 1998/1999.[138]

9.3 African Journal Online

This is the largest collection of African peer-reviewed journals, and it is indexed in the Directory of Open Access Journals.[139] African Journal Online (AJOL) became necessary to address the dearth of platforms providing visibility for knowledge developed by African to Africans and the global community. AJOL thus became the first African online journal dedicated to advancing African knowledge.[140] By means of this platform, it seeks to transform African Knowledge to African Development by increasing the potential accessibility, visibility, impact and utility of African research outputs. It is a platform on which Africans can showcase their works and in which Africans can search for works by other Africans.[141] The old saying that "he who blows the pipe dictates the tune" underscores the vision of AJOL as an African concern taking her destiny in her own hands. On the website of AJOL, it notes as follows that

> At the same time as online academic resources from the developed Global North are made available to Africa (such as HINARI, AGORA and OARE), there needs to be corresponding online availability of information from Africa. Important areas of research in Africa are not necessarily covered by publications from the developed world. African countries need to collectively play a greater role in the global online scholarly environment. African researchers also need access to their own continent's scholarly publications.
>
> Mainly due to difficulties accessing them, African-published research papers have been under-utilized, under-valued and under-cited in the international and African research arenas. The internet is a good way to change this, but many hundreds of worthy, peer-reviewed scholarly journals publishing from Africa cannot host their content online in isolation because of resource limitations and the digital divide.
>
> Valuable information has not reached the people who need it.[142]

AJOL achieves its vision by freely hosting African journals, it and currently hosts over 496 peer-reviewed journals in over 30 African countries. About 186 of these journals are open access journals. The journals are not restricted to any particular field. They cover the medical and health sciences, as well as social sciences, humanities, law, agriculture and virtually all fields. AJOL maximizes the benefits of the open environment by operating solely on open source software. It uses the open journal system (OJS) developed by the Public Knowledge Project in Canada and runs the PHP scripting language as well as MySQL for its Database Management System. It's Web server uses the Apache software and Linux is the operating System on which it runs.[143]

9.4 Access to Global Online Research in Agriculture

Several other initiatives have been born and are advancing the cause of not just access to knowledge but free access to knowledge. There is the Access to Global Online Research in Agriculture (AGORA), which was sponsored by the Food and Agriculture Organisation of the United Nations (FAO). This initiative is focused on providing the output of research on issues around food, agriculture, environmental sciences and related social sciences and it is designed to enhance scholarship in developing countries. It provides a collection of more than 3,500 key journals and 3,300 books to 2,500 institutions in over 116 countries.[144]

9.5 Online Access to Research in the Environment

This is another initiative focused on providing access to knowledge, and this time, knowledge about the environment. It was initiated in 2006 by the United Nations Environment Programme in partnership with the major publishers. It currently has over 5,710 peer-reviewed scientific journals made available by about 461 of its partners to over 100 eligible low-income countries. This initiative provides the world's largest collection of environmental scientific research and has the vision of providing access to this information, improving the quality and effectiveness of environmental sciences, research, education and training in low-income countries.[145]

9.6 Access to Research for Development and Innovation

There is also the Access to Research for Development and Innovation (ARDI) coordinated by the World Intellectual Property Organization in partnership with the major publishers for purposes of increasing availability to scientific and technical information in developing countries. It currently partners with about 17 publishers and has about 10,000 journals available to over 107 developing countries.[146]

9.7 Siyavula

Siyavula is another initiative focused on opening up the access gate to knowledge. Siyavula is not an initiative of any of the UN agencies. It is rather a private based

African initiative situated in South Africa, which provides educational resources to students at no cost. It seeks to join hands in the global action towards access to knowledge by developing and providing for free, educational resources to students on the Internet platform.[147]

9.8 The African Legal Information Institute

The African Legal Information Institute (African LII) provides free access to Kenyan legal resources and by this is helping to shape African Law and provides access to legal knowledge to all willing minds.[148]

9.9 Social Science Research Network

The world's largest repository, the Social Science Research Network (SSRN) recently set up a journal dedicated strictly to African law works. It was sponsored by seven law schools, six of which are American law schools and one is an African Law School. The Law African e-journal which was recently set up has received several visits and over 50,000 downloads.[149] SSRN hosts several other e-journals dedicated to African works.[150]

All of these initiatives provide a wider gate for access to knowledge, some merely provide better opportunities for access to knowledge through lower-price regimes (also referred to by Barbara Kirsop, Subbiah Arunachalam and Leslie Chan as donor access[151] and by John Willinsky as per capita open access),[152] while others comply with the expectation set for open access as contained in the Budapest, Bethesda and Berlin Statements and provide to users free, online, permanent and unrestricted use and reuse rights to their peer-reviewed literatures. These access gates pave a way for Nigerians to understand, join and contribute in the international discussion and also to freely build upon available knowledge in the interest of Nigeria and the global community.

10 Open access implications to Nigeria and developing countries

Up until now, we have considered the impact of open access as a concept on access to knowledge and have listed a number of initiatives that have been developed to further availability and accessibility to the output of scientific research. This next section will look at the likely implications of open access to Nigeria and other developing countries.

11 Likely effects (positive)

11.1 Increased accessibility, visibility, impact and utility

Open access has the potential to increase accessibility, visibility, impact and utility of work. These are four positive effects which, although different, are intertwined.

The potential for these four effects is possible considering that once an author makes a work available via self-archiving or open access journal, the work becomes freely available on the Internet, and anyone with Internet connectivity, a computer device, power supply (for those in developing countries) can easily access and use the information. This also means that the work becomes universally visible.[153] It creates the possibility for people from all over the world to gain from the knowledge, refer to it in their research and this in turn contributes to impact factors for both the author and his institution and provides the platform and possibility for the maximal utility of the work.[154]

11.2 Knowledge sharing

Other possible positive impacts for developing countries include what was captured in the BOAI "sharing the knowledge of the rich with the poor and the poor with the rich".[155] Put another way, *sharing the knowledge of members of the developed countries with members of the developing countries and the knowledge of member of the developing countries with the knowledge of the members of the developed countries*. I have suggested this new slant because the terms *rich* and *poor* are relative, and without a doubt, so is *developed* and *developing* countries, but since the article in question is knowledge, an ephemeral commodity, which is not easily quantifiable, the cloak of rich and poor appears to cast aspersion on the quality of knowledge with regards to "knowledge of the rich" and "knowledge of the poor" and has the possibility of giving an impression that knowledge of the rich is rich knowledge and that knowledge of the poor is poor knowledge. The possibility of such an interpretation could be sending a superiority/inferiority signal, thus laying the foundations on a wrong footing. It is however important not to lose focus of the actual intent of the initiative, which is the provision of the possibility of a platform for sharing knowledge, which brings with it limitless opportunities for development and is an important advantage to members of developing countries.[156]

11.3 Access to the World's Library

Open access will provide developing countries with the possibility for access to the vast resources of the world's wealth of knowledge, access to the World's Library.[157] It is an access which before now was locked up and for which institutions in developing countries could not afford, meaning that its people were locked out and were unable to access needed research materials.[158]

11.4 Global and local visibility

Open access provides the platform for global and local visibility to works authored by members of developing countries. Global visibility was particularly practically impossible prior to the open access initiative. Most journals published in developing countries were circulated within the associations that produced them and what compounded the problem was that the major publisher were not aware of such works and even when aware rarely indexed such works amongst their collection thus they were not within the rank and file of materials that could be located if a search was conducted.[159] Thanks to the Internet and to open access databases and indexes, works authored by members of developing countries can now enjoy both global and local visibility.[160] The possibility for local visibility is particularly interesting, because prior to the advent of open access, works authored within the same developing country jurisdictions were usually not visible due to poor channels of distribution and circulation and due to the fact that these works were not indexed in the major commercial indexes for journal articles.[161]

11.5 Digitization and preservation of works/heritage

The practice in so many developing countries is to conduct research, be it thesis and dissertation, research articles, government commissioned research or some other form of research, and the output of these research are then locked up in some cabinet where they rot away, and no one has access to them.[162] Open access provides several advantages to such works. First is the prospect for digitization and preservation of such works. Digitized works cannot be torn, burnt or eaten up by termites, and they are therefore better preserved.[163] It is true that digitized works can be destroyed due to corruption of the device on which such information is held, but this is often taken care of by backing up such documents.[164] Open access also provides such work the possibility of being read by anyone in the world and thus the product of such research is able to enjoy not only global visibility but has the potentials of been maximally utilized. In preserving works, one of the fundamental things achieved is the preservation of knowledge and for Nigerian's and nations with rich cultural heritage, preservation of knowledge provides an opportunity to preserve the cultural heritage of a people.[165] In a nutshell, open access provides the opportunity for bringing alive works that were virtually dead and for preserving works that will in turn preserve the cultural heritage of a people, heritage which in many cases are slowly gliding into extinction.

11.6 Avoiding duplicity

In the absence of a platform like open access which freely shares the output of research, duplication is inevitable. In so many organizations, whether in developed or developing countries, the duplication of research is an unfortunate incidence.[166] So often, what organization A is researching on is what organization B has worked on and may have produced credible and useful reports and data. However, because of the lack of a system to freely share such information and data, the same research is duplicated, and scarce resources which could have been deployed to some other highly needed areas are re-invested into the same research which simply amounts to re-inventing the wheels and wasting taxpayers' hard earned money.[167]

11.7 Learning without barriers

Open access through a related initiative, OER, affords members of developing countries the opportunity to learn from minds they otherwise would not have had access to. Examples abound with organizations such as KHAN Academy[168]

Similarly, we have several other initiatives that provide the opportunity for free learning via the Internet. There is the Wikiversity closely associated with Wikipedia,[169] the Open School of Learning (P2PU) run by the Creative Commons,[170] and CopyrightX providing lectures prepared and delivered by Prof William Fisher of Harvard.[171] All of these initiatives provide high-quality standard education at no cost to any willing mind and allow the reuse of these materials. The innovation to knowledge acquisition and learning is simply transformative and affords unprecedented learning opportunities to willing minds.[172]

12 Likely effects (negative)

Engaging with any initiative often has its pros and cons. Open access apparently is no exception; therefore, on the flip side of the impact, could an initiative such as this have any negative effects? Open access in its contextual form is meant to provide an avalanche of information and should provide it at the click of the mouse via the Internet. What negative effects could it have?

12.1 Consumption partners

The first negative effect is the tendency to turn developing countries into mere consumption partners in the knowledge creation and sharing relationship. Although this may not be the objective, the likelihood of its occurrence seems apparent, and this is so considering that the vast majority of information in the global north is already digitized and online and that the current stock of information in the world's major libraries are made up of writings from the global north.[173] The simple reasoning is that based on probability, if there are 10 balls in a basket with 9 of them red and only 1 is blue, the probability of my picking a blue ball is only 1 out of 10. This is the same probability rule with accessing knowledge from the open access pool. What is likely to be accessed is determined by the input, and as earlier noted, the global north is responsible for generating the majority of information and thus, the information likely to be located and accessed will often be that from the global north.

It is clear that open access affords the opportunity for all to share, use and where permitted reuse information, but when one considers what is within the pool of the world's vast resources of knowledge, there is a tendency that developing countries would become more of *knowledge consumers than knowledge contributors*. This is so because there is already the compliant of knowledge explosion[174] (also referred to as *infobesity*[175] and *infoxication*),[176] and there already exist within developing countries a tendency to tilt the educational system in favour of Western educational materials.[177]

It is also important to think about the fact that before developing countries are able to digitize and make their knowledge fully available, there is the fear that the knowledge accessible (that is knowledge within the global north) is the knowledge that would be accessed and utilized and that being the case, a pattern of knowledge consumption by members of the developing countries may have been established.

12.2 Cultural re-orientation/loss of cultural heritage

Open access from a global perspective should work towards promoting a knowledge-sharing relationship that is balanced and symbiotic in nature, not one that is lopsided.[178] It is a relationship which BOAI describes as sharing knowledge and not merely consuming knowledge. This concern is of particular interest when consideration is given to how Hollywood has invaded the cultural lives of many nations, influencing cultural and indigenous ideologies and sometimes eroding and even eradicating such cultures.[179] This concern of a cultural re-orientation and a possible loss of cultural heritage through the abundant availability, unrestricted accessibility and constant exposure to knowledge generated in the global north pose concerns to developing countries.[180]

12.3 Digital divide

The other challenge lies in the fact that open access is structurally built to function technologically, and it is widely known that the global south suffers from technological retardation and that the digital divide amongst other factors have decapacitated the global south from operating at the level of the global north.[181] One of the two major pillars of open access is the Internet.[182] Now, if open access is structured to work based on a technological leg which the global south is known not to have, the question then arises as to whether the global north actually contemplated the participation of the global south? One may answer that it is expected that the global south will eventually catch up with technological advancements and connect with the global open access move.

The rationality of catching up is however in question, when consideration is given to the rate of technological growth in the global north and the fact that people within the global north are barely able to keep pace with the technological changes.[183] This being the case, how then can it be reasonable expected for the global south to catch up with the technological advancements in the global north?

The problems associated with open access and the digital divide is further compounded by a lack of regular power supply in most developing countries, and it is even worsened by the lack of basic computer literacy.[184] It must be clearly noted that all these challenges are no fault of those who have initiated the idea of open access. In fact, the idea is intended to particularly provide platforms and a uniform playing ground for all, regardless of location, nationality, economic or social status. However, in taking advantage of these platforms, it is important for anyone engaging with the concept to understand the complexities around utilizing them and where necessary erect structures for the preservation and widest possible utility for the platforms. The aim is to ensure that open access does not amount to a creativity killer by its provision of free and reusable information. The concern is to ensure that researchers can look up works that have already been researched and yet take the next step to build upon it. The concern is for teachers to look up materials that have already been created and not just copy and paste them but take the time to adapt them to the local needs, improve upon them and also make them available for others to use and reuse, thereby adding value to the content and positively engaging in knowledge development. The concern is to ensure that developing countries do not become mere consumers of the already available and free knowledge but actual contributors to the vast wealth of the world's knowledge. The purpose of these concerns is not to distance developing countries from open access, but rather to build a consciousness for strategic engagement with open access to the end that the initiative will serve as a propelling force for development and will also ensure that the world's library which has now been opened up to everyone can serve as a mirror to reflect not only views of the global north, but also that of the global south.

13 Conclusion

The possibilities made available by open access are numerous. That free online unrestricted access to journal articles is possible provides like never before accessibility, visibility, impact and maximal utility on the output of research findings. These possibilities are particularly important to members of developing countries who prior to the open access era had been shot out from the world's library. Shot out from accessing journal articles and shot out by poor infrastructures frustrating visibility of their publications. This lockout, causing a lack of access to knowledge and heightened by the trio barriers of price, technical and legal is what the open access movement is taking steps to address. These initiatives open up the access gates that were shot and provide opportunities for all willing minds to access available information. Caution must however be taken by those in the global south who appear prone to becoming consuming partners in the open access knowledge market if proper strategies are not put in place to effectively harness, contribute and engage with the dynamics of open access. Open access no doubt provides an avalanche of information, and the more of one's information is put into the global poll, the more available such knowledge becomes and also the possibility for such knowledge achieving maximal impact. If this avalanche of information unfortunately breeds a sense of complacency in anyone, but particularly those in the global south and leads them to not develop their own knowledge, it could lead to a steady eradication of local knowledge, culture, heritage, creativity and innovation. This could bring about a gradual re-colonization, this time not one forcefully annexing the physical territories, but this time a willing surrender of the mind through lazy assimilation of ideas and information.

The central purport of open access is to democratize access to knowledge thereby enabling willing minds to explore without barriers. Maximizing the benefits of open access can be best achieved by engaging as contributors and not mere consumers to the pool of information within the open access to knowledge hemisphere.

Notes

1 National Institutes of Health (NIH), *About NIH*, available at www.nih.gov/about/.
2 NIH, *NIH Data Sharing Policy* (2003), available at http://grants.nih.gov/grants/policy/data_sharing/.
3 PubMed, *PubMed*, NIH, available at www.ncbi.nlm.nih.gov/pubmed/.
4 GenBank, *GenBank Overview*, available at www.ncbi.nlm.nih.gov/genbank/.
5 PubChem, *PubChem*, available at http://pubchem.ncbi.nlm.nih.gov/.
6 *Scientific Publications: Free for all? Tenth Report of Session 2003–04* (2004), available at www.publications.parliament.uk/pa/cm200304/cmselect/cmsctech/399/399.pdf.
7 Research Councils United Kingdom (RCUK), *RCUK Position Statement on Access to Research Outputs* (2005), available at www.rcuk.ac.uk/RCUK-prod/assets/documents/documents/2005statement.pdf.
8 P. Suber, *AHRC Announces Its OA Policy* (2007), available at http://legacy.earlham.edu/~peters/fos/2007/09/ahrc-announces-its-oa-policy.html.
9 Research Information Network & Stephane Goldstein, *Expanding Access to Published Research Findings* (2011), available at www.rin.ac.uk/news/press/expanding-access-published-research-findings.
10 Finch Report, *Report of the Working Group on Expanding Access to Published Research Findings* (2012), available at https://www.acu.ac.uk/research-information-network/finch-report-final
11 BIS & David Willetts, *Letter to Dame Janet Finch on the Government Response to the Finch Group Report: "Accessibility, Sustainability, Excellence: How to Expand Access to Research Publications"* (2012), available at www.gov.uk/government/uploads/system/uploads/attachment_data/file/32493/12-975-letter-government-response-to-finch-report-research-publications.pdf.
12 RCUK, *RCUK Policy on Open Access and Supporting Guidance* (2013), available at http://webcache.googleusercontent.com/search?q=cache:9mcesRxkWHgJ:www.rcuk.ac.uk/RCUK-prod/assets/documents/documents/RCUKOpenAccessPolicy.pdf+&cd=1&hl=en&ct=clnk&gl=uk.
13 House of Lords, *The Implementation of Open Access* (2013), available at www.publications.parliament.uk/pa/ld201213/ldselect/ldsctech/122/122.pdf.
14 Times Higher Education, *RCUK Open-Access Guidance Revised* (2013), available at www.timeshighereducation.co.uk/news/rcuk-open-access-guidance-revised/2002396.article.
15 Innovation and Skills Committee House of Commons Business, *Open Access* (2013), available at www.publications.parliament.uk/pa/cm201314/cmselect/cmbis/99/9902.htm.
16 BIS, *Open Access: Responses to the Committee's Fifth Report of Session 2013–14* (2013), available at https://www.rsb.org.uk/images/ResponsetoBIScom.pdf
17 BIS & David Willetts, *Letter to Dame Janet Finch on the Government Response to the Finch Group Report: "Accessibility, Sustainability, Excellence: How to Expand Access to Research Publications"* (2012), available at www.gov.uk/government/uploads/system/uploads/attachment_data/file/32493/12-975-letter-government-response-to-finch-report-research-publications.pdf.
18 BIS, *Progress Review: Implementing Finch Report Recommendations* (BIS, London, 2014).
19 SciELO, *Scientific Electronic Library Online*, available at www.scielo.br/.
20 Julie Caruso, Aurore Nicol & Eric Archambault, *Open Access Strategies in the European Research Area: RTD-B6-PP-2011–2: Study to Develop a Set of Indicators to Measure Open Access* (Science Metrix, 2013), available at www.science-metrix.com/

pdf/SM_EC_OA_Policies.pdf. Outside the ERA, the United States has passed the tipping point, and Canada is approaching. Brazil's proportion of open access articles is even more notable at 63 percent. See also, Global Open Access Portal, *Brazil*. "Brazil is the most active country of the region in open access implementations. And the first country to have a bill presented in 2007 to parliament proposing a national mandatory policy for open access, which is not yet approved."

21 Caralee Adams, 'Open Access in Latin America: Embraced as Key to Visibility of Research' *SPARC*, available at www.sparc.arl.org/news/open-access-latin-america-embraced-key-visibility-research-outputs.

> "SciELO proved to be a powerful tool in addressing the problem of locally-generated research being noticed and recognized by the international research community. Open Access soon showed it was the best way to raise the profile of Latin American-published journals," says Packer.
>
> Now, most all nationally published journals in Latin America are Open Access. "Today, if it's not on the web, it doesn't exist,"

22 NRC-CISTI, *NRC Publications Archive Statement of Responsibilites*, available at http://cisti-icist.nrc-cnrc.gc.ca/obj/cisti-icist/doc/nparc/NPArC-Statement-of-Responsibilities_e.pdf.

23 Government of Canada, *Minister Holder Announces New Open Access Policy for Research* (2015), available at www.science.gc.ca/default.asp?lang=En&n=415B5097-1.

24 Canadian Institutes of Health Research, *Tri-Agency Open Access Policy on Publications* (2015), available at www.cihr-irsc.gc.ca/e/32005.html.

25 European Union (EU), *Open Access to Scientific Information*, available at http://ec.europa.eu/digital-agenda/en/open-access-scientific-information.

26 EU, *FP7: Research and Innovation Funding 2014–2020*, available at http://ec.europa.eu/research/fp7/index_en.cfm.

27 EU, *The EU Framework Programme for Research and Innovation: Horizon 2020: Guidelines on Open Access to Scientific Publications and Research Data in Horizon 2020* (2012), available at http://ec.europa.eu/research/participants/data/ref/h2020/grants_manual/hi/oa_pilot/h2020-hi-oa-pilot-guide_en.pdf.

28 EU, *Communication from the Commission to the European Parliament, the Council, the European Economic and Social Committee and the Committee of the Regions: Towards Better Access to Scientific Information: Boosting the Benefits of Public Investments in Research* (2012), available at http://ec.europa.eu/research/science-society/document_library/pdf_06/era-communication-towards-better-access-to-scientific-information_en.pdf.

29 United Nations Educational, Scientific and Cultural Organization (UNESCO), *Global Open Access Portal*, available at www.unesco.org/new/en/communication-and-information/portals-and-platforms/goap/.

30 The World Bank, *World Bank Announces Open Access Policy for Research and Knowledge, Launches Open Knowledge Repository* (2012), available at www.worldbank.org/en/news/press-release/2012/04/10/world-bank-announces-open-access-policy-for-research-and-knowledge-launches-open-knowledge-repository.

31 The World Bank, *Open Knowledge Repository*, available at https://openknowledge.worldbank.org/.

32 Organisation for Economic Co-operation and Development (OECD), *Declaration on Access to Research Data from Public Funding: 30 March 2004 [C(2004)31/REV1]* (2004), available at http://acts.oecd.org/Instruments/ShowInstrumentView.aspx?InstrumentID=157.

The Ministers laid the following objectives and principles, namely, Openness, Transparency, Legal Conformity, Formal Responsibility, Professionalism, Protection of Intellectual Property, Interoperability, Quality and Security, Efficiency and Accountability.

33 OECD, *OECD Principles and Guidelines on Access to Research Data from Public Funding* (2007), available at www.oecd.org/science/sci-tech/38500813.pdf.

34 PubMed.
35 NIH, *NIH Mission*, available at www.nih.gov/about/mission.htm.
36 Michael Carrol, 'Complying with the NIH Public Access Policy – Copyright Considerations and Options' *SPARC Open Access Newsletter* (2008).
37 European Research Council (ERC), *About ERC*, available at http://erc.europa.eu/about-erc. See also, ERC, *ERC Work Programme 2015 (European Commission C(2014)5008 of 22 July 2014)* (2015).
38 ERC, *History*, available at http://erc.europa.eu/about-erc/history.
39 ERC, *Facts and Figures*, available at http://erc.europa.eu/about-erc/facts-and-figures.
40 The seven Research Councils in the United Kingdom are Arts and Humanities Research Council (AHRC), Biotechnology and Biological Sciences Research Council (BBSRC), Engineering and Physical Sciences Research Council (EPSRC), Economic and Social Research Council (ESRC), Medical Research Council (MRC), Natural Environment Research Council (NERC) and Science and Technology Facilities Council (STFC).
41 RCUK, *RCUK Aims & Objectives*, available at www.rcuk.ac.uk/about/aboutrcuk/aims/.
42 RCUK, *Open Access*, available at www.rcuk.ac.uk/research/openaccess/.
43 RCUK, *RCUK Policy on Open Access*, available at www.rcuk.ac.uk/research/Pages/outputs.aspx. See also, RCUK, *2014 Independent Review of Implementation*, available at www.rcuk.ac.uk/research/openaccess/2014review/.
44 Australian Research Council (ARC), *About ARC*, available at www.arc.gov.au/about_arc/default.htm.
45 ARC, *ARC Open Access Policy*, available at www.arc.gov.au/applicants/open_access.htm.
46 Id. at.
47 Wellcome Trust, *History*, available at www.wellcome.ac.uk/About-us/History/index.htm.
48 Wellcome Trust, *Our Vision*, available at www.wellcome.ac.uk/Our-vision/index.htm. See also, Wellcome Trust, *Funding*, available at www.wellcome.ac.uk/Funding/index.htm.
49 Wellcome Trust, *Strategic Plan 2010–2020* (2010), available at www.wellcome.ac.uk/stellent/groups/corporatesite/@policy_communications/documents/web_document/WTDV027438.pdf.
50 Wellcome Trust, *Open Access at the Wellcome Trust*, available at www.wellcome.ac.uk/about-us/policy/spotlight-issues/Open-access/index.htm. "[To] ensure that the work we fund can be read and utilized by the widest possible audience. We therefore support unrestricted access to the published outputs of research through our open access policy."
51 Wellcome Trust, *Open Access Policy: Position Statement in Support of Open and Unrestricted Access to Published Research*, available at www.wellcome.ac.uk/About-us/Policy/Policy-and-position-statements/WTD002766.htm.
52 Bill and Melinda Gate, *Bill & Melinda Gates Foundation Open Access Policy*, available at www.gatesfoundation.org/How-We-Work/General-Information/Open-Access-Policy. See where it was noted that "As of 1 January 2015 our Open Access policy will be effective for all new agreements."
53 Ford Foundation, *Issues*, available at www.fordfoundation.org/issues.
54 Ford Foundation, *Mission*, available at www.fordfoundation.org/about-us/mission.
55 Ford Foundation, *Ford Foundation Expand Creative Commons Licensing for All Grant-Funded Projects* (2015), available at www.fordfoundation.org/newsroom/news-from-ford/934. See where it was noted that "Beginning February 1, project grants from the foundation will include a requirement that the grantee widely disseminate all copyrightable products funded by the grant – including white papers, research reports, and websites – and license them under the CC BY 4.0 license."

56 The William and Flora Hewlett Foundation, *Open Educational Resources Initiative* (2005), available at https://hewlett.org/library/open-educational-resources-initiative/. See also, UNESCO, *Open Educational Resources*, available at www.unesco.org/new/en/communication-and-information/access-to-knowledge/open-educational-resources/.
57 The William and Flora Hewlett Foundation, *Programs*, available at www.hewlett.org/programs.
58 William & Flora Hewlett Foundation, *Commitment to Open Licensing*, available at www.hewlett.org/about-us/values-policies/commitment-open-licensing.
59 QS Topuniversities, *Top Universities in the World 2014/15* (2014), available at www.topuniversities.com/university-rankings-articles/world-university-rankings/top-universities-world-201415.
60 Budapest Open Access Initiative, *Ten Years on from the Budapest Open Access Initiative: Setting the Default to Open*, available at www.opensocietyfoundations.org/openaccess/boai-10-recommendations.
61 The STM Report, *An Overview of Scientific and Scholarly Publishing* (Mark Ware Consulting, 2012), available at www.markwareconsulting.com/articles-reports/the-stm-report-an-overview-of-scientific-and-scholarly-journal-publishing-2/. See page 14, where it notes that "The movement of information between the different participants in the journal publishing process is usually called 'the publishing cycle.'"
62 First Monday, *Peer-Reviewed Journal on the Internet*, available at http://firstmonday.org/index. See also, JOAL, *Journal of Open Access to Law, available at* https://ojs.law.cornell.edu/index.php/joal.
63 Gordon McIntyre et al., 'Library as Scholarly Publishing Partner: Keys to Success' 2 (2013) *Journal of Librarianship and Scholarly Comunication.*

> "Many academic libraries are looking at new ways to add value when they deliver services to faculty."

64 International Federation of Library Associations (IFLA), *IFLA/Brill Open Access Award 2015 Goes to DOAB*, available at www.ifla.org/node/9630.
65 Caruso et al. (2013). See page 25: "In response to the changing landscape of scholarly communication, publishers developed new products known as 'big deals', or journal bundles."
66 Y. Benkler, *The Wealth of Networks: How Social Production Transforms Markets and Freedom* (Yale University Press, 2006), 23–24.
67 Kenneth D. Crews, Reserving Rights of Use in Works Submitted for Publication: Negotiating Publishing Agreements. A Project of the IUPUI Copyright Management Center (Indiana University-Purdue University Indianapolis, 2004).
68 Anthony Austin et al., *Academic Authorship, Publishing Agreements and Open Access: Survey Results* (Queensland University of Technology, 2008). "Almost one-in-two respondents (49%) have not understood that terms of a publishing agreement but signed the agreement anyway."
69 Elsevier, *Copyright*, available at www.elsevier.com/about/company-information/policies/copyright#openaccess. See also, Springer, *Self-Archiving Policy*, available at www.springer.com/gp/open-access/authors-rights/self-archiving-policy/2124. See also, Harnad, Stevan, 'The Open Challenge: A Brief History. Public Service Review: European Science & Technology' 9 (2010) *Public Service Review: European Science & Technology*, 13–15. See also, Stevan Harnad & Nancy McGovern, 'Institutional Repository Success Is Dependent Upon Mandates' 36 (2009) *Bulletin of the American Society for Information Science and Technology* 27, where the author noted that "97% of journals have already given their assent to some form of immediate open access self-archiving, 63% for the final refereed, accepted draft."
70 Brian Fitzgerald et al., OAK LAW PROJECT NO. 1: Creating a Legal Framework for Copyright Management of Open Access Within the Australian Academic and Research

Sector (Report for the Department of Education and Science and Training (DEST) 116 (2006). "Copyright and contract law are central to the establishment and administration of open access systems."

71 See Article 5, Berne Convention for the Protection of Literary and Artistic Works, 9 September 1886, amended last on 28 September 1979.

72 Lawrence Liang, *Guide to Open Content Licenses v1.2 9* (Piet Zwart Institute, Institute for postgraduate studies and research, Willem de Kooning Academy Hogeschool, 2004). See where it was noted that "Even in countries where copyright may, by law, be non-transferable, most publishers effectively circumvent this regulation by requiring the author to sign a contract which grants the publisher exclusive distribution rights."

73 *Sybersound Records, Inc. v UAV Corp.*, 517 F. 3d 1137 – Court of Appeals, 9th Circuit 2008. Before Milan D. Smith, JR., Circuit Judge: "We also consider whether the transfer of an interest in a divisible copyright interest from a copyright co-owner to Sybersound, unaccompanied by a like transfer from the other copyright co-owners, can be an assignment or exclusive license that gives the transferee a co-ownership interest in the copyright. We hold that it cannot."

74 See *Brownmark Films, LLC v Comedy Partners*, 800 F. Supp. 2d 991 (D. Wis. 2011), where the defendants contend that "unless all the other co-owners of the copyright joined in granting an exclusive right to" a party, all Brownmark obtained from Mr. Ciraldo and Mr. Swant was a non-exclusive license in WWITB, which is insufficient to obtain standing to sue for a copyright violation. (Def.'s' Br. at 9–10) (citing *Sybersound Records*, 517 F.3d at 1145–46). The court, however, is unpersuaded by the defendants' first argument.

75 Ana Zoria, *Nigeria's Publishing Industry: Telling Our Own Stories*, available at www.pambazuka.net/en/category/books/93917.

76 Ben Okri, *F@T BEN OKRI, 19 Jan 2015, 06:42* (2015), available at http://first-thoughts.org/on/Ben+Okri/.

77 National Universities Commission, *List of Approved Universities in Nigeria*, National Universities Commission, 7 (2014), available at www.nuc.edu.ng/nucsite/File/Monday%20Bulletin/MB%202014/MONDAY%20Bulletin%2003-02-2014.pdf.

78 G. E. Christian, *Issues and Challenges to the Development of Open Access Institutional Repositories in Academic and Research Institutions in Nigeria*, 7 (2008), International Development Research Centre (IDRC), available at https://idl-bnc.idrc.ca/dspace/bitstream/10625/36986/1/127792.pdf, See also, J. I. Ezema, 'Trends in Electronic Journal Publishing in Africa: An Analysis of African Journal Online (AJOL)' *Webology*, available at www.webology.org/2010/v7n1/a74.html.

79 Justin Norrie, 'Harvard Decries the High Cost of Journal Subscription' *The Conversation* (2012), available at http://theconversation.edu.au/harvard-journal-subscription-fees-are-prohibitive-6659, 24 April. See also, John Willinsky, *The Access Principle: The Case for Open Access to Research and Scholarship* (MIT Press, 2006), 7.

80 Phil Davis, 'Publish-or-Perish Culture Promotes Scientific Narcissism' *The Scholarly Kitchen*, available at http://scholarlykitchen.sspnet.org/2012/05/07/publish-or-perish-culture-promotes-scientific-narcissism/.

81 Ezema (2010).

82 Willinsky, 143 (2006), where he noted that "access to knowledge is a human right that is closely associated with the ability to defend."

83 O. G. Ajao & B. T. Ugwu, 'Some Problems Facing Scientific Medical Publication in Nigeria' 1 (2011) *Journal of the West African College of Surgeons*.

84 Nigerian Field Society, *The Nigerian Field Society*, available at www.nigerianfield.org/.

85 Ayodejo Olukoju, 'The Crisis of Research and Academic Publishing in Nigerian Universities' (2004) *CiteSeer*, available at http://citeseerx.ist.psu.edu/viewdoc/download;jsessionid=31963D03475BE7DB5BE1EF1BBE75E8AD?doi=10.1.1.99.214&rep=rep1&type=pdf

86 AJOL, *Nigeria*, available at www.ajol.info/index.php/index/browse/country?countryId=156, www.ajol.info/index.php/index/browse/country?countryId=156, accessed on 20/02/2015.

87 Mark Ware & Mabe, 14. 2012. At p. 14 "research information, created by an author . . . passes through the journal editorial office of the author's chosen journal to its journal publisher subscribing institutional libraries – often via a subscription agent."

88 National Universities Commission NUC, 'FG Turning Brain Drain to Brain Gain' 9 (2014) *NUC Bulletin.*

89 Niyi Akinnaso, 'Still on ASUU vs Government' (2013) *PUNCH.*

90 *Nigeria Structural Adjustment Program: Policies, Implementation and Impact. No. 13053-UNI* (1994), available at www-wds.worldbank.org/external/default/WDSContentServer/WDSP/IB/1994/05/13/000009265_3961006113001/Rendered/PDF/multi0page.pdf, accessed on 20/02/2015.

91 Andrew Plume & Daphne Van Weijen, 'Publish or Perish? The Rise of the Fractional Author' 38 (2014) *Research Trend*, available at https://www.researchtrends.com/issue-38-september-2014/publish-or-perish-the-rise-of-the-fractional-author/

92 Olukoju (2004). See also, Ahmed Mohammed, 'The Development of Academic Journals in Institutions of Higher Learning in Kano State, Nigeria' *Library Philosophy and Practice (e-Journal)*, available at http://digitalcommons.unl.edu/cgi/viewcontent.cgi?article=1215&context=libphilprac.

93 Samuel Utulu & Omolara Bolarinwa, 'Open Access Initiatives: Adoption by Nigerian Academics' 58 (2009) *Emerald Law Review.*

94 Olukoju (2004).

95 Daisy Ouya, 'Open Access Survey of Africa-Published Journals' (2006) *INASP*, available at http://citeseerx.ist.psu.edu/viewdoc/summary?doi=10.1.1.490.6967

96 Ezema (2010). See where it says, "The paper recommends that in order to enhance the visibility of African research outputs more journals publishers should be encouraged to join AJOL." See also, AJOL, *African Journals Online*, available at www.ajol.info/, www.ajol.info/.

97 E. S. Gbaje, *Open Access Journal Publishing in Ahmadu Bello University, Zaria, Nigeria*, 76th IFLA: World Library and Information Congress, available at http://conference.ifla.org/past-wlic/2010/138-gbaje-en.pdf; UNESCO, 'Overview of OA in Nigeria' *UNESCO* (2013), available at www.unesco.org/new/en/communication-and-information/portals-and-platforms/goap/access-by-region/africa/nigeria/, www.unesco.org/new/en/communication-and-information/portals-and-platforms/goap/access-by-region/africa/nigeria/.

98 UNESCO, *Overview of OA in Nigeria* (2013), available at www.unesco.org/new/en/communication-and-information/portals-and-platforms/goap/access-by-region/africa/nigeria/.

99 EIFL, *Strategic Approach to Open Access in Nigeria: International Workshop On Open Access Repositories: New Models For Scholarly Communication*, 28–29 April, Ahmadu Bello University, Zaria, Nigeria (Electronic Information for Libraries (EIFL), 2008), www.eifl.net/20080512-strategic-approach-open-access-nigeria.

100 UNESCO, *Overview of OA in Nigeria* (2013), available at www.unesco.org/new/en/communication-and-information/portals-and-platforms/goap/access-by-region/africa/nigeria/.

101 ROARMAP, *Registry of Open Access Repositories Mandatory Archiving Policies*, available at http://roarmap.eprints.org/.

102 Directory of Open Access Journals (DOAJ), *Open Access Journal*, available at www.doaj.org/doaj?func=loadTemplate&template=faq&uiLanguage=en.

103 DSpace, *DSPACE*, available at www.dspace.org/.

104 Eprint, *Eprint*, available at www.eprints.org/software/.

105 Open Archives, *Open Archive Initiative*, available at www.openarchives.org/.

106 G. E. Christian, *Issues and Challenges to the Development of Open Access Institutional Repositories in Academic and Research Institutions in Nigeria*, 7 (2008), International Development Research Centre (IDRC), available at https://idl-bnc.idrc.ca/dspace/bitstream/10625/36986/1/127792.pdf. See also, C. P. Uzuegbu, 'Academic and Research Institutions Repository: A Catalyst for Access to Development Information in Africa' (2012) *IFLA*, available at http://conference.ifla.org/past-wlic/2012/191-uzuegbu-en.pdf. See also, Ivwighreghweta, O. & O. K. Onoriode, "Open Access and Scholarly Publishing: Opportunities and Challenges to Nigerian Researchers" 33 (2012) *Chinese Librarianship: An International Electronic Journal*. 1–13. See also, Ezema (2010). See also, Gbaje (2010).

107 See generally, Christian, 27 (2008). Issues identified includes, poor awareness of IR's, poor state of ICT, inadequate IR advocacy, poor funding, IP and Copyright issues.

108 Ivwighreghweta & Onoriode, 5 (2012). Where it was noted that "Most African countries cannot afford books. . . . This is where OA comes in. In Africa, researchers, students and scholars in general get materials via OA. This way they are able to obtain the latest, updated materials."

109 Uzuegbu, 1 (2012). "that an African-wide policy on IRs creation by concerned institutions, its visibility and interoperability should be made and signed by African countries through organs like the African Union (AU)."

110 UNESCO, *Overview of OA in Nigeria* (2013), available at www.unesco.org/new/en/communication-and-information/portals-and-platforms/goap/access-by-region/africa/nigeria/. The policy was adopted in January 2011 mandating all refereed publications in Journals, conferences and books to be deposited in the University's repository.

111 Tom G. Cochrane & Paula A. Callan, 'Making a Difference: Implementing the Eprints Mandate at QUT' 23 (2007) *International Digital Library Perspectives*.

112 Stevan Harnad et al., 'The Access/Impact Problem and the Green and Gold Roads to Open Access' 30 (2004) *Serial Review* 310-314.

113 AJOL, *African Journals Online*.

114 Bioline International, *Bioline International*, available at www.bioline.org.br/journals.

115 Academic Journals, *Academic Journals*, available at www.academicjournals.org/.

116 Academia Publishing, *Academia Publishing*, available at www.academiapublishing.org/.

117 AJOL, *Nigeria*.

118 BioMed Central, 'Article-Processing Charge' *BioMed Central*, available at www.biomedcentral.com/authors/apc.

119 Murdoch University, *Murdoch University Law Review*, available at https://mdulr.murdoch.edu.au/index.php/mdulr.

120 Public Knowledge Project, *Open Journal System*, available at http://pkp.sfu.ca/ojs/.

121 (DOAJ). See the section on Nigeria, particularly at publication charges.

122 Central.

123 OAU, *Obafemi Awolowo University*, available at www.oauife.edu.ng/.

124 UNIBEN, *University of Benin*, available at www.uniben.edu/.

125 Lou Frenzel, 'Drowning in Information but Starved for Knowledge' *Electronic Design* (2011), available at http://electronicdesign.com/blog/drowning-information-starved-knowledge.

126 The InterAcademy Partnership IAP, *IAP Statement on Access to Scientific Information* (2003), available at www.interacademies.net/10878/13916.aspx. "Access to the vast and varied literature . . . is essential to advances in human health, . . . agriculture, and the preservation of . . . our life. . . . Yet most scientists and research laboratories in developing countries cannot afford the journal subscriptions."

127 Kunle Ola, *Understanding Open Access for Africa*, SSRN 2476739, available at http://papers.ssrn.com/sol3/papers.cfm?abstract_id=2476739.

128 World Health Organization (WHO, *Publishers' Statement of Intent* (2014), available at www.who.int/hinari/statementofintent/en/.
129 WHO, *About HINARI* (2014), available at www.who.int/hinari/about/en/.
130 E. N. Anyaoku & C. V. Anunobi, 'Measuring HINARI Use in Nigeria Through a Citation Analysis of Nigerian Journal of Clinical Practice' 31 (2014) *Health Information and Libraries Journal.*
131 The World Bank, *Data & Statistics: Country Groups*, available at http://econ.worldbank.org/WBSITE/EXTERNAL/DATASTATISTICS/0,contentMDK:20421402~menuPK:64133156~pagePK:64133150~piPK:64133175~theSitePK:239419,00.html.
132 Health Internetwork Access to Research Initiative (HINARI, *HINARI Research in Health: Nigeria*, available at https://extranet.who.int/hinari/en/browse_institutions.php?cntry=81.
133 Ylann Schemm, *Leading the Way with HINARI*, available at http://exchanges.wiley.com/blog/2015/04/15/leading-the-way-with-hinari/.
134 International Network for the Availability of Scientific Publication (INASP), *About*, available at www.inasp.info/en/about/.
135 INASP, *Publishers*, available at www.inasp.info/en/network/publishers/.
136 AUTHORAID, *Supporting Developing Country Research in Publishing Their Work*, available at http://sites.nationalacademies.org/cs/groups/pgasite/documents/webpage/pga_085400.pdf
137 INASP Annual Review. (2012-13). available at http://www.inasp.info/uploads/filer_public/2013/10/24/2012-2013_annual_review.pdf
138 Ibid at 137.
139 AJOL, *African Journals Online*.
140 Margaret Cramption, 'An African Vison for African Journals OnLine (AJOL)' *INASP Newsletter*, available at http://r4d.dfid.gov.uk/PDF/Outputs/Peri/No-29-Newsletter.pdf.
141 Cumming, *African Journals Online* see id. at.
142 African Journal Online (AJOL), *About AJOL: Why Is AJOL Needed?* available at www.ajol.info/index.php/ajol/pages/view/AboutAJOL.
143 Project. The Open Journal Systems (OJS) is a management and publishing system aimed at expanding and improving access to research.
144 Access to Global Online Research In Agriculture, *About Agora* (2014), available at www.aginternetwork.org/en/.
145 OARE, *Online Access to Research in the Environment*, available at www.unep.org/oare/AboutOARE/tabid/129711/language/en-US/Default.aspx.
146 ARDI, *Access to Research for Development and Innovation*, available at www.wipo.int/ardi/en/.
147 Siyavula, *Who We Are Our Story*, available at http://siyavula.com/who-we-are/our-story/.
148 African Legal Information Institute (African LII), *African Law* (2014), available at www.africanlii.org/.
149 Social Science Research Network (SSRN), *Announcing New LSN African Law* (2014), available at www.ssrn.com/update/lsn/lsnann/annA004.html.
150 SSRN, *Social Science Research Network*, available at https://www.ssrn.com/en/
151 Barbara Kirsop et al., 'Access to Scientific Knowledge for Sustainable Development: Options for Developing Countries' *ARIADNE*, available at www.ariadne.ac.uk/issue52/kirsop-et-al.
152 Willinsky, 215–216 (2006).
153 Gutterman, Brian, 'Internet as a Catalyst for Change: Access, Development, Freedoms and Innovation' (Internet Governance Forum (IGF) 2011, available at www.intgovforum.org/cms/documents/publications/176-internet-as-a-catalyst-for-change-access-development-freedoms-and-innovations. See also, Michael Strangelove, 'The

Internet as Catalyst for a Paradigm Shift' 1 (1994) *Computer-Mediated Communication Magazine*. See also, Leavenworth Stuart, *Michelle Obama Urges Open Internet Access in China Speech*, available at www.smh.com.au/world/michelle-obama-urges-open-internet-access-in-china-speech-20140323-hvlvb.html.

154 Harnad et al., (2004).

155 Initiative.

156 Michael Finger & Philip Schuler, *Poor People's Knowledge Promoting Intellectual Property in Developing Countries* (World Bank and Oxford University Press, 2003).

157 See Ola, 17 (2014).

158 Okoye, M. O. & Ejikeme, A. N., 'Open Access, Institutional Repositories, and Scholarly Publishing: The Role of Librarians in South Eastern Nigeria' 2 (2011) *Library Philosophy and Practice (e-Journal)*, 1–9. See also, Datonye Dennis Alasia, 'The Impact of the Open Access Movement on Medical Based Scholarly Publishing in Nigeria' 12 (2007) *First Monday*. See also, EIFL (2008). See also, Gbaje (2010). See also, UNESCO, *Overview of OA in Nigeria* (2013), available at www.unesco.org/new/en/communication-and-information/portals-and-platforms/goap/access-by-region/africa/nigeria/.

159 Olukoju (2004).

160 Brian Fitzgerald et al., *Internet and E-Commerce Law Business and Policy* (Thomson Reuters, 2011), 4.

161 Barbara Kirsop et al., 'Towards Open and Equitable Access to Research and Knowledge for Development' 8 (3) *PLOS Medicine*, available at www.plosmedicine.org/article/fetchObject.action?uri=info%3Adoi%2F10.1371%2Fjournal.pmed.1001016&representation=PDF.

162 Willinsky (2006). See also, Forest Horton, *Public Access to Government Information and Information Literacy Training as Basic Human Rights* (2002), available at https://repository.arizona.edu/handle/10150/105882?show=full Sharif Read, *Maximizing the Value of Public Sector Information for Scientific and Socioeconomic Development in Africa*, available at www.hsrc.ac.za/uploads/pageContent/320/09aug11Sharifpaper.pdf

163 DDC Outsourcing Solutions, *5 Reasons to Digitise Your Documents* (2014), available at www.ddcos.com/5-reasons-to-digitise-your-documents/.

164 Bart Ooghe & Dries Moreels, 'Analysing Selection for Digitisation: Current Practices and Common Incentives' 15 (2009) *D-Lib Magazine*.

165 Matusiak K. K. & T. Johnston, 'Digitization for Preservation and Access: Restoring the Usefulness of the Nitrate Negative Collection at the American Geographical Society Library' 77 (2014) *The American Archivist* 241.

166 J. O. Nkwede, 'Approaches for Poverty Alleviation and Sustainable Development in Nigeria: A Study of Ebonyi State Community Based Poverty Reduction Agency (EB-CPRA)' 2 (2013) *International Journal of Social Science Studies* 7. See also, NSW Department of Education and Communities, *Research Partnership*, available at www.dec.nsw.gov.au/about-us/plans-reports-and-statistics/research-partnerships.

167 See, Z. O. Opafunso, 'An Assessment of the Impact of Government Interventon Projects on Poverty Alleviation/Reduction in Ekiti State, Nigeria' 5 (2014) *Mediterranean Journal of Social Sciences* 1.

168 Khan Academy, *Our Mission*, available at www.khanacademy.org/about.

169 Wikiversity, available at http://en.wikiversity.org/wiki/Wikiversity:Main_Page.

170 P2PU, *School of Open*, available at https://p2pu.org/en/schools/school-of-open/.

171 CopyrightX, available at http://blogs.law.harvard.edu/copyrightx/.

172 See, David W. Lewis, 'The Inevitability of Open Access' 73 (2012) *College & Research Libraries* 497–498. The author refers to it as disruptive innovation and notes that it makes products easier to access and cheaper to buy.

173 R. D. Christy & V. L. Bogan, *Financial Inclusion, Innovation, and Investments: Biotechnology and Capital Markets Working for the Poor* (World Scientific Publishing Company, 2011), 144. The Scopus database was used to measure knowledge based on countries and it was noted that North America (The United States and Canada) was responsible for the majority of knowledge output. They accounted for about 36 percent.

174 See A. Toffler, *Future Shock* (Bantam Books, 1990), 89. where he referred to the impact of knowledge explosion. See also, Dougald Hind, *What Good Is Information?* available at http://aeon.co/magazine/living-together/the-problem-with-too-much-information/.

175 Rogers Paul et al., 'Infobesity: The Enemy of Good Decisions' *Insight*, available at www.bain.com/publications/articles/infobesity-the-enemy-of-good-decisions.aspx.

176 See Area Manuel & Pessoa Teresa, 'From the Solid to the Liquid: New Literacies for the Cultural Changes of Web 2.0' *Comunicar*. Where it was noted that "One of the most remarkable phenomena marking the start of this century is the excess of information generated by the exponential increase of that information. . . . This has been dubbed 'infoxication' available at https://www.revistacomunicar.com/pdf/preprint/38/En-01-PRE-12378.pdf. See also, John Moravec, 'Infoxication 2.0' *Education Futures* (2008), available at www.educationfutures.com/2008/10/24/infoxication-20/.

177 Edward Shizha, 'Reclaiming Our Indigenous Voices: The Problem with Postcolonial Sub-Saharan African School Curriculum' 2 (2013) *Journal of Indigenous Social Development*.

178 See Barbara Kirsop et al., 'Access to Scientific Knowledge for Sustainable Development: Options for Developing Countries' *ARIADNE*, available at www.ariadne.ac.uk/issue52/kirsop-et-al. "Exchange of research findings must be bi-directional since research information generated in emerging countries is crucial to solving global problems. . . . Fortunately, the establishment of IRs in the developing world . . . and the conversion to OA of journals . . . help close the south-north digital divide that is too often considered unimportant and ignored by the development communities."

179 See, Olivia A. Cole, *Hollywood and the Shaping of perception of Racism* (2013), available at https://oliviaacole.wordpress.com/2013/12/24/hollywood-and-the-shaping-of-perceptions-about-racism/. "It is a known fact that the media we consume shapes our perception of the world: after all, media has economic, political, social and aesthetic purposes" See also, Mark Weber, *Hollywood's Agenda, and he Power Behind It*, available at www.ihr.org/hollywoodagenda_weber.html. "But his remark was another reminder of Hollywood's tremendous, global influence, and of how misleading its imagery can be." See also, Douglas S. Winnail, 'How the Media Mold the World' *Tomorrow's World* (2003), available at www.tomorrowsworld.org/magazines/2003/january-february/how-the-media-mold-the-world. "This small group of liberal-minded social revolutionaries has turned the Hollywood dream factory into a 'poison factory' that attacks religion, assaults the legitimacy of the family, promotes sexual perversions and glorifies ugliness."

180 Deborah Yakubu Dangana, *Nigeria: How Western Culture Erodes Values Among Nigerian Youths*, available at http://allafrica.com/stories/201408081141.html. "Man is essentially, the product of his culture. . . . Nigeria which is made up of rich and diverse cultural values is beginning to lose most its cultural ideals especially through the adoption of foreign culture showcased through the mass media."

181 Stephen Graham, 'Bridging Urban Digital Divides? Urban Polarisation and Information and Communications Technologies (ICTs)' 39 (2002) *Urban Studies* 39–40. "The societal diffusion of information and communication technologies (ICTs) remain starkly uneven at all scales." See also, Wenhong Chen & Barry Wellman, 'The Global

Digital Divide – Within and Between Countries' 1 (2004) *IT & Society* 18. "Telecommunications policies, infrastructures and education are prerequisites for marginalized communities to participate in the information age. High costs, English language dominance, the lack of relevant content, and the lack of technological support are barriers for disadvantaged communities using computers and the Internet."

182 Kunle Ola, 'Fundamentals of Open Access' 36 (2) (2014) *European Intellectual Property Review* 112, 113–115." The advent of digital technology and the internet altered the information sharing system and . . . no doubt influenced the open access movement"

183 Strangelove (1994).

184 J. Y. Oricha & G. A. Olarinoye, 'Analysis of Interrelated Factors Affecting Efficency and Stability of Power Supply in Nigeria' 2 (2012) *International Journal of Energy Engineering* 1. See also, E. O. George & J. E. Oseni, 'The Relationship Between Electricity Power and Unemployment Rates in Nigeria' 2 (2012) *Australian Journal of Business and Management Research* 10. See also, M. Emwanta & K. I. Nwalo, 'Influence of Computer Literacy and Subject Background on Use of Electronic Resources by Undergraduate Students in Universities in South-Western Nigeria' 5 (2012) *International Journal of Library and Information Science*. See also, L. A. Ogunsola et al., 'Information Literacy In Nigerian Higher Institutions – Any Role for Librarians?' 4 (2011) *Ozean Journal of Social Sciences*.

Bibliography

Academia Publishing, *Academia Publishing*, available at www.academiapublishing.org/.

Academic Journals, *Academic Journals*, available at www.academicjournals.org/.

Access to Global Online Research in Agriculture, *About Agora* (2014), available at www.aginternetwork.org/en/.

BIS & David Willetts, *Letter to Dame Janet Finch on the Government Response to the Finch Group Report: Accessibility, Sustainability, Excellence: How to Expand Access to Research Publications* (2012), available at www.gov.uk/government/uploads/system/uploads/attachment_data/file/32493/12-975-letter-government-response-to-finch-report-research-publications.pdf.Adams, Caralee, Open Access in Latin America: Embraced as Key to Visibility of Research, *SPARC*, available at www.sparc.arl.org/news/open-access-latin-america-embraced-key-visibility-research-outputs.

African Legal Information Institute (African LII), *African law* (2014), available at www.africanlii.org/.

Ajao, O. G. & B. T. Ugwu, 'Some Problems Facing Scientific Medical Publication in Nigeria' 1 (2011) *Journal of the West African College of Surgeons*.

AJOL, *About AJOL: Why Is AJOL Needed?* available at www.ajol.info/index.php/ajol/pages/view/AboutAJOL.

AJOL, *African Journals Online*, available at www.ajol.info/.

AJOL, *Nigeria*, available at www.ajol.info/index.php/index/browse/country?countryId=156.

Akinnaso, Niyi, Still on ASUU vs Government (2013) *Punch*.

Anyaoku, E. N. & C. V. Anunobi, 'Measuring HINARI Use in Nigeria Through a Citation Analysis of Nigerian Journal of Clinical Practice' 31 (2014) *Health Information and Libraries Journal*.

ARC, *About ARC*, available at www.arc.gov.au/about_arc/default.htm.

ARC, *ARC Open Access Policy*, available at www.arc.gov.au/applicants/open_access.htm.

ARDI, *Access to Research for Development and Innovation*, available at www.wipo.int/ardi/en/.

Austin, Anthony, et al., *Academic Authorship, Publishing Agreements and Open Access: Survey Results* (Queensland University of Technology, 2008).

AUTHORAID, *Supporting Developing Country Research in Publishing Their Work*, available at http://sites.nationalacademies.org/cs/groups/pgasite/documents/webpage/pga_085400.pdf.

Benkler, Y., *The Wealth of Networks: How Social Production Transforms Markets and Freedom* (Yale University Press, 2006).

Berne Convention for the Protection of Literary and Artistic Works, 9 September 1886, amended last on 28 September 1979.

Bill and Melinda Gate, *Bill & Melinda Gates Foundation Open Access Policy*, available at www.gatesfoundation.org/How-We-Work/General-Information/Open-Access-Policy.

Bioline International, *Bioline International*, available at www.bioline.org.br/journals.

BioMed Central, Article-Processing Charge, *BioMed Central*, available at www.biomedcentral.com/authors/apc.

BIS, *Open Access: Responses to the Committee's Fifth Report of Session 2013–14* (2013), available at https://www.rsb.org.uk/images/ResponsetoBIScom.pdf

BIS, *Progress Review: Implementing Finch Report Recommendations* (BIS, London, 2014),

BIS & David Willetts, *Letter to Dame Janet Finch on the Government Response to the Finch Group Report: "Accessibility, Sustainability, Excellence: How to Expand Access to Research Publications"* (2012), available at www.gov.uk/government/uploads/system/uploads/attachment_data/file/32493/12-975-letter-government-response-to-finch-report-research-publications.pdf.

Brownmark Films, LLC v Comedy Partners, 800 F. Supp. 2d 991 (D. Wis. 2011).

Budapest Open Access Initiative, *Ten Years on From the Budapest Open Access Initiative: Setting the Default to Open*, available at www.opensocietyfoundations.org/openaccess/boai-10-recommendations.

Canadian Institutes of Health Research, *Tri-Agency Open Access Policy on Publications* (2015), available at www.cihr-irsc.gc.ca/e/32005.html.

Carrol, Michael, 'Complying with the NIH Public Access Policy – Copyright Considerations and Options' (2008) *SPARC Open Access Newsletter*.

Chen, Wenhong & Barry Wellman, 'The Global Digital Divide – Within and Between Countries' 1 (2004) *IT & Society*.

Christian, G. E., *Issues and Challenges to the Development of Open Access Institutional Repositories in Academic and Research Institutions in Nigeria* (2008), International Development Research Centre (IDRC), available at https://idl-bnc.idrc.ca/dspace/bitstream/10625/36986/1/127792.pdf.

Christy, R. D. & V. L. Bogan, *Financial Inclusion, Innovation, and Investments: Biotechnology and Capital Markets Working for the Poor* (World Scientific Publishing Company, 2011).

Cochrane, Tom G. & Paula A. Callan, 'Making a Difference: Implementing the Eprints Mandate at QUT' 23 (2007) *International Digital Library Perspectives*.

Cole, Olivia A., *Hollywood and the Shaping of Perception of Racism* (2013), available at https://oliviaacole.wordpress.com/2013/12/24/hollywood-and-the-shaping-of-perceptions-about-racism/.

CopyrightX, available at http://blogs.law.harvard.edu/copyrightx/.

Cramption, Margaret, 'An African Vison for African Journals OnLine (AJOL)' *INASP Newsletter*, available at http://r4d.dfid.gov.uk/PDF/Outputs/Peri/No-29-Newsletter.pdf.

Cumming, Sioux, 'African Journals Online' *INASP Newsletter*, available at http://r4d.dfid.gov.uk/PDF/Outputs/Peri/No-29-Newsletter.pdf.

Davis, Phil, Publish-or-Perish Culture Promotes Scientific Narcissism, *The Scholarly Kitchen*, available at http://scholarlykitchen.sspnet.org/2012/05/07/publish-or-perish-culture-promotes-scientific-narcissism/.

DDC Outsourcing Solutions, *5 Reasons to Digitise Your Documents* (2014), available at www.ddcos.com/5-reasons-to-digitise-your-documents/.

Dennis Alasia, Datonye, 'The Impact of the Open Access Movement on Medical Based Scholarly Publishing in Nigeria' 12 (2007) *First Monday*.

'Directory of Open Access Journals (DOAJ)' *Open Access Journal*, available at www.doaj.org/doaj?func=loadTemplate&template=faq&uiLanguage=en.

Dspace, *DSPACE*, available at www.dspace.org/.

EIFL, *Strategic Approach to Open Access in Nigeria: International Workshop on Open Access Repositories: New Models for Scholarly Communication*, 28–29 April, Ahmadu Bello University, Zaria, Nigeria (Electronic Information for Libraries [EIFL], [2008]).

Elsevier, *Copyright*, available at www.elsevier.com/about/company-information/policies/copyright#openaccess.

Emwanta, M. & K. I. Nwalo, 'Influence of Computer Literacy and Subject Background on Use of Electronic Resources by Undergraduate Students in Universities in South-Western Nigeria' 5 (2012) *International Journal of Library and Information Science*.

Eprint, *Eprint*, available at www.eprints.org/software/.

ERC, *About ERC*, available at http://erc.europa.eu/about-erc.

ERC, *ERC Work Programme 2015 (European Commission C (2014)5008 of 22 July 2014)* (2015).

ERC, *Facts and Figures*, available at http://erc.europa.eu/about-erc/facts-and-figures.

ERC, *History*, available at http://erc.europa.eu/about-erc/history.

EU, *Communication from the Commission to the European Parliament, the Council, the European Economic and Social Committee and the Committee of the Regions: Towards Better Access to Scientific Information: Boosting the Benefits of Public Investments in Research* (2012), available at http://ec.europa.eu/research/science-society/document_library/pdf_06/era-communication-towards-better-access-to-scientific-information_en.pdf.

EU, *The EU Framework Programme for Research and Innovation: Horizon 2020: Guidelines on Open Access to Scientific Publications and Research Data in Horizon 2020* (2012), available at http://ec.europa.eu/research/participants/data/ref/h2020/grants_manual/hi/oa_pilot/h2020-hi-oa-pilot-guide_en.pdf.

EU, *FP7: Research and Innovation Funding 2014–2020*, available at http://ec.europa.eu/research/fp7/index_en.cfm.

EU, *Open Access to scientific information*, available at http://ec.europa.eu/digital-agenda/en/open-access-scientific-information.

Ezema, J. I., Trends in Electronic Journal Publishing in Africa: An Analysis of African Journal Online (AJOL) *Webology*, available at www.webology.org/2010/v7n1/a74.html.

Finch Report, *Report of the Working Group on Expanding Access to Published Research Findings* (2012), available at https://www.acu.ac.uk/research-information-network/finch-report-final.

Finger, Michael & Philip Schuler, *Poor People's Knowledge Promoting Intellectual Property in Developing Countries* (World Bank and Oxford University Press, 2003).

First Monday, 'Peer-Reviewed Journal on the Internet' available at http://firstmonday.org/index.

Fitzgerald, Brian, et al., *Internet and E-Commerce Law Business and Policy* (Thomson Reuters, 2011).

Fitzgerald, Brian, et al., OAK LAW PROJECT NO.1: Creating a Legal Framework for Copyright Management of Open Access Within the Australian Academic and Research Sector (Report for the Department of Education and Science and Training (DEST) (2006).

Ford Foundation, *Issues*, available at www.fordfoundation.org/issues.

Ford Foundation, *Ford Foundation Expand Creative Commons Licensing for All Grant-Funded Projects* (2015), available at www.fordfoundation.org/newsroom/news-from-ford/934.

Ford Foundation, *Mission*, available at www.fordfoundation.org/about-us/mission.

Frenzel, Lou, Drowning in Information but Starved for Knowledge, *Electronic Design* (2011), available at http://electronicdesign.com/blog/drowning-information-starved-knowledge.

Gbaje, E. S., *Open Access Journal Publishing in Ahmadu Bello University, Zaria, Nigeria*, 76th IFLA: World Library and Information Congress, available at http://conference.ifla.org/past-wlic/2010/138-gbaje-en.pdf.

GenBank, *GenBank Overview*, available at www.ncbi.nlm.nih.gov/genbank/.

George, E. O. & J. E. Oseni, 'The Relationship Between Electricity Power and Unemployment Rates in Nigeria' 2 (2012) *Australian Journal of Business and Management Research.*

Global Open Access Portal, *Brazil*.

Government of Canada, *Minister Holder Announces New Open Access Policy for Research* (2015), available at www.science.gc.ca/default.asp?lang=En&n=415B5097-1.

Graham, Stephen, 'Bridging Urban Digital Divides? Urban Polarisation and Information and Communications Technologies (ICTs)' 39 (2002) *Urban Studies*.

Gutterman, Brian, 'Internet as a Catalyst for Change: Access, Development, Freedoms and Innovation' *(Internet Governance Forum (IGF) 2011*, available at www.intgovforum.org/cms/documents/publications/176-internet-as-a-catalyst-for-change-access-development-freedoms-and-innovations

Harnad, Stevan, 'The Open Challenge: A Brief History. Public Service Review: European Science & Technology' 9 (2010) *Public Service Review: European Science & Technology*, 13–15.

Harnad, Stevan & Nancy McGovern, 'Institutional Repository Success Is Dependent Upon Mandates' 36 (2009) *Bulletin of the American Society for Information Science and Technology* 27.

Harnad, Stevan, et al., 'The Access/Impact Problem and the Green and Gold Roads to Open Access' 30 (2004) *Serial Review*, 310–314.

HINARI, *HINARI Research in Health: Nigeria*, available at https://extranet.who.int/hinari/en/browse_institutions.php?cntry=81.

Hind, Dougald, *What Good Is Information?* available at http://aeon.co/magazine/living-together/the-problem-with-too-much-information/.

Horton, Forest, *Public Access to Government Information and Information Literacy Training as Basic Human Rights* (2002), available at https://repository.arizona.edu/handle/10150/105882?show=full

House of Lords, *The Implementation of Open Access* (2013), available at www.publications.parliament.uk/pa/ld201213/ldselect/ldsctech/122/122.pdf.

IFLA, *IFLA/Brill Open Access Award 2015 Goes to DOAB*, available at www.ifla.org/node/9630.

INASP, *About*, available at www.inasp.info/en/about/.

INASP Annual Review (2012–13).

INASP, *Publishers*, available at www.inasp.info/en/network/publishers/.

Innovation and Skills Committee House of Commons Business, *Open Access* (2013), available at www.publications.parliament.uk/pa/cm201314/cmselect/cmbis/99/9902.htm.

The InterAcademy Partnership IAP, *IAP Statement on Access to Scientific Information* (2003), available at www.interacademies.net/10878/13916.aspx.

Ivwighreghweta, O. & O. K. Onoriode, 'Open Access and Scholarly Publishing: Opportunities and Challenges to Nigerian Researchers' 33 (2012) *Chinese Librarianship: An International Electronic Journal*, 1–13.

JOAL, *Journal of Open Access to Law*, available at https://ojs.law.cornell.edu/index.php/joal.

Khan Academy, *Our Mission*, available at www.khanacademy.org/about.

Kirsop, Barbara, et al., Access to Scientific Knowledge for Sustainable Development: Options for Developing Countries, *ARIADNE*, available at www.ariadne.ac.uk/issue52/kirsop-et-al.

Kirsop, Barbara, et al., 'Towards Open and Equitable Access to Research and Knowledge for Development' 8 (3) *PLOS Medicine*, available at www.plosmedicine.org/article/fetchObject.action?uri=info%3Adoi%2F10.1371%2Fjournal.pmed.1001016&representation=PDF.

Lewis, David W., 'The Inevitability of Open Access' 73 (2012) *College & Research Libraries*.

Liang, Lawrence, *Guide to Open Content Licenses v1.2* (Piet Zwart Institute, Institute for postgraduate studies and research, Willem de Kooning Academy Hogeschool, 2004).

Manuel, Area & Pessoa Teresa, 'From the Solid to the Liquid: New Literacies for the Cultural Changes of Web 2.0' *Comunicar*, available at https://www.revistacomunicar.com/pdf/preprint/38/En-01-PRE-12378.pdf

Matusiak, K. K. & T. Johnston, 'Digitization for Preservation and Access: Restoring the Usefulness of the Nitrate Negative Collection at the American Geographical Society Library' 77 (2014) *The American Archivist*.

McIntyre, Gordon, et al., 'Library as Scholarly Publishing Partner: Keys to Success' 2 (2013) *Journal of Librarianship and Scholarly Communication*, 1–12.

Mohammed, Ahmed, 'The Development of Academic Journals in Institutions of Higher Learning in Kano State, Nigeria' *Library Philosophy and Practice (e-Journal)*, available at http://digitalcommons.unl.edu/cgi/viewcontent.cgi?article=1215&context=libphilprac.

Moravec, John, Infoxication 2.0, *Education Futures* (2008), available at www.educationfutures.com/2008/10/24/infoxication-20/.

Murdoch University, *Murdoch University Law Review*, available at https://mdulr.murdoch.edu.au/index.php/mdulr.

National Universities Commission NUC, 'FG Turning Brain Drain to Brain Gain' 9 (2014) *NUC Bulletin*.

National Universities Commission NUC, *List of Approved Universities in Nigeria* (2014), National Universities Commission, 7, available at www.nuc.edu.ng/nucsite/File/Monday%20Bulletin/MB%202014/MONDAY%20Bulletin%2003-02-2014.pdf.

Nigerian Field Society, *The Nigerian Field Society*, available at www.nigerianfield.org/.

Nigeria Structural Adjustment Program: Policies, Implementation and Impact. No. 13053-UNI (1994).

NIH, *About NIH*, available at www.nih.gov/about/.

NIH, *NIH Data Sharing Policy* (2003), available at http://grants.nih.gov/grants/policy/data_sharing/.

NIH, *NIH Mission*, available at www.nih.gov/about/mission.htm.

Nkwede, J. O., 'Approaches for Poverty Alleviation and Sustainable Development in Nigeria: A Study of Ebonyi State Community Based Poverty Reduction Agency (EB-CPRA)' 2 (2013) *International Journal of Social Science Studies*.

Norrie, Justin, Harvard Decries the High Cost of Journal Subscription, *The Conversation* (2012), available at http://theconversation.edu.au/harvard-journal-subscription-fees-are-prohibitive-6659, 24 April.

NRC-CISTI, *NRC Publications Archive Statement of Responsibilities*, available at http://cisti-icist.nrc-cnrc.gc.ca/obj/cisti-icist/doc/nparc/NPArC-Statement-of-Responsibilities_e.pdf.

NSW Department of Education and Communities, *Research Partnership*, available at www.dec.nsw.gov.au/about-us/plans-reports-and-statistics/research-partnerships.

OARE, *Online Access to Research in the Environment*, available at www.unep.org/oare/AboutOARE/tabid/129711/language/en-US/Default.aspx.

OAU, *Obafemi Awolowo University*, available at www.oauife.edu.ng/.

Organisation for Economic Co-operation and Development, *Declaration on Access to Research Data from Public Funding: 30 March 2004 [C(2004)31/REV1]* (2004), available at http://acts.oecd.org/Instruments/ShowInstrumentView.aspx?InstrumentID=157.

Organisation for Economic Co-operation and Development, *OECD Principles and Guidelines on Access to Research Data from Public Funding* (2007), available at www.oecd.org/science/sci-tech/38500813.pdf.

Ogunsola, L. A., et al., 'Information Literacy in Nigerian Higher Institutions – Any Role for Librarians?' 4 (2011) *Ozean Journal of Social Sciences*.

Okoye, M. O. & Ejikeme, A. N., 'Open Access, Institutional Repositories, and Scholarly Publishing: The Role of Librarians in South Eastern Nigeria' 2 (2011) *Library Philosophy and Practice (e-Journal)*, 1–9.

Okri, Ben, *F@T BEN OKRI, 19 Jan 2015, 06: 42* (2015), available at http://first-thoughts.org/on/Ben+Okri/.

Ola, Kunle, 'Fundamentals of Open Access' 36 (2) (2014) *European Intellectual Property Review* 112.

Ola, Kunle, *Understanding Open Access for Africa*, SSRN 2476739, available at http://papers.ssrn.com/sol3/papers.cfm?abstract_id=2476739.

Olukoju, Ayodejo, 'The Crisis of Research and Academic Publishing in Nigerian Universities' (2004) *CiteSeer*, available at http://citeseerx.ist.psu.edu/viewdoc/download;jsessionid=31963D03475BE7DB5BE1EF1BBE75E8AD?doi=10.1.1.99.214&rep=rep1&type=pdf

Ooghe, Bart & Dries Moreels, 'Analysing Selection for Digitisation: Current Practices and Common Incentives' 15 (2009) *D-Lib Magazine*.

Opafunso, Z. O., 'An Assessment of the Impact of Government Intervention Projects on Poverty Alleviation/Reduction in Ekiti State, Nigeria' 5 (2014) *Mediterranean Journal of Social Sciences*.

Julie Caruso, Aurore Nicol & Eric Archambault, *Open Access Strategies in the European Research Area: RTD-B6-PP-2011–2: Study to Develop a Set of Indicators to Measure Open Access* (Science Metrix, 2013), available at www.science-metrix.com/pdf/SM_EC_OA_Policies.pdf

Open Archives, *Open Archive Initiative*, available at www.openarchives.org/.

Oricha, J. Y. & G. A. Olarinoye, 'Analysis of Interrelated Factors Affecting Efficiency and Stability of Power Supply in Nigeria' 2 (2012) *International Journal of Energy Engineering*.

Ouya, Daisy, 'Open Access Survey of Africa-Published Journals' (2006) *INASP*, available at http://citeseerx.ist.psu.edu/viewdoc/summary?doi=10.1.1.490.6967

P2PU, *School of Open*, available at https://p2pu.org/en/schools/school-of-open/.

Plume, Andrew & Daphne Van Weijen, *Publish or Perish? The Rise of the Fractional Author* 33 (2014) Research Trend, available at https://www.researchtrends.com/issue-38-september-2014/publish-or-perish-the-rise-of-the-fractional-author/

'Public Knowledge Project', *Open Journal System*, available at http://pkp.sfu.ca/ojs/.

PubChem, *PubChem*, available at http://pubchem.ncbi.nlm.nih.gov/.

PubMed, *PubMed*, National Institutes of Health (NIH), *available at* www.ncbi.nlm.nih.gov/pubmed/.

QS Topuniversities, *Top Universities in the World 2014/15* (2014), available at www.topuniversities.com/university-rankings-articles/world-university-rankings/top-universities-world-201415.

RCUK, *2014 Independent Review of Implementation*, available at www.rcuk.ac.uk/research/openaccess/2014review/.

RCUK, *Open Access*, available at www.rcuk.ac.uk/research/openaccess/.

RCUK, *RCUK Aims & Objectives*, available at www.rcuk.ac.uk/about/aboutrcuk/aims/.

RCUK, *RCUK Policy on Open Access*, available at www.rcuk.ac.uk/research/Pages/outputs.aspx.

RCUK, *RCUK Policy on Open Access and Supporting Guidance* (2013), available at http://webcache.googleusercontent.com/search?q=cache: 9mcesRxkWHgJ: www.rcuk.ac.uk/RCUK-prod/assets/documents/documents/RCUKOpenAccessPolicy.pdf+&cd=1&hl=en&ct=clnk&gl=uk.

RCUK, *RCUK Position Statement on Access to Research Outputs* (2005), available at www.rcuk.ac.uk/RCUK-prod/assets/documents/documents/2005statement.pdf.

Read, Sharif, *Maximizing the Value of Public Sector Information for Scientific and Socioeconomic Development in Africa*, available at www.hsrc.ac.za/uploads/pageContent/320/09aug11Sharifpaper.pdf.

Research Information Network & Stephane Goldstein, *Expanding Access to Published Research Findings* (2011), available at www.rin.ac.uk/news/press/expanding-access-published-research-findings.

Kenneth D Crews, *Reserving Rights of Use in Works Submitted for Publication: Negotiating Publishing Agreements. A Project of the IUPUI Copyright Management Center*. (Indiana University-Purdue University Indianapolis, 2004).

ROARMAP, *Registry of Open Access Repositories Mandatory Archiving Policies*, available at http://roarmap.eprints.org/.

Rogers, Paul, et al., 'Infobesity: The Enemy of Good Decisions' *Insight*, available at www.bain.com/publications/articles/infobesity-the-enemy-of-good-decisions.aspx.

Schemm, Ylann, *Leading the Way with HINARI*, available at http://exchanges.wiley.com/blog/2015/04/15/leading-the-way-with-hinari/.

SciELO, *Scientific Electronic Library Online*, available at www.scielo.br/.

Scientific Publications: Free for All? Tenth Report of Session 2003–04 (2004), available at www.publications.parliament.uk/pa/cm200304/cmselect/cmsctech/399/399.pdf.

Shizha, Edward, 'Reclaiming Our Indigenous Voices: The Problem with Postcolonial Sub-Saharan African School Curriculum' 2 (2013) *Journal of Indigenous Social Development*.

Siyavula, *Who We Are Our Story*, available at http://siyavula.com/who-we-are/our-story/.

Springer, *Self-Archiving Policy*, available at www.springer.com/gp/open-access/authors-rights/self-archiving-policy/2124.

SSRN, *Announcing New LSN African Law* (2014), available at www.ssrn.com/update/lsn/lsnann/annA004.html.

SSRN, *Social Science Research Network*, https://www.ssrn.com/en/

The STM Report, *An Overview of Scientific and Scholarly Publishing* (Mark Ware Consulting, 2012), available at www.markwareconsulting.com/articles-reports/the-stm-report-an-overview-of-scientific-and-scholarly-journal-publishing-2/

Strangelove, Michael, 'The Internet as Catalyst for a Paradigm Shift' 1 (1994) *Computer-Mediated Communication Magazine*.

Stuart, Leavenworth, *Michelle Obama Urges Open Internet Access in China Speech*, available at www.smh.com.au/world/michelle-obama-urges-open-internet-access-in-china-speech-20140323-hvlvb.html.

Suber, P., *AHRC Announces Its OA Policy* (2007), available at http://legacy.earlham.edu/~peters/fos/2007/09/ahrc-announces-its-oa-policy.html.

Sybersound Records, Inc. v UAV Corp., 517 F. 3d 1137 – Court of Appeals, 9th Circuit (2008).

Times Higher Education, *RCUK Open-Access Guidance Revised* (2013), available at www.timeshighereducation.co.uk/news/rcuk-open-access-guidance-revised/2002396.article.

Toffler, A., *Future Shock* (Bantam Books, 1990).

UNESCO, *Global Open Access Portal*, available at www.unesco.org/new/en/communication-and-information/portals-and-platforms/goap/.

UNESCO, *Open Educational Resources*, available at www.unesco.org/new/en/communication-and-information/access-to-knowledge/open-educational-resources/.

UNESCO, *Overview of OA in Nigeria* (2013), available at www.unesco.org/new/en/communication-and-information/portals-and-platforms/goap/access-by-region/africa/nigeria/, www.unesco.org/new/en/communication-and-information/portals-and-platforms/goap/access-by-region/africa/nigeria/.

UNIBEN, *University of Benin*, available at www.uniben.edu/.

Utulu, Samuel & Omolara Bolarinwa, *Open Access Initiatives: Adoption by Nigerian Academics*, 58 (2009) *Emerald Law Review*.

Uzuegbu, C. P., Academic and Research Institutions Repository: A Catalyst for Access to Development Information in Africa, *IFLA* (2012), available at http://conference.ifla.org/past-wlic/2012/191-uzuegbu-en.pdf.

Weber, Mark, *Hollywood's Agenda, and he Power Behind It*, available at www.ihr.org/hollywoodagenda_weber.html.

Wellcome Trust, *Funding*, available at www.wellcome.ac.uk/Funding/index.htm.

Wellcome Trust, *History*, available at www.wellcome.ac.uk/About-us/History/index.htm.

Wellcome Trust, *Open Access Policy: Position Statement in Support of Open and Unrestricted Access to Published Research*, available at www.wellcome.ac.uk/About-us/Policy/Policy-and-position-statements/WTD002766.htm.

Wellcome Trust, *Open Access at the Wellcome Trust*, available at www.wellcome.ac.uk/about-us/policy/spotlight-issues/Open-access/index.htm.

Wellcome Trust, *Our Vision*, available at www.wellcome.ac.uk/Our-vision/index.htm.

Wellcome Trust Strategic Plan 2010–2020 (2010), available at www.wellcome.ac.uk/stellent/groups/corporatesite/@policy_communications/documents/web_document/WTDV027438.pdf.

WHO, *About HINARI* (2014), available at www.who.int/hinari/about/en/.

WHO, *Publishers' Statement of Intent* (2014), available at www.who.int/hinari/statementofintent/en/.

wikiversity, available at http://en.wikiversity.org/wiki/Wikiversity: Main_Page.

The William and Flora Hewlett Foundation, *Commitment to Open Licensing*, available at www.hewlett.org/about-us/values-policies/commitment-open-licensing.

The William and Flora Hewlett Foundation, *Open Educational Resources Initiative* (2005), available at https://hewlett.org/library/open-educational-resources-initiative/

The William and Flora Hewlett Foundation, *Programs*, available at www.hewlett.org/programs.

Willinsky, John, *The Access Principle: The Case for Open Access to Research and Scholarship* (MIT Press, 2006).

Winnail, Douglas S., 'How the Media Mold the World' *Tomorrow's World* (2003), available at www.tomorrowsworld.org/magazines/2003/january-february/how-the-media-mold-the-world.

The World Bank, *Data & Statistics: Country Groups*, available at http://econ.worldbank.org/WBSITE/EXTERNAL/DATASTATISTICS/0,contentMDK: 20421402~menuPK: 64133156~pagePK: 64133150~piPK: 64133175~theSitePK: 239419,00.html.

The World Bank, *Open Knowledge Repository*, available at https://openknowledge.worldbank.org/.

The World Bank, *World Bank Announces Open Access Policy for Research and Knowledge, Launches Open Knowledge Repository* (2012), available at www.worldbank.org/en/news/press-release/2012/04/10/world-bank-announces-open-access-policy-for-research-and-knowledge-launches-open-knowledge-repository.

Yakubu Dangana, Deborah, *Nigeria: How Western Culture Erodes Values Among Nigerian Youths*, available at http://allafrica.com/stories/201408081141.html.

Zoria, Ana, *Nigeria's Publishing Industry: Telling Our Own Stories*, available at www.pambazuka.net/en/category/books/93917.

5 Open educational resources

1 Introduction

Open educational resources (OER) have been developed as tools and a means of addressing lack of access to educational materials globally and are a technological response to education in an era with unprecedented growth in technology. They provide an almost instantaneous solution to the financial, technical and access challenges faced by the educational system.[1] The imperatives for developing these tools are not unconnected to the enabling possibilities provided by Information Communication Technology (ICT), in particular the Internet, for information dissemination and distribution.

Education for all is important.[2] Particular emphasis is on the girl child due to their high illiteracy rate.[3] Although illiteracy has been successfully addressed in a number of developing nations where they are able to boast of an above 95 percent literacy level, this is not the case in several developing countries.[4] The countries with the highest need for education seem to be facing the greatest challenges to accessing education.[5] Thirteen countries account for the highest levels of illiteracy globally, and Nigeria is one of those countries.[6] The challenges faced in the pursuit for education for all in these countries include lack of political will on the part of government,[7] poverty, corruption, lack of infrastructure,[8] war[9] and the growing trend of terrorism exemplified by the activities of Boko Haram within the northern part of Nigeria, activities which are frustrating the strategies that are being put in place to address illiteracy.[10]

These clandestine activities allow the reign of illiteracy. Education for all is about turning on the light, but many factors including corruption, war, poverty, poor infrastructural facilities, lack of proper planning, budgeting, budgetary allocation, implementation and terrorism are destroying the structures providing "light", that is, education. The goal of education for all is a goal to turn on the light and is a goal that must not be frustrated. If conventional strategies to accessing knowledge are being frustrated, it is imperative on all well-meaning persons to seek alternative strategies, such as those provided by ICT and the Internet in delivering quality education. OER is one of such strategies.

Education is a right, it is an empowerment tool, and it is no surprise that the Obama Administration committed US$2 billion in support of OER which are tools that enable easy access, availability, use and reuse rights to educational resources. These tools address lack of access to knowledge and education and help in actualizing one of the fundamental rights; the right to education.[11]

2 Definition of OER

There are several definitions of OER. This section provides some of the definitions which will reflect the different perspectives of OER. Regardless of the perspective, fundamental issues run through each of these definitions, and will be explained.

The build up to the term OER can be linked to two terms: *learning object* and *Open Courseware*. In 1994, Wayne Hodgins birthed the learning object term which found deeper expression as educators and instructional designers began to make use of it.[12] The term learning objects refer to digital materials that can be created for use and reuse in a variety of pedagogical instances.[13]

The term Open Courseware comes from a Massachusetts Institute of Technology (MIT) initiative through which most of its educational course materials are openly made available for use and reuse.[14] It was the first of its kind and was named MIT OpenCourseWare (OCW).[15] The OCW consortium has emerged as an off-shoot of the MIT OCW under the leadership of MIT and the Hewlett Foundation. The OCW-consortium website provides useful information on OCW projects carried on in different parts of the world, especially in developing countries.[16]

The term OER was however first coined at a United Nations Educational, Scientific and Cultural Organization's (UNESCO) meeting held in 2002 in Paris, where educators meet in response to the feedbacks, impacts and inspirations from Open Courseware and decided on the need for greater access to educational resources for all of mankind especially to those from disadvantaged regions.[17] Johnstone noted that the meeting defined OER as "the open provision of educational resources, enabled by information and communication technologies, for consultation, use and adaptation by a community of users for non-commercial purposes".[18]

The United Nations Educational, Scientific and Cultural Organization (UNESCO) defines OER as "teaching, learning or research materials that are in the public domain or released with an intellectual property licence that allows for free use, adaptation, and distribution".[19]

The 2012 PARIS OER declaration defines the term as

> teaching, learning and research materials in any medium, digital or otherwise, that reside in the public domain or have been released under an open licence that permits no-cost access, use, adaptation and redistribution by others with no or limited restrictions.[20]

In a report commissioned by the Organisation for Economic Co-operation and Development (OECD), OER was defined as "[t]he open provision of educational resources, enabled by information and communication technologies, for consultation, use and adaptation by a community of users for non-commercial purposes".[21]

A definition of OER commonly used is, "open educational resources are digitized materials offered freely and openly for educators, students and self-learners to use and reuse for teaching, learning and research."

In the opinion of Atkins and as found on the William and Flora Hewlett Foundation website,

> OER are teaching, learning and research resources that reside in the public domain or have been released under an intellectual property licence that permit their free use or re-purposing by others. Open educational resources include full courses, course materials, modules, textbooks, streaming videos, tests, software and any other tools, materials, modules, textbooks, streaming videos, tests, software, and any other tools, materials, or techniques used to support access to knowledge.[22]

The definitions provided above all explain OER from similar but different perspectives. There are however fundamental issues when considering what an OER is. These fundamentals include the following.

2.1 Content

Characteristic of any OER is the element of providing usable and reusable resources/content for educational purposes, and they must be such that meet educational needs. These resources come in different languages depending on the source of creation, but may be translated, adapted and modified to meet specific needs. These resources vary in quality, style and packaging and may contain single topics, multiple topics, single courses, full courses, course materials, modules, textbooks, streaming videos, test sample and answers, software and any other tools. The onus is on the institutions or individuals to first locate and then appropriately adapt these resources.[23]

2.2 Target actors

The traditional model for creating educational materials have been for teachers to develop these materials and for students to use them. Sharing educational materials under the traditional model was common but was geographically restricted.[24] In today's ICT world, the development of educational resources has taken a totally different dimensions. Both teachers, students and independent minds are actively involved in the development of educational resources.[25] A simple search on the Internet of an educational-related topic is most likely to reveal several resources from professors (teachers), fellow students and from individuals who are neither teachers nor students (independent minds). Some of the definitions of OER infer a teacher creates, student use model; others suggest an all-inclusive creation model where students and teachers are seen both as creators and users. Understanding and adapting to the changes brought by technology to the educational sector would take some time, hence it is understandable and expected that the teacher creates, and student uses the model, which would continue to exist but with time the all-inclusive creation and use model is likely to become predominant. OER is best maximized when all available parties (teachers, students and independent minds) are involved in the creation, use and reuse of educational resources.

2.3 Platform/format

Information Communication Technology has enabled easy digitization, dissemination and distribution of millions of materials. One of the fundamental principles of the OER movement is built on distribution via the Internet and some definitions have tilted to this model.[26] The issue here is that the digital divide between the developed Western nations and the developing as well as the least developed nations place the latter group at the disadvantaged position with regards to accessing needed content.[27] The irony is that the greater need for OER rests with those who do not have easy access to the Internet. It may therefore be difficult or inappropriate at this stage to limit the format for OER to digitized materials as this may defeat the purpose.

2.4 Intellectual property

Intellectual property (IP) provides the legal framework that regulates how content is used and reused. The general rule for created content is that it is protected under intellectual property regimes which prohibit exploitation without prior consent.[28] Where creators of educational resources intend that such resources be OER, an active step must be taken to ensure that this happens. This is very important because by default, created contents are protected under proprietary rights and are therefore closed, that is, not freely available for use and reuse.[29] To make it open, creators have several options, they may choose to use works within the public domain (a free zone where no Intellectual Property Rights exist on contents) or apply an open licence to the work allowing for free access, use and reuse or whatever permission is intended to be granted.

2.5 Commercial or non-commercial

Use of a work is deemed commercial when it is used for profit, and non-commercial when it is used not-for-profit. The line between for profit and not for profit use often become blurred, especially with educational institutions that are registered as not-for-profit making entities, but yet charge some kind of fees. This raises issues as to whether or not use by these institutions would fall within commercial or non-commercial. As seen in two of the definitions above (UNESCO[30] and OECD[31]), use within the OER context need be for non-commercial purposes.

The legal sharing mechanism under which OER operates is open licensing, and the focus of open licensing just like that of open source software is not to prohibit or even discourage commercialization, but rather to enable access for use as well as reuse leading to further development.[32] It may therefore serve the wider interest if OER's are neutral sensitive to the issue of "commercial or non-commercial." OER should therefore not be restricted to non-commercial use as such restrictions are capable of limiting the enabling ability of the contents being created. Rather OER should focus on providing right of access, use and reuse and not limit the potential ability of the reuse right.

3 Components of OER

This section of the chapter examines three components of OER, that is, *open, educational* and *resources*. They are examined as individual concepts within the broader meaning of the OER movement and identified with what they stand for and how they impact the society, but specifically the education sector.

A critical look at definitions provided above shows that the term is quite broad and vague. What exactly does it cover, what does it entail, what are the ambits and limits? According to Johnstone, OER has been interpreted to include the following:

- Learning resources – courseware, content modules, learning objects, learner-support and assessment tools, online learning communities.
- Resources to support teachers – tools for teachers and support materials to enable them to create, adapt, and use OER, as well as training materials for teachers and other teaching tools.
- Resources to assure the quality of education and educational practices.[33]

3.1 Open

In the context of OER, the term open requires that educational resources are not just merely created, published and made available, but also structured to be freely open for viewing, use, reuse, adaptation, improvement and distribution and are to be shared among other things. In essence, authors or copyright owners are expected to exercise their discretion to make their educational resources available on terms that would allow access, use and reuse of such works. In practice, authors apply a licence to the work enabling would-be users identify the work as one free for access, use and reuse, subject to conditions where applicable.

Open within the OER context plays a role on the implications of rights granted on educational materials, it clarifies amongst other things the scope of access, use and reuse that has been permitted, its effect on the grantor (the one who granted the rights) whether any right still accrues to the copyright owner and the extent to which the materials are exploitable.[34]

The views are divergent as to the interpretation of open in OER. Walker opined that open should be "convenient, effective, affordable, sustainable and available to every learner and teacher worldwide".[35] Daniel referring to D'Antoni says it must have the 4A's: accessibility, appropriateness, accreditation and affordability.[36]

Downes appears to favour the view that open ought to be at no cost to the consumers. He says,

> It is not clear that resources which require some sort of payment by the user – whether that payment be subscription fees, contribution in kind, or even something simple, such as user registration – ought to be called 'open'. Even when the cost is low – or 'affordable' – the payment represents some sort of opportunity cost on the part of the user, an exchange rather than sharing.[37]

In Richard Stallman's opinion, open would need to comply with his "four freedoms", namely.

1 The freedom to run the program, for any purpose
2 The freedom to study how the program works and adapt it to your needs
3 The freedom to redistribute copies so you can help your neighbour
4 The freedom to improve the program and release your improvement to the public, so that the whole community benefits[38]

Tuomi distinguishes between two domains (social and technical), where 'open' has fundamental consequences. On the social side, he refers to Stallman's four freedoms where he said,

> A program is free software if users have all of these freedoms. Thus, you should be free to redistribute copies, either with or without modifications, either gratis or charging a fee for distribution, to anyone anywhere. Being free to do these things means (among other things) that you do not have to ask or pay for permission.[39]

On the other hand, the technical side is characterized by technical interoperability and functionality in contrast to the social side which is fundamentally motivated by the expected social benefits and ethical considerations related to human freedoms. In this domain, the interest is that products must be technically compatible and able to work with one another. Developing programs that work on restricted systems builds a technical divide and raises the issue of interoperability and functionality. An acceptable "open" within the OER movement would be required to be non-specialized in the technical sense. It would be required to conform to open standards, that is, standards that can operate and communicate with one another regardless of the format.[40]

On the other hand, some are of the opinion that "open" ought to be non-commercial,[41] others are of the view that the commerciality or non-commerciality of an OER is immaterial as one of the freedoms the user should have is a choice as to commercial or non-commercial distribution. As to whether or not the work would be in the public domain will be determined by the type of licence granted. It is noteworthy that open within the OER context seeks to ensure that educational resources are available, accessible, affordable, reusable, adaptable and distributable within accepted legal frameworks.

3.2 Educational

Education refers to the process of receiving or giving systematic instruction, especially at a school. This term is subject to multiple interpretations. The Federal Communications Commission's (FCC) second report and order (FCC 03–101, released on 30 April 2003) amended its rules to give clarity to the meaning and definition of educational purposes but did not define the term.[42] In the case of National Collegiate Athletic Association *(NCAA) v Kansas Dept of Revenue*, McFarland J gave an indication of the meaning of the term when he noted that *educational* refers to organized curriculum of classes and courses involving the systematic teaching and learning process.[43] In an attempt to clarify the meaning of the word, the judge referred to the K.A.R 9219–75, which provides that "educational institutions are not organizations that merely provide a series of classes or instructions on one topic, vocation or skill . . . impart knowledge to the public in a general manner through tours, seminars".[44]

Whereas the case was to establish if NCAA qualified as an educational institution, from the decision of McFarland, important facts on the word *educational* can be elicited to the effect that education refers to a process where organized teaching and learning is communicated. It could be through classes, courses, instructions on one or more topics, on vocations or skills. It should involve impartation of knowledge or information.

The content involved in delivering education is regulated by IP laws, which by default restrict use and reuse of such materials. In recognition of the importance of education to the common good and public interest, the national copyright laws of most countries provide limitations and exceptions to copyright, as well as compulsory licensing.[45] These provisions specify certain circumstances, such as educational purposes, where it would allow for the use of copyright protected materials without the need for prior permission. These provisions are often expressed within the doctrine of fair use and fair dealing depending on the jurisdiction.[46]

Educational purpose from the context of the United States Copyright Law,[47] allow for teaching (including multiple copies for classroom use), scholarship, or research. The Copyright laws of Canada,[48] Nigeria[49] and South Africa[50] amongst many others exclude from Copyright infringement, use without prior consent, of copyright protected work when it is used for educational purposes. The provisions of the three countries under "fair dealing" all have similar slants but are however different. While the Canadian Copyright Act provides for "research or private study",[51] that of Nigeria provides for "research and private use"[52] and South Africa's Copyright Act combines both providing for "research or private study, personal or private use".[53]

What is however common in all the legislation is the acknowledgement of the importance of education, the allowance for "use" provided by each legislation and the exclusion from infringement of such use. None of the legislations however define what educational purpose is but give an indication on what is excluded from copyright infringement under the auspices of educational purposes.

Considering the allowances provided for use under national legislations via limitations, exceptions and compulsory licences, one may have thought that with such provisions, OER have been catered for and further initiatives in this respect would be unnecessary. In reality, the scope of both concepts are different. While Limitations and exceptions are focused on *limited use and reuse*, OER are focused on *unlimited use and reuse*. OER provide a platform for unrestricted exercise of the human mind by the removal of barriers that could inhibit the creation, development, adaptation, translation, use and reuse of educational resources.

As can be deduced from the provisions in the above referred legislations, *educational* would entail research, teaching, private study, private use, personal use and scholarship. In the context of OER, educational purpose transcends use within the formal educational settings. It contemplates the non-formals considering that learning extends beyond formal settings and resources used within the non-formal settings are on all fours instances of OER.[54] Educational would therefore include teachers, students, adult education learners, distance learning education providers and receivers, private researchers, and curious minds.

3.3 Resources

Resources imply a pool from which can be drawn that which is required. They come in different forms and in this era of Information Communication technology where technological development has penetrated virtually all sectors, resources may be categorized into digital and non-digital resources.[55]

Non-digital resources are depletable with use. On the contrary, digital resources are not depletable as increased usage does not reduce its amounts but rather increases its value.[56] Resources in the OER context could therefore be understood as "resources that produce services that anyone can enjoy, without reducing the enjoyment of others".[57]

4 Rationale for OER

If one where to consider the schools of thought positing that a stronger IP regime incentivizes creativity and innovation,[58] one may then wonder why educational resources (which are primarily contents enjoying IP protection) should be made open as this may adversely affect creativity and innovation? Expressing the same thoughts in a different way, in an environment with strongly rooted consciousness of intellectual property protection for creativity and innovation, some may wonder why anyone will make freely available and grant others the right to use and reuse educational materials. The underlying rationale for such acts could be understood from the combination of several factors including the following.

4.1 Technological advancements

This refers to advancements in information communication technology, the Internet, newer and more sophisticated hardware and software, broadband networks and other ICT infrastructures. The combined effect of these gadgets, the software and hardware and the platform of the Internet have given interested individuals the opportunity for easier engagement in the process of producing and sharing content, thus bringing about the creation and distribution of content in an unprecedented dimension.[59] The argument in favour of free distribution of digital content is that outside the cost of Internet connection, sharing is virtually at no cost.[60] The current technologies responsible for production and dissemination of information has enabled the production and dissemination of multiple copies at little or no cost. This is one of the pillars that enables OER. The cost, time and quality implications involved in producing and disseminating information under previous technologies like the printing press has changed with the introduction of personal computers and the Internet.[61]

4.2 Cost

The increase in the cost of quality education and educational materials has excluded many from access to education. OER avail the opportunity of access to use and reuse quality educational resources at no cost. OER is therefore able to mitigate the rising cost of educational materials and subscription fees.[62] These costs have become prohibitive, and they place students' debt at one of the highest in America.[63] It also stands as a hindrance to students, researchers, teachers and learners interested in gaining access to useful and needed materials. On the other hand, the Internet is empowering the creation of new models such as open access publishing for the provision of access to knowledge.[64] Governments are recognizing the economic advantage of adopting OER policies and the huge savings they are able to make. A staff with the Creative Commons, Cable Green, explained the cost efficiency and effectiveness of adopting OER strategies by using his home state of Washington as an example. He noted that his state spends $130 million per year buying textbooks for about 1 million students, that is, $130 per child.[65] He suggests that instead of spending $130 million per year, it can be reduced to 10 million per year by adopting OER policies where a "Request for Proposal" would be put out for each book on the condition that books would be licensed under a Creative Commons licence and thus the IP would belong to the state, more so that it has been created with taxpayers' funds. Doing this will afford the students the opportunity to not only access the materials, but also to own copies. Cable estimates that the cost of making the materials available in e-version, paper print and other running cost would not be more than $10 million yearly, thus enabling a saving of about $120 million yearly.[66]

4.3 Adult education

As governments of the world strive to attain the Millennium Development Goal (MDG) of Universal Primary Education, more adults are showing interest in obtaining basic education and with economic resources dwindling globally, affordability is an issue. The other issue with adult education is the time and convenience. Most adult student have little time to spare as they are parents and workers. Technology provides them the opportunity to learn at their convenience and in the comfort of their home, while OER address the challenges of affordability of educational materials.

4.4 Growing competition between higher educational institutions

High educational institutions that provide OER are able to showcase the quality of their educational materials. This serves as some form of advertisement, and it breeds healthy competitions amongst the higher educational institutions.

4.5 Altruistic reasons

Not all authors are centred on the revenue they will generate from their writing. In fact, a lot of authors write basically for tenure purposes, while others do so for the mere pleasure of it. They love to write, and they would be satisfied knowing that others have read it and that it is able to help them. It is for this reason people licence their works and authorize not just the use, but also the reuse of their work through reproduction, public performance, translation, adaptation and other means.

4.6 A social responsibility through which the common good is served

An intrinsic characteristic of any OER is the interest to serve the common good, and this is achieved by ensuring that all OER content must be open for "use and reuse". It must be shareable and adaptable, and no barriers should stand in the way of these intrinsic characteristics of any OER.[67] The Free Open Source Software Movement (FOSS) is an organization and a platform that has spearheaded the ideology of sharing, and they are strong advocates for the Access to Knowledge (A2K) movement. They continue to raise awareness on the need to share, and that sharing is in the interest of the common good for all of humanity.

OER is built on the FOSS's sharing culture which allows not only free access to the use of software, but go even further to provide the source codes, thus allowing would-be users to alter the software for personal and even proprietary needs and further requires that such alterations be made available on the same term for other would-be users, thus ensuring not only a channel for continued access but entrenching a culture of sharing as against a locked up one.[68]

4.7 New business models created on the platform of the Internet

Technology affords the opportunity of delivering education via new business models in contradistinction to the old business model.[69] Initiatives like Khan Academy are able to offer first-class education for free. These are new business models enabled by the Internet providing quality educational services using OER. If a new business model avails the opportunity to get it for free why pay for it?

4.8 It has been mandated by my employers

Governments, employers and funding organizations are beginning to understand the value and importance of OER and are issuing policies requiring the development of OER. In such instance, these OER are developed in compliance with these policies.

4.9 Easy accessibility to a new licensing model allowing for development of OER

The development of open licensing and the ease in applying them on educational materials help in copyright clearance and resolves copyright uncertainties.[70] Educational resources are managed under the broad IP regime, specifically under copyright which controls "use and reuse" subject to limitations and exceptions.[71] Open content licensing (a licence granting permission in advance to would-be user based on specified conditions) is a tool that can be used to remove barriers to access. The introduction of standard licences by the Creative Commons has been very useful in simplifying rights clearance and enable users to "use and reuse" without violating current legal provisions.[72]

5 The role of the law and OER

The law provides standard, is an enabler and a disabler serving public and private interests. Copyright laws protect private interest by incentivizing creation and innovation. It also caters for public interest through limitations and exceptions to copyright. The rules of copyright are also able to enable use and reuse through open licensing and at the same time can be used as a disabler by simply doing nothing with copyright which is restrictive by default or by the application of a restrictive licence (NC-ND) restricting commercial use and reuse rights.[73]

5.1 As an enabler

In South Africa, the Department of Basic Education (the agency responsible for schools) embraced a policy which enabled the free distribution of science and math textbooks to all schools within the country.[74] The resources distributed included comprehensive set of workbooks and teacher's guides in both English and Afrikaans.[75] Siyavula's open education project which operates an open licence is what permitted and enabled the government of South Africa to freely print and distribute the educational materials all across South Africa.[76] Without this open licence, that is, the legal authorization, the South African government would have been in violation of copyright laws.

5.2 As a standard

The law governs societal behaviour to ensure peace and harmony. Without laws, everyone would do what seems right to him or her.[77] Some may describe such a state as freedom; where each person expresses himself or herself without reservation and without consideration of others. The lack of consideration of others is where the problem comes in. Although freedom is important, the exercise of freedom by A should not impinge on the freedom of B nor cause harm to B. Where this happens, a problem arises, and resolution is required. The mode of settlement is usually determined based on set of rules which the people have agreed would govern and regulate their behaviours.[78]

6 IP – the legal framework for OER

Access to education, sharing of knowledge and dissemination of information are governed by different but similar national legislations (usually the national copyright laws) as well as several international conventions such as the Berne Convention,[79] Trade-Related Aspects of Intellectual Property[80] and the World Intellectual Property Organization (WIPO) Internet Treaties.[81] These laws are connected in some way to several fields of law. IP laws however play a major role in the regulation of the exploitation of creativity and innovation and have to a large extent determined the scope of access and sharing of knowledge and information within the knowledge economy.[82]

WIPO refers to IP as "creations of the mind: inventions, literary and artistic works, and symbols, names, images and designs used in commerce."[83] IP can be divided into two, *industrial property* and *copyright*. Whilst industrial property covers inventions, trademarks, industrial designs and geographical indications of sources; copyright on the other hand covers literary, artistic and musical works (traditional copyright), as well as sound recordings, performances and broadcasts referred to as neighbouring rights or rights related to copyright.

IP laws are crucial to OER because the contents, software, methodologies and platforms created and used in the field of OER are covered by intellectual property laws.

7 Law as an enabler and disabler

The A2k, FOSS and open access movements acknowledge the importance of the law, but also acknowledges the way and manner in which the law has and is still used as a platform for restricting access to knowledge. The open source software movement is perhaps the inspiration behind the viral advocacy for free access and sharing of information. The genius within the open source software movement is the idea of the grant of prior approval,[84] leveraged on the principles of IP's proprietary rights, particularly copyright which grant owners the right to control exploitation of a work subject to certain exceptions and limitations.[85] In this sense, the law in its current state constitutes a disabler than an enabler and thus the need for developing mechanisms that are capable of working within the current legal framework and at the same time would fulfil the vision and mission of making provision for access, use and reuse of knowledge via the Internet at a near-zero cost.[86]

The core of OER is for it to be useable and reusable without restrictions. The open licensing mechanism has proved very useful in this regard, and Creative

Commons licences have been the focal point. It can therefore be said that OER builds upon the ideals of the A2k, FOSS and open access movements and utilizes tools such as open licences and policies to facilitate the creation and sharing of educational resources in the interest of all willing users and at the same time conforming to the requirements of the legal system. It is however the hope that our current legal framework will be amended to reflect the current societal realities, which now tilts in favour of a sharing culture in contrast to the former restrictive/ closed framework.

8 Licensing

Right owners and users often have to come to an agreement on the use of created or innovated works. Legal instruments are often drafted to reflect the terms and conditions between the right owners and users. The impracticability for right owners to regulate and administer all their works have necessitated the use of collecting societies to negotiate and grant licences as well as collect and distribute royalties on their behalf.[87] The terms of some licences are often very restrictive and sometimes prohibitive. The professional fees associated with concluding the licensing negotiations is often huge and could serve as a deterrence to otherwise interested users.

The movements towards free and open access, use and reuse have initiated licensing regimes that would achieve the legal necessities and at the same time overcome the challenges associated with legal fees, lengthy documentations and easy comprehension of the documents. The FOSS movement's licensing regime started of the process, with Richard Stallman's GNU Project releasing a GNU General Public Licence (GNU GPL). David Wiley converted FOSS's code-oriented licence from code to content and came up with an "Open Publication Licence" (OPL), birthing the Open Content Licence.[88] It is on these infrastructures Creative Commons licences are built.[89] A CC licence is one that provides the legal legitimacy and enables the sharing and use of knowledge and creativity. The permits granted are amenable to the wishes of the licensor who may place conditions on the grant of a permit. The architecture of this licensing model encourages a shift from the "all rights reserved" to a "some rights reserved" or a "no rights reserved" regime. One major aim of this licensing model is the provision of copyright compliant licences that are simple, standardized and free in the interest of the general public. The licences seek to take away the fears and worries about copyright infringement by providing permission in advance to would-be users.[90]

9 Policies

Achieving the vision of OER must be a collective effort. Leaving it to individuals will make the task a difficult one. The adoption of policies in favour of OER by organizations, institutions and governments would provide a spring board for OER. Policies are like well-constructed roads that aid easy movement from one point to the other. What an individual will struggle to achieve with regards to an idea by oneself is often easily accomplished when an institutional policy with regards to such idea is in place. The experience with institutional repositories and the issuance of mandates is a testimony to the effect institutional policies can have on an idea and not just on the idea but also on those who are both for and against such ideas. A clear example is that of Siyavula's open education policy which when embraced by the South African department of education enabled the free distribution of school textbooks to students all across South Africa.[91] Teacher Education in Sub-Saharan Africa (TESSA) is another policy initiative that seeks amongst other things to bring together teachers and educators from across sub-Saharan Africa and offers a range of OER in different languages.[92] The "High Level Workshop on OpenupEd OER and MOOCs for the National Open University of Nigeria" is another example of policy initiatives aimed at encouraging better understanding of OER and encouraging active participation in OER. The workshop was noted as a "first step to NOUN's roadmap of converting all of its 1800 courses to be completely OERized and MOOC formatted".[93]

10 The impact of OER

OER is not just a concept in the minds of some overzealous individuals. It is now widely accepted by governments, the public and private sector and is continually making great impact on not just the part of the students, but also on educators, government and independent learners. This section will highlight the growing acceptance and spread of OER and how it is impacting on everyday life.

10.1 OER Africa

This is an initiative that plays a leading role in supporting establishments across Africa in the understanding, development and use of OER in enhancing teaching and learning. It provides useful access to information and serves as a hub for locating relevant OER.[94] It was established by the South African Institute for Distance Education (Saide) and provides information on a wide range of issues. Through her partnerships with universities in Africa, OER Africa has been able to successfully share OER between Higher Educational Institutions.[95] This development is particularly important for Africa because of the lack of visibility of African works between Africans and Africans and Africans and the rest of the world.

10.2 African Virtual University

This is a Pan African intergovernmental organization established by charter with the mandate of significantly increasing access to quality higher education and training through the innovative use of information technologies. This charter has been signed by 18 African governments. The African Virtual University (AVU) operates from Nairobi, Kenya and Dakar Senegal, where it has its head and regional offices respectively. AVU was launched in 1997 as a World Bank project and later became an intergovernmental organization in 2003. AVU has the unique ability to work across the multi-lingual borders of Africa and has trained over 43,000 students since inception in 1997.[96] AVU has an OER architecture "through which the creation, organization, dissemination and utilization of OER is expected to lead to the development of a dynamic, rational and comprehensive strategy for collaborative partnerships for African higher education and training institutions". AVU has a repository which hosts the majority of AVU materials. In collaboration with the African Development Bank and the United Nations Development Programme, a number of professional courses have been developed and released as OER. These materials are available and accessible through the repository.[97]

10.3 Siyavula

Siyavula Education is an African OER success story that has impacted all of South Africa. With the aid of a Shuttleworth fellowship, the organization was born, and willing minds were able to share knowledge, produce them using the open licensing system and make them freely available online. This freedom is what enabled the South African government to put out these OER and distribute them freely to millions of students.[98]

10.4 Writing commons

This is an open education platform that provides free comprehensive, peer-reviewed, award-winning Open Text for students and faculty in college level courses that require writing and research. The mission is to help college students improve their writing, research and critical thinking, and this is done by publishing a variety of webtexts on writing pedagogy. The topics covered include writing, processes, information literacy, research methods and methodologies, collaboration, genres, style and new media. It was founded in 2008 by Joe Moxley and has been widely adopted. In 2013, 1,277, 591 users visited writing commons.[99]

10.5 OER-ization of four courses in Kenya

UNESCO and the University of Nairobi, Kenya successfully collaborated to transform four courses from static texts into dynamic online learning resources, and these materials have been released under an open licence that permits users to freely and legitimately access, use and reuse these materials. These four courses which are currently hosted in the OER commons platform are as follows:

- *Information Studies:* a course unit offered to masters students at the School of Biological and Physical Sciences,
- *Introduction to Business and Entrepreneurship:* a course unit offered to undergraduate students at the college of Biological;

- *Physical Sciences, Audit and Control:* a course unit offered to both undergraduate and master's students in different departments at the College of Biological
- *Physical Sciences and Database Systems:* a course unit offered to both undergraduate and graduate masters students in different departments at the College of Biological and Physical Sciences.[100]

10.6 National Open University of Nigeria and UNESCO

The National Open University of Nigeria (NOUN) is in collaboration with UNESCO to deepen understanding and facilitate the development of OER in Nigeria. In furtherance of the collaboration, UNESCO organized an intensive workshop on OER and massive open online courses (MOOCs) in Nigeria for the purposes of significantly enhancing the quality and access to higher education for thousands of Nigerian and African students. The workshop was attended by 30 senior faculty members of NOUN and was held from the 10–11 September 2014.[101]

10.7 MIT

The MIT OpenCourseWare (MIT OCW) contains virtually all of MIT's course content and is open and available to the world. The site contains 2,150 courses and has received over 125 million visitors.[102] The MIT OCW receives an average of 1 million visitors per month, with translation receiving about 500,000 more. Educators, students, self-learners and others are among the visitors.[103]

10.8 Obama Administration

The importance of OER was underscored when the Obama Administration pledged US$2 billion in its support. The amount released through the Trade Adjustment Assistance Community College and Career Training Grant Program (TAACCCT) is towards the development of educational materials that would be open and available to all learners. A condition of the grant is that all materials produced must be licensed under a creative commons 3.0 attribution licence.[104] This decision was prompted by the growing concern about the increased cost of education for the average student in the United States of America and the level of student indebtedness, which now surpasses auto and credit card debts.[105] This policy has brought about further development of OER, which have been made freely available to students, thereby cutting down on the need to purchase text books and other educational resources.

10.9 British Columbia

In 2012, British Columbia announced its OER policy by supporting the creation of 40 open textbook for the 40 most popular first- and second-year courses.[106]

10.10 California

Governor Jerry Brown of California assented to two bills in support of OER. The bills provide for the creation of free, openly licensed digital textbooks for the 50 most popular lower-division college courses offered by California colleges.[107]

10.11 OpenStax college

The OpenStax College, an OER initiative of Connextions currently run at Rice University, is creating high-quality, peer-reviewed open textbooks available under a Creative Commons Attribution licence (CC BY), allowing anyone to reuse, revise, remix and redistribute the books. Two of the textbooks have been downloaded over 110,000 times, by about 1.5 million learners and adopted by over 200 schools.[108]

10.12 US book project

Hilary Clinton launched the Open Book Project, an initiative which provides access to OER in Arabic. The initiative supports the creation of OER in Arabic language and the translation of existing OER into Arabic. It also offers training and support to governments, educators and students to put existing OER to use and to develop their own.[109]

10.13 World Bank

The World Bank announced its adoption of an open access policy requiring that all research outputs and knowledge products published by the Bank be licensed under a Creative Commons Attribution licence (CC BY) as a default and as a first phase of the policy, the Bank on the 10th of April, 2012, launched the Open Knowledge Repository[110] with more than 2,000 books, articles, reports and research papers under a CC BY licence,[111] thus making those materials freely available and accessible to the general public.[112]

OER continues to make financial impacts by the savings it makes possible and impacts on the social lives of many in developing countries through the opportunities it gives to study freely (without cost and at one's convenience) under some of the greatest minds. These opportunities before now were the exclusive preserve of the rich and for those in the Western society. OER is beginning to bridge the gap, and it is hoped that one day the divide would no more exist.

11 OER by and for developing countries

One of the focal objectives of OER Africa, the African Virtual University, Siyavula and several other OER initiatives that have been born in Africa is to ensure that Africans are able to develop and share their knowledge and to contribute to global knowledge.[113] Developing OER will require a purposeful, targeted and structured approach. OER will not happen by default. Most national laws allow use of copyright materials under limitations and exceptions or some form of compulsory or statutory licensing for educational purposes. However, permission is granted mostly for use, while reuse and other forms of adaptation are excluded. OER bridges these gaps by ensuring that the gains exemplified from the impacts made by OER so far can be replicated in Nigeria, the rest of Africa, other developing countries and indeed around the world, thereby eradicating (if possible) or at least reducing lack of access to education, illiteracy, poverty, poor health care and agriculture.

Developing countries stand at an advantaged position when it comes to developing OER because the OER movement is no more at its embryonic state and the possible fear of whether or not this initiative is workable is not an issue. The structures have been laid, millions of educational resources have been developed, used, reused, translated, adapted and distributed around the world. The following are therefore suggested for developing OER by developing countries.

11.1 Locate, adapt and build

Millions of OER have been developed already. Developing countries only need to locate the appropriate resource, translate where necessary and adapt them to the local needs. The MIT's OCW and KHAN Academy will come in very useful here. The courses have been translated into many languages including Spanish, Portuguese, Simplified Chinese, Traditional Chinese, Thai, Persian, Turkish and Korean.[114]

11.2 OER databases

Considering the vast amount of OER already developed and located on different websites, searching for these resources can be frustrating. To therefore maximize time, make the best out of already created OER, and to locate the most relevant resources, it would be best to search through OER databases which contain repositories such as Curriki,[115] OER Commons,[116] LeMill,[117] Connexions,[118] OpenCourseWare Consortium,[119] Index of OCW Websites,[120] JorumOpen[121] and The Encyclopedia of Life.[122]

Developing countries may wish to explore joining one of the existing consortiums. This will afford the opportunity for guidance in developing OER and to work with tested personnel.

It may also be useful to register and take as many MOOCs to obtain more knowledge on specific areas and methods. These courses will also afford the opportunity of acquiring firsthand experience of how OER are used and their multi-dimensional capabilities.[123]

11.3 Be innovative – tell your own story

No one ought to be able to tell your story better than you can. Unfortunately, this is not the case for most developing countries, whose stories are told by others and as you can expect, these stories no matter how sincerely delivered would still reflect the perspective of the story teller.[124] OER provides the platform for developing countries to write and tell their own stories. It provides the opportunity to develop teaching and learning tools that are tailored to local needs. In reality, developing countries already have content; such as teaching modules, articles, books, reports and others. The platform for sharing this knowledge has been the gap. University of Nairobi recently released four of her courses as OER under open licences, and Nigeria is working with the UNESCO to do the same.[125]

Inspiration can be found in Prof Ng's experience who noted that "I put one of my courses online and it reached an audience of 100,000 students," he says. "To put that number into context, I used to teach 400 students a year at Stanford, that means that to reach a comparable sized audience I would have had to teach at Stanford for 250 years."[126] Developing OER and making them available have the potentials of reaching the world. The challenges of finances, technical know-how, time on the part of academics, government support, donor support and general awareness are issues that must also be addressed in developing countries if OER would succeed.

12 OER challenges

In developing resources that are considered OER, developers are faced with several issues, including right clearance, universality of resources, cultural appropriateness, uncertainty as to choice of open licence and the digital divide. Similarly, would-be users are faced with issues of having to scavenge and locate purpose specific OER within reasonable time, taking cognizance of the fact that most of these materials are online. Some users are also faced with the challenge of adapting the material due to ICT skill deficiencies. Developing countries are faced with inability to access online available materials due to lack of infrastructural facilities. Finding ways to surmount these challenges is crucial to the continued success of OER.

12.1 Right clearance

Good and qualitative research often involve the work of others. Isaac Newton put it succinctly when he noted that "if I have seen farther it is by standing on the shoulders of giants."[127] OER is often made up of works from multiple authors. This is the very reason why it is imperative for OER developers to ensure that whatever is being put out as an OER material has obtained all the requisite authorizations.

Educational resources are proprietary by default and although the current legal framework provides limitations and exceptions to copyright allowing the use of copyright work for educational purposes, it is important to note that use is strictly for educational purpose only.[128]

In developing OER, the issues are usually to determine what is been used and how to either obtain appropriate authorization for use where authorization is required and to give the required credit to whom it is due. This issue of right clearance often serves as a bottleneck to the development of OER.

Rights clearance is very important in the development of OER because users of OER act on the belief that such materials are non-infringing materials. A duty is therefore placed on all OER developers to ensure that the proper legal freedoms exist in the content that is being put out as OER.[129] The process of rights clearance can be cumbersome, expensive and often confusing. Open content licensing provides a convenient solution to these legal challenges by satisfying the legal requirements and providing requisite permission in advance to would-be users. The Creative Commons licences are a very good example of open content licences.[130]

12.2 Uncertainty as to choice of open licence

The choice of the licence to affix to a work is an important decision which should be made with understanding. This is because the application of a CC licence implies that you have granted permission to everyone to use your work for the full duration of copyright on the work. The choice of what licence you will apply depends largely on the freedom you are minded to give. It is however fundamental to know that materials considered OER must bear licences that permit use and reuse rights. A number of resources have been developed to help in determining the most appropriate licences. Some of these resources include the flow chart developed by CC Australia,[131] a compilation by Creative Commons headquarters,[132] case studies which may be used for reference purposes and could serve as useful guides,[133] the CC community through its discussion lists[134] and also by engaging the services of a legal professional.

12.3 Digital divide and inability to access online available materials due to lack of infrastructural facilities and lack of ICT skills

The problem of the digital divide, lack of ICT infrastructure and issues of interoperability constitute a major barrier to access.[135] It is one thing for OER to be freely available online, and it is another for the intended audiences to be able to access the OER online. Inability to access freely available online material is a major challenge to members of some countries, particularly those from developing, least developed and under-developed countries.[136]

Lack of technical skills to develop and adapt OER also constitutes a major hindrance to the development and utility of OER. The creation of several resources require not just putting words and ideas together, but it requires a skilful, dynamic and artistic presentation which in several ways gives life to the actual knowledge that is sort to be communicated. These technical skills used in communicating letters, alphabets, sounds, words, images and graphs are often more impacting than the actual message being passed across.[137] Technical skills are vehicles that aid in effective delivery of communication. The lack of these skills in many academics have brought about challenges in developing OER and where they have been developed, they are often inappropriate and fail to achieve the desired purpose. Purposefully learning and re-learning these technical skills which include presentation styles, better computer appreciation, use of Microsoft Office software [word, power-point and excel] as well as other software will help in addressing some of these technical challenges. The need for continuous learning cannot be over-emphasized, seeing that technology keeps evolving, and the mode of delivering messages must be dynamic.

12.4 Universality of resources and cultural appropriateness

Developers often have a target audience in mind when developing resources. The multi-cultural nature of the world means that what is trash to one may be gold to another, and what is regarded as of no value to one may be highly regarded to some others.[138] For example, in the Indian culture, the Cow is sacred and worshipped and must not be killed, but other people see the Cow as a mere animal that is used for food as beef.[139] Similarly, in the development of OER, these challenges arise, and this is so because of the nature of the Internet where information uploaded in China can be retrieved in any other part of the world. The information uploaded in China is uploaded with probably a Chinese cultural slant and this is understandable as the views of individuals are greatly influenced by culture. Therefore, it is not for developers to develop OER that are globally applicable, but it is rather that user/developer, that is, users who then become developers should work at appropriately adapting the OER to suit their local/particular needs.[140] Some have advanced the idea that OER when developed should be tested within the locality of creation and within the initial target groups and where proved successful can be extended.[141] The drawback to these thoughts are that once a resource is put up on the Internet as an OER, it is available not just to a localized few but to the entire world.[142]

12.5 Locating OER

Another issue is the challenge of locating appropriate OER by interested users. Considering how search engines work, a seeking user would often input the available detail about a resource and hit search. This will bring out thousands and a times millions of related information. The "how" to sort through this information is often a challenge since time is always of the essence. Working through dedicated sites where specialized OER can be located and have been stored would be useful. Below is a list of OER databases that could serve as useful starting points:

1 Curriki[143]
2 OER Commons[144]
3 LeMill[145]
4 Connexions[146]
5 OpenCourseWare Consortium[147]
6 Index of OCW Websites[148]
7 JorumOpen[149]
8 The Encyclopedia of Life[150]

13 OER and MOOCs

MOOCs represents a model of delivering online courses to hundreds of thousands of interested minds via the Internet. Coursera, EdX, Udacity, Blackboard, Udemy and Educase are examples of MOOC providers.

Whereas traditional online education requires enrolment, payment of tuition fees, assignments and assessment leading to award of credits, MOOCs are usually (but not always) free, award no credits (some give a badge to acknowledge attendance) and have very high indication of interest.[151]

MOOC is defined in Wikipedia as

> a type of online course aimed at large scale participation and open access via the web. MOOCs are a recent development in the area of distance education, and a progression of the kind of open education ideals suggested by open educational resources. Though the design of participation in a MOOC may be similar to college or university courses, MOOCs typically do not offer credits awarded to paying students at schools. However, assessment of learning may be done for certification.

Sir John Daniel makes a distinction between two types of MOOCs, the cMOOCs and the xMOOCs. In his opinion, cMOOCs are focused on knowledge creation, while xMOOCs focus on knowledge duplication. The hype with regard to MOOCs have been in respect of xMOOCs, which gained centre stage in North America's educational system in 2012.[152] Although the hype is not unconnected to North America's worldwide media influence, the impact of MOOCs on participants and providers have played a critical role in the hype. A case in point is that of Prof Ng, one of the founders of Coursera and a Professor at Stanford who put up his lectures online and was able to reach 100,000 students as against his usually 400 students yearly. Prof Ng said, "to put that number into context, I used to teach 400 students a year at Stanford, that means that to reach a comparable sized audience I would have had to teach at Stanford for 250 years."[153] MOOCs have the capacity of impacting in a multiplying dimension.

On the flip side, if one professor is able to teach 100,000 students, the implications could be grave when it comes to jobs and employments. The number of professors needed may reduce, and so could the number of universities. The one thing though is that the high cost of education would likely drop significantly. The question then is where do we go from here and how can all these interests be accommodated?

MOOCs are not altogether a new phenomenon. Some argue that it is a recloned form of online distance learning. MOOCs play a significant role in the face of today's digital world and works alongside Open Distance Learning (ODL), open education and OER. MOOCs apparently are not anti-OER in that they seek "to make knowledge the common property of humankind, and to find a business model that generates money for doing it".[154] OER and MOOCs are however different in structure. While OER is content or resource based; MOOCs are course based, but they both seek to make knowledge available to curious minds. A major difference between MOOCs and OER is that while all OER are free/open source in structure, MOOCs are not necessarily free/open source.

Providers and participants of MOOCs need to be aware of the legal implications associated with providing and using these massive open online courses. MOOCs may be built using purely OER, thus those resources are free to use but may also be built with a mix. In such cases, the final output is a work containing proprietary interest with IP laws coming to the fore. The issue is for creators to clarify the type of resources made available and to identify the rights that exist on such resources. Where there are rights, clearance needs to be obtained. A convenient option in the spirit of openness is to stick to contents/resources licensed under one of the open licensing regimes and to licence the materials within the courses under an open licence.

14 Future of OER

Where OER will go from here cannot be accurately predicted. The fact that educational resources are open and freely available for curious minds to tinker with provides the world an endless opportunity for development and transformation. It is also already changing the educational system, with initiatives like MOOCs providing alternative ways of providing courses to students. It is also already impacting on the cost of education through its free availability of resources. Whether MOOCs will one day translate into award of degrees is still not yet certain but the dynamic changes taking place within the educational sector with the quick adoption of open courses by several universities is an indication that open education has come to stay.

On the social side, globalization has contributed to a decline in most indigenous languages in favour of the major languages especially, the English language. Whether this is good or bad is not the focus here. OER provides the platform for preservation of languages and the culture. Using the OER platform, knowledge can be provided in creative ways about indigenous languages and cultures and this information can be further developed by other contributors. The usefulness of this type of information will be most valuable to nationals in diasporas who are desirous of learning their language or teaching their children the language. Other interested learners would also have the opportunity to do so.

At the introduction of this article, I referred to the quotation by Nelson Mandela that "education is the most powerful weapon which you can use to change the world." The OER movement has begun a global change and seeks to put this weapon in the hands of every willing mind by providing unrestricted and unlimited opportunities to educational resources.

Notes

1 Greg Edwards, 'Fed: Student Loan Debt Surpasses Auto, Credit Card Debt' *St. Louis Business Journal*, available at www.bizjournals.com/stlouis/blog/2013/04/fed-student-loan-debt-surpasses-auto.html. See also, Cable Green, *OER K-12 Bill Passes in U.S.*

Washington State, available at http://creativecommons.org/weblog/entry/31756. See also, Cable Green, *The Impact of Open Textbooks at OpenStax College*, available at http://creativecommons.org/tag/open-textbooks.

2 UNESCO, EFA Global Monitoring Report 2015: Education for all 2000–2015: Achievements and Challenges (2015), http://unesdoc.unesco.org/images/0023/002322/232205e.pdf UNESCO Institute for Statistics, *International Literacy Data*, UNESCO (2013), available at www.uis.unesco.org/literacy/Pages/data-release-map-2013.aspx.

3 United Nations Educational, Scientific and Cultural Organization's (UNESCO) Institute for Statistics, *International Literacy Data*, UNESCO (2013), available at www.uis.unesco.org/literacy/Pages/data-release-map-2013.aspx.

4 See generally, Hans Botnen Eide, *Literacy Rates Are Rising – but Not Fast Enough*, available at http://efareport.wordpress.com/2012/05/31/literacy-rates-are-rising-but-not-fast-enough/. Norway, 100 percent; Luexembourg, 100 percent; Finland, 100 percent; Andorra, 100 percent; Greenland 100 percent; North Korea 100 percent; Russia, 99.7 percent; United States, 99 percent; United Kingdom, 99 percent; Ireland, 99 percent; Switzerland, 99 percent; Sweden, 99 percent; Japan, 99 percent; New Zealand, 99 percent; Australia, 96 percent. See also, Wikipedia, *List of Countries by Literacy Rate*, available at http://en.wikipedia.org/wiki/List_of_countries_by_literacy_rate.

5 The foreword to the EFA 2015 reports notes that "There are still 58 million children out of school globally and around 100 million children who do not complete primary education. Inequality in education has increased, with the poorest and most disadvantaged shouldering the heaviest burden."

6 John Alechenu, 'Nigeria, Still in the Throes of Illiteracy' *Punch*, available at www.punchng.com/education/nigeria-still-in-the-throes-of-illiteracy/. See also, UNESCO, 'Major Push for Adult and Youth Literacy in Nigeria' *UNESCO* (2012), available at www.unesco.org/new/en/dakar/about-this-office/single-view/news/major_push_for_adult_and_youth_literacy_in_nigeria/.

7 S. O. Labo-Popoola et al., 'Universal Basic Education in Nigeria: Challenges and Way Forward' 6 (2009) *Pakistan Journal of Social Sciences* 252.

8 Ige Akindele, 'Challenges Facing the Achievement of Education for All (EFA) and Education Related Millennium Development Goals (MDG) in Nigeria' 3 (2014) *Journal of Poverty, Investment and Development*.

9 See generally, Brian Lai & Clayto Thyne, 'The Effect of Civil War on Education, 1980–97' 44 (2007) *Journal of Peace Research*. See also, Mark Tran, *War Denying Millions of Children an Education*, available at www.theguardian.com/global-development/2013/jul/12/war-denying-children-education.

10 IRIN, *NIGERIA: School Attendance Down After Boko Haram Attacks*, available at www.irinnews.org/report/95327/nigeria-school-attendance-down-after-boko-haram-attacks.

11 See Article 26, UN General Assembly, *UDHR Universal Declaration of Human Rights*, 10 December (1948), 217 A (III), available at www.unhcr.org/refworld/docid/3ae6b3712c.html

12 Organisation for Economic Co-operation and Development (OECD), *Giving Knowledge for Free The Emergence of Open Educational Resources* (OECD Publishing, 2007), 30.

13 See generally, Stephen Downes, 'Learning Objects: Resources for Distance Education Worldwide' 2 (2001) *The International Review of Research in Open and Distributed Learning (IRRODL)*. See also, J. L. Moore et al., 'E-Learning, Online Learning, and Distance Learning Environments: Are They the Same?' 14 (2011) *Internet and Higher Education*.

14 Massachusetts Institute of Technology (MIT), *About OCW*, available at http://ocw.mit.edu/about/.accessed on 19/7/2013. The site currently hosts 2150 courses and has had over 125 million visitors.

15 Sally Johnstone, 'Open Educational Resources Serve the World' 3 (2005) *Educase Quarterly*.

16 MIT, *About the OpenCourseWare Consortium*, available at http://ocw.mit.edu/about/ocw-consortium/.
17 UNESCO, *Open Educational Resources*, available at www.unesco.org/new/en/communication-and-information/access-to-knowledge/open-educational-resources/. accessed on 19/7/2013.
18 Sally Johnstone, *Open Eductional Resources Conversation in Cyberspace* (UNESCO Publishing, 2009), 30.
19 UNESCO, *Open Educational Resources.*
20 UNESCO World Open Educational Resources (OER) Congress (2012). It was held in Paris, 20–22 June 2012.
21 OECD, Giving Knowledge for Free: The Emergence of Open Educational Resources (2007), available at www.oecd.org/education/ceri/38851849.pdf
22 Daniel E. Atkins et al., *A Review of the Open Educational Resources (OER) Movement: Achievements, Challenges, and New Opportunities*, available at www.hewlett.org/uploads/files/ReviewoftheOERMovement.pdf. Prepared by Atkins, Brown & Hammond. See P. 4.
23 *A Basic Guide to Open Educational Resoources (OER)*, A Report Commissioned by the Commonweath of Learning and the UNESCO, prepared by Neil Butcher and Edited by Asha Kanwar (COL) and Stamenka Uvalic-Trumbic (UNESCO). (2011).
24 Fadokun James Banji, *Open Education Resources and Teacher Professional Development in Nigeria: Prospects and Challenges, a Paper Delivered at the 7th Pan-Commonwealth Forum on Open Learning (PCF7)*, available at http://pcfpapers.colfinder.org/bitstream/handle/5678/125/Paper%20460%20%20%28Supplementary%20File%29.pdf?sequence=1. See the abstract which notes that OER amongst other things obviates demographic, economic and geographical educational boundaries.
25 Ilkka Tuomi, 'Open Educational Resources and the Transformation of Education' 48 (2013) *European Journal of Education* 70.
26 *Budapest Open Access Initiative*, available at www.opensocietyfoundations.org/openaccess/read.
27 Wenhong Chen & Barry Wellman, 'The Global Digital Divide – Within and Between Countries' 1 (2004) *IT & Society*.
28 Kunle Ola, 'Evolution and Future Trends of Copyright In Nigeria' 36 (2) (2014) *Journal of Open Access to Law (JOAL)* 1, 4.
29 See, Lawrence Liang, *Guide to Open Content Licenses v1.2 43* (Piet Zwart Institute, Institute for postgraduate studies and research, Willem de Kooning Academy Hogeschool, 2004). "Every open content license therefore asserts the copyright of the author and states that without a license from the author, any user using the work would be in violation of copyright." Lucie Guilbault & Christina Angelopoulos, *Open Content Licensing* (Amsterdam University Press, 2011), 8."This new licensing model purports to rectify the shortcomings of the copyright regime by allowing, through contracts increased access to and use of artistic and scientific works."
30 Johnstone, *UNESCO Publishing* (2009).
31 OECD (2007).
32 Richard Stallman, *The GNU Project*, available at www.gnu.org/gnu/thegnuproject.html.
33 Johnstone, 16 (2005).
34 Alek Kwi, Open Lesson Launched in Poland with 30 Workshops, *European Open Edu Policy Project*, available at http://oerpolicy.eu/open-lesson-do-it-yourself-workshop-materials-on-open-education/. "The kids let it go a little bit and stopped being copyright extremist. What is more, the teacher used our scenario also to discuss how to protect one's personal data on Facebook, and why this is so important."
35 OECD, 32 (2007).
36 John Daniel et al., *eLearning and Free Open Source Software the Key to Global Mass Higher Education*, available at www.col.org/PublicationDocuments/pub_JDspeeches_Vol2_web.pdf, 2 COL (2006).

37 Stephen Downes, *Models for Sustainable Open Educational Resources*, available at www.oecd.org/edu/ceri/36781698.pdf.
38 Stallman (2010).
39 Ilkka Tuomi, *Open Educational Resources: What They Are and Why Do They Matter: Report prepared for the OECD*, available at www.meaningprocessing.com/personalPages/tuomi/articles/OpenEducationalResources_OECDreport.pdf. at 8.
40 Anne Fitzgerald & Kylie Pappalardo, 'Open Standards in Government' in Brian Fitzgerald ed., *Access to Public Sector Information: Law, Technology & Policy* (Sydney University Press, 2007), 304.
41 Downes (2006).
42 Federal Communications Commission, *Federal Communications Commission's (FCC) Second Report and Order (FCC 03–101, Released on the 30th of April, 2003) 47 C.F.R. § 54.500(b)*. available at www.sl.universalservice.org/reference/educational_purposes.asp.
43 *The National Collegiate Athletic Association v Kansas Department of Revenue*, 781 P. 2d 726, 245 Kan. 553 (Supreme Court).
44 Id. at.
45 See P. B. Hugenholtz & Ruth L. Okediji, *Conceiving an International Instrument on Limitations and Exceptions to Copyright* (2008), 19, available at https://www.ivir.nl/publicaties/download/limitations_exceptions_copyright.pdf. where it was noted that "In all likelihood, the term applies first and foremost to statutory limitations that curtail the rights of right holders in specific circumstances to cater for the interests of certain user groups or the public at large."
46 Jerome H. Reichman & Ruth L. Okediji, 'When Copyright Law and Science Collide: Empowering Digitally Integrated Research Methods on a Global Scale' 96 (2012) *Minnesota Law Review*.
47 Section 107, The United States of America, Copyright Act of 1976 Title 17 of United States Code (1976).
48 Canadian Copyright Act, C-42 (1985).
49 Nigerian Copyright Act, Cap C28 (2004).
50 South African Copyright Act No. 98 of 1978 (1978).
51 Section 29, C-42 (1985).
52 Second Schedule, Cap C28 (2004).
53 Section 12(1)a, (1978).
54 OECD (2007).
55 David W. Barnes, 'Congestible Intellectual Property and Impure Public Goods' 9 (2011) *Northwestern Journal of Technology and Intellectual Property* 533.
56 Peter Suber, 'Knowledge as a Public Good' *SPARC* (2009), available at www.sparc.arl.org/resources/articles/knowledge#sthash.R1nBSlQF.dpuf.
57 OECD (2007).
58 See Fitzgerald Brian, 'Copyright 2010: The Need for Better Negotiability/Usability Principles' in *Knowledge Policy Challenges for the 21st Century* (Greg Hearn & David Rooney eds., 2008), 152. Where he noted, "As the mantra goes, copyright law is needed as an incentive or a reward for creators in a world where it is hard to control information."
59 David Bollier, *Viral Spiral: How the Commoners Built a Digital Republic of Their Own* (New Press, 2008), 3–4.
60 Peter Suber, *Open Access Overview: Focusing on Open Access to Peer-Reviewed Research Articles and Their Preprints*, Peter Suber ed., available at www.earlham.edu/~peters/fos/overview.htm.
61 Joel Waldfogel, 'The Four P's of Digital Distribution in the Internet Era: Piracy, Pricing, Pie-Splitting, and Pipe Control' 7 (2010) *Student's Guides to the U.S. Government Series 3* 17.

62 Justin Norrie, 'Harvard Decries the High Cost of Journal Subscription' *The Conversation* (2012), available at http://theconversation.edu.au/harvard-journal-subscription-fees-are-prohibitive-6659, 24 April.
63 Edwards (2013).
64 Gutterman, Brian, 'Internet as a Catalyst for Change: Access, Development, Freedoms and Innovation' (Internet Governance Forum (IGF) 2011, available at www.intgovforum.org/cms/documents/publications/176-internet-as-a-catalyst-for-change-access-development-freedoms-and-innovations.
65 Green, *OER K-12 Bill Passes in U.S. Washington State* (2012)
66 Simon Owens, 'The Growing Adoption of Creative Commons Textbooks' (2013) *US News*.
67 See generally, Susan D'Antoni, *Open Educational Resources: The Way Forward, Deliberations of an International Community of Interest* (2008), available at www.pontydysgu.org/wp-content/uploads/2008/03/oer-way-forward-final-version-for-printing.pdf.
68 Stallman (2010).
69 Bollier, 3–4 (2008).
70 (CC) Creative Commons, *About the Licenses: What Our Licenses Do*, available at http://creativecommons.org/licenses/.
71 See Divisions 3, 4 and 4A of the Australian Copyright Act 1968 Act No. 63 of 1968 as amended Act No 63 (1968). See Sections 40–47A (Division 3), Sections 45–47A (Dvision 4), Sections 47AB-47H (Division 4A) See also, Sections 29–32.2 of the C-42 (1985). See also, S.107–122Title 17 of United States Code (1976). See Specifically Section 107 for Fair Use, 108–112, 117, 119, 121 ad 122 for other limitations on exclusive rights to copyright. See also, the second schedule to the Cap C28 (2004). See also, sections 12–19 of the (1978).
72 Brian Fitzgerald, 'A Short Overview of Creative Commons' in Brian Fitzgerald ed., *Open Content Licensing: Cultivating the Creative Commons* (Sydney University Press, 2007), 3.
73 Brian Fitzgerald, *Open Content Licensing (OCL) for Open Educational Resources: A Paper Commissioned by the OECD's Centre for Educational Research and Innovation (CERI) for the project on Open Educational Resources*, 7 (2007).
74 Rob Farrow, *National Uptake of Siyavula Textbooks in South Africa* (2014), available at http://oermap.org/evidence/national-uptake-of-siyavula-textbooks-in-south-africa/.
75 Institute for the Study of Knowledge Management in Education (ISKME), *Siyavula: Building Communities to Support Teacher Use Localization and Sharing of OER*, available at www.iskme.org/our-work/siyavula-project-formative-and-summative-research-study.
76 See Siyavula, *Who We Are Our Story*, available at http://siyavula.com/who-we-are/our-story/.
77 Judges 21:25, *The Holy Bible: Authorized King James Version, Containing the Old and New Testaments* (Holman Bible Publishers Read-to-me ed., 1984).
78 H. L. A. Hart, *Law, Liberty, and Morality* (Stanford University Press, 1963), 14, 47.
79 Berne Convention for the Protection of Literary and Artistic Works, 9 September 1886, amended last on 28 September 1979.
80 World Trade Organization (WTO), Agreement on Trade-Related Aspects of Intellectual Property Rights (WTO ed., 1994).
81 World Intellectual Property Organisation (WIPO), *WIPO Internet Treaties*, available at www.wipo.int/copyright/en/activities/wct_wppt/wct_wppt.html.
82 Internet Industry Association (IIA), *Principles for a Digitial Economy: A Manifesto on Internet Policy and Regulation with Principles and Recommendations to Guide Decision Making*, available at http://iia.net.au/sites/default/files/manifesto-2010-6.pdf.
83 WIPO, *What Is Intellectual Property*, available at www.wipo.int/about-ip/en/.
84 Fitzgerald, 10–11 (2007).

85 Kunle Ola, *Copyright Collective Administration in Nigeria Lessons for Africa* (Springer, 2013), 4.
86 Waldfogel, 17 (2010).
87 O. Ola, *Copyright Collective Administration in Nigeria: Lessons for Africa* (Springer, London, 2013), 8.
88 Till Kreutzer, 'User-Related Assets and Drawbacks of Open Content Licensing' in Lucie Guilbault & Christina Angelopoulos eds., *Open Content Licensing from Theory to Practice* (Amsterdam University Press, 2011), 109.
89 Esther Hoorn, 'Contributing to Conversational Copyright: Creative Commons Licenses and Cultural Heritage Institutions', see id. at 206.
90 Fitzgerald, 3 (2007).
91 Michael Carrol, 'Creative Commons Licenses Opening Access to Education in Sub-Saharan Africa and India' *Creative Commons* (2015), available at http://us.creativecommons.org/archives/1062.
92 TESSA, *Primary Education Materials*, available at www.tessafrica.net/.
93 UNESCO, *High Level Workshop on OpenupEd OER and MOOCs for the National Open University of Nigeria* (2014), available at http://en.unesco.org/events/high-level-workshop-openuped-oer-and-moocs-national-open-university-nigeria.
94 OER Africa, *Building African Education Capacity Through Openness*, available at www.oerafrica.org/Home/tabid/36/Default.aspx.
95 Aurelia J. Schultz, *Back to School: Open Educational Resources in Africa*, available at http://creativecommons.org/weblog/entry/17273.
96 African Virtual University (AVU), *About: Introduction*, available at www.avu.org/About-AVU/introduction.html.
97 AVU, *The AVU OER Repository*, available at www.avu.org/the-avu-oer-repository.html.
98 ISKME. See also, Siyavula. See also, Farrow (2014). See also, Carrol (2015).
99 Writing Commons, *About*, available at http://writingcommons.org/about.
100 UNESCO, *The University of Nairobi Enhances Education for All with Open Educational Resources* (2015), available at www.unesco.org/new/en/nairobi/about-this-office/single-view/news/the_university_of_nairobi_enhances_education_for_all_with_op-1/
101 UNESCO, *Massive Open Education Opportunities at the National Open University of Nigeria* (2014), available at www.unesco.org/new/en/communication-and-information/resources/news-and-in-focus-articles/all-news/news/massive_open_education_opportunities_at_the_national_open_university_of_nigeria/#.VVBqdvmqqko.
102 MIT, *MITOPENCOURSEWARE*, available at http://ocw.mit.edu/index.htm.
103 MIT, *Site Statistics*, available at http://ocw.mit.edu/about/site-statistics/.
104 Timothy Vollmer, *New Federal Education Fund Makes Available $2 Billion to Create OER Resources in Community Colleges*, available at http://creativecommons.org/weblog/entry/26100.
105 Edwards (2013).
106 Cable Green, *British Columbia Government Lends Support to Open Textbooks*, available at http://creativecommons.org/weblog/entry/34566?utm_campaign=newsletter_1210&utm_medium=blog&utm_source=newsletter.
107 Timothy Vollmer, *California Passes Groundbreaking Open Textbook Legislation*, available at http://creativecommons.org/weblog/entry/34288.
108 Green (2013).
109 Cable Green, *US Department of State Unveils Open Book Project*, available at http://creativecommons.org/weblog/entry/36421.
110 The World Bank, *Open Knowledge Repository*, available at https://openknowledge.worldbank.org/.

111 (CC) Creative Commons, *About the Licenses*, available at http://creativecommons.org/licenses/.
112 The World Bank, *World Bank Announces Open Access Policy for Research and Knowledge, Launches Open Knowledge Repository* (2012), available at www.worldbank.org/en/news/press-release/2012/04/10/world-bank-announces-open-access-policy-for-research-and-knowledge-launches-open-knowledge-repository.
113 Examples of other OER initiatives in Africa include but are not limited to the following:

1) ACEMaths Project www.oerafrica.org/acemaths; 2) Free Courseware Project, http://freecourseware.uwc.ac.za/; 3) African Health OER Network, www.oerafrica.org/healthoer; and 4) MERLOT African Network, http://man.merlot.org/index.html

114 MIT, Site Statistics. See also, Khan Academy, *Our Mission*, available at www.khanacademy.org/about.
115 *Curriki*, available at www.curriki.org/.
116 *OER Commons*, available at www.oercommons.org/.
117 *LeMIll*, available at http://lemill.net/.
118 *Connexions*, available at http://cnx.org/.
119 *Open Courseware Consortium*, available at www.ocwconsortium.org/.
120 *Opencourseware Websites*, available at www.ocwconsortium.org/courses/ocwsites.
121 *Jorum*, available at www.jorum.ac.uk/.
122 *Encyclopedia of Life*, available at http://eol.org/.
123 See OpenupEd, *Our Framework*, available at www.openuped.eu/mooc-features.
124 Chimamanda Ngozi Adichie, 'The Danger of a Single Story' *TEDGlobal*, available at www.ted.com/talks/chimamanda_adichie_the_danger_of_a_single_story?language=en." if we hear only a single story about another person or country, we risk a critical misunderstanding."
125 UNESCO (2015). See also, UNESCO (2014).
126 David Grossman, *Massive Open Online Courses – Threat or Opportunity?* available at www.bbc.co.uk/news/education-23069542.
127 Isaac Newton, *From a Letter Written by Isaac Newton to Robert Hooke*, 5 February (1676).
128 See the Second Schedule to the Nigerian Copyrght Act, Cap C28 (2004).
129 Fitzgerald, 14 (2007)."We need to be clear that the person or entity that provides permission under a Creative Commons license is indeed the copyright owner."
130 See, Fitzgerald (2007). See also, Creative Commons, About the Licenses. See also, Owens, *US News* (2013).
131 CC Australia, *Which Creative Commons Licence Is Right for Me? Poster*, available at http://creativecommons.org.au/learn/fact-sheets/licensing-flowchart/.
132 Creative Commons, *Examples of Creative Commons License Use*, available at http://creativecommons.org/examples.
133 Creative Commons, *The Power of Open*, available at http://thepowerofopen.org/.
134 Creative Commons, *Contact*, available at http://creativecommons.org/contact#discuss.
135 Wenhong Chen & Wellman (2004).
136 Barbara Kirsop et al., 'Access to Scientific Knowledge for Sustainable Development: Options for Developing Countries' *ARIADNE*, available at www.ariadne.ac.uk/issue52/kirsop-et-al.
137 Sherwyn P. Morreale et al., 'Why Communication Is Important: A Rationale for the Centrality of the Study of Communication' 29 (2000) *Journal of the Association for Communication Administration* 6–7.
138 Joshua Reno, 'Your Trash Is Someone's Treasure: The Politics of Value at a Michiga Landfill' 14 (2009) *Journal of Material Culture* 29.

139 G. Agoramoorthy & M. J. Hsu, 'The Significance of Cows in Indian Society Between Sacredness and Economy' 18 (2012) *Anthropological Notebooks* 5.

140 Neil Butcher, 12 (2011)."In the final analysis, responsibility for assuring the quality of OER used in teaching and learning environments will reside with the institution, programme/course coordinators, and individual educators responsible for delivery of education."

141 Open Educational Resources: Open Content for Higher Education, Forum 1 Final Report of The Virtual University, Prepared by Paul Albright, Western Interstate Commission for Higher Education, CO, February (2006), available at www.unesco.org/iiep/virtualuniversity/forumsfiche.php?queryforumspages_id=23. "You can't create educational materials that function effectively in every single context any more than you can write software that runs on every single platform. . . . [W]e should focus on solving specific instruction problems, and make sure that our solution at least works for someone. Then other developers can 'port' our materials to their 'platform.'"

142 Downes (2006).

143 *Curriki.*

144 *OER Commons.*

145 *LeMIll.*

146 *Connexions.*

147 *Open Courseware Consortium.*

148 *Opencourseware Websites.*

149 *Jorum.*

150 *Encyclopedia of Life.*

151 Laura Pappano, The Year of the MOOC, available at www.nytimes.com/2012/11/04/education/edlife/massive-open-online-courses-are-multiplying-at-a-rapid-pace.html?_r=0

152 John Daniel, Daniel's Comprehensive Review of MOOC Developments, available at https://www.tonybates.ca/2012/10/01/daniels-comprehensive-review-of-mooc-developments/

153 David Grossman, What Is a Mooc?, available at https://www.bbc.com/news/education-23069542

154 John Daniel, Daniel's Comprehensive Review of MOOC Developments, available at https://www.tonybates.ca/2012/10/01/daniels-comprehensive-review-of-mooc-developments/

Bibliography

African Virtual University, *About: Introduction*, available at www.avu.org/About-AVU/introduction.html.

African Virtual University, *The AVU OER Repository*, available at www.avu.org/the-avu-oer-repository.html.

Agoramoorthy, G. & M. J. Hsu, 'The Significance of Cows in Indian Society Between Sacredness and Economy' 18 (2012) *Anthropological Notebooks*.

Akindele, Ige, 'Challenges Facing the Achievement of Education for All (EFA) and Education Related Millennium Development Goals (MDG) in Nigeria' 3 (2014) *Journal of Poverty, Investment and Development*.

Alechenu, John, Nigeria, Still in the Throes of Illiteracy, *Punch*, available at www.punchng.com/education/nigeria-still-in-the-throes-of-illiteracy/.

Atkins, Daniel E., et al., *A Review of the Open Educational Resources (OER) Movement: Achievements, Challenges, and New Opportunities*, available at www.hewlett.org/uploads/files/ReviewoftheOERMovement.pdf.

Australian Copyright Act 1968 Act No. 63 of 1968 as amended Act No 63 (1968).

Barnes, David W., 'Congestible Intellectual Property and Impure Public Goods' 9 (2011) *Northwestern Journal of Technology and Intellectual Property* 533.

A Basic Guide to Open Educational Resources (OER), A Report Commissioned by the Commonweath of Learning and the UNESCO, prepared by Neil Butcher and Edited by Asha Kanwar (COL) and Stamenka Uvalic-Trumbic (UNESCO) (2011).

Berne Convention for the Protection of Literary and Artistic Works, 9 September 1886, amended last on 28 September 1979.

Bollier, David, *Viral Spiral: How the Commoners Built a Digital Republic of Their Own* (New Press, 2008).

Botnen Eide, Hans, *Literacy Rates Are Rising – But Not Fast Enough*, available at http://efareport.wordpress.com/2012/05/31/literacy-rates-are-rising-but-not-fast-enough/.

Brian, Fitzgerald, '*Copyright 2010:* The Need for Better Negotiability/Usability Principles' in Greg Hearn & David Rooney eds., *Knowledge Policy Challenges for the 21st Century* (Edward Elgar, 2008).

Budapest Open Access Initiative, available at www.opensocietyfoundations.org/open access/read.

Cable Green, *British Columbia Government Lends Support to Open Textbooks*, available at http://creativecommons.org/weblog/entry/34566?utm_campaign=newsletter_1210&utm_medium=blog&utm_source=newsletter.

Cable Green, *The Impact of Open Textbooks at OpenStax College*, available at http://creativecommons.org/tag/open-textbooks.

Cable Green, *OER K-12 Bill Passes in U.S. Washington State*, available at http://creativecommons.org/weblog/entry/31756.

Cable Green, *US Department of State Unveils Open Book Project*, available at http://creativecommons.org/weblog/entry/36421.

Canadian Copyright Act, C-42 (1985).

Carrol, Michael, Creative Commons Licenses Opening Access to Education in Sub-Saharan Africa and India, *Creative Commons* (2015), available at http://us.creativecommons.org/archives/1062.

(CC) Creative Commons, *About the Licenses*, available at http://creativecommons.org/licenses/.

(CC) Creative Commons, *About the Licenses: What Our Licenses Do*, available at http://creativecommons.org/licenses/.

(CC) Creative Commons, *Contact*, available at http://creativecommons.org/contact#discuss.

(CC) Creative Commons, *Examples of Creative Commons License Use*, available at http://creativecommons.org/examples.

(CC) Creative Commons, *The Power of Open*, available at http://thepowerofopen.org/.

CC Australia, *Which Creative Commons License Is Right for Me? Poster*, available at http://creativecommons.org.au/learn/fact-sheets/licensing-flowchart/.

Chen, Wenhong & Barry Wellman, 'The Global Digital Divide – Within and Between Countries' 1 (2004) *IT & Society*.

Connexions, available at http://cnx.org/.

Curriki, available at www.curriki.org/.

Daniel, John, et al., *ELearning and Free Open Source Software the Key to Global Mass Higher Education* (2006), available at www.col.org/PublicationDocuments/pub_JDspeeches_Vol2_web.pdf, 2 COL.

Downes, Stephen, 'Learning Objects: Resources for Distance Education Worldwide' 2 (2001) *The International Review of Research in Open and Distributed Learning (IRRODL)*.

Downes, Stephen, *Models for Sustainable Open Educational Resources*, available at www.oecd.org/edu/ceri/36781698.pdf.

Edwards, Greg, 'Fed: Student Loan Debt Surpasses Auto, Credit Card Debt' *St. Louis Business Journal*, available at www.bizjournals.com/stlouis/blog/2013/04/fed-student-loan-debt-surpasses-auto.html.

UNESCO, EFA Global Monitoring Report 2015: Education for all 2000–2015: Achievements and Challenges (2015), available at http://unesdoc.unesco.org/images/0023/002322/232205e.pdf*Encyclopedia of Life*, available at http://eol.org/.

Farrow, Rob, *National Uptake of Siyavula Textbooks in South Africa* (2014), available at http://oermap.org/evidence/national-uptake-of-siyavula-textbooks-in-south-africa/.

Federal Communications Commission, *Federal Communications Commission's (FCC) Second Report and Order (FCC 03–101, Released on the 30th of April, 2003) 47 C.F.R. § 54.500(b)*, available at www.sl.universalservice.org/reference/educational_purposes.asp.

Fitzgerald, Brian, 'A Short Overview of Creative Commons' in Brian Fitzgerald ed., *Open Content Licensing: Cultivating the Creative Commons* (Sydney University Press, 2007).

Fitzgerald, Brian, *Open Content Licensing (OCL) for Open Educational Resources: A Paper Commissioned by the OECD's Centre for Educational Research and Innovation (CERI) for the Project on Open Educational Resources* (2007), available at www.oecd.org/education/ceri/38645489.pdf

Fitzgerald, Anne & Kylie Pappalardo, 'Open Standards in Government' in Brian Fitzgerald ed., *Access to Public Sector Information: Law, Technology & Policy* (Sydney University Press, 2010).

OECD, Giving Knowledge for Free: The Emergence of Open Educational Resources (2007), available at www.oecd.org/education/ceri/38851849.pdf

Grossman, David, *Massive Open Online Courses – Threat or Opportunity?* available at www.bbc.co.uk/news/education-23069542.

Guilbault, Lucie & Christina Angelopoulos, *Open Content Licensing* (Amsterdam University Press, 2011).

Gutterman, Brian, 'Internet as a Catalyst for Change: Access, Development, Freedoms and Innovation' Internet Governance Forum (IGF) 2011, available at www.intgovforum.org/cms/documents/publications/176-internet-as-a-catalyst-for-change-access-development-freedoms-and-innovations

Hart, H. L. A., *Law, Liberty, and Morality* (Stanford University Press, 1963).

The Holy Bible: Authorized King James Version, Containing the Old and New Testaments (Holman Bible Publishers Read-to-me ed., 1984).

Hoorn, Esther, 'Contributing to Conversational Copyright: Creative Commons Licenses and Cultural Heritage Institutions' in Lucie Guilbault & Christina Angelopoulos eds., *Open Content Licensing from Theory to Practice* (Amsterdam University Press, 2011).

Hugenholtz, P. B. & Ruth L. Okediji, *Conceiving an International Instrument on Limitations and Exceptions to Copyright* (2008), available at https://www.ivir.nl/publicaties/download/limitations_exceptions_copyright.pdf

Institute for the Study of Knowledge Management in Education (ISKME), *Siyavula: Building Communities to Support Teacher Use Localization and Sharing of OER*, available at www.iskme.org/our-work/siyavula-project-formative-and-summative-research-study.

Internet Industry Association (IIA), *Principles for a Digital Economy: A Manifesto on Internet Policy and Regulation with Principles and Recommendations to Guide Decision Making*, available at http://iia.net.au/sites/default/files/manifesto-2010-6.pdf.

IRIN, *NIGERIA: School Attendance Down After Boko Haram Attacks*, available at www.irinnews.org/report/95327/nigeria-school-attendance-down-after-boko-haram-attacks.

James Banji, Fadokun, *Open Education Resources and Teacher Professional Development in Nigeria: Prospects and Challenges, a Paper Delivered at the 7th Pan-Commonwealth Forum on Open Learning (PCF7)*, available at http://pcfpapers.colfinder.org/bitstream/handle/5678/125/Paper%20460%20%20%28Supplementary%20File%29.pdf?sequence=1.

Jerome H. Reichman & Ruth L. Okediji, 'When Copyright Law and Science Collide: Empowering Digitally Integrated Research Methods on a Global Scale' 96 (2012) *Minnesota Law Review*.

Johnstone, Sally, *Open Educational Resources Conversation in Cyberspace* (UNESCO Publishing, 2009).

Johnstone, Sally, 'Open Educational Resources Serve the World' 3 (2005) *Educase Quarterly*.

Jorum, available at www.jorum.ac.uk/.

Khan Academy, *Our Mission*, available at www.khanacademy.org/about.

Kirsop, Barbara, et al., Access to Scientific Knowledge for Sustainable Development: Options for Developing Countries, *ARIADNE*, available at www.ariadne.ac.uk/issue52/kirsop-et-al.

Kreutzer, Till, 'User-Related Assets and Drawbacks of Open Content Licensing' in Lucie Guilbault & Christina Angelopoulos eds., *Open Content Licensing from Theory to Practice* (Amsterdam University Press, 2011).

Kwi, Alek, Open Lesson Launched in Poland with 30 Workshops, *European Open Edu Policy Project*, available at http://oerpolicy.eu/open-lesson-do-it-yourself-workshop-materials-on-open-education/.

Labo-Popoola, S. O., et al., 'Universal Basic Education in Nigeria: Challenges and Way Forward' 6 (2009) *Pakistan Journal of Social Sciences*.

Lai, Brian & Clayto Thyne, 'The Effect of Civil War on Education, 1980–97' 44 (2007) *Journal of Peace Research*.

LeMIll, available at http://lemill.net/.

Liang, Lawrence, *Guide to Open Content Licenses v1.2* (Piet Zwart Institute, Institute for postgraduate studies and research, Willem de Kooning Academy Hogeschool. 2004).

(MIT) Massachusetts Institute of Technology, *About OCW*, available at http://ocw.mit.edu/about/.

(MIT) Massachusetts Institute of Technology, *About the OpenCourseWare Consortium*, available at http://ocw.mit.edu/about/ocw-consortium/.

(MIT) Massachusetts Institute of Technology, *Mitopencourseware*, available at http://ocw.mit.edu/index.htm.

(MIT) Massachusetts Institute of Technology, *Site Statistics*, available at http://ocw.mit.edu/about/site-statistics/.

Moore, J. L., et al., 'E-Learning, Online Learning, and Distance Learning Environments: Are They the Same?' 14 (2011) *Internet and Higher Education*.

Morreale, Sherwyn P., et al., 'Why Communication Is Important: A Rationale for the Centrality of the Study of Communication' 29 (200) *Journal of the Association for Communication Administration*.

The National Collegiate Athletic Association v Kansas Department of Revenue, 781 P. 2d 726, 245 Kan. 553 (Supreme Court).

Newton, Isaac, *From a Letter Written by Isaac Newton to Robert Hooke*, 5 February (1676).

Ngozi Adichie, Chimamanda, The Danger of a Single Story, *TEDGlobal*, available at www.ted.com/talks/chimamanda_adichie_the_danger_of_a_single_story?language=en.

Nigerian Copyright Act, Cap C28 (2004).

Norrie, Justin, Harvard Decries the High Cost of Journal Subscription, *The Conversation* (2012), available at http://theconversation.edu.au/harvard-journal-subscription-fees-are-prohibitive-6659, 24 April.

Organisation for Economic Co-operation and Development, *Giving Knowledge for Free the Emergence of Open Educational Resources* (OECD Publishing, 2007).

OER Africa, *Building African Education Capacity Through Openness*, available at www.oerafrica.org/Home/tabid/36/Default.aspx.

OER Commons, available at www.oercommons.org/.

Ola, Kunle, *Copyright Collective Administration in Nigeria Lessons for Africa* (Springer, 2013).

Ola, Kunle, 'Evolution and Future Trends of Copyright in Nigeria' 36 (2) (2014) *Journal of Open Access to Law (JOAL)* 1.

Ola, O., *Copyright Collective Administration in Nigeria: Lessons for Africa* (Springer, London, 2013).

Open Courseware Consortium, available at www.ocwconsortium.org/.

Opencourseware Websites, available at www.ocwconsortium.org/courses/ocwsites.

Open Educational Resources: Open Content for Higher Education, Forum 1 Final Report of The Virtual University, Prepared by Paul Albright, Western Interstate Commission for Higher Education, CO, February (2006), available at www.unesco.org/iiep/virtualuniversity/forumsfiche.php?queryforumspages_id=23.

UNESCO, Open Educational Resources: The Way Forward, Deliberations of an International Community of Interest (2008), available at http://unesdoc.unesco.org/images/0015/001579/157987e.pdf

OpenupEd, *Our Framework*, available at www.openuped.eu/mooc-features.

Owens, Simon, 'The Growing Adoption of Creative Commons Textbooks' (2013) *US News*.

Reno, Joshua, 'Your Trash Is Someone's Treasure: The Politics of Value at a Michigan Landfill' 14 (2009) *Journal of Material Culture*.

Schultz, Aurelia J., *Back to School: Open Educational Resources in Africa*, available at http://creativecommons.org/weblog/entry/17273.

Siyavula, *Who We Are Our Story*, available at http://siyavula.com/who-we-are/our-story/.

South African Copyright Act No.98 of 1978 (1978).

Stallman, Richard, *The GNU Project*, available at www.gnu.org/gnu/thegnuproject.html.

Suber, Peter, Knowledge as a Public Good, *SPARC* (2009), available at www.sparc.arl.org/resources/articles/knowledge#sthash.R1nBSlQF.dpuf.

Suber, Peter, *Open Access Overview: Focusing on Open Access to Peer-Reviewed Research Articles and Their Preprints*, available at www.earlham.edu/~peters/fos/overview.htm (Peter Suber ed.).

TESSA, *Primary Education Materials*, available at www.tessafrica.net/.

Tran, Mark, 'War Denying Millions of Children an Education' *The Guardian*, available at www.theguardian.com/global-development/2013/jul/12/war-denying-children-education.

Tuomi, Ilkka, 'Open Educational Resources and the Transformation of Education' 48 (2013) *European Journal of Education*.

Tuomi, Ilkka, *Open Educational Resources: What They Are and Why Do They Matter: Report Prepared for the OECD*, available at www.meaningprocessing.com/personalPages/tuomi/articles/OpenEducationalResources_OECDreport.pdf.

UN General Assembly, UDHR Universal Declaration of Human Rights 217 A (III), 10 December 1948, available at www.unhcr.org/refworld/docid/3ae6b3712c.html.

UNESCO, *High Level Workshop on OpenupEd OER and MOOCs for the National Open University of Nigeria* (2014), available at http://en.unesco.org/events/high-level-workshop-openuped-oer-and-moocs-national-open-university-nigeria.

UNESCO, Major Push for Adult and Youth Literacy in Nigeria, *UNESCO* (2012), available at www.unesco.org/new/en/dakar/about-this-office/single-view/news/major_push_for_adult_and_youth_literacy_in_nigeria/.

UNESCO, *Massive Open Education Opportunities at the National Open University of Nigeria* (2014), available at www.unesco.org/new/en/communication-and-information/resources/news-and-in-focus-articles/all-news/news/massive_open_education_opportunities_at_the_national_open_university_of_nigeria/#.VVBqdvmqqko.

UNESCO, *Open Educational Resources*, available at www.unesco.org/new/en/communication-and-information/access-to-knowledge/open-educational-resources/.

UNESCO, *The University of Nairobi Enhances Education for All with Open Educational Resources* (2015), available at www.unesco.org/new/en/nairobi/about-this-office/single-view/news/the_university_of_nairobi_enhances_education_for_all_with_op-1/

UNESCO, World Open Educational Resources (OER) Congress (2012), http://www.unesco.org/new/en/communication-and-information/events/calendar-of-events/events-websites/world-open-educational-resources-congress/.

UNESCO Institute for Statistics, International Literacy Data, *UNESCO* (2013), available at www.uis.unesco.org/literacy/Pages/data-release-map-2013.aspx.

The United States of America, Copyright Act of 1976 Title 17 of United States Code (1976).

Vollmer, Timothy, *California Passes Groundbreaking Open Textbook Legislation*, available at http://creativecommons.org/weblog/entry/34288.

Vollmer, Timothy, *New Federal Education Fund Makes Available $2 Billion to Create OER Resources in Community Colleges*, available at http://creativecommons.org/weblog/entry/26100.

Waldfogel, Joel, 'The Four P's of Digital Distribution in the Internet Era: Piracy, Pricing, Pie-Splitting, and Pipe Control' 7 (2010) *Student's Guides to the U.S. Government Series* 3.

Wikipedia, *List of Countries by Literacy Rate*, available at http://en.wikipedia.org/wiki/List_of_countries_by_literacy_rate.

WIPO, *What Is Intellectual Property*, available at www.wipo.int/about-ip/en/.

WIPO, *WIPO Internet Treaties*, available at www.wipo.int/copyright/en/activities/wct_wppt/wct_wppt.html.

The World Bank, *Open Knowledge Repository*, available at https://openknowledge.worldbank.org/.

The World Bank, *World Bank Announces Open Access Policy for Research and Knowledge, Launches Open Knowledge Repository* (2012), available at www.worldbank.org/en/news/press-release/2012/04/10/world-bank-announces-open-access-policy-for-research-and-knowledge-launches-open-knowledge-repository.

World Trade Organization (WTO), *Agreement on Trade-Related Aspects of Intellectual Property Rights* (World Trade Organization (WTO) ed., 1994).

Writing Commons, *About*, available at http://writingcommons.org/about.

6 Public sector information

1 Introduction

Information has become the most important commodity in this dispensation. The reign of a global knowledge economy coupled with technological advancements like the Internet, the World Wide Web, Web 2.0, and many other technological discoveries and inventions have contributed to the ascendency of information as the most important commodity in this generation, and information within the custody of government is an important part of the information structure.[1] Public sector information (PSI) refer to government-held information, which is information collated, generated, sourced and funded in part or fully by taxpayers.

The trade currency of the world today is information, content, knowledge.[2] The sayings "knowledge is power",[3] "information is key"[4] and "my people perish for a lack of knowledge"[5] couldn't be more relevant in this generation. The concern today about information revolves amongst other things around how to access, use and reuse PSI within legally accepted boundaries. These concerns have been discussed at several fora and have become topical internationally. The governments of the United States of America,[6] European Union,[7] United Kingdom,[8] Canada,[9] New Zealand,[10] Australia[11] and Brazil[12] have all embraced the principles enabling access, use and reuse of PSI and continue to build better frameworks and principles that would enable access, use and reuse of their PSI. After 51 years of independence and several years of lobby, Nigeria passed a freedom of information (FOI) bill, which provides a legal regime for access to information subject to issues of confidentiality, intellectual property rights, right of privacy and national security.[13]

In a speech delivered at the University of Westminster, the Former Prime Minister of the United Kingdom, the Rt Hon. Gordon Brown MP, said "this is the century of information. Our ability to compete in the global economy, to protect ourselves against crime and terrorist attack, depends not just on natural wealth or on walls or fences but on our ability to use information."[14] This statement was captured in "Information matters", a government document jointly signed by the heads of the Cabinet Office, National Archive and National Audit Office in which it was noted that "Public servants are . . . guardians of public sector information, not the owners of it, and we will be judged by how well we manage this invaluable asset."[15]

Government cannot function in isolation of its people. Government is really about the people, it is about the active participation of citizens, accountability, transparency and openness. The reality however is that many citizens are cut off from the information flow channel. Access to information within the direct or indirect control of government enables citizenry participation in governance and also enables them make contributions to the society by turning around the information into value-added services and resources. The incentive to provide these services is even stronger when the information is freely accessible. Therefore, making this information available and accessible for use and reuse at a near zero price is imperative for development in this information age.

2 Definition and scope of PSI

PSI refers to information within the custody of the public service of a government inclusive of materials created as a result of public funding.[16] The Organisation for Economic Co-operation and Development particularly defines the term as "information, including information products and services, generated, created, collected, processed, preserved, maintained, disseminated, or funded by or for the Government or public institution".[17] These materials include legislations, judicial decisions, regulations, reports, official gazettes, policy documents, memoranda's, minutes, proceedings and reports of meetings, draft bills, submissions, public registers, maps, datasets, meteorological and geospatial information, census report, budget, fiscal policy and several other informational materials that enable citizens to be better informed of their environment, the activities and decisions of their elected leaders.[18]

PSI is wide and has been described as the "PSI complexity".[19] The public service includes the federal or central government, state or regional government, quasi or non-quasi-governmental structures, local governments, councils, wards and agencies. Information emanating from any of these sources inclusive of government owned public sector companies or private sector companies funded by government are information generated based on taxpayers' monies and hence may be regarded as public-sector information.

Government gathers information in multi-faceted ways; through its own platform, by directly procuring them from citizens, by mandating collation of it for instance through population census exercises, vaccination exercises, statistical surveys, birth, death, marriage, vehicle and company registrations.[20] These collated pieces of information in the custody of government is information gathered from the people for the people, and they should be available to the people to access, use and reuse.[21] The exact extent of access, use and reuse to certain information is however precluded due to reasons of national security, privacy, confidentiality and intellectual property rights protection. These exclusions shall be explained later in the chapter. The definition of PSI encapsulates information under the direct or indirect control of government in the broadest sense but at the same time recognizes the limitations placed on releasing certain information due to statutory or common law prohibitions. This chapter therefore discusses PSI from the broadest perspective but takes into cognizance the aforementioned legal limitations.

3 Importance of enabling access to PSI

Access to information is a fundamental right of all humans and governments have noted the need to make information available to their citizens for use and reuse as this enables *greater citizen participation, transparency of governance, promotion of democratic ideals and values (equality, democracy, openness), government accountability and transparency, and it allows for commercial development* through value-added services that are developed from information and knowledge made available and accessible and which allows for reuse.[22] Governments in recognition of the impact and dynamic nature of the Internet and the World Wide Web are adopting these platforms for information dissemination.[23]

Making information in the public sector readily available and accessible to the general public is crucial to national development. The reality is that not all of such information can be made available due to legal restrictions such as privacy, confidentiality, intellectual property protection, national security and such other considerations. Assuming information that falls within this category is excluded, there is still a lot of PSI, that is, information with no legal restrictions, that is, "publicly accessible information, the use of which would not infringe any legal right, or any obligation of confidentiality".[24] This class of information is of great value and if made available by PSI holders for use and reuse, it would enhance both the public and private sector, as well as governmental and individual well-being.

3.1 Consumer protection

The importance of enabling PSI could be construed from an economic or non-economic perspective. The latter perspective is best understood by looking at the protection of consumers. Legislations protecting consumers provide for certain terms which must be complied with to protect the interest of consumers.[25] It also provides for remedies in the event that a consumer has been wrongly treated. One of the best ways to protect the interest of the consumer is to provide adequate information when due and in all available formats. The availability of information to consumers puts them in a position to take informed decisions.

From the economic perspective, a large portion of PSI form the raw materials for value-added services. Meteorological data are a good example. The US government makes this information available to the general public, and it has built an economically viable navigation industry employing millions and making turnovers in the billions.[26]

3.2 Transparency in governance

Transparency is manifested through timely freedom of access to information. This enables good governance, curbs corruption and other illegal activities. Uhlir noted that "the more information that is openly available from the government and about the government, the less likely it will be that government is able to hide illegal acts, corruption and misrule. Conversely, excessive secrecy breeds tyranny."[27]

3.3 Promotion of democratic ideals

Qualitative participation in governance by members of the society is a fundamental part of democracy.[28] The recognition of the equality of all citizens as well as openness are integral parts of the democratic mechanism.[29] Qualitative participation is however best achieved when information is made available and accessible and the people are fully and duly informed. Protest or support for certain decisions of government is basically determined by access to information on such issues by the general public; therefore, access to PSI promotes democratic ideals.[30]

3.4 Enhances public health, safety and general social welfare

The free flow of information has been attributed as one of the key factors that aided in Nigeria's ability to arrest the unfortunate Ebola virus imported into Nigeria by Patrick Sawyer from Liberia.[31] Bankole noted that "We were in our office on Friday evening when we got word that Ebola had come to Lagos. Twenty-four hours later, Ebolafacts.com went live. In the next week, the infographic website explaining the causes, symptoms and preventive measures to be taken against Ebola would be seen by hundreds of thousands of Nigerians across the website, Twitter and Facebook".

The government does not belong to those who govern it. Those in position of power are merely servants to the generality of people and are to represent the public interest.[32] Provision of basic amenities such as health care facilities, security, welfare, education, good roads and water are some of the responsibilities of leaders. In most developing countries where there is a high level of lack of access to PSI, there is a trend where political candidates promise the people these basic amenities for their votes and once elected they renege on their promises.[33] One would expect that such persons would be voted out at the next election, but due to a lack of access to PSI, such leaders are able to deceive the uninformed publics. Access to PSI would enable ordinary citizens determine whether or not the electoral promises made have been fulfilled, and if not, they are thus empowered with facts to challenge government. This enhances public health, security and general social welfare.[34]

3.5 Serves essential scientific and technical research function

Some of the most expensive scientific and technical researches are carried out by government agencies. The data collated during the research as well as the reports of the research form very important information capable of enhancing innovation, creativity and development. The challenge often encountered by those eager to innovate, create and develop is that of a lack of access to this information. When access is granted, reuse rights may be withheld with technological protection measures requiring some payments and thereby restricting the use and reuse of such contents. For these reasons many governments are taking positive steps to ensure that the output of funded research is freely available for use and reuse.[35]

3.6 Socio-political development

Access to PSI has the potential of closing the information gap between the information rich and the information poor. It therefore provides social development to specific communities, which also extends in principle to the entire world. This is achieved by means of expanding access to the amount and quality of information available to the ordinary person.

3.7 Pragmatic feedback

Government is able to get pragmatic feedback from citizens when PSI is made accessible in a format that is easily retrievable. The need for the PSI to be accessible not just on a government website but in a retrievable and easily searchable format is crucial. With billions of data stored online, it is imperative that information storage patterns be compatible.

3.8 Sense of duty

The subconscious awareness created by ready accessibility and availability of PSI to the citizenry, raises caution in the mind of government officials to be up and doing on their jobs and this in turn sets in motion a sense of duty to service.

3.9 Accountability

The knowledge that every policy made and decision taken is openly available and would most likely be scrutinized by the people builds a sense of accountability on government officer holders. This is pertinent because poor decisions may cause protests, litigations, civil unrest or some form of reaction by the people. The mere awareness of this raises the accountability bar for government and its officials.

3.10 Reduced cost

Government agencies often expend taxpayers' monies carrying out the same findings. This is often done due to a lack of interagency collaboration and more often due to a lack of knowledge by each agency of the activities of the other. This lack of knowledge is not unconnected with the absence of information-sharing system between government agencies, which often results in duplication of activities, research findings and public funds. Interoperable and easy access to PSI will no doubt reduce government expenditure and save taxpayers' monies.

In a white paper prepared for United Nations Education and Scientific Cultural Organisation (UNESCO), the US National Commission on Libraries and Information Science and the National Forum on Information Literacy, Horton highlighted five main uses of public service information as follows:

1 To document for public accountability purposes how government conducts its business;

2 To inform public policy-makers and program managers so that they can do their job better;
3 To inform the general public so that it can do a wide variety of things with the information, such as apply for benefits for which they are entitled under the nation's laws, comply with various laws, obtain permits, and so forth;
4 To provide citizens with an independent, unmediated way to know what the government is doing, beyond reliance on the popular media, scholarly journals, and trade magazines, and which the public is paying for with its tax payer dollars; and
5 To provide the internal information necessary for conduct of an agency's responsibility.

According to Horton (2002), some of the imperatives for enabling access, use and reuse of public information and knowledge resources are as follows:

i Sustaining the competitive competency of the country's businesses and industries, in both domestic and global marketplaces;
ii Attaining the highest levels of educational excellence for all the nation's children and adults in a lifelong learning context;
iii Enabling citizens to participate more effectively in all facets of a democratic society;
iv Informing public officials at all levels of government so that they can enact better laws, formulate and enact enlightened public policies, monitor the programs they authorize effectively, and govern fairly, equitably, and wisely; and
v Enhancing the quality of life of all a country's citizens, including responsibility to the special government information needs of disadvantaged and disabled individuals.[36]

Accessibility to PSI has numerous values to the public. It gives power to the citizens, the power to be informed and to make informed decisions. Access to PSI allow citizens to participate in governance.

PSI represents some of the largest volumes of raw materials used in the private sector. It enhances commerce and employment and generates additional funds to the government through tax.[37] PSI serves as the databank for a lot of businesses and non-governmental organizations (NGO) who are desirous of providing some form of service to the community. Access to the number of people in a community, gender, health situation, layout, mapping, land size and other demographic information go along away in aiding these organizations provide highly needed services.[38] Access to PSI will enable anyone anywhere in the world to access information about that government and this increases the opportunity for social development, particularly education.

4 Global outlook on PSI

Prior to the movement for access to, use and reuse PSI, government establishments considered information within their custody as privileged information and hence kept it safely under locks and inaccessible to the public. The FOI movement altered this position by providing a platform to obtain requisite information on a request and need to know basis. The current movement builds on the "request and need to know" principles of the FOI and goes further to establish a default where PSI is made freely available and accessible without the requirement for request; free from all governmental bureaucratic challenges, technological barriers and where possible at a zero or marginal cost to users. This is made possible by the unique abilities of the Internet. Government agencies are therefore able via the Internet to make PSI available. However, the ability to fully access data provided by government is in question, as "most of the information relevant to the rulemaking process remain locked away in computer files that are images of printed documents, which cannot be easily reused."[39] Also observed is the fact that the right to use and reuse these materials is mostly restricted and where allowed, the terms permitting use/reuse are often times unclear to users. The need to therefore clarify these ambiguities through properly thought out information policies by government is imperative. The reality is that the value of PSI increases when price, technical and intellectual property (more particularly copyright) restrictions on access and reuse are removed, and it is made available in user-friendly digital formats downloadable from Internet websites.[40] The policies and strategies adopted by different nations to enable greater access to PSI will now be considered.

4.1 United States

Dissemination of information generated by or under the influence of the United States government is actively encouraged by the absence of copyright on all information generated by the federal government.[41] This model encourages openness and has enabled free dissemination of government information. Section 105 of the Copyright Act particularly provides that copyright protection is not available for any work of the United States Government. It places these works in the public domain and allows for free and unrestricted use. It is however important to note that this section does not extend to states within the United States. One of the famous year 2000 circulars issued by the Office of Management and Budget (OMB), Circular A-130, established the data access and reuse policy framework for executive-branch departments and agencies of the US federal government.[42] The document acknowledged the government as the largest single producer, collector, consumer and disseminator of information and took cognizance of the role of free-flowing information in the strengthening of a democratic nation. It further pointed out that government information is a valuable national resource which provides the public with requisite knowledge (past, present and future) about the government, society and the economy.[43]

On 21 January 2009, President Obama in a "Memorandum on Transparency and Open Government"[44] expressed his determination to establish a more open government and noted that government should be transparent, participatory and collaborative. He directed the OMB to issue an "Open Government Directive",[45] which was issued on 8 December 2009. The directive instructed executive departments and agencies to take specific actions to implement the principles of transparency, participation and collaboration, as set forth in the President's Memorandum.[46]

Prior to the 2009 Open Government Directive, the National Institute of Health in 2008 had issued an open access policy, mandating that all research funded by the agency should be made available on the PubMed Central website[47] where it becomes globally, freely, available and accessible.[48]

4.2 European Union

The European Union (EU) has been at the forefront of expanding the access gate to knowledge and has adopted mechanisms for information dissemination, administration and management within the EU. The European Commission Vice-President Neelie Kroes said: "Opening up public data means opening up business opportunities, creating jobs and building communities. I welcome the Council's agreement to this culture change."[49] The press-release referred to the Public-Sector Information Directive, which was issued on 17 November 2003, as EU Directive 2003/98/EC on the reuse of PSI.[50] The Directive which came into force on 31 December 2003 addressed materials in the custody of public sector organizations at all tiers of governments including national, regional local, ministries, agencies, municipalities and entities funded in part or wholly from taxpayers' funds.[51] This directive focused on maximizing the economic possibilities inherent in PSI. The directive encouraged members to make as much information available for reuse as possible and encouraged that such reusable information by made available in electronically compatible formats, at no cost and where inevitable at a near zero cost and that whatever cost must be charged should not exceed the cost of production and a reasonable return on investment.[52]

In 2013, the PSI directive was revised.[53] The intent of the revision was to open up the market for services based on PSI by the inclusion of new bodies in the scope of the application of the directive such as libraries (including university libraries), museums and archives; limiting the fees that can be charged by the public authorities at the marginal costs as a rule; introducing independent oversight over reuse rules in the Member States and making machine-readable formats for information held by public authorities the norm.[54]

This review builds on the strong policies set out in 2003 but makes certain clarifications. In addition to the definition section, it strategically identifies PSI as documents within the scope of public task by public sector bodies but notes that such public task must however be transparent and subject to review.[55] The revision also noted that documents restricted from the access regime in member states by virtue of national security, defence, public security, statistical or commercial confidentiality and personal data are excluded from the scope of PSI.[56] Also excluded are documents held by educational and research establishments but notes that university libraries are not included.[57]

It provides an improvement on the mode of release of information by stipulating the inclusion of metadata and that such information be released in machine-readable formats in addition to other open formats.[58] It further clarifies that machine-readable format means "a file format structured so that software applications can easily identify, recognize and extract specific data, including individual statements of fact, and their internal structure".[59]

In July 2014, the Commission published guidelines for the purposes of helping Member States transpose the revised 2013 PSI directives and to indicate best practices in several fields of importance for the reuse of PSI. The guidelines recommend the use of available open standard licences, datasets and how to make them more readily reusable and the application of marginal cost rules in charging for the reuse of documents.[60]

4.3 United Nations

The United Nations (UN) was established in 1945 after the Second World War, and it is a multinational intergovernmental platform that promotes international peace and security, social progress, better living standards and human rights. It carries out its daily operations through several bodies, such as the General Assembly, the Security Council, and the Economic and Social Council.

> The organization works on a broad range of fundamental issues, from sustainable development, environment and refugees protection, disaster relief, counter terrorism, disarmament and non-proliferation, to promoting democracy, human rights, gender equality and the advancement of women, governance, economic and social development and international health, clearing landmines, expanding food production, and more.[61]

The Economic and Social Council through the United Nations Department of Economic and Social Affairs (UNDESA) and the Division for Public Administration and Development Management (DPADM) oversees the United Nation Public Administration Programme (UNPAP), which amongst other things support open government data (OGD) and services.[62] OGD has been one of the focal points of the DPADM as it seeks to offer online government service for purposes of strengthening participatory governance. OGD provides a platform for greater citizenry participation as it

> allows citizens to monitor data streams and thereby improves the accountability and transparency of government. OGD also allows citizens to be aware of important issues and to be part of the decision-making process to address policy issues (e-participation). DPADM's work on open government is divided into four pillars: policies and regulatory framework; organizational framework; channels & modalities; and case studies.[63]

The UN is not a sovereign nation, but it is an umbrella body that complies, generates and analyzes a broad range of data and information from which member states can freely draw upon in taking policy decisions. It provides practical steps on how to implement issues at national levels. One of such practical steps is the Guidelines on Open Government Data for Citizen Engagement. This guideline issued in 2013 provides relevant information on OGD and helps member states in designing, implementing and sustaining OGD initiatives. "It contains the core principles of openness, best practices and case studies, checklists, step-by-step guidelines and practical policy recommendations."[64]

The UN is yet to adopt an organization-wide policy that enables accessibility, availability, use and reuse of knowledge products generated under its supervision. It however is a strong supporter for the use and reuse of information it generates. In the governance lab, it was noted that "The UN has been opening up statistical and programmatic data for years now, and as experts learn more about the field of open data, it is important to reflect on the opportunities to maximize open data adoption within the UN." [65] The guideline referred to above, provides an express prior permission for use and reuse subject to attribution.[66] In 2013, UNESCO adopted a policy which provides unrestricted access to millions of its digital publications to the general publication. It was noted that the new policy will enable increased visibility, accessibility and distribution of the agency's publications.[67] Although the World Bank is not one of the traditional UN agencies but rather a specialized UN agency, it nonetheless has noted the importance of openness[68] and transparency in national, economic and social development. In 2012, the World Bank President, Robert B. Zoellick remarked that the Bank is "opening up more and more".[69] He further noted that "making our knowledge widely and readily available will empower others to come up with solutions to the world's toughest problems".[70] The adoption of the CC-BY licence as the standard licensing model for works made available through World Bank's Open Knowledge Repository testifies to the Banks commitment to make available and enable use and reuse of their data.[71] The guidelines and policies by UN agencies are clear manifestations of the commitment of the UN to openness, transparency, collaboration and greater citizenry participation in governance and development.

4.4 Organisation for Economic Co-operation and Development

OECD was established in 1961 with headquarters in Paris, France. It currently has 34 members, and it seeks to promote policies that foster socio-economic development of the global community.[72] In recognition of the need to optimize the value of publicly funded research amongst other things, the organization made the *Declaration on Access to Research Data from Public Funding* and committed to working towards the establishment of access regimes for publicly funded digital research data.[73] As a result of this ministerial declaration by Ministers of Science and technology of OECD member states, the OECD was mandated to develop a set of guidelines which would provide a platform that would enable cost efficient and effective access to digital products of research data generated from public funding. The guideline was developed and approved by the OECD Council on the 14th of December 2006.[74] The organization as a further step to both the declaration and the guideline mandated the Committee for Information, Computer and

Communication Policy to review policies regarding access, use and reuse of PSI. A report by the working party on the information economy was presented to the Council in June 2015.[75] The recommendation of the committee was adopted as the OECD Recommendation of the Council for Enhanced Access and More effective use of Public Sector Information (c[2008]36) by the OECD Council at the 1,172nd session on the 30th of April 2008.[76]

The Guidelines of 2006 adopted the principles and objectives laid out in the 2004 Declaration. It addressed issues of openness, transparency, legal conformity, formal responsibility, professionalism, protection of intellectual property, interoperability, quality and security, efficiency and accountability. The 2008 Recommendation built on the guidelines introduced the issues of reuse. It emphasized the need for interoperability addressing new technologies and long-term preservation, international access and use, citizenry participation through public–private partnership, best practice, and provides mechanisms for redress.

The 2005 report titled "Digital Broadband Content: Public Sector Information and Content"[77] presented by the working party on Information Economy as well as the recommendation of the Council dealing with enhanced access and more effective use of PSI particularly addresses the issue of reuse rights and takes cognizance of the fact that access to use and reuse PSI increases the return on public investment, increases social and economic development through better access and wider use and reuse rights which is particularly made possible through the avenues, which the Internet and technology has provided for efficient distribution, enhanced innovation and the development of new uses. The development of new uses which is enabled by reuse rights is particularly important as it aids the development of new knowledge products and services (value-added products and

Table 6.1 A comparison of the 2004 Declaration and 2006 Guidelines

S/N	*Declaration/ Guidelines*	*Recommendation on Enhanced Use of Psi*	*Comments*
1	Openness	Openness	Common to both
2	Transparency	Access & transparent condition for reuse	Common to both, but reuse is introduced in the latter
3	Legal Conformity	Redress mechanism	Working towards similar ends
4	Quality and Security	Quality	Common to both
5	Professionalism	Integrity	Upholds the same ideal
6	Protection of Intellectual Property	Copyright pricing	Aims at the same thing but the scope of the former is wider than the latter
7	Interoperability	New technologies and long-term preservation	Pursues the same goal
8	Formal responsibility	Best practice	Same focus
9	Efficiency	Asset lists	
10	Accountability	Public–private partnership	
11		International access and use	
12		Competition	

services) and provides the opportunity for healthy competition among reusers of information. Enhanced access to PSI not only maximizes the use of such information, but it provides the opportunity for collaboration and greater citizen participation, leading to better governance as well as social and economic developments.

4.5 United Kingdom

Information within the public sector in the United Kingdom is governed by crown copyright.[78] The United Kingdom has been proactive in making policies that enhance access for the use and reuse of PSI.[79] The Office of Public Sector Information (OPSI) which is a part of the National Archive is at the heart of UK's information policy. It is responsible for setting standards, creating platforms for access to government-held information and encouraging the use and reuse of such information. The office provides a number of services to the general public and enables curious minds locate, use, reuse, share and add value to PSI.[80]

The UK government has developed a licensing framework for dissemination of PSI known as the UK Government Licensing Framework.[81] Under this framework, it has adopted an open government licence which permits the use and reuse of PSI and grants a worldwide, royalty-free, perpetual, non-exclusive licence to the licensee subject to a few conditions.[82]

The leadership of the government of the United Kingdom has shown understanding of the relevance of enabling access to PSI. In a speech at the University of Westminster in 2007, Gordon Brown noted that

> this is the century of information. Our ability to compete in the global economy, to protect ourselves against crime and terrorist attack, depends not just on natural wealth or in walls or fences but on our ability to use information. . . . If government is to maintain the confidence of the public and to operate accountably and efficiently, then our management of information must be no less than excellent.[83]

David Cameron while the Prime Minister of the United Kingdom demonstrated Government's commitment to enabling access to PSI when he noted that

> Greater transparency across Government is at the heart of our shared commitment to enable the public to hold politicians and public bodies to account; to reduce the deficit and deliver better value for money in public spending; and to realise significant economic benefits by enabling businesses and no-profit organizations to build innovative applications and websites using public data.[84]

It is clear that the government of the United Kingdom appreciates the value that access to PSI is capable of contributing to global development. The potentials in PSI are better and easily harnessed when government's like those in the United Kingdom understand and appreciate the nexus between access to PSI and economic, social and political developments. By creating platforms for individuals and groups to access, use and reuse government-held information, people are able to express the genius within them by rearranging and realigning this information to bring about value-added services, new businesses and new lines of discussion.[85]

4.6 New Zealand

In 2008, the government of New Zealand released the Digital Strategy 2.0 expressing government's commitment to "making public information accessible to everyone . . . and open up authoritative data sources for others to use, while protecting privacy and the security of information".[86] Prior to the Digital strategy 2.0, government information was regulated under 11 guiding principles set out within the "Policy Framework for Government-held Information (PFGHI).[87] The growth in the dependence on digital technology quickly elicited the inadequacies in the policy, for example, the policy made no provision for "licensing publicly available information, offering it for reuse or for ensuring secure management of personal government-held information".[88] These inadequacies prompted the government to review the policy framework and in line with its open and transparent perspective, the cabinet on 8 August 2011 approved new principles for regulating New Zealand's information system.[89] The new policy addressed issues of ready availability and openness of government data and information for public access. Unlike the 1997 policy, the 2011 policy addresses the issue of reuse rights noting that

> data and information can be discovered, shared, used and reused over time and through technology change. Copyright works are licensed for reuse and open access to and reuse of non-copyright materials is enabled, in accordance with the New Zealand Government Open Access and Licensing framework.[90]

The policy discourages fee charging for access to use and reuse of government-held information. The combined effect of the Digital Strategy 2.0 and the 2011 updated information policy provides a strong policy framework for New Zealand to harness the possibilities made available through digital technology and to support the growth of creativity, innovation and development as a whole through the use and reuse of government-held data and information.

4.7 Australia

The Office of the Australian Information Commissioner (OAIC) is responsible for Australia's information management policies.[91] Although the OAIC is a recent creation, Australia has been committed to the principles of sharing information having passed its Freedom of Information Act (FOIA) in 1982.[92] In the same vein, it has been noted that "from the emergence of the World Wide Web in the early 1990's, the Australian government embraced the internet as a medium for communicating with citizens, civil society and business."[93] The importance of providing access to use and reuse PSI was emphasized in a 2008 report that reviewed the National Innovation System.[94] In the report, it was noted that "Good information is crucial to the efficiency of markets and the ability of discerning consumers to drive innovation by providers."[95] The report amongst other things recommended the establishment of a National Information Strategy to maximize the flow of information in the Australian economy.[96] The report further noted in recommendation 7.14 that "to the maximum extent practicable, information, research and content funded by Australian governments -including national collections- should be made freely available over the internet as part of the global public commons."[97] The government's response to the 2008 Venturous Report was documented in a white paper titled "Powering Ideas: An Innovation Agenda for the 21st century" and released as part of the 2009 budget. The response by government was generally supportive of the recommendations and particularly noted that "Better information produces better decisions. The Australian Government controls mountains of information, and it is determined to make more of this vast national resource accessible to citizens, business people, researchers and policy-makers."[98] It is in furtherance of this determination, that the Office of the Australian Commissioner for Information was established in 2011 to maximize and optimize amongst other things access to use and reuse PSI. Several government agencies like the Australian Bureau of Statistics[99] and the Bureau of Meteorology and Geoscience Australia[100] have adopted strategies that allow for free flow of information. In the same vein since 2011, the Australian budget and other associated documents have been made available to the general public by the parliament under a CC BY licence. Similarly, all information on the Australian National Data Service website is also licensed under a CC BY licence, except where otherwise noted. This particular organization seeks to "make Australia's research data collections more valuable by managing, connecting, enabling discovery and supporting reuse of this data".[101]

Australia's resolve to make available for use and reuse PSI is not in doubt. Consequent upon the "Venturous Australia report"[102] and the response of government through "Powering ideas"[103] the steps taken by government to ensure free and open flow of information speaks volumes.

4.8 Nigeria

Access to freely use and reuse information generated and held by government is a challenge in Nigeria. On 28 May 2011, Nigeria after 51 years of independence and years of lobbying[104] passed the FOIA, 2011.[105] This act ensures the rights of Nigerian's to access information subject to certain limitations. Providing citizens with "the right to know" underpins the fundamental principles of democracy. It is the hallmark of any administration that seeks to follow "the four magic words of development" namely accountability, transparency, participation and inclusion.[106] The issue of access to information can be viewed from two standpoints, the first being the right to access, that is to use information and the second being the right to reuse information. It is important to make this distinction because the legal regime which the FOIA in Nigeria establishes allows for restrictive access to use and does not provide reuse rights. The global campaigns with regards to PSI focuses on both "access to use and reuse" as seen in the analysis above of the UN, EU, OECD, United States, United Kingdom, Australia and New Zealand.

Nigeria currently has no national policy that covers both use and reuse rights but has increased efforts to provide the general public with PSI through e-Governance. This has been principally aimed at increasing and improving transparency as well as the flow of information within government ministries, departments and agencies; between government and its citizens and the citizens to government. The Nigeria Extractive Industries Transparency Initiative (NEITI) set up in 2004 under the administration of the former President Olusegun Obasanjo is an example of an initiative seeking to build transparency by government.[107] The passage of the Public Procurement Act[108] as well as the establishment of the Bureau of Public Procurement an agency saddled with the responsibility of ensuring fairness, competition, transparency, accountability and probity in the procurement process is another example of government's drive to run an accountable, transparent, open and inclusive government.[109] These initiatives are laudable, and they have provided a form of window for transparency, and for the citizens to know and probably to be involved in governance. These initiatives as well as the FOIA do not however provide Nigerians with the needed opportunities to build upon and turnaround available and accessible information. This information are the building blocks and navigational tools used by curious minds in developing value-added services and products, which in turn develops and strengthens creativity industries as well as national innovation systems.

Although there is no national policy in the above respect, one of the state governments, namely Edo State, recently has set up an Open Data Portal under its open government initiative.[110] The portal is the official data repository for the state government, and it provides an easy way for the public to find, access and reuse public datasets. The first phase of the initiative which commenced in 2011 is what culminated in the launch of the Open Data Portal in September 2013. The focus of the initiative is "to establish a broader framework for an Open Government ecosystem in the state."[111] It is said to be the first sub-national portal in Africa, and it contains more than 100 datasets which is freely available and accessible to the public for use and reuse.[112] The data and information available on the site is licensed under a creative commons attribution (CC-BY) licence.[113] It has been reported that the "Edo State Open Data Portal is now being reused by the developer's community and is providing citizens of Edo state with free access to high-value, government data."[114]

5 Nigeria's Freedom of Information Act Structure

The FOIA is a victory to the public and particularly to the Nigerian media industry who have suffered severely at the hands of many dictatorial leaders.[115] The FOIA was initiated as a private bill in 1999.[116] The struggle for what is now FOIA took so many years during which many activist's had to pay the ultimate price in their quest to ensure there was free speech.[117] The Chairman of *Thisday Newspapers*, explained that FOI is

> the right of a citizen to ask for information on how he is governed and thereby be in a position to hold government accountable. The Act is therefore one of the most important tools citizens and reporters can have in demanding for transparency and accountability in governance.[118]

As noted earlier, the FOIA 2011 has no legal framework for reuse rights. The act was structured to provide access to use information. The FOI clearly does not provide all possible access, but considering where Nigerians have come from, it is worth celebrating and can be one of the building blocks for greater access.

The FOIA gives every Nigerian the legal right to access or request information, records and documents held by government bodies and private bodies carrying our public functions.[119] These include the three arms of government, the executive, legislative and judiciary, as well as the three tiers of government namely, federal, state and local governments.[120] Applicants are not required to demonstrate any specific interest in the information they seek,[121] and such applicants are entitled to institute proceedings in court to compel compliance.[122] The procedure for applying for information, the time for granting or refusing an application, transfer of an application, extension of time limit for granting or refusing an application, what can be done when access is refused and the fees payable are all covered under Sections 3, 4, 5, 6, 7 and 8 of the Act, respectively.

Public institutions are mandated to facilitate access to information by properly documenting and keeping information about all its activities, operations and businesses. These institutions are to ensure that the information is widely disseminated and made readily available through various means including print, electronic, online sources and at the office of the public institution.[123]

The Act makes an attempt at striking a balance between making information more freely available and national security,[124] protecting public records,[125] as well as the protection of personal privacy[126] and intellectual property rights.[127] It also protects serving public officers from adverse consequences for disclosing certain kinds of official information without authorization.[128]

5.1 Nigeria's FOIA implementation

Although the legislation on FOI is common place globally, its passage in Nigeria stirred understandable celebration across Nigeria.[129] A few years have rolled by now, and the implementation of the FOIA has attracted mixed reactions from the government, the people and the courts. Some government agencies still act as if the repealed Official Secrets Act is still in force. Several demands have been declined and the courts may have complicated matters by its interpretation on applicability of the FOIA.[130] A great number of requests have been granted, but there have been instances where government agencies have refused requests for information. In such cases, the FOIA which entitles an applicant to institute a proceeding to compel the grant of the request has been activated.

Adekoya v Governor of Ogun State,[131] *Osita Okechukwu v Petroleum Resources Minister,*[132] *India Garba v SA to Governor of Benue State*[133] are examples of proceedings that were instituted.

5.2 National applicability of FOIA

The national applicability of the FOIA across Nigeria has been considered by the courts and have brought about opposing judgements.[134]

In *Yomi Ogunlola v Clerk of Oyo State,* Justice S.A Akinteye of the Ibadan High Court held that the Act has general application throughout Nigeria and "does not need to be domesticated by any state before taking effect in all states across the federation."[135] Justice Adekeye in the same case noted that

> the supreme court had made it clear that the National assembly has the legal competence to make laws for the peace, order and good government of Nigeria that is applicable to all states of Nigeria without infringing on the autonomy of the states, if such a legislation is designed to correct a malaise plaguing the country.[136]

In an interesting twist from Justice Adekeye's decision as noted above, Justice Okon Abang of the Federal High Court of Lagos in *Legal Defence and Assistance Project Limited/GTE v AG Lagos State & 5 Others* ruled that the FOIA is non-binding on the 36 sates of the federation. He explained that since the Act was passed by the National Assembly, it binds the federal government and its agencies. The judge noted that the FOIA is not a residual law, neither is it on the concurrent list of the Constitution. He noted that the houses of assembly of the states were empowered to make laws for their respective states and as a result, the FOIA enacted by the federal legislature was non-binding on the states.[137]

FOIA provides Nigeria and Nigerians with a framework for access to knowledge. The challenge is that this access is restricted to "use rights" and considering where Nigeria has come from, this form of access is worth celebrating and have indeed been a cause for celebration. Notwithstanding the celebration, if Nigeria is going to maximize the potentials of her people in this globalized and knowledge-based economy, a framework that provides for both use and reuse rights must be put in place.

6 PSI and FOI

Whereas FOI refers to the right of all citizens to access government-held information by requesting for it, the philosophy to PSI is that all citizens should have the right to access government-held information without the requirement of having to ask for the information as the information should be made available online, and there will therefore be no need to request for it. Therefore, information under FOI is not available to the public by default, but under PSI, it is by default available to the public.

Whereas, FOI provides users with the right to use government-held information and nothing more, PSI goes further to provide not just the right to use, but the right to reuse such government-held information. The objective of FOI, which is to enable the right of citizens to know, thereby creating a conducive environment for transparency, accountability, greater citizenry participation and inclusion is fully encapsulated within the objectives of PSI. The objective of PSI is however broader as it contains that of the FOI and also focuses on building on the accessible and available government information. It seeks to encourage economic development through value-added services developed by the reuse of government-held information. It also seeks to develop and strengthen the creative industries and innovation systems by providing raw materials (data) for further creativity and innovations.[138]

7 PSI and intellectual property law

PSI in its drive for free and open access to use and reuse government-held information recognizes the intellectual property legal framework that protect works of creativity and innovation. It utilizes licensing as a tool to provide access within the current legal framework. Licensing is the grant of permission or authorization subject to terms and conditions. The cost, technicalities and other legal issues surrounding licences have led to the development of free and open licences.[139] The Creative Commons licences have been the most effective and impacting of these licences.[140] There are however other licensing models which clarify the rights that are available to the public. The open movement has been proactive to ensure compatibility in the licences that have been issued.[141]

8 PSI and privacy law/issues: confidentiality

A large portion of the information in government custody is about individuals and this information are protected under privacy laws. This information includes general medical, educational, financial and employment records. The law also recognizes the need for confidentiality which exists between doctors and patients, lawyers and clients, journalists and source as well as between spiritual leaders and their members. Access to the above type of information in not within the contemplation of PSI as this type of information is legally protected and therefore excluded. Where individuals attempt to hide fraud under the guise of privacy or confidentiality the law provides for processes where warrants and orders may be issued, and information would be obtained as deemed necessary.[142]

9 PSI and government business interest

Deregulation of businesses run by government has brought about greater efficiency and effectiveness. The campaign for free and open access to government-held information may therefore not go down well with agencies whose trading product is information. The simple argument would be if we give away for free our trading product, then how would we generate funds and how would the agency continue to operate? It is for this reason the EU recognized the need to address pricing. It is generally recommended that as much as practicable all government information is to be made available and accessible free of charge, at a near zero cost or at the least minimum cost. Where a cost applies it should not be beyond the cost of production and a reasonable amount to cover administration costs.[143] In a country like Nigeria where a number of the government agencies trade in government-held information, for instance the Corporate Affairs Commission, it would be impracticable for it to make available and accessible all the information in her custody for free. The pricing model adopted by the EU when dealing with particular types of PSI would be a recommended model.

10 PSI and national interest/national security

When Snowden leaked classified information in the United States and about many other nations, the explanation was that

> the more information he saw about what he viewed as . . . mass surveillance, the more disillusioned he became. He says quite explicitly that he thought that (President Barack) Obama would roll back some of these programs when he came into the White House, and when this didn't happen, essentially Snowden decided he would take things into his own hands and become a whistle-blower.[144]

Every citizen has the "right to know" and is guaranteed the freedom of expression and liberty. Nonetheless, there must be mutual respect for the right of others. Government's operation requires a high level of intelligence and surveillance to uphold the national interest and for purposes of national security. The laws of each land support prioritization of making decisions and policies based on national interest and national security. It is for this reason that individual citizens who work in positions where they handle privileged information are sworn to an oath of secrecy and they have no right to take laws into their hands as Snowden did because such decisions affect not just the individual but the entire nation.[145] Access to PSI takes cognizance of this fact and adds to its exclusion list information which is considered to be restricted due to national interest or national security.

The importance of access to PSI cannot be contested when cognizance is taken of its effect on creativity, innovation and good governance. The need however for balance has been highlighted in the discussion above about national security, intellectual property rights, and with privacy and confidentiality issues. The dynamics of accessing PSI has its own challenges but the importance of accessing such information cannot be over-emphasized. The three stories told hereunder brings to life the importance of access to information particularly public-sector information.

11 Conclusion

Government holds some of the largest and most important pieces of information, and information is an essential commodity in all spheres of life. Access to this information is crucial as it creates an enabling environment for accountability, transparency, participation and inclusion. The passage of the FOIA in Nigeria established a legal framework for the right to access and use information. This Act left out an important component of access to information, which is the right to reuse information. The reuse right enables communities to build upon government-held information. It encourages the growth of strong creative industries and viable innovation systems. Nigeria's progress with the passage of the FOIA bill is a step in the right direction and must be built upon to ensure a national open government policy. The open government policy currently been implemented in Edo State can serve as a guide for a national policy initiative.

Notes

1 *The Economist*, 'Knowledge Is Power: Do We Need a New Competition Policy for the New Economy?' available at www.economist.com/node/375597. The article noted that "Whatever the outcome of the battle between Microsoft and the American government, some economists worry that because of the very nature of information and knowledge, which form the building bricks of the new economy, more and more monopolies like Microsoft are likely to emerge."

2 Kunle Ola, 'Evolution and Future Trends of Copyright in Nigeria' in Brian Fitzgerald & John Gilchrist eds., *Copyright Perspectives* (Springer, 2015), 122. The author noted that "Acquiring knowledge is therefore imperative for development and the currency to acquiring knowledge is access. No knowledge no development, no access, no knowledge."

3 See generally, J. Henry, *Knowledge Is Power: Francis Bacon and the Method of Science* (Icon, 2002).

4 Subbiah Arunachalam, *Information Poverty the Story: How the Internet Is failing the Developed World*, available at www.abc.net.au/science/slab/infopoverty/story.htm. The author noted that "If we agree that it is very important for researchers to get to know what is happening around the world as well as to let others know what they are doing, that *information is key* [emphasis mine] to the growth of knowledge, and dissemination of information is crucial for the scientific enterprise, then scientists in the developing world are currently being starved of opportunities and vital resources. I would not be surprised if very soon the gulf between the scientifically advanced nations and the others widens even further."

5 See, Hosea 4:6; *The Holy Bible: Authorized King James Version, containing the Old and New Testaments* (Holman Bible Publishers Read-to-me ed., 1984).

6 *Coordination of Federal Information Policy* (2002), available at www.archives.gov/about/laws/fed-information-policy.html.

7 Directive 2013/37/EU of the European Parliament and of the Council of 26 June (2013), available at http://eur-lex.europa.eu/legal-content/EN/TXT/PDF/?uri=CELEX:02003L0098-20130717&from=EN (2013). The 2003 EU directive was amended in 2013. See DIRECTIVE 2013/37/EU of 26 June 2013 at http://eur-lex.europa.eu/LexUriServ/LexUriServ.do?uri=OJ:L:2013:175:0001:0008:EN:PDF.

8 The National Archives, *Who We Are*, available at www.nationalarchives.gov.uk/about/who-we-are.htm. See also, OPSI, *Office of Public Sector Information*, available at www.opsi.gov.uk/psi/. See also, The National Archives, *Open Government Licenses for Public Sector Information*, available at www.nationalarchives.gov.uk/doc/open-government-licence/version/2/. See also, The National Archives, 'About Us' *legislation.gov.uk*, available at www.legislation.gov.uk/aboutus.

9 Treasury Board of Canada Secretariat Canada, *Information Management Policy*, available at www.tbs-sct.gc.ca/im-gi/imp-pgi/imp-pgi-eng.asp.

10 New Zealand Government NZ, *New Zealand Data and Information Management Principles* (2011), available at http://ict.govt.nz/guidance-and-resources/open-government/new-zealand-data-and-information-management-princi/.

11 Office of the Australian Information Commission Australian Government, *Information Policy Report*, available at www.oaic.gov.au/information-policy/information-policy-resources/information-policy-reports/. See also, Queensland Government, *Information Management Policy Framework* (2009), available at www.qgcio.qld.gov.au/products/qgea-documents/548-information/2349-information-management-policy-framework.

12 Federal Government Brazil, *Open Data*, available at http://dados.gov.br/noticia/dados-abertos-permitem-que-cidadaos-conhecam-melhor-as-acoes-e-os-resultados-do-mj/.

13 Freedom of Information Act 2011.

14 Cabinet Office, Information Matters, Speech by the Prime Minister, the Rt Hon. Gordon Brown MP at Liberty, University of Westminster, October 2007 4 (Cabinet Office ed., Cabinet Office 2007), available at www.nationalarchives.gov.uk/documents/information-matters.pdf.

15 See the Foreword, id. at, 2. Sir Gus O'Donnell (Cabinet Secretary and Head of the Cabinet Office; Sir John Bourn, Comptroller and Auditor General; Natalie Ceeney, CEO, The National Archives.

16 Judge Elizabeth, 'Enabling Access to Public Sector Information in Canada' in Michael Geist ed., *From Radical Extremism to Balance Copyright: Canadian Copyright and the Digital Agenda* (Irwin Law, Canada, 2010). See also, *Digital Broadband Content: Public Sector Information and Content* (2006).

17 Organisation for Economic Co-operation and Development (OECD), *Recommendation of the Council for Enhanced Access and More Effective Use of Public Sector Information. [C(2008) 36]* (2008), available at www.oecd.org/internet/ieconomy/4082 6024.pdf.

18 Fitzgerald Anne, 'Open Access and Public Sector Information: Policy Developments In Australia and Key Jurisdictions' in Fitzgerald Brian ed., *Access to Public Sector Information: Law, Technology & Policy* (Sydney University Press, 2010).

19 Corbin Chris, *PSI Policy Principles: European Best Practice*, see id. at (165).

20 The Coercive Information-Gathering Powers Of Government Agencies: Report No: 48 of May 2008 Prepared by the Administrative Review Council (2008).

21 See, Maureen Henninger, 'The Value and Challenges of Public Sector Information' 5(2013) *Cosmopolitan Civil Societies Journal* 75, where it was noted that "There is a notion that all government information belongs to its citizens because it is derived through governmental processes and therefore should be freely accessible and re-useable by them."

22 Open Government Working Group, *Eight Principles of Open Government Data* (2007), available at https://public.resource.org/8_principles.html. See also, OECD, *Recommendation of the Council for Enhanced Access and More Effective Use of Public Sector Information [C(2008) 36]* (2008). Where it was noted that the aim is "to increase returns on public investments in public sector information and increase economic and social benefits from better access and wider use and re-use in particular through more efficient distribution." See also, United Nations (UN), *United Nations E-Government Survey 2014: E-Government for the Future We Want* (2014), available at http://unpan3.un.org/egovkb/Portals/egovkb/Documents/un/2014-Survey/E-Gov_Complete_Survey-2014.pdf. " The recent recognition of the importance of Open Government Data (OGD) in meeting the rights of individuals, businesses and civil organizations to access and use government information to engage in policy making . . . is significant."

23 The White House, *Office of E-Government and Information Technology* (2002), available at www.whitehouse.gov/omb/e-gov/.

24 United Nations Educational, Scientific and Cultural Organization (UNESCO), 'The UNESCO Recommendation on Promotion and Use of Multilingualism and

Universal Access to Cyberspace' *UNESCO* (2004), available at www.unesco.org/new/fileadmin/MULTIMEDIA/HQ/CI/CI/pdf/official_documents/Eng%20-%20Recommendation%20concerning%20the%20Promotion%20and%20Use%20of%20Multilingualism%20and%20Universal%20Access%20to%20Cyberspace.pdf.

25 Australian Consumer Law and Fair Trading Act 2012 (Vic).

26 See *Open Data for Economic Growth* (2014), available at www.worldbank.org/content/dam/Worldbank/document/Open-Data-for-Economic-Growth.pdf., where it was noted that "A study of the importance of the Global Positioning System to the US Economy found that it was difficult to estimate the total economic value of GPS because it had become so pervasive and because it was still increasing at a high rate. However, the best estimate as of June 2011 was that there were $96 billion in annual direct economic benefits attributable to GPS and 3.3 million US jobs were dependent on it: the agriculture sector alone had productivity and cost-saving gains of $19.9 billion a year due to GPS."

27 Paul Uhlir, 'Policy Guidelines for the Development and Promotion of Governmental Public Domain Information' in Fitzgerald Brian ed., *Access to Public Sector Information: Law, Technology & Policy* (Sydney University Press, 2010), 216.

28 Anks Michels, 'Innovations in Democratic Governance: How Does Citizen Participation Contribute to a Better Democracy?' 77 (2011) *International Review of Administrative Sciences* 275. See where it was noted that "Citizen participation is usually considered a valuable element of democratic citizenship and democratic decision-making. Many theorists claim that citizen participation has positive effects on the quality of democracy."

29 U.S. Congress, *Declaration of Independence* (1776), available at www.archives.gov/exhibits/charters/declaration_transcript.html.

30 J. DeBardeleben & J. Pammett, *Activating the Citizen: Dilemmas of Participation in Europe and Canada* (Palgrave Macmillan, 2009), 17–41. See generally, the chapter on "Citizen Participation and Democratic Deficits: Considerations from the Perspective of Democratic Theory by Mark E Warren and specifically at page 17 where he noted that "Governments should be responsive to citizens as a consequence of citizen participation, through elections, pressure, public deliberation, petitioning, or other conduits. For these forms of participation to function democratically, all affected by the decisions of a government should have the opportunity to influence those decisions, in proportion to their stake in the outcome."

31 Oluwafemi Bankole, *Nigeria: How Information Conquered Ebola* (2014), available at http://techcabal.com/2014/10/20/nigeria-information-conquered-ebola/.

32 T. Jefferson et al., *The Writings of Thomas Jefferson* (Issued under the auspices of the Thomas Jefferson Memorial Association of the United States, 1904). Thomas Jefferson in his writing Politics & Government noted in Section 5: "The Sovereignty of the People" that "The purpose of government is to enable the people of a nation to live in safety and happiness. Government exists for the interests of the governed, not for the governors. As Benjamin Franklin wrote, 'In free governments the rulers are the servants and the people their superiors and sovereigns.' The ultimate powers in a society, therefore, rest in the people themselves, and they should exercise those powers, either directly or through representatives, in every way they are competent and that is practicable."

33 Raymond Tatalovic, 'Presidents and Promises: From Campaign Pledge to Presidential Performance' 48 (1986) *The Journal of Politics* 189.

34 Patrick McGroarty, *Muhammadu Buhari Defeats Goodluck Jonathan in Nigeria Election*, available at www.wsj.com/articles/officials-tally-remaining-votes-in-nigeria-presidential-election-1427796882.

35 See, Federal Ministry of Health, *National Strategic Health Development Plan (NSHDP 2010–2015)*, available at www.health.gov.ng/doc/NSHDP.pdf. See also, NIH, *NIH Public Access Policy*, available at http://publicaccess.nih.gov/. See also RCUK, *RCUK Policy on Open Access*. See also, ARC, *ARC Open Access Policy*, available at

www.arc.gov.au/applicants/open_access.htm. See also, ERC, *Open Access Guidelines for Researchers Funded by the ERC* (2012), available at http://erc.europa.eu/sites/default/files/document/file/open_access_policy_researchers_funded_ERC.pdf. See also, Government of Canada, *Minister Holder Announces New Open Access Policy for Research* (2015), available at www.science.gc.ca/default.asp?lang=En&n=415B5097-1.

36 Forest Horton, Public Access to Government Information and Information Literacy Training as Basic Human Rights (2002), https://repository.arizona.edu/handle/10150/105882?show=full

37 Stott (2014). See page 12 where it was noted that "Revenues from the publication of data are nil, but the data may lead to increased levels of customer engagement and loyalty, with revenue gains. There is also the opportunity to sell value-added services based on the supplier's intimate understanding of the data."

38 Henninger (2013). "In general terms governments have recognised the transformational potential of access to their own data to drive efficiency in the public sector, to provide better and new community services and basic infrastructure. There are many examples of the use of OGD to deliver weather and transport and environmental impact benefits, to support national and international economies, the development of technological innovations, and the contribution of new knowledge."

39 Ed Felten et al., 'Government Data and the Invisible Hand' 11 (2009) *Yale Journal of Law and Technology* 160, 164.

40 Ibid., 164.

41 The United States of America, Copyright Act of 1976 Title 17 of United States Code (1976).

42 Office of Management and Budget (OMB), Circular No. A-130, Revised, (Transmittal Memorandum No. 4) (November 28, 2000), Memorandum For Heads Of Executive Departments and Agencies (United States Office of Managment and Budget ed., 2000).

43 Ibid. See Para 7, Considerations and Assumptions.

44 OMB, *Memorandum on Transparency and Open Government* (United States Office of Managment and Budget ed., 2009).

45 OMB, *Open Government Directive* (United States Office of Managment and Budget ed., 2009).

46 OMB, *Open Government* (United States Office of Managment and Budget ed., 2009).

47 PubMed, *PubMed*, National Institutes of Health (NIH), available at www.ncbi.nlm.nih.gov/pubmed/.

48 NIH.

49 European Union, *Commission Welcomes Member States' Endorsement of EU Open Data Rules* (2013), available at http://europa.eu/rapid/press-release_IP-13-316_en.htm.

50 Directive 2003/98/Ec of the European Parliament and of the Council on the Re-Use of Public Sector Information (2003), available at http://eur-lex.europa.eu/LexUriServ/LexUriServ.do?uri=OJ:L:2003:345:0090:0096:EN:PDF.

51 Ibid. See Article 2 (1&2).

52 Ibid. See Article 6.

53 Directive 2003/98/Ec Of The European Parliament And Of The Council On The Re-Use Of Public Sector Information, available at http://eur-lex.europa.eu/LexUriServ/LexUriServ.do?uri=OJ:L:2003:345:0090:0096:EN:PDF (2003).

54 European Union, *Revision of the PSI Directive* (2012), Newsroom Editor ed., available at http://ec.europa.eu/digital-agenda/en/news/revision-psi-directive.

55 Directive 2003/98/Ec Of The European Parliament And Of The Council On The Re-Use Of Public Sector Information, available at http://eur-lex.europa.eu/LexUriServ/LexUriServ.do?uri=OJ:L:2003:345:0090:0096:EN:PDF (2003). See Article 1 (2) a.

56 Ibid. See Article 1 (2) c, ca, cb, cc.

57 Ibid. See Article 1 (2) e.

58 Ibid. See Article 5 (1).

59 Ibid. See Article 2 (6).

60 EU European Union, *Commission Notice: 'Guidelines on Recommended Standard Licences, Datasets and Charging for the Re-Use of Documents* (2014), Newsroom Editor ed., available at https://ec.europa.eu/digital-agenda/en/news/commission-notice-guidelines-recommended-standard-licences-datasets-and-charging-re-use.
61 UN, *UN at a Glance*, available at www.un.org/en/aboutun/index.shtml.
62 UN, *The United Nations Committee of Experts on Public Administration (CEPA)*, available at www.unpan.org/cepa.asp.
63 UN, *UN Public Administration Programme: Open Government Data and Services*, available at www.unpan.org/DPADM/Themes/OpenGovernmentDataandServices/tabid/1536/language/en-US/Default.aspx.
64 United Nations Department for Economic and Social Affairs, *Guidelines on Open Government Data for Citizen Engagement, ST/ESA/PAD/SER.E/177*, available at http://workspace.unpan.org/sites/Internet/Documents/Guidenlines%20on%20OGDCE%20May17%202013.pdf.
65 GOVLAB, *Open Data and the United Nations: Experts Reflect on Current Open Data Challenges Within the UN and Outline a Path Forward* (2014), available at http://thegovlab.org/open-data-and-the-united-nations-experts-reflect-on-current-open-data-challenges-within-the-un-and-outline-a-path-forward/.
66 Affairs, See Page 3, where it states "(the Guidelines on OGDCE) may be used, reused, copied, distributed, adopted, and adapted."
67 UNESCO, *UNESCO Adopts Open Access Policy* (2013), available at http://openscience.com/unesco-adopts-open-access-policy/.
68 UN, *Structure and Organisation*, available at www.un.org/en/aboutun/structure/index.shtml.
69 World Bank, *World Bank Announces Open Access Policy for Research and Knowledge, Launches Open Knowledge Repository*, Press-Release No:2012/379/EXTOP (2012).
70 World Bank, *World Bank Announces Open Access Policy for Research and Knowledge, Launches Open Knowledge Repository* (2012), available at www.worldbank.org/en/news/press-release/2012/04/10/world-bank-announces-open-access-policy-for-research-and-knowledge-launches-open-knowledge-repository.
71 World Bank, *Open Knowledge Repository*, available at https://openknowledge.worldbank.org/.
72 OECD, *About the OECD*, available at www.oecd.org/about/.
73 OECD, *Declaration on Access to Research Data from Public Funding: 30 March 2004 [C(2004)31/REV1]* (2004), available at http://acts.oecd.org/Instruments/ShowInstrumentView.aspx?InstrumentID=157.
74 OECD, *Recommendation of the Council concerning Access to Research Data from Public Funding: 14 December 2006 – C(2006)184* (2006), available at http://webnet.oecd.org/OECDACTS/Instruments/ShowInstrumentView.aspx?InstrumentID=159&Lang=en&Book=False.
75 OECD (2006).
76 OECD, *Recommendation of the Council for Enhanced Access and More Effective Use of Public Sector Information. [C(2008) 36]* (2008).
77 OECD, *Digital Broadband Content*.
78 See Section 163, Copyright, Designs and Patents Act C.48 (1988), available at www.legislation.gov.uk/ukpga/1988/48/data.pdf. See also, Archives, 'About Us' *legislation.gov.uk*, where it was noted that "Her Majesty's Stationery Office (HMSO) was founded in 1786. It is the holder of Crown copyright and has been the official printer and publisher of all Acts of Parliament since 1889." See generally, The National Archives, *Crown Copyright, available at* www.nationalarchives.gov.uk/information-management/re-using-public-sector-information/copyright/crown-copyright/.
79 GOV.UK, *10 Policies About Government Efficiency, Transparency and Accountability*, available at www.gov.uk/government/policies?topics%5B%5D=government-efficiency-transparency-and-accountability.
80 OPSI, available at www.opsi.gov.uk/psi/.

81 The National Archives, *UK Government Licensing Framework for Public Sector Information* (2013), available at www.nationalarchives.gov.uk/documents/information-management/uk-government-licensing-framework.pdf.
82 The National Archives, *Open Government Licence for Public Sector Information*, available at www.nationalarchives.gov.uk/doc/open-government-licence/.
83 Office, 4, (2007).
84 Simon Rogers, 'Government Data: Full Text of David Cameron's Letter Pledging to Open Up the Datasets' *The Guardian* (2010), available at www.theguardian.com/news/datablog/2010/jun/01/government-data-david-cameron-letter.
85 See generally, *The Power of Information: An Independent Review by Ed Mayo and Tom Steinberg* (2007), available at www.opsi.gov.uk/advice/poi/power-of-information-review.pdf.
86 Digital Strategy 2.0. (2008), available at www.aotearoapeoplesnetwork.org/sites/aotearoapeoplesnetwork.org/files/Digital-Strategy.pdf.
87 New Zealand Government, *Policy Framework for New Zealand Government-Held Information* (1997), available at www.ssc.govt.nz/Documents/policy_framework_for_Government_.htm. The 11 policies are as follows: availability, ownership, coverage, preservation, pricing, quality, copyright, integrity, stewardship, privacy and collection.
88 Keitha Booth, 'NZ Government Information Policy and Data Re-Use Project Background Paper' in Fitzgerald Brian ed., *Access to Public Sector Information: Law, Technology & Policy* (Sydney University Press, 2010), 139.
89 New Zealand Government, *New Zealand Data and Information Management Principles* (2011), available at https://ict.govt.nz/guidance-and-resources/open-government/new-zealand-data-and-information-management-principles/.
90 New Zealand Cabinet, Open Government, CAB Min (11) 29/12 (Cabinet Office ed., 2011).
91 Australian Information Commissioner Act 2010 Act No.52 of 2010 C2014C00382, available at www.comlaw.gov.au/Details/C2014C00382. See also, Office of the Australian Information Commissioner OAIC, *About us, available at* www.oaic.gov.au/home/about-us.
92 Freedom of Information Act 1982 Act No.3 of 1982 (1982).
93 See Anne, 49 (2010).
94 *Venturous Australia Report: Building Strength in innovation* (2008), available at www.business.nsw.gov.au/__data/assets/pdf_file/0016/5407/NIS_review_Web3.pdf. The review was commisisoned by Hon. Senator Kim Carr, Minister for Innovation, Industry, Science and Research on the 22nd of January 2008.
95 Id. at, 101.
96 See Recommendation 7.7, id. at, 115.
97 Id. at, 118.
98 *Powering Ideas An Innovation Agenda for the 21st Century* (2009), available at http://sydney.edu.au/documents/about/higher_education/2012/20120308%20PoweringIdeas.pdf.
99 See Australian Bureau of Statistics, *ABS Copyright* (2010), available at www.abs.gov.au/websitedbs/D3310114.nsf/Home/%A9+Copyright?opendocument#from-banner=GB. All information on the ABS website is licensed under a CC BY licence except otherwise stated.
100 Bureau of Meterology, *Copyright Notice: Your Rights to Use Material on Bureau Websites*, available at www.bom.gov.au/other/copyright.shtml?ref=ftr.
101 Australian National Research Services ANDS, *About Us*, available at www.ands.org.au/about-ands.html.
102 Cutler (2008).
103 Government (2009).

104 Article19, *Memorandum on the Nigerian Freedom of Information Bill* (2000), available at www.article19.org/data/files/pdfs/analysis/nigeria.foi.00.pdf. This memorandum expressing support for the passage of the FOI bill in Nigeria was published in 2000. It noted that "Information is the oxygen of democracy, we therefore fully support the initiative to introduce FOI legislation in Nigeria" See also, Article19, *The Public's Right to Know Principles on Freedom of Information Legislation* (1999), available at www.article19.org/data/files/pdfs/standards/righttoknow.pdf. See also, Article 19 & Media Rights Agenda, *Unshackling the Nigerian Media*, Article 19 & Media Rights Agenda (1997), available at www.article19.org/data/files/pdfs/publications/nigeria-unshackling-the-media.pdf.
105 Freedom of Information Act, 2011 FOI Act (2011).
106 Thomas Carothers & Saskia Brechenmacher, 'The Four Magic Words of Development' *World Bank* (2014), available at http://blogs.worldbank.org/publicsphere/four-magic-words-development-tom-carothers-and-saskia-brechenmacher.
107 The Presidency, *Nigeria Extractive Industries Transparency Initiative (NEITI)*, available at http://neiti.org.ng/index.php?q=pages/about-neiti.
108 Public Procurement Act 2007 Act No.14 (2007).
109 Bureau of Public Procurement, *About BPP*, available at www.bpp.gov.ng/index.php?option=com_content&view=article&id=110&Itemid=740.
110 Edo State Open Data Portal, *Terms of Use*, available at www.data.edostate.gov.ng/terms-of-use.
111 Bujoreanu, Lyudmila, et al., *Open Government Initiative in Edo State: Fostering an Ecosystem of Collaboration and Transparency* (2014), available at https://openknowledge.worldbank.org/handle/10986/18713. See the introductory section on page 1
112 Ibid. 11.
113 Portal, available at www.data.edostate.gov.ng/terms-of-use.
114 Bujoreanu, Lyudmila, et al., *Open Government Initiative in Edo State: Fostering an Ecosystem of Collaboration and Transparency* (2014), available at https://openknowledge.worldbank.org/handle/10986/18713.
115 Dan Agbese, When the Sun Set in Nigeria: Dele Giwa's Awful Murder (Committee to Protect Journalists, CPJ 2009), https://cpj.org/blog/2009/10/nigerian-editor-dele-giwas-unsolved-murder.php
116 Bayo Oladeji, *The Importance of Freedom of Information Act*, available at http://leadership.ng/blogposts/390236/importance-freedom-information-act.
117 CPJ, *10 Journalists Killed in Nigeria Since 1992/Motive Confirmed*, Committee to Protect Journalists, available at www.cpj.org/killed/africa/nigeria/.
118 Oladeji.
119 See Section1(1), FOI Act, (2011).
120 Ibid. Section 2(7).
121 Ibid. Section 1(2).
122 Ibid. Section 1(3).
123 Ibid. Section 2 (1, 2 & 4).
124 Ibid. Section 11(1).
125 Ibid. Section 12.
126 Ibid. Section 14.
127 Ibid. Section 15.
128 Ibid. See Section 27, as well as the explanatory notes to the FOI Act.
129 See Elliot Ross, *Nigeria's New FOIA: Reporters Enjoy New Freedoms in a Long-Repressive Society*, available at www.cjr.org/behind_the_news/nigerias_new_foia.php, where he noted that "Journalism in Nigeria has never been easy work, and the new Freedom of Information Act (FOIA), which finally became law in May 12 years after the bill was first drafted, isn't about to change that overnight. But having struggled through decades of repression under military rule, advocates of press freedom

in Nigeria are in unusually optimistic mood. . . . Senior figures in Nigerian journalism have celebrated the law's passing, but stress that the work of opening up their country has only just begun." See also, Lanre Idowu, 'Nigeria's new FOI law brings celebration, challenges' (Committee to Protect Journalists 2011), Where it was noted that "There is a deserved celebration in the Nigerian media over the recently passed Freedom of Information Act, which provides citizens with broad access to public records and information held by a public official or institution. It is the climax of an 11-year struggle to pass such a law in the Nigerian parliament."

130 The Citizen, *Undermining Freedom of Information Act-Punch*, available at http://thecitizenng.com/public-affairs/undermining-freedom-of-information-act-punch/.

131 Joseph Emmanuel, *Ogun State Govt fined by Court Over Freedom of Information Act* (2014), available at www.thetrentonline.com/foi-ogun-state-govt-fined-court/.

132 Sahara Reporters, 'Freedom of Information: APC Chieftain Drags Alison-Madueke to Court' *Sahara Reporters* (2014), available at http://saharareporters.com/2014/09/24/freedom-information-apc-chieftain-drags-alison-madueketo-court.

133 *India Garba v SA to Governor Benue State* MHC/2565M/2012 (Makurdi High Court 9th October, 2014).

134 Davidson Iriekpen, 'Nigeria: In Conflicting Judgement, Court Says FOI Act not Binding on States' *AllAfrica*, available at http://allafrica.com/stories/201411030673.html.

135 *Yomi Ogunlola v Clerk of the Oyo State House of Assembly*, (High Court Ibadan).

136 Ibid.

137 *Legal Defence and Assistance Project Limited/GTE v AG Lagos State & 5 Others* (Federal High Court of lagos).

138 See, *The Sources of Innovation and Creativity: National Center on Education and the Economy (NCEE) Research Summary and Final Report* (2005), available at www.ncee.org/wp-content/uploads/2010/04/Sources-of-Innovation-Creativity.pdf. See pages 3&4, where knowledge was identified as one of the three components for creativity and described "as all the relevant information that an individual brings to bear on a problem."

See also, Isaac Newton, *From a Letter Written by Isaac Newton to Robert Hooke*, 5 February (1676), which emphasizes the importance of collaboration and building on the works of others.

139 Free Software Foundation, *GNU Free Documentation License*, available at www.gnu.org/licenses/fdl.html. See also, Richard Stallman, *The GNU Project*, available at www.gnu.org/gnu/thegnuproject.html

140 Lucie Guilbault & Christina Angelopoulos, *Open Content Licensing from Theory to Practice* (Amsterdam University Press, 2011), 8. See where it was noted that "Among the numerous licensing models based on open content, the most successful application so far is the Creative Commons initiative."

141 European Commission, 'Open-Source Software: Licence Compatibility and Interoperability' *Joinup*, available at https://joinup.ec.europa.eu/software/page/licence_compatibility_and_interoperability%20.

142 ACT Australian Capital Territory Government, *Open Data Policy: Draft Proactve Information Disclosure (Open Data) Policy*, available at http://actgov.github.io/opendatapolicy/ (GitHub). The policy provides for exemptions from public disclosure which include issues of privacy, commercial confidentiality, security and Cabinet Data. It also notes that the publication of data must not breach legislation or security classifications and that staff should be aware unauthorized disclosure could breach several legislations, including Public Sector Management Act 1994, Privacy Act 1988, Health Records (Privacy and Access) Act 1997, The Territory Workplace Privacy Act 2011, The Territory Children and Young People Act 2008, or the Territory Public Interest Disclosure Act 2012.

143 European Union (2014). The guideline expands upon Article 6 of Directive 2003/98/EC of the European Parliament and the of the Council of 17 November 2003 on the reuse of public sector information which covers the principles governing charging and states at Article 6 (1) that "where charges are made for the re-use of documents, those charges shall be limited to the marginal costs incurred for their reproduction, provision and dissemination." The guidelines provide guidance to agencies who charge fees and notes that although Article 6 (2) exempts public sector bodies that generate revenue to cover a substantial part of their costs, it does not however prevent them from implementing a wilful zero-cost policy. It allows for documents to be made available for reuse free of charge. At the same time, it limits any charges to the marginal costs incurred for the reproduction, provision and dissemination of documents.

144 Mark Morgenstein, 'Edward Snowden: World's Most Wanted Man, Says New Book' *CNN* (2014), available at http://edition.cnn.com/2014/02/02/world/europe/uk-snowden-book/.

145 Barbara Miller, 'Fugitive Edward Snowden Meets with Human Rights Groups at Moscow Airport' *ABC News* (2013), available at www.abc.net.au/news/2013-07-12/snowden-meets-with-human-rights-groups/4817674. See where he noted that "That moral decision to tell the public about spying that affects all of us has been costly, but it was the right thing to do and I have no regrets."

Bibliography

ACT Australian Capital Territory Government, Open Data Policy: Draft Proactive Information Disclosure (Open Data) Policy, GitHub, available at http://actgov.github.io/opendatapolicy/.

Dan Agbese, When the Sun Set in Nigeria: Dele Giwa's Awful Murder (Committee to Protect Journalists, CPJ 2009), available at https://cpj.org/blog/2009/10/nigerian-editor-dele-giwas-unsolved-murder.php

ARC, *ARC Open Access Policy*, available at www.arc.gov.au/applicants/open_access.htm.

Article19, *Memorandum on the Nigerian Freedom of Information Bill* (2000), available at www.article19.org/data/files/pdfs/analysis/nigeria.foi.00.pdf.

Article19, *The Public's Right to Know Principles on Freedom of Information Legislation* (1999), available at www.article19.org/data/files/pdfs/standards/righttoknow.pdf.

Article 19 & Media Rights Agenda, *Unshackling the Nigerian Media*, Article 19 & Media Rights Agenda (1997), available at www.article19.org/data/files/pdfs/publications/nigeria-unshackling-the-media.pdf.

Arunachalam, Subbiah, *Information Poverty the Story: How the Internet Is Failing the Developed World*, available at www.abc.net.au/science/slab/infopoverty/story.htm.

Australian Bureau of Statistics, *ABS Copyright* (2010), available at www.abs.gov.au/websitedbs/D3310114.nsf/home/%C2%A9%20Copyright

Australian Consumer Law and Fair Trading Act 2012 (Vic).

Australian Information Commissioner Act 2010 Act No.52 of 2010 C2014C00382.

Australian National Research Services ANDS, *About Us*, available at www.ands.org.au/about-ands.html.

Bankole, Oluwafemi, *Nigeria: How Information Conquered Ebola* (2014), available at http://techcabal.com/2014/10/20/nigeria-information-conquered-ebola/.

Bollier, David, *Viral Spiral: How the Commoners Built a Digital Republic of Their Own* (New Press, 2008).

Booth, Keitha, 'NZ Government Information Policy and Data Re-Use Project Background Paper' in Fitzgerald Brian ed., *Access to Public Sector Information: Law, Technology & Policy* (Sydney University Press, 2010).

Bujoreanu, Lyudmila, et al., *Open Government Initiative in Edo State: Fostering an Ecosystem of Collaboration and Transparency* (2014), available at https://openknowledge.worldbank.org/handle/10986/18713.

Bureau of Meteorology, *Copyright Notice: Your Rights to Use Material on Bureau Websites*, available at www.bom.gov.au/other/copyright.shtml?ref=ftr.

Bureau of Public Procurement, *About BPP*, available at www.bpp.gov.ng/index.php?option=com_content&view=article&id=110&Itemid=740.

Cabinet Office, Information Matters, Speech by the Prime Minister, the Rt Hon. Gordon Brown MP at Liberty, University of Westminster, October 2007 (Cabinet Office ed., Cabinet Office 2007).

Carothers, Thomas & Saskia Brechenmacher, The Four Magic Words of Development, *World Bank* (2014), available at http://blogs.worldbank.org/publicsphere/four-magic-words-development-tom-carothers-and-saskia-brechenmacher.

Chris, Corbin, 'PSI Policy Principles: European Best Practice' in Fitzgerald Brian ed., *Access to Public Sector Information: Law, Technology & Policy* (Sydney University Press, 2010).

The Citizen, *Undermining Freedom of Information Act-Punch*, available at http://thecitizenng.com/public-affairs/undermining-freedom-of-information-act-punch/.

The Coercive Information-Gathering Powers of Government Agencies: Report No: 48 of May 2008, Prepared by the Administrative Review Council (2008).

Coordination of Federal Information Policy (2002), available at www.archives.gov/about/laws/fed-information-policy.html.

Copyright, Designs and Patents Act C.48 (1988).

CPJ, *10 Journalists Killed in Nigeria Since 1992/Motive Confirmed*, Committee to Protect Journalists, available at www.cpj.org/killed/africa/nigeria/.

DeBardeleben, J. & J. Pammett, *Activating the Citizen: Dilemmas of Participation in Europe and Canada* (Palgrave Macmillan, 2009).

Digital Broadband Content: Public Sector Information and Content (2006), OECD Digital Economy Papers, No 112, OECD Publishing, Paris, available at https://doi.org/10.1787/231534841283

Digital Strategy 2.0 (2008).

Directive 2003/98/EC of the European Parliament and of the Council on the Re-Use of Public Sector Information (2003), available at http://eur-lex.europa.eu/LexUriServ/LexUriServ.do?uri=OJ: L: 2003: 345: 0090: 0096: EN: PDF.

Directive 2013/37/EU of the European Parliament and of the Council of 26 June (2013), available at http://eur-lex.europa.eu/legal-content/EN/TXT/PDF/?uri=CELEX: 02003L0098-20130717&from=EN.

The Economist, 'Knowledge Is Power: Do We Need a New Competition Policy for the New Economy?' available at www.economist.com/node/375597.

Edo State Open Data Portal, *Terms of Use*, available at www.data.edostate.gov.ng/terms-of-use.

Emmanuel, Joseph, *Ogun State Govt Fined by Court over Freedom of Information Act* (2014), available at www.thetrentonline.com/foi-ogun-state-govt-fined-court/.

ERC, *Open Access Guidelines for Researchers Funded by the ERC* (2012), available at http://erc.europa.eu/sites/default/files/document/file/open_access_policy_researchers_funded_ERC.pdf.

European Commission, Open-Source Software: Licence Compatibility and Interoperability, *Joinup*, available at https://joinup.ec.europa.eu/software/page/licence_compatibility_and_interoperability%20.

European Union, *Commission Notice: 'Guidelines on Recommended Standard Licences, Datasets and Charging for the Re-Use of Documents*, available at https://ec.europa.eu/digital-agenda/en/news/commission-notice-guidelines-recommended-standard-licences-datasets-and-charging-re-use (Newsroom Editor ed., 2014).

European Union, *Commission Welcomes Member States' Endorsement of EU Open Data Rules* (2013), available at http://europa.eu/rapid/press-release_IP-13-316_en.htm.

European Union, *Revision of the PSI Directive*, available at http://ec.europa.eu/digital-agenda/en/news/revision-psi-directive (Newsroom Editor ed., 2012).

Federal Government Brazil, *Open Data*, available at http://dados.gov.br/noticia/dados-abertos-permitem-que-cidadaos-conhecam-melhor-as-acoes-e-os-resultados-do-mj/.

Federal Ministry of Health, *National Strategic Health Development Plan (NSHDP 2010–2015)*, available at www.health.gov.ng/doc/NSHDP.pdf.

Felten, Ed, et al., 'Government Data and the Invisible Hand' 11 (2009) *Yale Journal of Law and Technology* 160.

Forest, Horton, *Public Access to Government Information and Information Literacy Training as Basic Human Rights* (2002), available at https://repository.arizona.edu/handle/10150/105882?show=full

Freedom of Information Act 1982 Act No.3 of 1982 (1982).

Freedom of Information Act 2011.

Free Software Foundation, *GNU Free Documentation License*, available at www.gnu.org/licenses/fdl.html.

Fitzgerald, Anne, 'Open Access and Public Sector Information: Policy Developments in Australia and Key Jurisdictions' in Fitzgerald Brian ed., *Access to Public Sector Information: Law, Technology & Policy* (Sydney University Press, 2010).

GOV.UK, *10 Policies About Government Efficiency, Transparency and Accountability*, available at www.gov.uk/government/policies?topics%5B%5D=government-efficiency-transparency-and-accountability.

Government of Canada, *Minister Holder Announces New Open Access Policy for Research* (2015), available at www.science.gc.ca/default.asp?lang=En&n=415B5097-1.

GOVLAB, *Open Data and the United Nations: Experts Reflect on Current Open Data Challenges Within the UN and Outline a Path Forward* (2014), available at http://thegovlab.org/open-data-and-the-united-nations-experts-reflect-on-current-open-data-challenges-within-the-un-and-outline-a-path-forward/.

Guilbault, Lucie & Christina Angelopoulos, *Open Content Licensing from Theory to Practice* (Amsterdam University Press, 2011).

Henninger, Maureen, 'The Value and Challenges of Public Sector Information' 5 (2013) *Cosmopolitan Civil Societies Journal* 75.

Henry, J., *Knowledge Is Power: Francis Bacon and the Method of Science* (Icon, 2002).

The Holy Bible: Authorized King James Version, Containing the Old and New Testaments (Holman Bible Publishers Read-to-me ed., 1984).

Idowu, Lanre, *Nigeria's New FOI Law Brings Celebration, Challenges* (Committee to Protect Journalists 2011), available at https://cpj.org/blog/2011/07/nigerias-new-foi-law-brings-celebration-challenges.php

India Garba V SA to Governor Benue State MHC/2565M/2012 (Makurdi High Court 9 October 2014).

Iriekpen, Davidson, Nigeria: In Conflicting Judgement, Court Says FOI Act Not Binding on States, *AllAfrica*, available at http://allafrica.com/stories/201411030673.html.

Jefferson, T., et al., *The Writings of Thomas Jefferson* (Issued Under the Auspices of the Thomas Jefferson Memorial Association of the United States, 1904).

Judge Elizabeth, 'Enabling Access to Public Sector Information in Canada' in Michael Geist ed., *From Radical Extremism to Balance Copyright: Canadian Copyright and the Digital Agenda* (Irwin Law, Canada 2010).

Legal Defence and Assistance Project Limited/GTE V AG Lagos State & 5 Others (Federal High Court of Lagos).

McGroarty, Patrick, *Muhammadu Buhari Defeats Goodluck Jonathan in Nigeria Election*, available at www.wsj.com/articles/officials-tally-remaining-votes-in-nigeria-presidential-election-1427796882.

Michels, Anks, 'Innovations in Democratic Governance: How Does Citizen Participation Contribute to a Better Democracy?' 77 (2011) *International Review of Administrative Sciences* 275.

Miller, Barbara, 'Fugitive Edward Snowden Meets with Human Rights Groups at Moscow Airport' (2013) *ABC News*, available at www.abc.net.au/news/2013-07-12/snowden-meets-with-human-rights-groups/4817674.

Morgenstein, Mark, 'Edward Snowden: World's Most Wanted Man, Says New Book' *CNN* (2014), available at http://edition.cnn.com/2014/02/02/world/europe/uk-snowden-book/.

The National Archives, About Us, *Legislation.gov.uk*, available at www.legislation.gov.uk/aboutus.

The National Archives, *Crown Copyright*, available at www.nationalarchives.gov.uk/information-management/re-using-public-sector-information/copyright/crown-copyright/.

The National Archives, *Open Government License for Public Sector Information*, available at www.nationalarchives.gov.uk/doc/open-government-licence/.

The National Archives, *Open Government Licenses for Public Sector Information*, available at www.nationalarchives.gov.uk/doc/open-government-licence/version/2/.

The National Archives, *UK Government Licensing Framework for Public Sector Information* (2013), available at www.nationalarchives.gov.uk/documents/information-management/uk-government-licensing-framework.pdf.

The National Archives, *Who We Are*, available at www.nationalarchives.gov.uk/about/who-we-are.htm.

Newton, Isaac, *From a Letter Written by Isaac Newton to Robert Hooke*, 5 February (1676).

New Zealand Cabinet, Open Government, CAB Min (11) 29/12 (Cabinet Office ed., 2011).

New Zealand Government, *Policy Framework for New Zealand Government-Held Information* (1997), available at www.ssc.govt.nz/Documents/policy_framework_for_Government_.htm.

New Zealand Government, *New Zealand Data and Information Management Principles* (2011), available at https://ict.govt.nz/guidance-and-resources/open-government/new-zealand-data-and-information-management-principles/.

NIH, *NIH Public Access Policy*, available at http://publicaccess.nih.gov/.

Organisation for Economic Co-operation and Development (OECD), *About the OECD*, available at www.oecd.org/about/.

OECD, *Declaration on Access to Research Data from Public Funding: 30 March 2004 [C(2004)31/REV1]* (2004), available at http://acts.oecd.org/Instruments/ShowInstrumentView.aspx?InstrumentID=157.

OECD, *Recommendation of the Council Concerning Access to Research Data from Public Funding: 14 December 2006 – C(2006)184* (2006), available at http://webnet.oecd.org/

OECDACTS/Instruments/ShowInstrumentView.aspx?InstrumentID=159&Lang=en&Book=False.

OECD, *Recommendation of the Council for Enhanced Access and More Effective Use of Public Sector Information [C(2008) 36]* (2008), available at www.oecd.org/internet/ieconomy/40826024.pdf.

Office of the Australian Information Commission Australian Government, *Information Policy Report*, available at www.oaic.gov.au/information-policy/information-policy-resources/information-policy-reports/.

Office of the Australian Information Commissioner OAIC, *About Us*, available at www.oaic.gov.au/home/about-us.

Ola, Kunle, 'Evolution and Future Trends of Copyright in Nigeria' in Brian Fitzgerald & John Gilchrist eds., *Copyright Perspectives* (Springer, 2015).

Oladeji, Bayo, *The Importance of Freedom of Information Act*, available at http://leadership.ng/blogposts/390236/importance-freedom-information-act.

OMB, Circular No. A-130, Revised, Transmittal Memorandum No. 4, 28 November, Memorandum for Heads of Executive Departments and Agencies (United States Office of Management and Budget ed., 2000).

OMB, *Memorandum on Transparency and Open Government* (United States Office of Management and Budget ed., 2009).

OMB, *Open Government* (United States Office of Management and Budget ed., 2009).

OMB, *Open Government Directive* (United States Office of Management and Budget ed., 2009).

Open Data for Economic Growth (2014), available at www.worldbank.org/content/dam/Worldbank/document/Open-Data-for-Economic-Growth.pdf.

Bujoreanu, Lyudmila, et al., *Open Government Initiative in Edo State: Fostering an Ecosystem of Collaboration and Transparency* (2014), available at https://openknowledge.worldbank.org/handle/10986/18713.

Open Government Working Group, *Eight Principles of Open Government Data* (2007), available at https://public.resource.org/8_priciples.html.

OPSI, *Office of Public Sector Information*, available at www.opsi.gov.uk/psi/.

United Nations Economic Commission for Europe (UNECE), *The Power of Information: An Independent Review by Ed Mayo and Tom Steinberg* (2007), available at https://aarhusclearinghouse.unece.org/resources/power-of-information-an-independent-review

Powering Ideas an Innovation Agenda for the 21st Century (Canberra: Dept of innovation, Industry, Science and Research, 2009), available at https://sydney.edu.au/documents/about/higher_education/2012/20120308%20PoweringIdeas.pdf

The Presidency, *Nigeria Extractive Industries Transparency Initiative (NEITI)*, available at http://neiti.org.ng/index.php?q=pages/about-neiti.

Public Procurement Act 2007 Act No. 14 (2007).

PubMed, *PubMed*, National Institutes of Health (NIH), available at www.ncbi.nlm.nih.gov/pubmed/.

Queensland Government, *Information Management Policy Framework* (2009), available at www.qgcio.qld.gov.au/products/qgea-documents/548-information/2349-information-management-policy-framework.

RCUK, *RCUK Policy on Open Access*, available at www.library.qmul.ac.uk/s-3807/research-councils-uk-rcuk-policy-on-open-access/

Rogers, Simon, 'Government Data: Full Text of David Cameron's Letter Pledging to Open Up the Datasets' (2010) *The Guardian*, available at www.theguardian.com/news/datablog/2010/jun/01/government-data-david-cameron-letter.

Ross, Elliot, *Nigeria's New FOIA: Reporters Enjoy New Freedoms in a Long-Repressive Society*, available at www.cjr.org/behind_the_news/nigerias_new_foia.php.

Sahara Reporters, Freedom of Information: APC Chieftain Drags Alison-Madueke to Court, *Sahara Reporters* (2014), available at http://saharareporters.com/2014/09/24/freedom-information-apc-chieftain-drags-alison-madueketo-court.

The Sources of Innovation and Creativity: National Center on Education and the Economy (NCEE) Research Summary and Final Report (2005), available at www.ncee.org/wp-content/uploads/2010/04/Sources-of-Innovation-Creativity.pdf.

Stallman, Richard, *The GNU Project*, available at www.gnu.org/gnu/thegnuproject.html.

Tatalovic, Raymond, 'Presidents and Promises: From Campaign Pledge to Presidential Performance' 48 (1986) *The Journal of Politics* 189.

Treasury Board of Canada Secretariat Canada, *Information Management Policy*, available at www.tbs-sct.gc.ca/im-gi/imp-pgi/imp-pgi-eng.asp.

Uhlir, Paul, 'Policy Guidelines for the Development and Promotion of Governmental Public Domain Information' in Fitzgerald Brian ed., *Access to Public Sector Information: Law, Technology & Policy* (Sydney University Press, 2010).

UNESCO, *UNESCO Adopts Open Access Policy* (2013), available at http://openscience.com/unesco-adopts-open-access-policy/.

UNESCO, The UNESCO Recommendation on Promotion and Use of Multilingualism and Universal Access to Cyberspace, *UNESCO* (2004), available at www.unesco.org/new/fileadmin/MULTIMEDIA/HQ/CI/CI/pdf/official_documents/Eng%20-%20Recommendation%20concerning%20the%20Promotion%20and%20Use%20of%20Multilingualism%20and%20Universal%20Access%20to%20Cyberspace.pdf.

United Nations UN, *Structure and Organisation*, available at www.un.org/en/aboutun/structure/index.shtml.

United Nations UN, *UN at a Glance*, available at www.un.org/en/aboutun/index.shtml.

United Nations UN, *UN Public Administration Programme: Open Government Data and Services*, available at www.unpan.org/DPADM/Themes/OpenGovernmentDataandServices/tabid/1536/language/en-US/Default.aspx.

United Nations UN, *The United Nations Committee of Experts on Public Administration (CEPA)*, available at www.unpan.org/cepa.asp.

United Nations UN, *United Nations E-Government Survey 2014: E-Government for the Future We Want* (2014), available at http://unpan3.un.org/egovkb/Portals/egovkb/Documents/un/2014-Survey/E-Gov_Complete_Survey-2014.pdf.

United Nations Department for Economic and Social Affairs, *Guidelines on Open Government Data for Citizen Engagement, ST/ESA/PAD/SER.E/177*, available at http://workspace.unpan.org/sites/Internet/Documents/Guidenlines%20on%20OGDCE%20May17%202013.pdf.

The United States of America, Copyright Act of 1976 Title 17 of United States Code (1976).

U.S. Congress, *Declaration of Independence* (1776), available at www.archives.gov/exhibits/charters/declaration_transcript.html.

The White House, *Office of E-Government and Information Technology* (2002), available at www.whitehouse.gov/omb/e-gov/.

The World Bank, *Open Knowledge Repository*, available at https://openknowledge.worldbank.org/.

The World Bank, World Bank Announces Open Access Policy for Research and Knowledge, Launches Open Knowledge Repository, Press Release No. 2012/379/EXTOP (2012).

The World Bank, *World Bank Announces Open Access Policy for Research and Knowledge, Launches Open Knowledge Repository* (2012), available at www.worldbank.org/en/news/press-release/2012/04/10/world-bank-announces-open-access-policy-for-research-and-knowledge-launches-open-knowledge-repository.

Venturous Australia Report: Building Strength in Innovation (2008), available at www.voced.edu.au/content/ngv%3A12472

Yomi Ogunlola v Clerk of the Oyo State House of Assembly (High Court Ibadan).

7 Guidelines for developing a framework for access to knowledge in Nigeria

1 What is a framework?

Framework is a document detailing how an action may be carried out. It provides samples and simplifies the adaptation and implementation of actions:

> It is not a detailed hypothesis or set of hypotheses; rather, it is a suggested point of view. . . . A good framework is one that sounds reasonably plausible relative to available scientific data. . . . It is unlikely to be correct in all the details. A framework often contains unstated (and often unrecognized) assumptions, but this is unavoidable.[1]

It is a supporting or underlying structure.[2] A framework refers to interlinked systems or items supporting an action, a process or/and an approach. It serves as a guide and is modifiable to meet various types of objectives. A framework is meant to provide a broad overview, outline or skeleton of an issue.[3]

2 Why develop a framework?

Developing standards is an integral part of any organization, particularly government who operates through its ministries, departments and agencies (MDA).[4] These different segments of government (MDA) are meant to work towards the same goal but are often unaware of what other segments are doing and of how actions are being implemented. It is not uncommon to have multiple agencies of government working on the same issues and for the same goal but due to lack of interface and the unavailability of a functioning central structure, agencies of government are made to re-invent the wheel, and the issue(s) in question may then have to be redeveloped and re-implemented using different structures and strategies. This often results in duplicity of human effort, loss of manpower time, duplicity of taxpayers' funds and a lack of uniformity of policies and strategies.[5] The development of a framework provides a uniform standard and thereby makes it easier to work within complex settings. It encourages coercion by bringing together various components as one and thereby compels a team to implement issues in a uniform way. It also therefore allows for a unified system of checks and balances.

3 Key stakeholders for the framework

In the context of this, research open access to knowledge the key stakeholders include the following:

1. Government
2. Universities
3. Research institutions
4. Libraries
5. International and intergovernmental organizations
6. Teachers
7. Students
8. Independent researchers
9. Journalists
10. Curious minds (which includes user publics)

4 Scope of the framework

This research focuses on *legal, regulatory* and *policy frameworks* and provides clarity as to how far it may go and at the same time restricts its scope to the identified research-focused areas.

5 Legal framework

Expressions in written form are generally protected as literary works by copyright laws.[6] These laws protect the works of authors from unauthorized use. It is however this same works that needs to be disseminated and since it must be done within the confines of legally accepted rules and with due regard for the legal system, a framework that provides an enabling environment for use and reuse and at the same time gives due respect to the legal system is required.[7] Developing such a legally acceptable and appropriate strategy is the central focus, and open licensing is what has been globally adopted.[8]

6 Regulatory framework

When structures and standards are established, a major milestone is accomplished, but the challenges of compliance, monitoring and evaluation arise. A system that provides standards but provides no checks and balances to such standards is set to fail.[9] The process that facilitates checks and balances is what the regulatory framework addresses, and it addresses it from both a process and positional point of view. Process in the sense that it would analyze how the checks and balances may be implemented and positional, from the point of view that it will advise on what type of offices, officers, ministries, departments and agencies should be responsible for its administration.

7 Policy framework

The development of clear expressions of expectations and how actions may be developed and implemented can be referred to as policies. Policies may be made and used by individuals, organizations and nations. A policy establishes a settled way of doing things for certain people. It is accepted worldwide that those to whom the policy applies are expected to do things in a certain way. It therefore provides amongst many other things a platform for otherwise weaker parties to negotiate with stronger parties.[10]

8 Features of the framework

8.1 Title of the framework

It gives the reader and the general public a bird-eye preview of what is expected in the larger document. It is therefore useful to title a framework and use titles that portray the central theme of the framework.

8.2 Purpose

Expressing the underlying rationale for pursuing a framework is crucial to every framework. It is the purpose that gives meaning to an activity. Organizations may be carrying out the exact same activity, but for different reasons. Understanding the underlying rationale prompting the organizations to carry out the actions is what gives true meaning to the activities. Understanding the purpose, the rationale, the reason, the why a thing is done strengthens and sharpens an individual's resolve and dedication. In the words of Myles Munroe, "Where purpose is not known, abuse is inevitable. Without purpose activity has no meaning and time and energy are misused."[11] It is therefore advisable to develop purpose specific statements or adapt from organizations with identical or similar purposes. The purpose statement of an organization is often expressed through their aims, objectives and goals. It is therefore important to clearly enunciate the purpose of any framework. What follows is an example.

Example: The United States Government Memorandum for Heads of Executive Departments and Agencies on Management of Federal Information Resources

> This Circular establishes policy for the management of Federal information resources. OMB includes procedural and analytic guidelines for implementing specific aspects of these policies as appendices.[12]

8.3 Applicability and scope

Providing clarity as to how far the intended action or process will go and to whom it is directed is an important part in the development of any framework. In making this clarification, it is however important to make provision for unforeseen circumstances. In defining the scope and applicability of any framework, cognizance must be taken of cultural, economic, technological and other related factors which may have effect on the development of an open access to knowledge framework. For instance, in developing such a framework in Nigeria and in other nations endowed with a rich folklore heritage, it will be important to duly regard the cultural believes and factor these believes into whatever frameworks are being developed. Disregard of local beliefs and practices could be very antithetical to the success of an idea and could inhibit its implementation. It would also be crucial to identify who the target audiences are and who may be excluded. These target audiences have been identified earlier in the section above on key stakeholders for the framework.

8.4 Definitions

Understanding the meaning of words and terminologies in a document is paramount in optimizing the utility of such documents. Many of these terms used in the open movement are new. Most of these terms are not defined in the conventional dictionaries. It is therefore important to provide a definition section within the framework.[13]

8.5 Commencement date

In developing a framework, tracking the timelines of how and when certain decisions are made could be important; it is therefore important for the framework to have a commencement date. It would usually be the date after the appropriate authority has granted the requisite approvals. The style in which the date is expressed is not of critical importance. The expression of the date would however usually conform to the drafting style of the organization or nation. What is important is that the actual dates when the framework was approved, executed and deemed to take effect be clearly expressed. If these dates are one and the same, it should be so stated, and if the dates are different, the different dates should be indicated accordingly. See Table 7.1 capturing a single date inserted into the New South Wales Open Data Policy to indicate the commencement date.[14]

See Table 7.2, which provides multiple dates indicating the timeline for the United Kingdom Government Licensing Framework for Public Sector Information.[15]

8.6 Governing principles

Individuals and organizations operate based on certain guiding principles. These principles determine mode of operation, priorities and influences the kind of

Table 7.1 Document history (NSW)

Date	*Version No*	*Description*	*Author*
September 2013	**1.0**	**Final**	**Department of Finance and Services**

Table 7.2 Document control/ Change summary

Version	*Date*	*Author/Editor*	*Change Summary*
1.0	**30/09/2010**	**TNA**	**First published edition**
2.0	**29/07/2011**	**TNA**	**Second published edition**
3.0	**28/06/2013**	**TNA**	**Third published edition**
4.0	**01/09/2013**	**TNA**	**Fourth published edition**
4.1	**30/10/2014**	**TNA**	**Updated to reflect launch of OGLv3.0**

partners to collaborate with. It is also instrumental to the general decision-making process. The framework should capture an organization's governing principles. Putting this information out will help prospective partners know and understand the idiosyncrasies of particular organizations. These principles are often captured within the overarching policy statements of the organization. The United Nation's Department of Economic and Social Affair's Guideline on Open Government Data for Citizen Engagement issued in 2013 captures the governing principles of the organization.[16] In a 2006 court case, which bordered on the recognition of access to information as a human right by the Inter-American Court of Human Rights, the need to include essential principles within frameworks was noted by the courts. The court enunciated the need to design an access to information regime which would include essential principles.[17]

8.7 Action plan

An implementation strategy should be developed and captured in the framework. Equally important is how the idea will be implemented, the step-by-step strategy or at least a rough map on an implementation strategy. Failure to develop and make such a plan is planning to fail.[18] The implementation strategy can always be sharpened, revamped and redeveloped to accommodate new ideas, recent changes and include unforeseen circumstances. Providing these implementation strategies in the framework provide the needed tools for implementation and helps the general public avoid the problem of wrong, misdirected or incomplete implementation. Please find below the action plan provided in the Budapest Open Access Treaty.

> Open access to peer-reviewed journal literature is the goal. Self-archiving (I.) and a new generation of open-access journals (II.) are the ways to attain this goal. They are not only direct and effective means to this end, they are within the reach of scholars themselves, immediately, and need not wait on changes brought about by markets or legislation. While we endorse the two strategies just outlined, we also encourage experimentation with further ways to make the transition from the present methods of dissemination to open access. Flexibility, experimentation, and adaptation to local circumstances are the best ways to assure that progress in diverse settings will be rapid, secure, and long-lived.

8.8 Licensing framework

In developing a framework for access to knowledge anywhere in the world, content is central. As discussed earlier in Chapters 3, 4, 5 and 6, content is protected under the legal regime of intellectual property and more particularly copyright which covers literary works (journal articles, books, reports and other types of written works). One of the most important aspects of an open access to knowledge framework would be making provision for the grant of authorization (licensing) and the type(s) of authorization. Providing for this would not only establish a legal platform for the operation of the framework but it will allay any fears of uncertainty as to what can be done and what can be used by current and prospective users. The licensing framework should therefore put into consideration and capture the following issues:

8.8.1 Management of copyright

i In developing an access to knowledge framework, understanding and managing copyright is crucial.

8.8.2 Clarify rights

ii Once a work has been identified, it is important to clarify what rights are likely to be exploited. This is important because copyright is comprised of a bundle of rights and therefore works may enjoy multiple rights. With each right comes distinct privileges which enjoy distinct protection. Therefore, unbundling these rights by clarifying them will help in identifying what type of authorization should be sought and obtained.

8.8.3 Payment

iii The goal of a more open world is that all content be available for free. It is however currently impracticable for all content to be freely available. It is therefore important for the framework to indicate what is free and what is not and for the framework to express its goal as to payments.

8.8.4 Licences

The grant of authorization for works is often done through licensing, and a licence is a permit/document evidencing the authorization granted. The current copyright legal framework has a default *all rights reserved,* and authors are able through this exclusive right to exclude others from accessing, using and reusing the work. It is therefore important that a framework focused on open access to knowledge should shift the default to *no rights reserved* or *some rights reserved.*[19] This is achievable through the instrumentality of licensing via the law of contract and would enable users' free access to use and reuse knowledge. The choice of what open licence to adopt would depend on the organization, but the Creative Commons

(CC) licences has been noted as the most effective of the open licences.[20] There are several other licences which can be adapted including GNU General Public Licence,[21] the UK Government Licensing Framework for Public Sector Information,[22] the Open Government Licence,[23] and the New Zealand Government Open Access and Licensing Framework (NZGOAL).[24]

The above are the general factors to be considered in the development of any open access to knowledge framework. These factors are broad enough to capture most of the issues that may arise with respect to open access to knowledge. However, it is important to note that the different fields within the open movement and the access to knowledge movement may require special slants to the general factors discussed above. This next segment will consider issues pertinent to each of the three areas mentioned above.

9 Open access framework

Chapter 4 explained journal articles and noted that they play a major role in academic research.[25] It further noted that they are instrumental to knowledge development on a global scale and forms part of the critical building blocks used in evaluating competence and progress in the academic world. It is critical to academic tenure, promotion and research. The economic successes and the many millions of dollars attributed to the publishing industry is not unconnected to journal articles.[26] It is a major lifeline for the publishing industry and forms a major part of the content used by the publishing industry.[27] The issues surrounding the creation, production, distribution, and access to use and reuse content expressed via journal articles are multi-faceted and affect many parties. It is therefore important to consider these issues, factors and parties when crafting a framework that would enable access to these journal articles. Yes, access to journal articles is imperative in this age for development, but access must be obtained within the confines of the law and with due regard for the legal system. An effective open access framework would necessarily factor in most of the issues already discussed but should pay attention to the following aspects.

10 Academic and research communities

The academic and research community constitute the core of those who generate majority of the content in journal articles and are therefore major stakeholders when it comes to journal articles. They are not only responsible for generating the ideas that crystalize in the creation of the content, but they are also responsible for its quality assurance through the peer-review mechanism process[28] and are equally the major consumer market through its staff, students and researchers.[29] It is therefore important for these institutions to develop policy statements that drive their individual open access initiatives. There are several examples to help in developing such policies, for example,

1 National Institute of Health (NIH) in the United States[30]
2 Australian Research Council (ARC)[31]

3 European Research Council (ERC)[32]
4 Research Council UK (RCUK)[33]

11 Institutional repository

Accessing content from a convenient place and at the time of ones choosing is central to the success of any open access framework. Institutional repositories provide a convenient platform for anytime and anyplace access; however, populating the repository is the task because the value of a repository increases with its volume.[34] It is therefore important for the framework to provide for the creation, maintenance and deposit of contents into the repository. It should also provide for terms of access to use and reuse of such contents. These are best achieved by developing a policy statement by the individual or organization on institutional repositories (IR). The IR Policy may be drafted in a way that deposits into the repository by staff, students, researchers, members or beneficiaries are mandatory or persuasive. The choice of whether the policy should be mandatory or persuasive would be left to each individual entity. It may however be best to make it mandatory as research has shown that the level of deposits drastically increases with a mandate,[35] and it will eventually serve the greater good. There are ready examples of institutional repository policies which can be studied and adapted as the need arises. Examples of IR policies include the following:

1 The IR policy by the Queensland University of Technology[36]
2 The Institutional Research Repository Policy of the University of Otago[37]
3 The University of South Africa[38]
4 The Covenant University in Nigeria[39]

Useful information on IR policies can be obtained from the Registry of Open Access Repositories,[40] Registry of Open Access Repositories Mandates and Policies (ROARMAP)[41] as well as from the Directory of Open Access Repositories.[42] IRs will be particularly instrumental for Nigeria and other developing countries because it provides immediate access to information.[43] Granted it may not provide the published version, but it provides without any delay immediate access to at least read information of cutting edge technology, recently discovered issues and a host of other information. Most Nigerian libraries are unable to afford the cost of subscriptions to the major publishers and are therefore cut off from the global information flow channel. Establishing functional IRs re-establishes this link. Access is a fundamental need and IRs provides a functional and immediate platform for access.[44] It is little wonder that the number of IR policies have continually been on the increase as indicated on the ROARMAP website.[45]

12 Framework for open educational resources

In Chapter 5, it was noted that the reign of the knowledge economy has brought to the fore the growing relevance of education. To properly embrace OER and make the best of it, the general factors discussed in Chapter 5 should be borne in mind.

Attention should be paid to understanding OER, its purpose, how it intersects with intellectual property, its scope, the role of government and higher education institutions.

12.1 Higher education institutions

Higher education institutions (HEI) are responsible for developing and implementing teaching and learning modules. They develop curriculum and enjoy academic freedom. With this freedom comes the responsibility to ensure that the educational system is provided with the best opportunities that exist. Considering the many challenges in the current educational system inclusive of, the high cost of textbooks, the high cost of fees, the rising number of applicants and the trend towards globalization in the educational system, open educational resources (OER) provide useful tips on how to address these challenges and advance the current educational system. The following under-listed issues will be useful in crafting an OER framework in Nigeria.

1. *Develop individual institutional strategies on how to integrate OER:* An easy way to achieve this is to view the strategy of a university that has already adopted one. The MIT Open Courseware is a good example.[46] It has been adopted by many other institutions, and the contents have been mirrored by many other websites and translated into various languages.[47]
2. *Provide adequate funding for the development, acquisition and adaptation of high-quality learning and teaching materials*: Considering the fact that a huge amount of educational resources is already openly available, HEI interested in OER should adequately fund the development, acquisition and adaptation of these materials.
3. *Incentive System*: Establish an incentive system (promotion, tenure, appointments) for developing and adapting OER.
4. *Institutional Repository*: Provide an effective and efficient institutional repository for the OERs.
5. *OER Textbooks*: Encourage use of OER textbooks as the recommended texts.
6. *Publishing as OER*: Promote the publication of educational, learning and other teaching materials as OER within the institution.
7. *Quality Control*: Establish a quality control mechanism for the contents that are developed and adapted. This will ensure that OER are not substandard materials.
8. *Adopt an institution-wide licensing framework*: It is important for staff members to know that copyright and other intellectual property issues have been catered for on an institutional level. The uncertainty on the part of staff and students as to copyright infringement could be a major hindrance to getting involved in developing and adapting OER. An institutional licensing framework, preferable one that is open such as the Creative Commons attribution licence puts such fears to rest.
9. *Active and continuous capacity building for staff and students*: HEI will need to actively engage with staff and students on a regular basis. The process of

getting people on board a vision is not always easy, but with persistence, interaction and networking, people begin to see the relevance and advantages. When staff and student are exposed to what others are doing and have done, it often serves as a challenge and inspiration.

10 *Provide the needed ICT infrastructure and training*: It has been shown in a research that lack of ICT infrastructure and training are amongst some of the factors that discourage academic staff from embracing a culture of sharing on the open platform.[48] Without these infrastructures and the requisite training, HEI will find it next to impossible to make any success in implementing an OER strategy.

11 *Review institutional OER policies regularly*: Due to human dynamism, environmental and technological changes and taking cognizance of the role of these factors especially technology in the development, use, reuse and adaptation of OER, it would be instructive for HEI to regularly review their policies and practices. It is also important to assess what has worked well and what has not worked.

12.2 Academic staff

The value of OER is directly linked to the volume of content made available. Academic staff members play a major role in content development. They are mostly the ones who write, review, edit and make comments on school textbooks. They are responsible for preparing the curriculum, the course outlines, assessment tools, choosing the textbooks and other teaching and learning materials. Combining all these often place a heavy burden on academic staff and yet they need to address the different cultural needs of students and get themselves updated with relevant ICT skills.

The integration of OER into the academic system rests heavily on the shoulders of academic staff. The choice of what OER to select, acquire, adapt and repurpose is on them. The job of ensuring that the materials are properly adapted to suit the specific institutional need is also that of the academic staff. It can be conveniently concluded that the quality of OER in most HEI depends on academic staff members. In view of the important roles and responsibilities on academic staff members, the following are suggested in developing an OER framework in Nigeria:

1 Enlighten Academic staff members about the meaning, making and use of OER.

2 Encourage the development of requisite OER skills. This will help to sieve out important information from the vast stock.[49]

3 Begin to publish OER. It may be best to start with small materials such as course outlines or course information booklets.

4 Maximize the use of existing OER. There is no need to re-invent the wheel when what is required already exists. The important thing to note is that after adapting the existing OER, ensure that the adapted work is also made available. That way, the OER global bank is made richer.

5 Enlist students in the crusade. Students appear to understand today's technology better than the teachers.
6 Develop a practice of providing feedback on the OER acquired, adapted and developed. This will ensure that the quality of OER is at its highest. It will also help in identifying effective ways of managing OER.

12.3 Students

Students have always played a major role in the education system. Today the role they play is increasingly expanding. Students post explanations of topics on YouTube which are accessible to the whole world. Students provide commentaries to recommended texts and also provide several other learning aids online. Students have a role to play in developing, using, reusing and adapting OER. To effectively play this role, cognizance should be taken of the following:

1 Understand OER by gaining insights on how to develop, use, reuse and adapt OER.
2 Advocate for the development, use and adaptation of OER: Students have a strong voice for advocacy. This voice should be used to advocate for the development, use and adaptation of OER. It is advisable that the students maximize the use of social media in their advocacy.
3 Encourage the student community to publish OER works
4 Encourage the student community to comment on OER works thereby participating in quality assurance of OER works.
5 Maximize the platform of social network for OER.
6 Encourage students to join local and international OER networks
7 Understand intellectual property and particularly copyright issues.

12.4 Supervisory ministry and agencies and accreditation bodies

Government plays a major role in the regulation of the educational system. It does this by formulating and coordinating education policies. It prescribes and ensures maintenance of a minimum standard of educational quality throughout the nation. It encourages domestic and international cooperation on educational matters, and it also oversees the development of curricula and syllabuses. The Federal and State Ministries of Education in Nigeria are responsible for delivering sound education for public good. They are to ensure that education is used as a tool for fostering development of all Nigerians. The federal government carries out its education mandate through the instrumentality of a number of parastatal or agencies. These agencies include the National Universities Commission,[50] National Commission for Colleges of Education, National Board for Technical Education, and Nigerian Education Research and Development Council.[51]

Considering the critical role of these supervisory ministries, agencies and accreditation bodies in regulating the day-to-day affairs of education in a country, OER is a veritable tool that these agencies can adopt, and it has the potential of not only reducing the high cost of education on the part of government, but it also has high potentials of increasing the quality of education as well as the number of citizens who can be provided with access to quality educational resources. In developing an OER framework, these entities would need to pay attention to the following:

1 Understand OER.
2 Explore existing OER policies.
3 Study the successes and failures of existing OER policies.
4 Provide incentives for the development of OER: An example is the Obama Administrations pledge of US$2 billion towards the development of OER.[52]
5 Strategic Engagement with HEI. An assessment of the local circumstances is important in the development and implementation of OER policies. It may not be realistic to legislate the development, use and reuse of OER, but a strategic engagement with the management of HEI's can begin the process of the change in culture. Where outright legislation is possible, this would be more effective, but the important thing is to understand the local circumstances and approach the development and implementation of an OER framework with these circumstances in mind.
6 Licensing Regime: Adopt a national open licensing regime. See the licensing frameworks for the United Kingdom[53] and that of New Zealand.[54]
7 Establish a monitoring mechanism.

13 Public sector information framework

In Chapter 6, we discussed that government holds some of the largest stock of information and that this information serves educational, research, technological, meteorological and several other purposes.[55] Also noted was that the quest for information by citizens is a major part of democracy with underpinning ideals of citizenry participation, transparency, accountability and openness.[56] To successfully develop a public sector information (PSI) framework for Nigeria, the general factors discussed earlier must be noted, but the following factors will also need to be considered and the following steps taken.

14 Factors to consider

14.1 Transparency

Government is about the people; therefore, the proposed plan for implementing an access regime should be laid bare before the people. The plan should not be shrouded with high-sounding words characteristic of bureaucratic complexities. The plan however complex should be set out in as plain a language as possible. The step-by-step process of how to obtain access should be explained in no unequivocal terms. If fees are to be paid, and if there are limitations to use and reuse, it must be clearly spelt and laid out.

14.2 Participation

Opportunities for participation should be provided.

14.3 Collaboration

Too many agencies of government continue to re-invent the wheel because of a lack of institutional collaboration. Providing an enabling environment for collaboration either through a systemic submission mechanism of information or through deposits and retrievals in and from a central governmental repository will be an important part of the framework. Collaboration is however not limited to government to government relationship. It should extend to government and non-profits, as well as private organizations. The general public should also be made active players in this collaboration.

14.4 Accountability

A credible feedback mechanism allowing the public to verify and assess the promises of the strategy should be put in place.

14.5 Openness

Government and private entities may not be able to disclose all the information they hold due to matters of security, privacy or intellectual property protections. The information that falls outside the purview of the above-mentioned information are still a large stock of information which if made properly available and accessible will spur development in no small way. Making this kind of information not just available but openly accessible, which is ensuring no restrictions are placed on such information is important for the success of the framework. Openness is best achieved by adopting an open government initiative. The open government initiatives of the United States,[57]Australia,[58] and the United Kingdom,[59]as well as the Open Government Declaration of the Open Government Partnership[60] endorsed by over 65 nations provide useful tools on openness in government.[61]

14.6 Legal conformity (use and reuse rights)

The legal framework that protects information is quite detailed. It is therefore important that there be unequivocal clarity as to what can and cannot be done with the information that is put out. The major points of clarity will border on the right to use and reuse information.

14.7 Intellectual property protection

Understanding intellectual property can make the difference between a well-structured framework and a badly structured framework. No matter how well intentioned an objective, if it offends the letter and spirit of the law, it is illegal. Obtaining the relevant consent, focusing on works within the public domain, clarifying what rights in a work are required and identifying the most effective licensing model to adopt are factors to be deliberated upon and properly considered.

14.8 Interoperability

The format in which an information is made accessible must be one that can easily interact with other formats.

14.9 Cost

It is preferable that every possible barrier to access inclusive of cost barriers be removed. Not all information providers are however currently making the information within their custody available and accessible for free. The reason for placing cost varies from one entity to the other. It will be instructive for the framework to contain information as to whether or not access is provided at no cost, and if at a cost, what the cost will be or is likely to be and if possible provide a standardized mode of ascertaining cost. Absolute freedom as to price is the goal, but where this is not possible, the cost should be as close as possible to the cost of production plus a fair value.

15 Steps to be taken

15.1 Publish government information online

To ensure that access is truly available, government should work towards making information available online.

15.2 Provide quality information

The information that would be made available should be of high quality. It should not be the draft copy, but rather the final and approved copy.

15.3 Create and institutionalize an open government culture

Making information available online should be made the standard practice. A deadline for making information available should be set. The format and quality of information uploaded should be standardized. A system for maintaining and updating the information should be put in place. Where possible, a specific officer(s) should be designated to oversee the implementation of this task. As each entity deems fit, a new agency may be set up to administer the implementation of this task. On the other hand, it may be fused into the responsibility of an existing agency, ministry or department.

15.4 Create awareness about PSI

To maximize the potential of PSI it is important that people know they have access to use and reuse information held by government. Public awareness by the public, private and civil societies is important.

At the beginning of this chapter, we considered general factors for developing a framework for open access to knowledge in Nigeria. We also highlighted specific factors to be considered in developing a framework with respect to the three different fields considered in this research. The next section of this chapter discusses the option of adopting an international treaty pathway for the development of an open access to knowledge framework in Nigeria.

16 International treaties

Another pathway to the development of frameworks is through International treaties which are legal binding documents with textual specifications of legal obligations. They result from a general process governed by rules of law and itself sets forth particular rules of law.[62] Member states who ratify such treaties agree to be bound by them.[63] Some states then go on to domesticate these laws by enacting an adapted version of the treaty as part of their national laws. Nigeria for example provides for domestication of international treaties before such treaties can be enforced in Nigeria.[64] A major incentive for the international treaty pathway is its global applicability.[65] There has been the push to capture the essence of the open movement as an international instrument through the draft treaty on Access to Knowledge.[66]

17 World Intellectual Property Organization

17.1 World Intellectual Property Organization development agenda

The World Intellectual Property Organization (WIPO) has been instrumental in the vanguard for access to knowledge. It captured the need for improved access to knowledge amongst the 45 recommendations under the WIPO development agenda adopted at WIPO's General Assembly in 2007.[67] Cluster C of the agenda particularly focused on Technology Transfer, Information and Communication Technologies and Access to Knowledge. It specifically provided in recommendation 19 for WIPO "to initiate discussion on how, within WIPO's mandate, to further facilitate access to knowledge and technology for developing countries and LDCs to foster creativity and innovation and to strengthen such existing activities within WIPO".

17.2 Marrakesh Treaty

In 2013, a treaty that would enable better access to knowledge for Visually Impaired Persons (VIP) was adopted by (WIPO).[68] The Diplomatic conference leading to its adoption brought together more than 600 negotiators from WIPO's 186 member.

The treaty called the *Marrakesh Treaty to Facilitate Access to Published Works for Persons Who Are Blind, Visually Impaired, or otherwise Print Disabled*, enables reproduction, distribution and the making available of published works in compatible formats for VIP.[69] The treaty has been reported as the first of its kind. Other copyright treaties have focused on minimum requirements to be granted to copyright owners and the minimum requirements for enforcing such copyright, but this treaty requires member states to grant certain rights to VIP, thereby curtailing the traditional rights of copyright owners.[70] The treaty addresses a major access to knowledge challenge and requires contracting parties to domesticate the treaty as national laws permitting reproduction, distribution and making available of published works in accessible formats through limitations and exceptions to the rights of copyright owners.

WIPO is not alone in the access to knowledge movement. The World Trade Organization and World Health Organization have both been identified with the access to knowledge movement. The rallying point for these organizations has been the drafted A2K treaty.[71]

18 Access to Knowledge Treaty (A2K)

This is a treaty that seeks to enable access to knowledge. The treaty is still in its draft form and underscores the importance of knowledge as an essential tool in the daily activities of all global citizens. It recognizes the role of the law in knowledge transactions and seeks to bridge the divide between the rich and the poor with regards to knowledge goods.[72] The Preamble to the draft treaty states that the treaty seeks to "enhance participation in cultural, civic and educational affairs, and sharing of the benefits of scientific advancement".[73] The objective of the draft treaty is to protect and expand access to knowledge and to facilitate transfer of technology to developing countries.[74] Part 5 of the draft article focuses on expanding and enhancing the knowledge commons. It encapsulates a host of issues revolving around knowledge inclusive of distance education, government funded research, scholarly publications, PSI, databases, open access journals, open access archives/repositories, open knowledge projects, public domain, access to archives of broadcasting works, interoperability and several other issues that would enable access to knowledge.[75] The minds behind the draft were able to capture the multi-disciplinary perspective of access to knowledge.

18.1 Guidelines for adapting A2K

In an attempt to developing a national open access framework, the A2K draft framework route may be an option. The general factors discussed above will be relevant and have to a large extent been captured in the draft A2K treaty. As the draft is wide in scope, there is the need to

1 Delineate areas of interest and focus on what will best serve the national interest.

2 Set up public enlightenment groups to carry out public enlightenment campaigns about the meaning and importance of open access to knowledge.
3 Set up advocacy groups to lobby the executive arm of government to present the bill and the legislative arm to speedily pass them. This is important considering the fact that Nigeria requires domestication of international treaties.

The challenge, however, is that reliance on such a treaty brings along the bureaucracies of international organizations and sovereign nations. Firstly, the document is still a draft and has not been passed as a treaty by any of the international bodies. It may require a number of diplomatic meetings and probably a conference to achieve this. Assuming the treaty has been adopted and is in force, it may not be enforceable in Nigeria until it has been domesticated in line with Section 12(1) of the constitution. The same may apply to other nations.[76] The process of achieving this often takes time. It is therefore important to weigh the odds before deciding to build a framework around an international treaty. The advantage of using this framework is that it serves as qualitative and tested precedence having undergone rigorous reviews by international experts.

19 Conclusion

This chapter has explored general and special factors to consider and has provided draft guidelines to aid in developing an open access to knowledge framework. Whereas the general factors were considered from a broad perspective and apply to the three fields of the open access movement discussed in Chapters 4, 5 and 6 of this chapter, the special factors laid emphasis on each of these fields. Lastly, an international instrument/treaty pathway was considered using the "A2K draft treaty as the working precedence."

Notes

1 Francis Crick & Christof Koch, 'A Framework for Consciousness' 6 (2003) *Nature Neurosicence.*
2 Catherine Soanes & Sara Hawker, *Compact Oxord English Dictionary* (Oxford University Press, 2005).
3 The Law Dictionary, *What Is Framework*, available at http://thelawdictionary.org/framework/.
4 R. F. Ola, *Local Administration in Nigeria* (Kegan Paul International, 1984).
5 Kunle Ola, *Understanding Open Access for Africa*, SSRN 2476739, available at http://papers.ssrn.com/sol3/papers.cfm?abstract_id=2476739.
6 Kunle Ola, *Copyright Collective Administration in Nigeria Lessons for Africa* (Springer, 2013), 5. He noted that "Copyright controls the grant of rights in respect of certain 'works' – works such literary works."
7 Lessig Lawrence, 'The Vision for the Creative Commons: What Are We and Where Are We Headed? Free Culture' in Fitzgerald Brian ed., *Open Content Licensing: Cultivating the Creative Commons* (Sydney University Press, 2007).
8 Ibid. Brian Fitzgerald, *A short Overview of Creative Commons* (Sydney University Press, 2007).

9 G. A. Maxwell, 'Checks and Balances: The Role of Managers in Work – Life Balance Policies and Practices' 12 (2005) *Journal of Retailing and Consumer Services*. "managers apparently play a pivotal role in translating . . . policies into practice and in ensuring there are appropriate checks and balances in the management of such practices."

10 Peter Suber, 'Knowledge as a Public Good' *SPARC* (2009), available at www.sparc.arl.org/resources/articles/knowledge#sthash.R1nBSlQF.dpuf. The author states that "It makes a huge difference who can say "take it or leave it" in a negotiation."

11 M. Munroe, *Rediscovering the Kingdom: Ancient Hope for Our 21st Century World* (ReadHowYouWant.com Limited, 2010), 116.

12 Office of Management and Budget (OMB), Circular No. A-130, Revised, (Transmittal Memorandum No. 4) (November 28, 2000), Memorandum For Heads Of Executive Departments And Agencies (United States Office of Managment and Budget ed., 2000).

13 See the Glossary of words at the Appendix section for a definition of terminologies used in the open movement.

14 New South Wales Government, *NSW Government Open Data Policy* (2013), available at www.finance.nsw.gov.au/ict/sites/default/files/NSW%20Government%20Open%20Data%20Policy%201.0.pdf.

15 The National Archives, *UK Government Licensing Framework for Public Sector Information* (2013), available at www.nationalarchives.gov.uk/documents/information-management/uk-government-licensing-framework.pdf.

16 United Nations Department for Economic and Social Affairs, *Guidelines on Open Government Data for Citizen Engagement, ST/ESA/PAD/SER.E/177*, available at http://workspace.unpan.org/sites/Internet/Documents/Guidenlines%20on%20OGDCE%20May17%202013.pdf.

17 *Claude-Reyes et al. v Chile*, (Inter-American coourt of Human Rights 19 September 2006).

18 Churchill Winston has been attributed as the one who said, "If you fail to plan, you are planning to fail".

19 Brian Fitzgerald, *Open Content Licensing (OCL) for Open Educational Resources: A Paper Commissioned by the OECD's Centre for Educational Research and Innovation (CERI) for the project on Open Educational Resources*, 4 & 5. (2007). He noted that "The key to seamless access to knowledge – through open access, new business models or e commerce mechanisms – is to work out how that permission process can be automated."

20 Lucie Guilbault & Christina Angelopoulos, *Open Content Licensing from Theory to Practice* (Amsterdam University Press, 2011), 8.

21 Free Software Foundation, *GNU Free Documentation License*, available at www.gnu.org/licenses/fdl.html.

22 Archives (2013).

23 The National Archives, *Open Government Licence for Public Sector Information*, available at www.nationalarchives.gov.uk/doc/open-government-licence/.

24 NZGOAL, *New Zealand Government Open Access and Licensing Framework (NZGOAL)* (2010), available at https://ict.govt.nz/assets/Uploads/Documents/NZGOAL.pdf.

25 Peter Suber, *Open Access* (MIT Press, 2012), 44, where he noted that "for 350 years, scholars have willingly, even eagerly published journal articles without payments."

26 Livres Hebdo, 'The Global Ranking of the Publishing Industry 2014' *Rüdiger Wischenbart Content and Consulting* (2014), available at http://wischenbart.com/upload/Global-Ranking-of-the-Publishing-Industry_2014_Analysis.pdf.

27 International Publishers Association IPA, *Annual Report October 2013|October 2014* (2014), available at www.internationalpublishers.org/images/reports/2014/IPA-annual-report-2014.pdf.

28 Richard Smith, 'Peer-Review: A Flawed Process at the Heart of Science and Journals' 99 (2006) *Journal of the Royal Society of Medicine*.

29 Ray Spier, 'The History of the Peer-Review Process' 20 (2002) *Trends in Biotechnology*.
30 National Institutes of Health (NIH), *NIH Public Access Policy*, available at http://publicaccess.nih.gov/.
31 ARC, *ARC Open Access Policy*, available at www.arc.gov.au/applicants/open_access.htm.
32 European Research Council (ERC), *Open Access Guidelines for Researchers Funded by the ERC* (2012), available at http://erc.europa.eu/sites/default/files/document/file/open_access_policy_researchers_funded_ERC.pdf.
33 Research Councils United Kingdom (RCUK), *RCUK Policy on Open Access*, available at www.rcuk.ac.uk/research/Pages/outputs.aspx.
34 Alma Swan & Sheridan Brown, *Open Access Self-Archivng: An Author Study* (Key Perspective Limited, 2005), 70, where it was noted that the "current open access archives contain so little content. Once the volume of research deposited in these archives increases, usage will rise." See also, Stevan Harnad & Nancy McGovern, 'Institutional Repository Success Is Dependent Upon Mandates' 36 (2009) *Bulletin of the American Society for Information Science and Technology*, 27. "The measure of that success is accordingly the proportion of the faculty's annual journal article output being deposited in the IR."
35 Arthur Sale, *Comparison of Content Policies for Institutional Repositories in Australia* (2006), available at http://firstmonday.org/ojs/index.php/fm/article/view/1324/1244. "A requirement to deposit research output into a repository coupled with effective author support policies works in Australia and delivers high levels of content."
36 Queensland University of Technology, *QUT ePrints*, available at http://eprints.qut.edu.au/.
37 University of Otago, *Institutional Research Repository Policy*, available at www.otago.ac.nz/administration/policies/otago014455.html.
38 University of South Africa (UNISA), *Unisa Institutional Repository*, available at http://uir.unisa.ac.za/.
39 Covenant University, *Covenant University Repository*, available at http://eprints.covenantuniversity.edu.ng/.
40 ROAR, *Registry of Open Access Repositories*, available at http://roar.eprints.org/cgi/roar_search/advanced?location_country=&software=&type=institutional&order=-recordcount%2F-date.
41 ROARMAP, *Registry of Open Access Repositories Mandatory Archiving Policies*, available at http://roarmap.eprints.org/.
42 OpenDOAR, *Directory of Open Access Repositories*, available at www.opendoar.org/countrylist.php.
43 Stevan Harnad et al., *The Green and Gold Roads to Open Access*, Nature Publishing Group, available at www.nature.com/nature/focus/accessdebate/21.html?a_aid=3598aabf.
44 Stevan Harnad, *Gold Open Access Publishing Must Not Be Allowed to Retard the Progress of Green Open Access Self-Archiving*, available at http://eprints.soton.ac.uk/271818/1/logospaper.pdf.
45 ROARMAP.
46 Massachusetts Institute of Technology (MIT), *Mitopencourseware*, available at http://ocw.mit.edu/index.htm.
47 MIT), *About the OpenCourseWare Consortium*, available at http://ocw.mit.edu/about/ocw-consortium/.
48 Okoye, M. O. & Ejikeme, A. N., 'Open Access, Institutional Repositories, and Scholarly Publishing: The Role of Librarians in South Eastern Nigeria' 2 (2011) *Library Philosophy and Practice (e-Journal)*, 1–9. See also, Ivwighreghweta, O. & O. K. Onoriode, 'Open Access and Scholarly Publishing: Opportunities and Challenges to Nigerian Researchers' 33 (2012) *Chinese Librarianship: An International Electronic Journal*, 1–13.

49 See generally, A. Toffler, *Future Shock* (Bantam Books. 1990). See also, Rogers Paul et al., 'Infobesity: The Enemy of Good Decisions' *Insight*, available at www.bain.com/publications/articles/infobesity-the-enemy-of-good-decisions.aspx. See also, John Moravec, 'Infoxication 2.0' *Education Futures* (2008), available at www.educationfutures.com/2008/10/24/infoxication-20/.

50 National Universities Commission Act, Cap N.81, Laws of the Federation of Nigeria (LFN) (2004), available at www.placng.org/lawsofnigeria/node/507 Cap N.81 LFN.

51 Federal Republic of Nigeria, *Federal Ministry of Education*, available at www.nigeria.gov.ng/2012-10-29-11-06-51/executive-branch/93-federal-ministry-of-education/116-federal-ministry-of-education.

52 Timothy Vollmer, *New Federal Education Fund Makes Available $2 Billion to Create OER Resources in Community Colleges*, available at http://creativecommons.org/weblog/entry/26100.

53 Archives(2013).

54 NZGOAL (2010).

55 Fitzgerald Anne, 'Open Access and Public Sector Information: Policy Developments in Australia and Key Jurisdictions' in Fitzgerald Brian ed., *Access to Public Sector Information: Law, Technology & Policy* (Sydney University Press, 2010).

56 Thomas Carothers & Saskia Brechenmacher, 'The Four Magic Words of Development' *World Bank* (2014), available at http://blogs.worldbank.org/publicsphere/four-magic-words-development-tom-carothers-and-saskia-brechenmacher.

57 The White House, *Open Government Initiative*, available at www.whitehouse.gov/open.

58 AusGOAL, *Australian Governments Open Access ad Licensing Framework*, available at www.ausgoal.gov.au/overview.

59 DATA.GOV.UK, *Opening up Government*, available at http://data.gov.uk/.

60 Open Government Partnership, *Open Government Declaration*, available at www.opengovpartnership.org/about/open-government-declaration.

61 See the example of the Open Government Partnership, *Australia*, available at www.opengovpartnership.org/country/australia. See also that of the Open Government Partnership, *United States of America*, available at www.opengovpartnership.org/country/united-states. See also the Open Government Partnership, *United Kingdom*, available at www.opengovpartnership.org/country/united-kingdom.

62 John K. Setear, 'An Iterative Perspective on Treaties: A Synthesis of International Relations Theory and International Law' 37 (1996) *Harvard International Law Journal* 139.

63 United Nations (UN), *Vienna Convention on the Law of Treaties*, 23 May 1969, United Nations, Treaty Series, vol. 1155, p. 331, (1969). See also, H. L. A. Hart, *The Concept of Law* (Clarendon Press, 1961), 219.

64 See Section 12(1) of *The Constitution of the Federal Republic of Nigeria*, available at www.nigeria-law.org/ConstitutionOfTheFederalRepublicOfNigeria.htm. It states that "No treaty between the Federation and other country shall have the force of law except to the extent to which any such treaty has been enacted into law by the National Assembly." See also, Olawale Adebambo, 'Domesticating International Treaties' *The Nation* (2013), available at http://thenationonlineng.net/new/domesticating-international-treaties/.

65 Setear (1996). See page 215 where John noted that "Treaties may not only mandate meetings among all the parties to a treaty but may also direct efforts by particular parties embroiled in specific disputes. The Provision of treaties often include specific mechanisms." See also, pages 166–167 where he noted that "the rule of the law of treaties, rather than being treaties are binding everywhere in all circumstances is actually treaties are binding, except when terminated by fundamental change in circumstances or by inconsistency with a peremptory norm"

66 World Intellectual Property Organisation (WIPO), 'The Third Access to Knowledge (A2K3) Conference' Wipo Magazine (2008), available at www.wipo.int/wipo_magazine/

en/2008/06/article_0007.html. The magazine noted that the conference was "Organized by ten international partners, the Third Access to Knowledge (A2K3) Conference, held in Geneva from September 8 to 10, attracted over 400 participants."

67 WIPO, *Member States Adopt a Development Agenda for WIPO*, Geneva, 1 October (2007), PR/2007/521, available at www.wipo.int/pressroom/en/articles/2007/article_0071.html.

68 Marrakesh Treaty to Facilitate Access to Published Works for Persons Who Are Blind, Visually Impaired, or Otherwise Print Disabled, adopted by the Diplomatic Conference to Conclude a Treaty to Facilitate Access to Published Works by Visually Impaired Persons and Persons with Print Disabilities on 27 June (2013), available at www.wipo.int/edocs/lexdocs/treaties/en/marrakesh/trt_marrakesh_001en.pdf.

69 World Intellectual Property Organization (WIPO), *Summary of the Marrakesh Treaty to Facilitate Access to Published Works for Persons Who Are Blind, Visually Impaired, or Otherwise Print Disabled (MVT)* (2013). See also, WIPO, Historic Treaty Adopted, Boosts Access to Books for Visually Impaired Persons Worldwide, Marrakesh/Geneva, June 27, 2013, PR/2013/741(2013), WIPO ed., available at www.wipo.int/pressroom/en/articles/2013/article_0017.html.

70 Michael Carrol, *PIJIP's Marrakesh Treaty Event – Teaching Resource and Thanks*, available at http://infojustice.org/archives/30682.

"The treaty is the first of its kind. A series of multilateral agreements on intellectual property have established the minimum rights that Member States must grant to authors, inventors or other owners. Other bilateral and plurilateral agreements have focused on minimum requirements for enforcing these rights. Now, this treaty pushes in the opposite direction by requiring Member States to cut back on the scope of protection under copyright law so as to allow 'authorized entities' within their territory to make print resources available to the blind and print disabled without the consent of the publisher or other copyright owner. Currently less than 2% of the published literature is available to this population in an accessible format. The negotiation was particularly hard fought because of the larger context concerning the future direction of international intellectual property law."

71 See the WIPO (2008). The A2K Challenge by Maximiliano Santa Cruz, where it was noted that "A2K now has a strong influence in intergovernmental processes at WIPO, the WTO and the WHO."

72 CPTech, *Access to Knowledge: Overview*, available at www.cptech.org/a2k/.

73 Draft Treaty on Access to Knowledge A2K Treaty (9 May 2005). See the Preamble, P. 3 at Part 1.

74 Ibid. See Article 1–1: Objectives.

75 Ibid. See Articles 5–1–5–6.

76 UN, *United Nations Treaty Collection: Glossary*, available at https://treaties.un.org/pages/Overview.aspx?path=overview/glossary/page1_en.xml#adoption.

Bibliography

Adebambo, Olawale, Domesticating International Treaties, *The Nation* (2013), available at http://thenationonlineng.net/new/domesticating-international-treaties/.

Anne, Fitzgerald, 'Open Access and Public-Sector Information: Policy Developments in Australia and Key Jurisdictions' in Fitzgerald Brian ed., *Access to Public Sector Information: Law, Technology & Policy* (Sydney University Press, 2010).

ARC, *ARC Open Access Policy*, available at www.arc.gov.au/applicants/open_access.htm.

AusGOAL, *Australian Governments Open Access and Licensing Framework*, available at www.ausgoal.gov.au/overview.

Carothers, Thomas & Saskia Brechenmacher, The Four Magic Words of Development, *World Bank* (2014), available at http://blogs.worldbank.org/publicsphere/four-magic-words-development-tom-carothers-and-saskia-brechenmacher.

Carrol, Michael, *PIJIP's Marrakesh Treaty Event – Teaching Resource and Thanks*, available at http://infojustice.org/archives/30682.

Claude-Reyes, et al. v Chile (Inter-American court of Human Rights 19 September 2006).

The Constitution of the Federal Republic of Nigeria (1999), available at www.nigeria-law.org/ConstitutionOfTheFederalRepublicOfNigeria.htm

Covenant University, *Covenant University Repository*, available at http://eprints.covenant university.edu.ng/.

CPTech, *Access to Knowledge: Overview*, available at www.cptech.org/a2k/.

Crick, Francis & Christof Koch, 'A Framework for Consciousness' 6 (2003) *Nature Neuroscience* (2003).

DATA.GOV.UK, *Opening up Government* (2005), available at http://data.gov.uk/.

Draft Treaty on Access to Knowledge A2K Treaty, 9 May.

ERC, *Open Access Guidelines for Researchers Funded by the ERC* (2012), available at http://erc.europa.eu/sites/default/files/document/file/open_access_policy_researchers_funded_ERC.pdf.

Federal Republic of Nigeria, *Federal Ministry of Education*, available at www.nigeria.gov.ng/2012-10-29-11-06-51/executive-branch/93-federal-ministry-of-education/116-federal-ministry-of-education.

Fitzgerald, Brian, *Open Content Licensing (OCL) for Open Educational Resources: A Paper Commissioned by the OECD's Centre for Educational Research and Innovation (CERI) for the Project on Open Educational Resources* (2007), available at www.oecd.org/education/ceri/38645489.pdf

Fitzgerald, Brian, 'A Short Overview of Creative Commons' in Fitzgerald Brian ed., *Open Content Licensing: Cultivating the Creative Commons* (Sydney University Press, 2007).

Free Software Foundation, *GNU Free Documentation License*, available at www.gnu.org/licenses/fdl.html.

Guilbault, Lucie & Christina Angelopoulos, *Open Content Licensing from Theory to Practice* (Amsterdam University Press, 2011).

Harnad, Stevan, *Gold Open Access Publishing Must Not Be Allowed to Retard the Progress of Green Open Access Self-Archiving*, available at http://eprints.soton.ac.uk/271818/1/logospaper.pdf.

Harnad, Stevan & Nancy McGovern, 'Institutional Repository Success Is Dependent Upon Mandates' 36 (2009) *Bulletin of the American Society for Information Science and Technology* 27.

Harnad, Stevan, et al., *The Green and Gold Roads to Open Access*, Nature Publishig Group, available at www.nature.com/nature/focus/accessdebate/21.html?a_aid=3598aabf.

Hart, H. L. A., *The Concept of Law* (Clarendon Press, 1961).

Hebdo, Livres, *The Global Ranking of the Publishing Industry 2014*, Rüdiger Wischenbart Content and Consulting (2014), available at http://wischenbart.com/upload/Global-Ranking-of-the-Publishing-Industry_2014_Analysis.pdf.

International Publishers Association IPA, *Annual Report October 2013|October 2014* (2014), available at www.internationalpublishers.org/images/reports/2014/IPA-annual-report-2014.pdf.

Ivwighreghweta, O. & O. K. Onoriode, 'Open Access and Scholarly Publishing: Opportunities and Challenges to Nigerian Researchers' 33 (2012) *Chinese Librarianship: An International Electronic Journal*. 1–13.

The Law Dictionary, *What Is Framework*, available at http://thelawdictionary.org/framework/.

Lawrence, Lessig, 'The Vision for the Creative Commons: What Are We and Where Are We Headed? Free Culture' in Fitzgerald Brian ed., *Open Content Licensing: Cultivating the Creative Commons* (Sydney University Press, 2007).

Marrakesh Treaty to Facilitate Access to Published Works for Persons Who Are Blind, Visually Impaired, or Otherwise Print Disabled, adopted by the Diplomatic Conference to Conclude a Treaty to Facilitate Access to Published Works by Visually Impaired Persons and Persons with Print Disabilities on (27 June 2013), available at www.wipo.int/edocs/lexdocs/treaties/en/marrakesh/trt_marrakesh_001en.pdf.

Maxwell, G. A., 'Checks and Balances: The Role of Managers in Work – Life Balance Policies and Practices' 12 (2005) *Journal of Retailing and Consumer Services.*

(MIT) Massachusetts Institute of Technology, *About the OpenCourseWare Consortium*, available at http://ocw.mit.edu/about/ocw-consortium/.

(MIT) Massachusetts Institute of Technology, *MITOPENCOURSEWARE*, available at http://ocw.mit.edu/index.htm.

Moravec, John, Infoxication 2.0, *Education Futures* (2008), available at www.educationfutures.com/2008/10/24/infoxication-20/.

Munroe, M., *Rediscovering the Kingdom: Ancient Hope for Our 21st Century World* (ReadHowYouWant.com Limited, 2010).

The National Archives, *Open Government Licence for Public Sector Information*, available at www.nationalarchives.gov.uk/doc/open-government-licence/.

The National Archives, *UK Government Licensing Framework for Public Sector Information* (2013), available at www.nationalarchives.gov.uk/documents/information-management/uk-government-licensing-framework.pdf.

National Universities Commission Act, Cap N.81, Laws of the Federation of Nigeria (LFN), available at www.placng.org/lawsofnigeria/node/507 Cap N.81 Laws of the Federation of Nigeria (LFN) (2004).

New South Wales Government, *NSW Government Open Data Policy* (2013), available at www.finance.nsw.gov.au/ict/sites/default/files/NSW%20Government%20Open%20Data%20Policy%201.0.pdf.

NIH, *NIH Public Access Policy*, available at http://publicaccess.nih.gov/.

NZGOAL, *New Zealand Government Open Access and Licensing Framework (NZGOAL)* (2010), available at https://ict.govt.nz/assets/Uploads/Documents/NZGOAL.pdf.

Okoye, M. O. & Ejikeme, A. N., 'Open Access, Institutional Repositories, and Scholarly Publishing: The Role of Librarians in South Eastern Nigeria' 2 (2011) *Library Philosophy and Practice (e-Journal)*, 1–9.

Ola, Kunle, *Copyright Collective Administration in Nigeria Lessons for Africa* (Springer, 2013).

Ola, Kunle, *Understanding Open Access for Africa*, SSRN 2476739, available at http://papers.ssrn.com/sol3/papers.cfm?abstract_id=2476739.

Ola, R. F., *Local administration in Nigeria* (Kegan Paul International, 1984).

OMB, Circular No. A-130, Revised, Transmittal Memorandum No. 4, 28 November, Memorandum for Heads of Executive Departments and Agencies (United States Office of Management and Budget ed., 2000).

OpenDOAR, *Directory of Open Access Repositories*, available at www.opendoar.org/countrylist.php.

Open Government Partnership, *Australia*, available at www.opengovpartnership.org/country/australia.

Open Government Partnership, *Open Government Declaration*, available at www.opengovpartnership.org/about/open-government-declaration.

Open Government Partnership, *United Kingdom*, available at www.opengovpartnership.org/country/united-kingdom.

Open Government Partnership, *United States of America*, available at www.opengovpartnership.org/country/united-states.

Paul, Rogers, et al., Infobesity: The Enemy of Good Decisions, *Insight*, available at www.bain.com/publications/articles/infobesity-the-enemy-of-good-decisions.aspx.

Queensland University of Technology, *QUT ePrints*, available at http://eprints.qut.edu.au/.

RCUK, *RCUK Policy on Open Access*, available at www.rcuk.ac.uk/research/Pages/outputs.aspx.

ROAR, *Registry of Open Access Repositories*, available at http://roar.eprints.org/cgi/roar_search/advanced?location_country=&software=&type=institutional&order=-recordcount%2F-date.

ROARMAP, *Registry of Open Access Repositories Mandatory Archiving Policies*, available at http://roarmap.eprints.org/.

Sale, Arthur, *Comparison of Content Policies for Institutional Repositories in Australia* (2006), available at http://firstmonday.org/ojs/index.php/fm/article/view/1324/1244.

Setear, John K., 'An Iterative Perspective on Treaties: A Synthesis of International Relations Theory and International Law' 37 (1996) *Harvard International Law Journal* 139.

Smith, Richard, 'Peer-Review: A Flawed Process at the Heart of Science and Journals' 99 (2006) *Journal of the Royal Society of Medicine*.

Soanes, Catherine & Sara Hawker, *Compact Oxford English Dictionary* (Oxford University Press, 2005).

Spier, Ray, 'The History of the Peer-Review Process' 20 (2002) *TRENDS in Biotechnology*.

Suber, Peter, Knowledge as a Public Good, *SPARC* (2009), available at www.sparc.arl.org/resources/articles/knowledge#sthash.R1nBSlQF.dpuf.

Suber, Peter, *Open Access* (MIT Press, 2012).

Swan, Alma & Sheridan Brown, *Open Access Self-Archiving: An Author Study* (Key Perspective Limited, 2005).

Timothy Vollmer, *New Federal Education Fund Makes Available $2 Billion to Create OER Resources in Community Colleges*, available at http://creativecommons.org/weblog/entry/26100.

Toffler, A., *Future Shock* (Bantam Books, 1990).

UNISA, *Unisa Institutional Repository*, available at http://uir.unisa.ac.za/.

United Nations UN, *United Nations Treaty Collection: Glossary*, available at https://treaties.un.org/pages/Overview.aspx?path=overview/glossary/page1_en.xml#adoption.

United Nations UN, *Vienna Convention on the Law of Treaties*, 23 May 1969, United Nations, Treaty Series, vol. 1155, p. 331.

United Nations Department for Economic and Social Affairs, *Guidelines on Open Government Data for Citizen Engagement, ST/ESA/PAD/SER.E/177*, available at http://workspace.unpan.org/sites/Internet/Documents/Guidenlines%20on%20OGDCE%20May17%202013.pdf.

University of Otago, *Institutional Research Repository Policy*, available at www.otago.ac.nz/administration/policies/otago014455.html.

The White House, *Open Government Initiative*, available at www.whitehouse.gov/open.

WIPO, *Historic Treaty Adopted, Boosts Access to Books for Visually Impaired Persons Worldwide* (2013), Marrakesh/Geneva, 27 June, PR/2013/741, available at www.wipo.int/pressroom/en/articles/2013/article_0017.html (WIPO ed., 2013).

WIPO, *Member States Adopt a Development Agenda for WIPO* (2007), Geneva, 1 October PR/2007/521, available at www.wipo.int/pressroom/en/articles/2007/article_0071.html.

WIPO, *Summary of the Marrakesh Treaty to Facilitate Access to Published Works for Persons Who Are Blind, Visually Impaired, or Otherwise Print Disabled (MVT) (2013)* (2013).

WIPO, 'The Third Access to Knowledge (A2K3) Conference' (2008) *Wipomagazine*, available at www.wipo.int/wipo_magazine/en/2008/06/article_0007.html.

8 Conclusion

"Let us hear the Conclusion of the whole matter."

1 Introduction

2 The frustrations are still there

As I was concluding this work, I got an email from a Nigerian who now lives and lectures in the United Kingdom. He had read one of my works that was freely available online and discovered it had many Nigerian-decided cases. He had been trying to collate information on a particular area of Nigeria's case law but was unable to access any of those cases. He therefore sent me an email asking that I kindly assist him with the Nigerian cases I have. I have since pulled up the cases and sent them to him, but this is not how it should be. The Nigerian judiciary is funded by taxpayers' money, and the records of the court are public documents that should be accessible to the public. Chapter 6 on public sector information (PSI) addressed the need for openness and transparency and explained how valued-added services through access to use and reuse government-held information can foster development and good governance. The Nigerian judiciary and the other arms of government can bring about a better Nigeria if they adopt an open government policy. My colleague in the United Kingdom and several others will be able to access useful information and the utility and impact of such information will be maximized.

3 Chibok girls still missing

Although agitations by Nigerians about the government's lackadaisical attitude towards the kidnapped Chibok girls brought about a change of government during the April 2015 Nigerian presidential election, some of the girls are still missing and Boko Haram is still bombing different parts of Nigeria. People are afraid to go to school; people are not learning, education is lacking. Chapter 5 discussed open educational resources (OER) as an alternative route to the traditional route of acquiring education. OER cannot pretend to be a panacea to global education, but it definitely provides tools to tackling challenges to accessing education. A high population of Nigerians in the areas where Boko Haram operates have mobile phones. These phones can receive OER and can therefore serve as learning portal. Desperate situations require desperate measures.

4 Retrospect

This work examined three major areas within the open movement, namely open access journal articles, OER and PSI.

This work set out to achieve three things namely:

1. To demonstrate the potential benefits of the open access movement to Nigeria's national development.
2. To investigate, explain and propose a legal, regulatory and policy framework for Nigeria that would enable open access to the output of journal articles, OER and PSI.
3. To situate Nigeria within the current open access movement by engaging in local pragmatic projects capable of advancing the development of Nigerians, other developing countries and the world at large. (For instance, the establishment of institutional repositories in most Nigerian Tertiary Institutions.)

To actualize the above aims and objectives, three problem statements were developed, namely:

1. What role(s) can open access play in Nigeria's national development?
2. What are the possible challenges to the implementation of open access in Nigeria?
3. What legal, regulatory and policy frameworks are required or needed to be strengthened for the successful implementation of open access in Nigeria?

Chapter 1 laid the background for the work explaining the origin and development of open access. It expatiated on the strategies to achieving open access and provided information on the dynamics of the open access movement.

Chapter 2 considered the theory of open access from a social, economic, legal and political perspective. It laid out the reasoning of certain scholars and philosophers towards sharing of knowledge, and it argues that open access is a practical way of implementing the ideologies.

Chapter 3 examined specific Nigerian legal, regulatory and policy frameworks against the background of the open access movement in Nigeria to ascertain how these frameworks work in tandem or otherwise with the overall objective of open access.

Chapters 4–6 examined different aspects of knowledge management and how knowledge can be maximized from the perspective of open scholarly publishing, PSI and OER. They emphasized the need to conform to the rule of law and deploy open licensing to grant the requisite permissions. The duo strategy of self-archiving and open access publishing in the implementation of open access is investigated, as well as the importance of providing use and reuse rights to publicly funded research and all government-held information that do not fall within legally excluded materials. The impracticability to keep up with the high cost of educational materials and the need for a more globalized and integrated educational system was noted. Understanding and deploying OER as strategic educational tools was explored as a pathway to alleviating the cost as well as providing the platform for the development and sharing of educational resources on a global scale.

Chapter 7 provides guidance and useful tools for developing open access frameworks, be it that of an individual, a university, research institute, an agency of government, the private sector or even the public service. It provides links to a number of draft policy statements that could be helpful in developing a draft but draws attention to the need to customize and localize such draft policy statements.

The implementation of open access to knowledge in Nigeria can transform Nigeria if properly implemented. Below are some recommendations that would aid in maximizing open access to knowledge in Nigeria.

5 Recommendations

1 Government to develop a national open access policy, open government initiatives and OER policy. The objective is to develop a policy with national applicability. In implementing this recommendation, government may wish to empanel a committee made up of public servants, private sector and international experts to undertake surveys and research and adapt the guidelines provided in this work. For funding, the first preference would be that it be funded by government. The second option would be local (Nigerian) private sector funding. The third option would be from international donor organizations and non-governmental organizations.
2 Universities to adopt open access policies. The aim is to institutionalize open access in the Nigerian academic environment. In implementing this recommendation, the office of the Vice Chancellor (VC) or that of the Deputy Vice Chancellor (DVC) should direct the policy development and delegate implementation to the Dean of each faculty, but the VC or DVC should take responsibility for supervising its implementation.
3 All Nigerian research agencies to adopt open access policies, to ensure that the output of Nigeria's publicly funded research is made freely available. The Head of the agency or an officer at management level should be saddled with the responsibility of organizing the development and implementation of the policy.
4 All higher educational institutions, research institutes and government agencies to establish institutional repositories (IR) for purposes of providing an online platform for free global visibility and accessibility of Nigerian works.

In the development of the IR, agencies should avail themselves of open source software platforms such as

- Dspace and Eprint for their repositories (Green OA)
- Ubuntu for the operating system
- Open Journal System as the publishing platform (Gold OA)

The Head of the agency or an officer at management level should be saddled with the responsibility of organizing the development and implementation of the policy.

5 Embark on aggressive enlightenment to the private sector in Nigeria on the benefits of adopting open cultures and to build business models using available open platforms such as open source licences, open educational resources etc.

6 PSI held by government agencies should be made available for use and reuse. To encourage citizenry participation, accountability, transparency and good governance by the provision for use and reuse of government-held information. In the implementation of this recommendation, the Head of the agency or an officer at management level should be saddled with the responsibility of providing this information via the government's website.

7 Government to adopt a standard licensing regime for PSI preferably the creative commons licences to simplify and standardize the mode of obtaining authorization for use and reuse of works. Implementation will require understanding and adoption of suitable Creative Commons licences taking cognizance of the peculiarities of certain ministries, departments and agencies of government.

8 All libraries and informatics centres in Nigeria to work towards digitizing all documents in their custody and should works towards going online.

9 All government agencies to be encouraged to begin to use open source software.

10 Develop a national advocacy program on understanding open access.

11 Develop a national portal capable of harvesting content from all the university IR. This will provide a single platform where all data in IR in Nigeria can be harvested and systematically accessed. In implementing this recommendation, the national portal could be jointly managed by government and the Nigerian private sector (GLO, MTN, MainOne Cable, SubUrban). The RIAN in Ireland, OpenAIRE, DartEurope, Driver and Base in Europe as well as NORA in Norway are examples of national portals that may be adapted. In developing this national portal, open source platforms should be used, such as

- Dspace and Eprint for the portal
- Ubuntu for the operating system
- Open Journal System for the publishing platform

12 Adoption of open policy by the judiciary thereby making the cases available for free online.
13 Adoption of open policy by the legislature thereby making legislations, draft bills and other legislative materials freely available online. This will promote transparency, good governance and greater citizen participation.
14 Encourage individual authors to set up individual websites and upload their works.
15 Open access policies in the universities to include a mandate on deposits of works.
16 Enlist the support of Nigerian publishers to adopt open access publishing models.
17 Old and new work in Nigerian universities should be made available in their respective institutional repositories.
18 Establish a monitoring mechanism to access the level of open access compliance in Nigeria. See MTMT in Hungary as an example.
19 Encourage all Nigerian journal publishers to register with one of the global indexing outlets to enhance the global visibility of works published in Nigeria.
20 Government in collaboration with the private sector to provide proper infrastructure, such as power and better Internet service.
21 Government to encourage publicly funded schools to use OES.

Index

For Product Safety Concerns and Information please contact our EU representative GPSR@taylorandfrancis.com Taylor & Francis Verlag GmbH, Kaufingerstraße 24, 80331 München, Germany